Office of Government Commerce

Service Transition

London: TSO

TSO

Published by TSO (The Stationery Office) and available from:

Online
www.tsoshop.co.uk

Mail, Telephone, Fax & E-mail
TSO
PO Box 29, Norwich, NR3 1GN
Telephone orders/General enquiries: 0870 600 5522
Fax orders: 0870 600 5533
E-mail: customer.services@tso.co.uk
Textphone 0870 240 3701

TSO Shops
123 Kingsway, London, WC2B 6PQ
020 7242 6393 Fax 020 7242 6394
16 Arthur Street, Belfast BT1 4GD
028 9023 8451 Fax 028 9023 5401
71 Lothian Road, Edinburgh EH3 9AZ
0870 606 5566 Fax 0870 606 5588

TSO@Blackwell and other Accredited Agents

Published for the Office of Government Commerce under licence from the Controller of Her Majesty's Stationery Office.

First published 2007

ISBN 978 0 11 331048 7

Printed in the United Kingdom for The Stationery Office

Contents

List of figures

All diagrams in this publication are intended to provide an illustration of ITIL Service Management Practice concepts and guidance. They have been artistically rendered to visually reinforce key concepts and are not intended to meet a formal method or standard of technical drawing. The ITIL Service Management Practices Intergrated Service Model conforms to technical drawing standards and should be referred to for complete details. Please see www.best-management-practice.com/itil for details.

List of tables

OGC's foreword

Since its creation, ITIL has grown to become the most widely accepted approach to IT Service Management in the world. However, along with this success comes the responsibility to ensure that the guidance keeps pace with a changing global business environment. Service Management requirements are inevitably shaped by the development of technology, revised business models and increasing customer expectations. Our latest version of ITIL has been created in response to these developments.

This publication is one of five core publications describing the IT Service Management practices that make up ITIL. They are the result of a two-year project to review and update the guidance. The number of Service Management professionals around the world who have helped to develop the content of these publications is impressive. Their experience and knowledge have contributed to the content to bring you a consistent set of high-quality guidance. This is supported by the ongoing development of a comprehensive qualifications scheme, along with accredited training and consultancy.

Whether you are part of a global company, a government department or a small business, ITIL gives you access to world-class Service Management expertise. Essentially, it puts IT services where they belong – at the heart of successful business operations.

Peter Fanning

Acting Chief Executive

Office of Government Commerce

Chief Architect's foreword

This publication, ITIL Service Management Practices Service Transition, sits at the centre of the ITIL lifecycle structure. Transition, is not an everyday word – words like 'design' and 'operate', describing the lifecycle stages on either side of transition, are more familiar. But these more familiar terms that bracket transition can also serve to help define and explain its goals and purpose.

The need to design a service, totally new or changed, is accepted – without a vision of the service's purpose that purpose will always remain undelivered. And over the last 17 years (since the inception of ITIL) the need has been firmly established for ongoing management of the services. This has been recognized as the 'core' of IT Service Management – providing and supporting the 'business as usual' delivery of the organization's requirements from IT.

And so, it is readily apparent that successfully moving from the concept of 'how' – developed by design – into 'what' – as supported by operations – is going to be the key element of delivering the business support we are charged with. And so there is always a need for a Service Transition.

The importance of actually delivering a design, adapting it as needed, assuring and ensuring its continued relevance, has been less obvious to many. Service Transition concentrates on delivering the service vision in a relevant and cost-effective fashion. As such, Service Transition is effectively defined by the service delivery concepts that supply its inputs and the Service Operations expectations that serve as recipients of its outputs   which are usable services.

The best way of achieving Service Transition will vary between organizations and has to reflect the risks, resources and other parameters pertaining to that organization in general and the service to be transitioned in particular.

A useful analogy is a relay race, where the team of runners must carry a baton round the track – passing it from hand-to-hand between team members. The initial expectation might be that victory in such a race relies on having the fastest athletes. However, important as speed

and fitness of the runners are, it is equally important not to drop the baton. Conversely, total concentration on careful and risk-free passing of the baton will also not make a winning team. To win the race requires the right combination of speed and handover of the baton.

In a similar way, Service Transition must deliver relevant services with the appropriate balance of speed, cost and safety.

The priorities, concerns, constraints and conditions that dictate the decisions and focus of Service Transition will vary between service providers. For those in safety-critical industries, such as medical technological support and nuclear power station control, the focus will be on thoroughness and risk reduction – the main priority here is not to drop the baton: 'take it carefully' is the correct approach. This is typical where competition is low, such as in the public sector, or where governmental controls insist on caution, or the customer perception of their reliability requirement is high.

Alternatively, in highly competitive industries, such as online product sales or mobile telephone facilities, speed may be more important. In a relay race with 100 teams, concentration on safe handover will bring you in consistently in the first 20%, but you will probably never win. The customer's business needs may dictate that it makes more sense to drop the baton 80% of the time but come first for the rest.

This may seem tangential, but it is important to set the scene here, and recognize that this publication of best practice, based on successful practices followed in many organizations, will not deliver absolute guidance in all areas. Rather, guidance rests on judging a service provider's correct transitional parameters and then helping to build and implement the best approach for their circumstances.

By following this logic, the publication addresses itself to the full range of different circumstances and allows for flexible interpretation. It should be read, understood and followed in a flexible and pragmatic way, aware that Service Transition is, in effect, offering an internal service; taking design outputs and delivering them to an operational state, in order to best support business requirements. This requires sufficient understanding of design outputs and operational inputs, and of the true and final business requirement. This knowledge is required in assessment and assurance (or rejection) of requirements and design specification, constraints and parameters.

The success of Service Transition is in the ability of Service Operations to support the business processes via the installed service base. The mechanism for achieving the goal is secondary and adaptive – and this applies whether an organization is transitioning service designs into business support or components and materials into motorcycles (see the Service Strategy publication). The aim of this publication is to support Service Transition managers and practitioners in their application of Service Transition practices.

Sharon Taylor

Chief Architect, ITIL Service Management Practices

Preface

'They always say that time changes things, but you actually have to change them yourself' Andy Warhol, *The Philosophy of Andy Warhol*. US artist (1928–1987).

Effective Service Transition does not happen until an organization recognizes the need for it and the benefits it will bring them.

And effective Service Transition is needed because business environments are in a constant state of transition. The quest for competitive advantage, best of breed innovation and self-preservation are eternal catalysts for change that must then be delivered.

Service Transition is the Information Technology Service Management (ITSM) professional's guide to delivering those changes through transition lifecycle steps, which help them manage change in a broader context. Large-scale IT change is often driven through project or programme initiatives. These are mistakenly seen to be outside 'Change Management', and too often not considered a Service Management concern until it is time to implement. However, experience teaches that this approach rarely yields the best possible benefit to the business.

This publication supplies answers to managing Service Transition from designed specifications, change, configuration, test, release and deployment and every step in between.

Effective Service Transition ensures that meeting business need, cost and efficiency are achieved with minimal risk, maximum optimization and the highest degree of confidence possible.

Service Transition also requires effective management of knowledge, organizational culture and transition in difficult or unusual circumstances. Every ITSM professional knows the major part of any change – that can make or break its success – is related to the human factor, especially cultural aversion to change.

This publication explores industry practices for all sizes and types of organizations and will benefit anyone involved in Service Management. The practices contained in these pages culminate from decades of experience, evolving knowledge and emerging research in the field of IT Service Management.

Contact information

Full details of the range of material published under the ITIL banner can be found at www.best-management-practice.com/itil

For further information on qualifications and training accreditation, please visit www.itil-officialsite.com. Alternatively, please contact:

APMG Service Desk
Sword House
Totteridge Road
High Wycombe
Buckinghamshire
HP13 6DG

Tel: +44 (0) 1494 452450
E-mail: servicedesk@apmg.co.uk

Acknowledgements

Chief Architect and authors

Sharon Taylor (Aspect Group Inc)   Chief Architect

Shirley Lacy (ConnectSphere)   Author

Ivor MacFarlane (Guillemot Rock)   Author

ITIL authoring team

The ITIL authoring team contributed to this guide through commenting on content and alignment across the set. So thanks are also due to the other ITIL authors, specifically Jeroen Bronkhorst (HP), David Cannon (HP), Gary Case (Pink Elephant), Ashley Hannah (HP), Majid Iqbal (Carnegie Mellon University), Vernon Lloyd (Fox IT), Michael Nieves (Accenture), Stuart Rance (HP), Colin Rudd (ITEMS), George Spalding (Pink Elephant) and David Wheeldon (HP).

Mentors

Malcolm Fry and Robert Stroud.

Further contributions

A number of people generously contributed their time and expertise to this Service Transition publication. Jim Clinch, as OGC Project Manager, is grateful for the support provided by Jenny Dugmore, Convenor of Working Group ISO/IEC 20000, Janine Eves, Carol Hulm, Aidan Lawes and Michiel van der Voort.

The authors would also like to thank Jane Clark, Michelle Hales and Carol Chamberlain of ConnectSphere, Dr Paul Drake, Lyn Jackson, LJ Training, Amanda Robinson, Luciana Abreu, EXIN Brasil, Kate Hinch, kFA and Candace Tarin, Aspect Group Inc.

In order to develop ITIL v3 to reflect current best practice and produce publications of lasting value, OGC consulted widely with different stakeholders throughout the world at every stage in the process. OGC would also like to thank the following individuals and their organizations for their contributions to refreshing the ITIL guidance:

The ITIL Advisory Group

Pippa Bass, OGC; Tony Betts, Independent; Signe-Marie Hernes Bjerke, Det Norske Veritas; Alison Cartlidge, Xansa; Diane Colbeck, DIYmonde Solutions Inc; Ivor Evans, DIYmonde Solutions Inc; Karen Ferris, ProActive; Malcolm Fry, FRY-Consultants; John Gibert, Independent; Colin Hamilton, RENARD Consulting Ltd; Lex Hendriks, EXIN; Carol Hulm, British Computer Society-ISEB; Tony Jenkins, DOMAINetc; Phil Montanaro, EDS; Alan Nance, ITPreneurs; Christian Nissen, Itilligence; Don Page, Marval Group; Bill Powell, IBM; Sergio Rubinato Filho, CA; James Siminoski, SOScorp; Robert E. Stroud, CA; Jan van Bon, Inform-IT; Ken Wendle, HP; Paul Wilkinson, Getronics PinkRoccade; Takashi Yagi, Hitachi.

Reviewers

Terry Adams, iCore Ltd; Tina Anderson, IBM; Daniel Andrade, Pink Elephant; Deborah Anthony, HP; Graham Barnett, Fujitsu Services; James Biglin, Lloyds TSB; Signe-Marie Hernes Bjerke, Det Norske Veritas; Roland Boettcher, Fachhochschule Bochum; Maarten Bordewijk, Getronics PinkRoccade NL; Alison Cartlidge, Xansa; Chia-jen liu Chyan, HP; David Clifford, PRO-ATTIVO; Lynda Cooper, Fox IT; Helen Curran, IBM; James Doss, UD Defense Intelligence Agency; Jenny Ellwood-Wade, Bowood Ltd; James Finister, PA Consulting; John Gibert, Independent; Frank Gogola, Mayer, Brown, Rowe & Maw, LLP; Ian Gunning, Standard Life Assurance plc; Susan Hall, University of Dundee; Liz Holmes, iCore Ltd; Wim Hoving, BHVB; Alison Howitt, The Scottish Parliament; Michael Hughes, Sensis; Robin Hysick, Pink Elephant; Horacio Laprea, HP; Kerry Litten, INS Ltd; Brenda McCabe, McCain Foods; Peter McLoughlin, ConnectSphere; Vinay Nikumbh, Quint Wellington Redwood India Consulting; Tsuyoshi Ohata, NEC; Christian Piechullek, Prinovis Ahrensburg GmbH & Co KG; Glen Purdy, Fujitsu Consulting; Jonathan Ridler, HP; Sergio Rubinato Filho, CA; Frances Scarff, OGC; Moira Shaw, Xansa plc; Marco Smith, iCore Ltd; John Sowerby, DHL Information Services; George Stark, IBM; Randy Steinberg, ITSM Strategies Inc; Michal Tepczynski, Nokia Finland; Adrian van de Rijken, Plexent; Bruce Weiner, GEICO; Natalie Welch, Severn Trent Systems; Kathleen Wilson, Microsoft; Abbey Wiltse, ITpreneurs; Grover Wright, Computacenter Services.

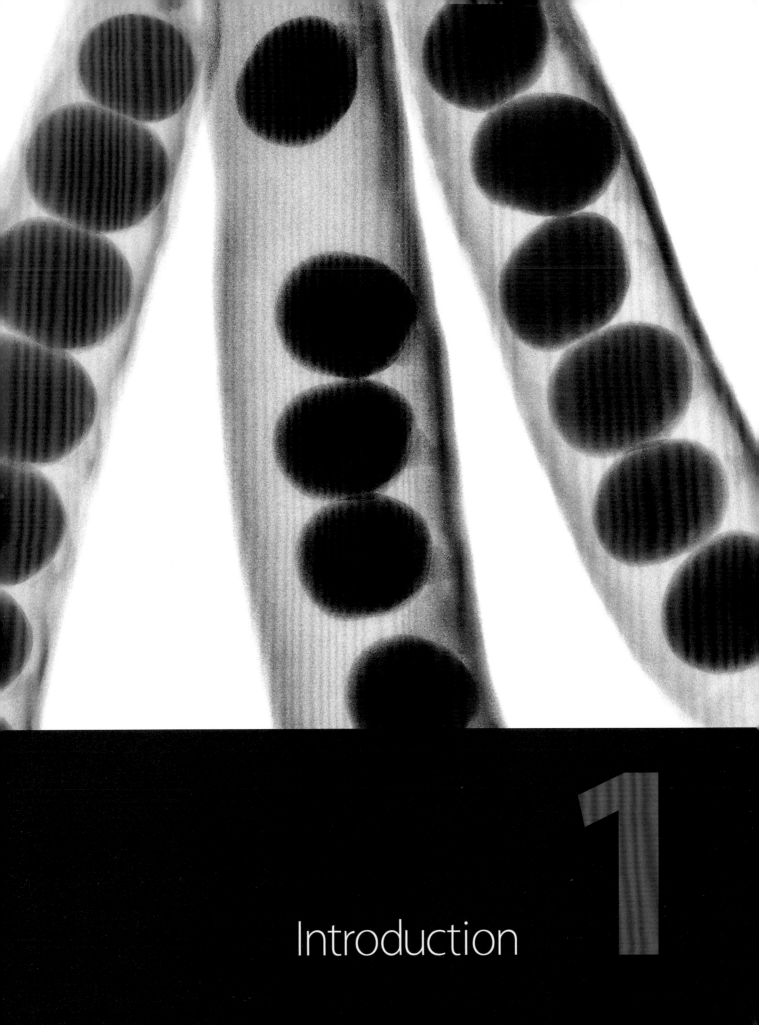

Introduction

1 Introduction

The Service Transition publication is part of the ITIL Service Management Practices, which document industry best practice for the service lifecycle management of IT enabled services. Although this publication can be read in isolation, it is recommended that it be used in conjunction with the other ITIL publications. Service Management is a generic concept and the guidance in the new ITIL publications applies generically. The guidance is also scalable – applicable to small and large organizations. It applies to distributed and centralized systems, whether in-house or supplied by third parties. It is neither bureaucratic nor unwieldy if implemented wisely and in full recognition of the business needs of your organization.

Adopting Service Transition best practices can enable improvements to services and Service Management capability by ensuring that the introduction, deployment, transfer and decommissioning of new or changed services is consistently well managed.

1.1 OVERVIEW

Service providers are increasingly focusing on service quality while adopting a more business and customer oriented approach to delivering services and cost optimization.

Many organizations deliver significant change through formal projects, and the failure to ensure that projects address the full Service Management and operational requirements as well as the functional requirements can be a costly, or even fatal, mistake to an organization. Service Transition ensures that the transition processes are streamlined, effective and efficient so that the risk of delay is minimized. It establishes assurance of the expected and actual service deliverables, and integrated elements that each service depends on to deliver and operate the service successfully. These elements include applications, infrastructure, knowledge, documentation, facilities, finance, people, processes, skills and so on.

Where there is major change there will be complexity and risk. There are usually many interdependencies to manage and conflicting priorities to resolve, particularly as new and changed services transition and go live. Service Transition takes into consideration aspects such as organizational change and adaptation of the wider environment in which they operate that would influence an organization's use of the services and the associated risks. More is required than merely receiving a design containing detailed Acceptance Criteria, implementing according to that design and measuring against the criteria. This would be the case if stability could be assured but in the real world the design and Acceptance Criteria may be affected by changes to IT, other services, the business or other external factors. Observation, interpretation and manipulation of the broader services environment are often necessary to deliver the benefits from the services required by the customer and envisaged by design.

At all stages the likelihood of success is balanced against the consequences of failure and the costs (financial and other). The assessment and prediction of performance and risk is therefore an essential and day-to-day element of the Service Transition process.

Successful Service Transition rests on effective understanding and application of Change Management, quality assurance, and risk management and effective programme and project management. This makes it possible, at every stage through the Service Transition process, to plan, track and confirm progress against current requirements, not just for one service but across all services in transition.

Service Transition does not end abruptly when a new or changed service goes live; rather it works with Service Operations to deliver early life support.

1.2 CONTEXT

1.2.1 Service Management

Information technology (IT) is a commonly used term that changes meaning with context. From the first perspective, IT systems, applications and infrastructure are components or sub-assemblies of a larger product. They enable or are embedded in processes and services. From the second perspective, IT is an organization with its own set of capabilities and resources. IT organizations can be of various types such as business functions, shared services units and enterprise-level core units.

From the third perspective, IT is a category of services used by business. They are typically IT applications and infrastructure that are packaged and offered as services by internal IT organizations or external service providers. IT costs are treated as business expenses. From the fourth perspective, IT is a category of business assets that provide a stream of benefits for their owners, including but not limited to revenue, income and profit. IT costs are treated as investments.

1.2.2 Good practice in the public domain

Organizations operate in dynamic environments with the need to learn and adapt. There is a need to improve performance while managing trade-offs. Under similar pressure, customers seek advantage from service providers. They pursue sourcing strategies that best serve their own business interest. In many countries, government agencies and non-profits have a similar propensity to outsource for the sake of operational effectiveness. This puts additional pressure on service providers to maintain a competitive advantage with respect to the alternatives that customers may have. The increase in outsourcing has particularly exposed internal service providers to unusual competition.

To cope with the pressure, organizations benchmark themselves against peers and seek to close gaps in capabilities. One way to close such gaps is to adopt good practices in wide industry use. There are several sources for good practices including public frameworks, standards and the proprietary knowledge of organizations and individuals (Figure 1.1).

Public frameworks and standards are attractive compared with proprietary knowledge.

Proprietary knowledge is deeply embedded in organizations and therefore difficult to adopt, replicate or transfer even with the cooperation of the owners. Such knowledge is often in the form of tacit knowledge, which is inextricable and poorly documented.

- Proprietary knowledge is customized for the local context and specific business needs to the point of being idiosyncratic. Unless the recipients of such knowledge have matching circumstances, the knowledge may not be as effective in use.
- Owners of proprietary knowledge expect to be rewarded for their long-term investments. They may make such knowledge available only under commercial terms through purchases and licensing agreements.
- Publicly available frameworks and standards such as ITIL, Control Objectives for Information and related Technology (COBIT), Capability Maturity Model Integration (CMMI), eSourcing Capability Model for Service Providers (eSCM-SP), PRINCE2, ISO 9000, ISO 20000 and ISO 27001 are validated across a diverse

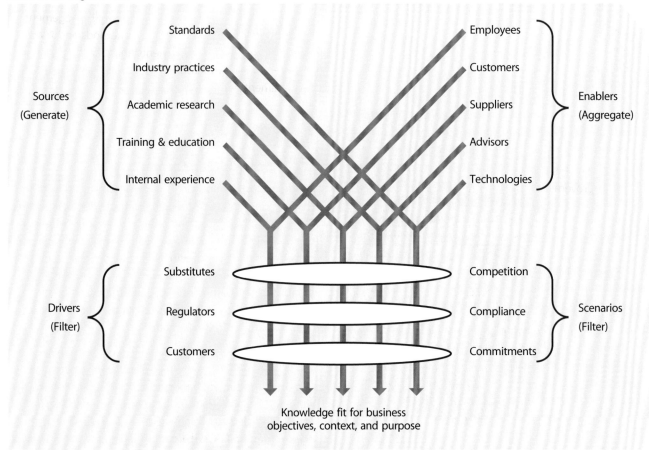

Figure 1.1 Sourcing of Service Management practice

set of environments and situations rather than the limited experience of a single organization. They are subject to broad review across multiple organizations and disciplines. They are vetted by diverse sets of partners, suppliers and competitors.

■ The knowledge of public frameworks is more likely to be widely distributed among a large community of professionals through publicly available training and certification. It is easier for organizations to acquire such knowledge through the labour market.

Ignoring public frameworks and standards can needlessly place an organization at a disadvantage. Organizations should cultivate their own proprietary knowledge on top of a body of knowledge based on public frameworks and standards. Collaboration and coordination across organizations are easier on the basis of shared practices and standards.

1.2.3 ITIL and good practice in Service Management

The context of this publication is the ITIL Framework as a source of good practice in Service Management. ITIL is used by organizations world-wide to establish and improve capabilities in Service Management. ISO/IEC 20000 provides a formal and universal standard for organizations seeking to have their Service Management capabilities audited and certified. While ISO/IEC 20000 is a standard to be achieved and maintained, ITIL offers a body of knowledge useful for achieving the standard.

The ITIL Library has the following components:

■ The ITIL Core: best practice guidance applicable to all types of organizations that provide services to a business

■ The ITIL Complementary Guidance: a complementary set of publications with guidance specific to industry sectors, organization types, operating models and technology architectures.

The ITIL Core consists of five publications (Figure 1.2). Each provides the guidance necessary for an integrated approach as required by the ISO/IEC 20000 standard specification:

■ Service Strategy
■ Service Design
■ Service Transition
■ Service Operation
■ Continual Service Improvement.

Each publication addresses capabilities that have a direct impact on a service provider's performance. The structure of the core is in the form of a lifecycle. It is iterative and multidimensional. It ensures organizations are set up to leverage capabilities in one area for learning and improvements in others. The core is expected to provide structure, stability and strength to Service Management capabilities with durable principles, methods and tools. This serves to protect investments and provide the necessary basis for measurement, learning and improvement.

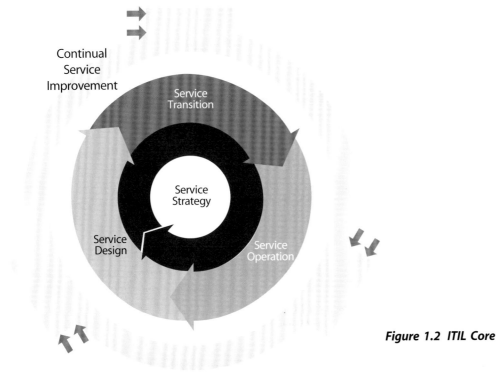

Figure 1.2 ITIL Core

The guidance in ITIL can be adapted for use in various business environments and organizational strategies. The Complementary Guidance provides flexibility to implement the core in a diverse range of environments. Practitioners can select Complementary Guidance as needed to provide traction for the core in a given business context, much like tyres are selected based on the type of automobile, purpose and road conditions. This is to increase the durability and portability of knowledge assets and to protect investments in Service Management capabilities.

1.2.3.1 Service Strategy

The Service Strategy publication provides guidance on how to design, develop and implement Service Management not only as an organizational capability but as a strategic asset. Guidance is provided on the principles underpinning the practice of Service Management which are useful for developing Service Management policies, guidelines and processes across the ITIL service lifecycle. Service Strategy guidance is useful in the context of Service Design, Service Transition, Service Operation and Continual Service Improvement. Topics covered in Service Strategy include the development of markets, internal and external, service assets, service catalogue, and implementation of strategy through the service lifecycle. Financial management, Service Portfolio management, organizational development and strategic risks are among other major topics.

Organizations use the guidance to set objectives and expectations of performance towards serving customers and market spaces, and to identify, select and prioritize opportunities. Service Strategy is about ensuring that organizations are in position to handle the costs and risks associated with their Service Portfolios, and are set up not just for operational effectiveness but for distinctive performance. Decisions made about Service Strategy have far-reaching consequences including those with delayed effect.

Organizations already practising ITIL use this publication to guide a strategic review of their ITIL-based Service Management capabilities and to improve the alignment between those capabilities and their business strategies. This ITIL publication encourages readers to stop and think about why something is to be done before thinking of how. Answers to the first type of questions are closer to the customer's business. Service Strategy expands the scope of the ITIL framework beyond the traditional audience of IT Service Management professionals.

1.2.3.2 Service Design

The Service Design publication provides guidance for the design and development of services and Service Management processes. It covers design principles and methods for converting strategic objectives into portfolios of services and service assets. The scope of Service Design is not limited to new services. It includes the changes and improvements necessary to increase or maintain value to customers over the lifecycle of services, the continuity of services, achievement of service levels, and conformance to standards and regulations. It guides organizations on how to develop design capabilities for Service Management.

1.2.3.3 Service Transition

The Service Transition publication provides guidance for the development and improvement of capabilities for transitioning new and changed services into operations. This publication provides guidance on how the requirements of Service Strategy encoded in Service Design are effectively realized in Service Operations while controlling the risks of failure and disruption. The publication combines practices in release management, programme management and risk management and places them in the practical context of Service Management. It provides guidance on managing the complexity related to changes to services and Service Management processes, preventing undesired consequences while allowing for innovation. Guidance is provided on transferring the control of services between customers and service providers.

1.2.3.4 Service Operation

This publication embodies practices in the management of Service Operations. It includes guidance on achieving effectiveness and efficiency in the delivery and support of services so as to ensure value for the customer and the service provider. Strategic objectives are ultimately realized through Service Operations, therefore making it a critical capability. Guidance is provided on how to maintain stability in Service Operations, allowing for changes in design, scale, scope and service levels. Organizations are provided with detailed process guidelines, methods and tools for use in two major control perspectives: reactive and proactive. Managers and practitioners are provided with knowledge allowing them to make better decisions in areas such as managing the availability of services, controlling demand, optimizing capacity utilization, scheduling of operations, and fixing problems. Guidance is provided on supporting operations through new models and architectures such as shared services, utility computing, web services and mobile commerce.

1.2.3.5 Continual Service Improvement

The Continual Service Improvement publication provides instrumental guidance in creating and maintaining value for customers through better design, introduction and operation of services. It combines principles, practices and methods from quality management, Change Management and capability improvement. Organizations learn to realize incremental and large-scale improvements in service quality, operational efficiency and business continuity. Guidance is provided for linking improvement efforts and outcomes with Service Strategy, design and transition. A closed-loop feedback system, based on the Plan–Do–Check–Act (PDCA) model specified in ISO/IEC 20000, is established and capable of receiving inputs for change from any planning perspective.

1.3　GOAL AND SCOPE OF SERVICE TRANSITION

1.3.1　Goal

The goal of this publication is to assist organizations seeking to plan and manage service changes and deploy service releases into the production environment successfully.

1.3.2　Scope

This publication provides guidance for the development and improvement of capabilities for transitioning new and changed services into the production environment, including release planning building, testing, evaluation and deployment. The guidance focuses on how to ensure the requirements of Service Strategies, set out in Service Design, are effectively realized in Service Operations while controlling the risks of failure and disruption.

Consideration is given to:

■ Managing the complexity associated with changes to services and Service Management processes
■ Allowing for innovation while minimizing the unintended consequences of change
■ The introduction of new services
■ Changes to existing services, e.g. expansion, reduction, change of supplier, acquisition or disposal of sections of user base or suppliers, change of requirements or skills availability
■ Decommissioning and discontinuation of services, applications or other service components

■ Transfer of services.

Guidance on transferring the control of services includes transfer in the following circumstances:

■ Out to a new supplier, e.g. outsourcing, off-shoring
■ From one supplier to another
■ Back in from a supplier, e.g. insourcing
■ To or from an external service provider
■ Moving to a shared service provision (e.g. partial outsource of some processes)
■ Multiple suppliers, e.g. smart-sourcing
■ Joint venture/secondment
■ Partnering
■ Down-sizing, up-sizing (right-sizing)
■ Merger and acquisition.

In reality, circumstances generate a combination of several of the above options at any one time and in any one situation.

The scope also includes the transition of fundamental changes to the service provider's Service Management capability that will change the ways of working, the organization, people, projects and third parties involved in Service Management.

1.4　USAGE

1.4.1　Target audience

This publication is relevant to organizations involved in the development, delivery or support of services, including:

■ Service providers, both internal and external
■ Organizations that aim to improve services through the effective application of Service Management and service lifecycle processes to improve their service quality
■ Organizations that require a consistent managed approach across all service providers in a supply chain
■ Organizations that are going out to tender for their services.

The publication is relevant to IT service managers and to all those working in Service Transition or areas supporting the objectives of Service Transition including:

■ Staff working in programmes and projects that are responsible for delivering new or changed services and the services environment
■ Transition managers and staff

- Testing managers and testing practitioners, including test environment and test data managers and librarians
- Quality assurance managers
- Asset and Configuration Management staff
- Change Management staff
- Release and deployment staff
- Procurement staff
- Relationship managers and supplier managers
- Suppliers delivering services, support, training etc.

1.4.2 Benefits of this publication

Selecting and adopting the best practices in this publication will assist organizations in delivering significant benefits. Adopting and implementing standard and consistent approaches for Service Transition will:

- Enable projects to estimate the cost, timing, resource requirement and risks associated with the Service Transition stage more accurately
- Result in higher volumes of successful change
- Be easier for people to adopt and follow
- Enable Service Transition assets to be shared and re-used across projects and services
- Reduce delays from unexpected clashes and dependencies, e.g. in test environments
- Reduce the effort spent on managing the Service Transition test and pilot environments
- Improve expectation setting for all stakeholders involved in Service Transition including customers, users, suppliers, partners and projects
- Increase confidence that the new or changed service can be delivered to specification without unexpectedly affecting other services or stakeholders
- Ensure that new or changed services will be maintainable and cost-effective.

The publication will help its readers to set up Service Transition and the processes that support it, and to make effective use of those processes to facilitate the effective transitioning of new, changed or decommissioned services.

It sets out guidance on the establishment and operation of Service Transition and specifically addresses the processes that are substantially focused on supporting Service Transition. Specifically, in addition to this chapter's high-level introduction to the subject, subsequent chapters in the publication address the following topics.

Chapter 2 – Service Management as a practice

This chapter introduces the concept of Service Management as a practice. Here Service Management is positioned as a strategic and professional component of any organization. It illustrates elements of the Service Transition lifecycle stages. The goal and scope of the topic are set out together with key success measures. Interfaces to other ITIL Core topics are described and the processes that support transition are listed, placed in context and outlined in terms of their range of applicability across the lifecycle and their interface and relevance to transition.

Chapter 3 – Service Transition principles

This chapter sets out the key tenets and concepts within Service Transition, specific terminology and usage.

Chapter 4 – Service Transition processes

A separate section is dedicated to each of the processes that support Service Transition.

Some of these processes are almost wholly contained within the transition area, e.g. deployment. Others are effectively whole lifecycle processes that support the full service lifecycle: Change Management for example (see paragraph 2.4.6).

Chapter 5 – Service Transition common operation activities

Activities, information and other matters relevant to Service Transition, including the management of organizational change during transition.

Chapter 6 – Organizing for Service Transition

Roles and responsibilities together with other appropriate organizational options are considered with reference to relevant adaptations for size, industry sector etc.

Chapter 7 – Service Transition technology considerations

All aspects of IT Service Management rely, to a greater or lesser extent, on appropriate technological support. This chapter sets out the typical technology requirements for effective Service Transition and how technology can deliver constructive support.

Chapter 8 – Implementing Service Transition

This chapter considers the elements required and suitable approaches of an organization implementing Service Transition.

Chapter 9 – Challenges, critical success factors and risks

In order to ensure successful, effective and efficient Service Transitions it is essential to be able to establish the performance against targets and costs against budgets of transitioning services and of the process overall.

Afterword

Appendix A: Description of asset types

Further information

This appendix references external (to ITIL) concepts and approaches that are relevant to Service Transition. Included are:

- Formal standards such as ISO/IEC 20000 and ISO/IEC 27000
- Best practice guidance such as COBIT
- Processes and methods such as project and programme management.

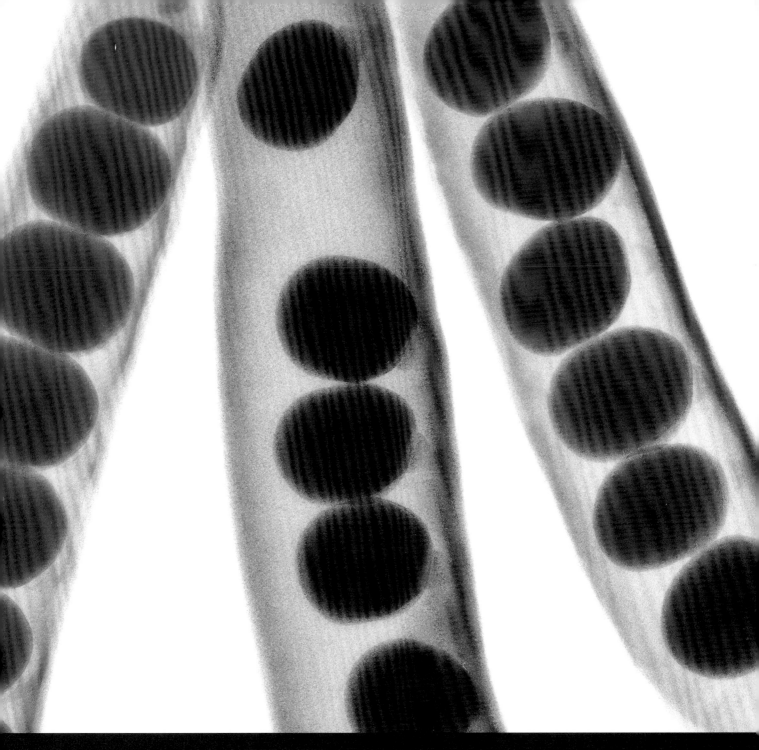

Service Management as a practice

2

2 Service Management as a practice

2.1 WHAT IS SERVICE MANAGEMENT?

Service Management is a set of specialized organizational capabilities for providing value to customers in the form of services. The capabilities take the form of functions and processes for managing services over a lifecycle, with specializations in strategy, design, transition, operation and continual improvement. The capabilities represent a service organization's capacity, competency and confidence for action. The act of transforming resources into valuable services is at the core of Service Management. Without these capabilities, a service organization is merely a bundle of resources that by itself has relatively low intrinsic value for customers.

> **Service Management**
>
> 'A set of specialized organizational capabilities for providing value to customers in the form of services.'

Organizational capabilities are shaped by the challenges they are expected to overcome. An example of this is how in the 1950s Toyota developed unique capabilities to overcome the challenge of smaller scale and financial capital compared to its American rivals. Toyota developed new capabilities in production engineering, operations management and managing suppliers to compensate for its inability to afford large inventories, make components, produce raw materials or own the companies that produced them (Magretta 2002). Service Management capabilities are similarly influenced by the following challenges that distinguish services from other systems of value creation such as manufacturing, mining and agriculture:

- The intangible nature of the output and intermediate products of service processes; this is difficult to measure, control and validate (or prove).
- Demand is tightly coupled with customer's assets; users and other customer assets such as processes, applications, documents and transactions arrive with demand and stimulate service production.
- High level of contact for producers and consumers of services; there is little or no buffer between the customer, the front-office and back-office.
- The perishable nature of service output and service capacity; there is value for the customer from assurance on the continued supply of consistent quality. Providers need to secure a steady supply of demand from customers.

Service Management, however, is more than just a set of capabilities. It is also a professional practice supported by an extensive body of knowledge, experience and skills. A global community of individuals and organizations in the public and private sectors fosters its growth and maturity. Formal schemes exist for the education, training and certification of practising organizations and individuals influence its quality. Industry best practices, academic research and formal standards contribute to its intellectual capital and draw from it.

The origins of Service Management are in traditional service businesses such as airlines, banks, hotels and phone companies. Its practice has grown with the adoption by IT organizations of a service-oriented approach to managing IT applications, infrastructure and processes. Solutions to business problems and support for business models, strategies and operations are increasingly in the form of services. The popularity of shared services and outsourcing has contributed to the increase in the number of organizations that are service providers, including internal organizational units. This in turn has strengthened the practice of Service Management and at the same time imposed greater challenges on it.

2.2 WHAT ARE SERVICES?

2.2.1 The value proposition

> **Service**
>
> 'A means of delivering value to customers by facilitating outcomes customers want to achieve without the ownership of specific costs and risks.'

Services are a means of delivering value to customers by facilitating outcomes customers want to achieve without the ownership of specific costs and risks. Services facilitate outcomes by enhancing the performance of associated tasks and reducing the effect of constraints. The result is an increase in the probability of desired outcomes (Figure 2.1).

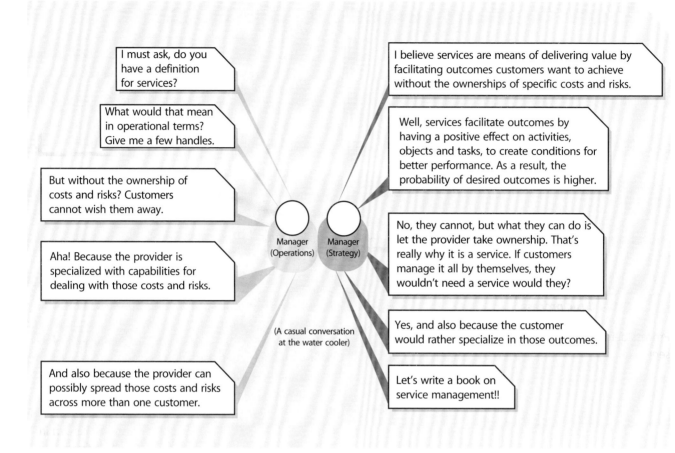

Figure 2.1 A conversation about the definition and meaning of services

2.3 FUNCTIONS AND PROCESSES ACROSS THE LIFECYCLE

2.3.1 Functions

Functions are units of organizations specialized to perform certain types of work and responsible for specific outcomes. They are self-contained with capabilities and resources necessary to their performance and outcomes. Capabilities include work methods internal to the functions. Functions have their own body of knowledge, which accumulates from experience. They provide structure and stability to organizations.

Functions are means to structure organizations to implement the specialization principle. Functions typically define roles and the associated authority and responsibility for a specific performance and outcomes. Coordination between functions through shared processes is a common pattern in organization design. Functions tend to optimize their work methods locally to focus on assigned outcomes. Poor coordination between functions combined with an inward focus leads to functional silos that hinder alignment and feedback critical to the success of the organization as a whole. Process models help avoid this problem with functional hierarchies by improving cross-functional coordination and control. Well-defined processes can improve productivity within and across functions.

2.3.2 Processes

Processes are examples of closed-loop systems because they provide change and transformation towards a goal, and use feedback for self-reinforcing and self-corrective action (Figure 2.2). It is important to consider the entire process or how one process fits into another.

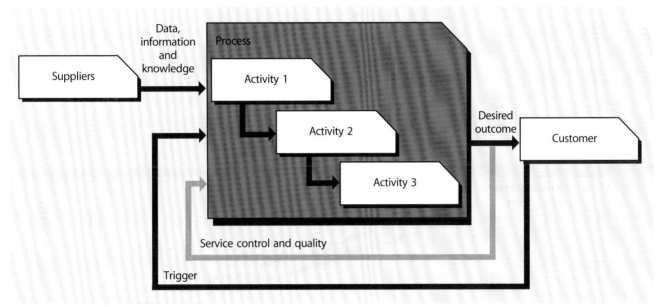

Figure 2.2 A basic process

Process definitions describe actions, dependencies and sequence. Processes have the following characteristics:

- They are measurable. We are able to measure the process in a relevant manner. It is performance driven. Managers want to measure cost, quality and other variables while practitioners are concerned with duration and productivity.

- They have specific results. The reason a process exists is to deliver a specific result. This result must be individually identifiable and countable. While we can count changes, it is impossible to count how many service desks were completed.

- They deliver to customers. Every process delivers its primary results to a customer or stakeholder. They may be internal or external to the organization but the process must meet their expectations.

- They respond to a specific event. While a process may be ongoing or iterative, it should be traceable to a specific trigger.

Functions are often mistaken for processes. For example, there are misconceptions about capacity management being a Service Management process. First, capacity management is an organizational capability with specialized processes and work methods. Whether or not it is a function or a process depends entirely on organization design. It is a mistake to assume that capacity management can only be a process. It is possible to measure and control capacity and to determine whether it is adequate for a given purpose. Assuming that is always a process with discrete countable outcomes can be an error.

2.3.3 Specialization and coordination across the lifecycle

Specialization and coordination are necessary in the lifecycle approach. Feedback and control between the functions and processes within and across the elements of the lifecycle make this possible. The dominant pattern in the lifecycle is the sequential progress starting from Service Strategy (SS) through Service Delivery (SD)–Service Transition (ST)–Service Operation (SO) and back to SS through Continual Service Improvement (CSI). That, however, is not the only pattern of action. Every element of the lifecycle provides points for feedback and control.

The combination of multiple perspectives allows greater flexibility and control across environments and situations. The lifecycle approach mimics the reality of most organizations where effective management requires the use of multiple control perspectives. Those responsible for the design, development and improvement of processes for Service Management can adopt a process-based control perspective. For those responsible for managing agreements, contracts and services may be better served by a lifecycle-based control perspective with distinct phases. Both these control perspectives benefit from systems thinking. Each control perspective can reveal patterns that may not be apparent from the other.

2.4 SERVICE TRANSITION FUNDAMENTALS

2.4.1 Purpose, goals, and objectives

The purpose of Service Transition is to:

- Plan and manage the capacity and resources required to package, build, test and deploy a release into production and establish the service specified in the customer and stakeholder requirements
- Provide a consistent and rigorous framework for evaluating the service capability and risk profile before a new or changed service is released or deployed
- Establish and maintain the integrity of all identified service assets and configurations as they evolve through the Service Transition stage
- Provide good-quality knowledge and information so that change, Release and Deployment Management

can expedite effective decisions about promoting a release through the test environments and into production

- Provide efficient repeatable build and installation mechanisms that can be used to deploy releases to the test and production environments and be rebuilt if required to restore service
- Ensure that the service can be managed, operated and supported in accordance with the requirements and constraints specified within the Service Design.

The goals of Service Transition are to:

- Set customer expectations on how the performance and use of the new or changed service can be used to enable business change

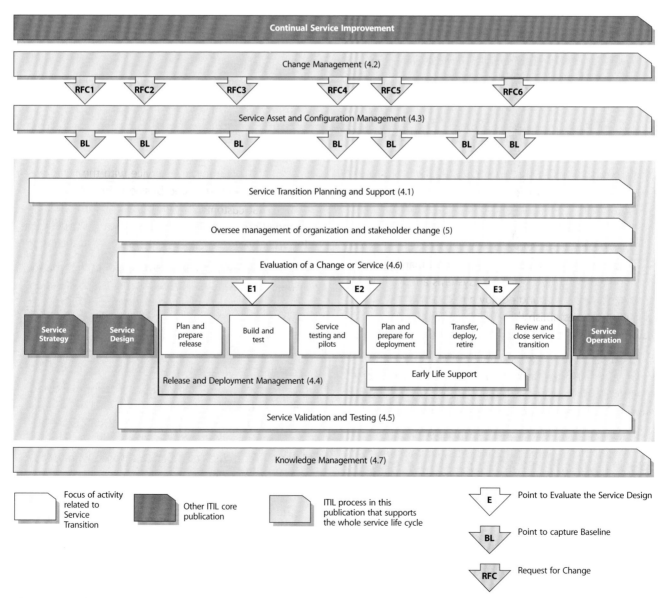

Figure 2.3 The scope of Service Transition

■ Enable the business change project or customer to integrate a release into their business processes and services

■ Reduce variations in the predicted and actual performance of the transitioned services

■ Reduce the known errors and minimize the risks from transitioning the new or changed services into production

■ Ensure that the service can be used in accordance with the requirements and constraints specified within the service requirements.

The objectives are to:

■ Plan and manage the resources to establish successfully a new or changed service into production within the predicted cost, quality and time estimates

■ Ensure there is minimal unpredicted impact on the production services, operations and support organization

■ Increase the customer, user and Service Management staff satisfaction with the Service Transition practices including deployment of the new or changed service, communications, release documentation, training and knowledge transfer

■ Increase proper use of the services and underlying applications and technology solutions

■ Provide clear and comprehensive plans that enable the customer and business change projects to align their activities with the Service Transition plans.

2.4.2 Scope

The scope of Service Transition includes the management and coordination of the processes, systems and functions to package, build, test and deploy a release into production and establish the service specified in the customer and stakeholder requirements.

The scope of the Service Transition lifecycle stage is shown in Figure 2.3. Service Transition activities are shown in the white boxes. The black boxes represent activities in the other ITIL core publications.

There may be situations when some activities do not apply to a particular transition. For example the transfer of a set of services from one organization to another may not involve release planning, build, test and acceptance.

The following lifecycle processes in this publication support all lifecycle stages:

■ Change Management

■ Service Asset and Configuration Management

■ Knowledge Management.

Service Transition uses all the processes described in the other ITIL publications as it is responsible for testing these processes, either as part of a new or changed service or as part of testing changes to the Service Management processes. Service level management is important to ensure that customer expectations are managed during Service Transition. Incident and problem management are important for handling incidents and problems during testing, pilot and deployment activities.

The following activities are excluded from the scope of Service Transition best practices:

■ Minor modifications to the production services and environment, e.g. replacement of a failed PC or printer, installation of standard software on a PC or server, or a new user

■ Ongoing Continual Service Improvements that do not significantly impact the services or service provider's capability to deliver the services, e.g. request fulfilment activities driven from Service Operations.

2.4.3 Value to business

Effective Service Transition can significantly improve a service provider's ability to handle high volumes of change and releases across its customer base. It enables the service provider to:

■ Align the new or changed service with the customer's business requirements and business operations

■ Ensure that customers and users can use the new or changed service in a way that maximizes value to the business operations.

Specifically, Service Transition adds value to the business by improving:

■ The ability to adapt quickly to new requirements and market developments ('competitive edge')

■ Transition management of mergers, de-mergers, acquisitions and transfer of services

■ The success rate of changes and releases for the business

■ The predictions of service levels and warranties for new and changed services

■ Confidence in the degree of compliance with business and governance requirements during change

■ The variation of actual against estimated and approved resource plans and budgets

■ The productivity of business and customer staff because of better planning and use of new and changed services

- Timely cancellation or changes to maintenance contracts for hardware and software when components are disposed or de-commissioned
- Understanding of the level of risk during and after change, e.g. service outage, disruption and re-work.

2.4.4 Optimizing Service Transition performance

Service Transition, in order to be effective and efficient, must focus on delivering what the business requires as a priority and doing so within financial and other resource constraints.

2.4.4.1 Measurements for alignment with the business and IT plans

The Service Transition lifecycle stage and release plans need to be aligned with the business, Service Management and IT strategies and plans.

Typical measures that can be used in measuring this alignment are:

- Increased percentage of Service Transition plans that are aligned with the business, IT, Service Management strategies and plans
- Percentage of customer and stakeholder organizations or units that have a clear understanding of the Service Transition practice and its capabilities
- Percentage of service lifecycle budget allocated to Service Transition activities
- Index of quality of the plans including adherence to structured approach, compliance with the plan templates and completeness of the plans
- Percentage of planning meetings where stakeholders have participated
- Percentage of Service Transition plans that are aligned with the Service Transition policy
- Percentage of strategic and tactical projects that adopt the Service Transition service practices
- Percentage of release planning documents that are quality assured by the Service Transition function or role.

2.4.4.2 Measurements for Service Transition

Measuring and monitoring the performance of the Service Transition lifecycle stage should focus on the delivery of the new or changed service against the predicted levels of warranty, service level, resources and constraints within the Service Design or release package. Measurements should therefore be aligned with the measures for Service

Design, and may include the variation in predicted vs actual measures for:

- Resources utilization against capacity
- Capabilities
- Warranties
- Service levels
- Cost against approved budget
- Time
- Quality of service, e.g. satisfaction rating or service levels met, breached and near misses
- Value
- Errors and incidents
- Risks.

Examples of other measures to optimize the performance of Service Transition are:

- Cost of testing and evaluation vs cost of live incidents
- Delays caused by Service Transition, e.g. lack of Service Transition resources
- Operational problems that could have been identified by the Service Transition processes
- Stakeholder satisfaction with the transition stage
- Cost savings by targeted testing of changes to the Service Design
- Reduction in urgent or late changes and releases – reducing unplanned work
- Reduced cost of transitioning services and releases – by type
- Increased productivity of staff
- Increased re-use and sharing of service assets and Service Transition process assets
- More motivated staff and improved job satisfaction
- Improved communications and inter-team working (IT, customer, users and suppliers)
- Enhanced performance of Service Transition processes.

2.4.5 Interfaces to other service lifecycle stages

Service Transition 'sits between' Service Design and Service Operations in the service lifecycle and the major day-to-day interfaces are with those stages. However, there is interface with all of the other service lifecycle stages, delineated by inputs and outputs that flow between them.

2.4.5.1 Inputs to Service Transition

Inputs from Service Strategy influence the overall approach, structures and constraints that apply to Service Transitions and include:

- Service Portfolio
- Customer portfolio
- Contract portfolio
- Service Lifecycle model
- Policies
- Strategies
- Constraints
- Architectures
- Service Transition requirements
- Service Management Plan (as required by ISO/IEC 20000).

Service Design is the principal source of the triggers that initiate work elements within the Service Transition lifecycle stage, i.e. they input the Service Design packages that need to be transitioned. The Service Design package includes:

- Service definition
- Service structure (including core and supporting services)
- Financial/economic/cost model (with Total Cost of Ownership/Total Cost of Utilization)
- Capacity/resource model – combined with performance and availability
- Service Management integrated process model (as in ISO/IEC 20000)
- Service Operations model (includes support resources, escalation procedures and critical situation handling procedures)
- Design and interface specifications
- Release design
- Deployment plan
- Acceptance Criteria – at all levels at which testing and acceptance have been foreseen
- Requests for Change (RFCs) to instigate required changes to the environment within which the service functions or will function.

The key input, in terms of initiating action, which would normally be channelled through Service Design is the authorization to start Service Transition (e.g. RFC). However this authorization may come directly from the business customers, through a strategy change or from audit or Continual Service Improvement (CSI).

Continual Service Improvement will deliver inputs in terms of suggested improvements to transition policy, practices and processes, based on audit and other improvement exercises, possibly in liaison with customer and other stakeholders via techniques such as a stakeholder survey.

Service Operation will provide input to testing and especially to service acceptance in terms of establishing whether operations requirements have been met before handover can be made.

2.4.5.2 Outputs from Service Transition

The clearest set of outputs from Service Transition are to Service Operations and the customer and user community to whom services are delivered following successful Service Transition. These outputs include:

- Approved service release package and associated deployment packages
- Updated Service package or service bundle that defines the end-to-end service(s) offered to customers
- Updated Service Portfolio and service catalogue
- Updated contract portfolio
- Documentation for a transferred or decommissioned service.

Outputs to Continual Service Improvement will comprise suggestions and observations on changes required to improve processes, especially those within Service Design and Service Transition, but possibly also within Service Strategy and in business processes and relationship management.

2.4.6 Processes within Service Transition

There are two types of significant Service Management process that are described in this publication as indicated below.

2.4.6.1 Processes that support the service lifecycle

The first group are whole service lifecycle processes that are critical during the transition stage but influence and support all lifecycle stages. These comprise:

- Change Management
- Service Asset and Configuration Management
- Knowledge Management.

2.4.6.2 Processes within Service Transition

The following processes are strongly focused within the Service Transition stage:

- Transition Planning and Support
- Release and Deployment Management
- Service Testing and Validation
- Evaluation.

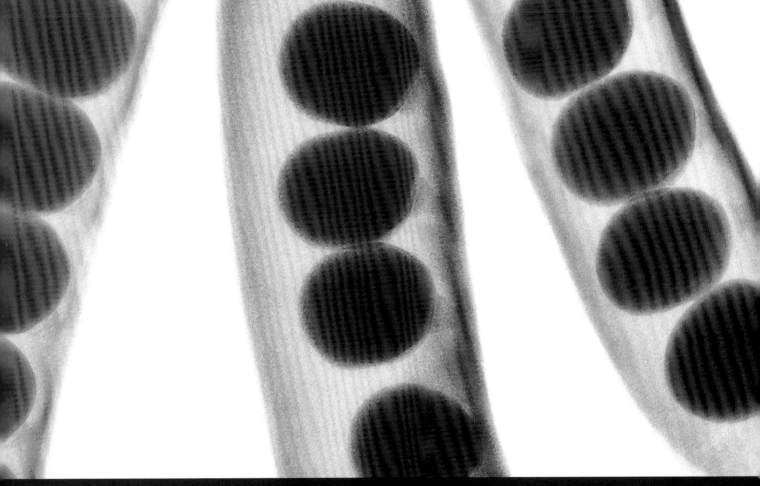

Service Transition
principles

3 Service Transition principles

This section describes some of the key principles of Service Transition that will enable service providers to plan and implement the Service Transition best practices. These principles are the same irrespective of the organization; however, the approach may need to be tailored to circumstances, including the size, distribution, culture and resources.

3.1 PRINCIPLES SUPPORTING SERVICE TRANSITION

Service Transition is supported by underlying principles that evolve from Service Strategy considerations and underpin the Service Transition practices and approach. These principles, around understanding what a service is and how it delivers value to the business, provide the foundation for Service Transition.

3.1.1 Define a service

The Service Strategy publication describes the framework for defining a service. The value of a service is defined within the context of customers and contracts within an eco-system that is commonly referred to as the business environment. Figure 3.1 illustrates the service provider assets used to deliver services to the business and customers.

Resources are tangible and intangible assets that are owned or controlled by the service provider or the organization for conversion into final products or services that are utilized by customers. Resources are converted into goods and services using knowledge, skills, experience, processes, systems and technologies, which are by themselves a special category of intangible assets called capabilities. This is described further in Service Strategy.

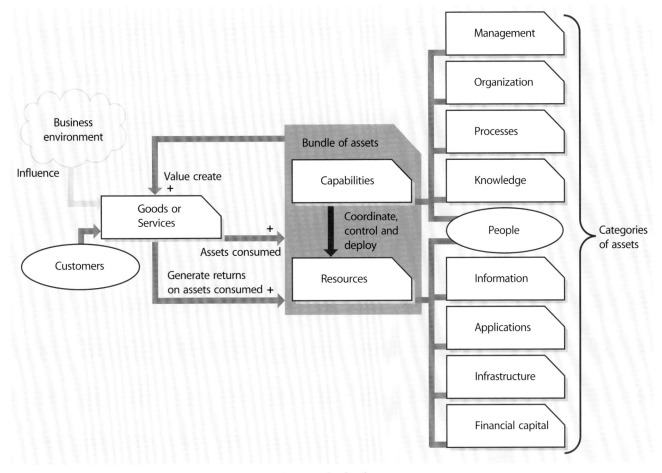

Figure 3.1 Service assets required to deliver services to the business

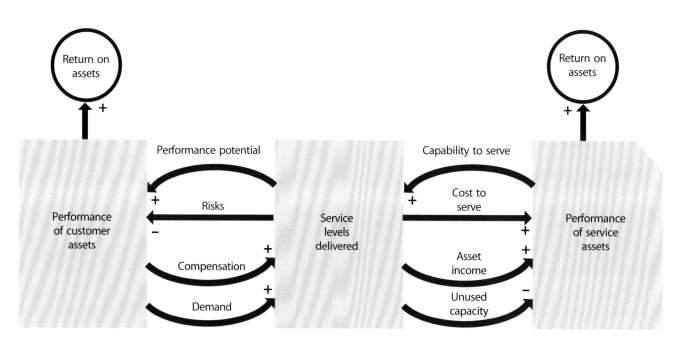

Value = Potential increased + risks reduced
Value ≥ Compensation

ROA = Compensation/Cost to serve

Figure 3.2 Services provide value by increasing the performance of customer assets and removing risks

The term asset is used to refer either to capabilities or resources, or both depending on the surrounding context.

Services are a means for providing value to customers as shown in Figure 3.2. They are a means by which one business unit delivers value to one or more other business units, or to sub-units within itself. In this publication, business units that deliver services are commonly referred to as service providers or service units and those that use services are called customers or simply business units.

3.1.2 Service utilities and warranties

The utility of a service is defined in terms of the business outcomes that customers expect the service to support and the constraints it will remove. This utility is in the form of enhancing or enabling the performance of the customer assets, and contributing to the realization of business outcomes.

> **Example of utility**
>
> In the case of the lending division of a bank (customer), the utility of a credit-check service is that it allows the lending process (customer assets) to determine the credit-worthiness of borrowers so that loan applications may be approved in a timely manner after calculating all the risks associated with the borrower (supported outcome).

A warranty is an assurance that some product or service will be provided or will meet certain specifications. Three characteristics of warranty are that it:

■ is provided in terms of the availability and capacity of services

■ ensures that customer assets continue to receive utility, even if at degraded service levels, through major disruptions or disasters

■ ensures security for the value-creating potential of customer assets.

It is important to understand that the three aspects of warranty are valid for all services though one aspect may be more critical than another. Indeed, the primary value proposition in some services is high-availability, continuity and security.

3.2 POLICIES FOR SERVICE TRANSITION

The following aspects constitute fundamental principles of Service Transition. Their endorsement and visible support from senior management contributes to the overall effectiveness. Each principle is explicitly stated and its suggested application and approach is illustrated by applicable principles and best practices that help an organization to deliver that principle.

3.2.1 Define and implement a formal policy for Service Transition

Policy:

- A formal policy for Service Transition should be defined, documented and approved by the management team, who ensure that it is communicated throughout the organization and to all relevant suppliers and partners.

Principles:

- Policies should clearly state the objectives and any non-compliance with the policy shall be remedied.
- Align the policies with the overall governance framework, organization and Service Management policies.
- Sponsors and decision makers involved in developing the policy must demonstrate their commitment to adapting and implementing the policy. This includes the commitment to deliver predicted outcomes from any change in the Services.
- Use processes that integrate teams; blend competencies while maintaining clear lines of accountability and responsibility.
- Deliver changes in releases.
- Address deployment early in the release design and release planning stages.

Best practice:

- Obtain formal sign off from the management team, sponsors and decision makers involved in developing the policy.

3.2.2 Implement all changes to services through Service Transition

Policy:

- All changes to the Service Portfolio or service catalogue are implemented through Change Management and the changes that are managed by the Service Transition lifecycle stage are defined and agreed.

Principles:

- A single focal point for changes to the production services minimizes the probability of conflicting changes and potential disruption to the production environment.
- People that do not have the authority to make a change or release into the production environment should be prevented from having access.

- Familiarity with the Service Operations organization enhances mobilization and enables organizational change.
- Increasing knowledge and experience of the services and production environment improves efficiency.
- Each release package will be designed and governed by a Request for Change raised via the Change Management process to ensure effective control and traceability.
- Standardized methods and procedures are used for efficient and prompt handling of all changes, in order to minimize the impact of change-related incidents on business continuity, service quality and re-work.
- All updates to changes and releases are recorded against service assets and/or configuration items in the Configuration Management System.

Best practices:

- The definition of a change is clearly defined.
- Internal and external changes are differentiated.
- Changes are justified through the development of a clear Business Case.
- Changes to services are defined in a Service Design Package that Service Transition can use to measure the actual vs predicted progress and performance.
- The existing Change Management process may need to be standardized and enforced.
- Management commitment to enforcing the process is essential, and it must be clearly visible to all stakeholders.
- Configuration auditing aims to identify unauthorized changes.
- Do not accept late requests for changes that cannot be properly managed.

3.2.3 Adopt a common framework and standards

Policy:

- Base Service Transition on a common framework of standard re-usable processes and systems to improve integration of the parties involved in Service Transition and reduce variations in the processes.

Principles:

- Implement industry best practices as the basis of standardization to enable integration across the supply chain.
- Control the Service Transition framework and standards under Change and Configuration Management.

■ Ensure processes are adopted consistently by scheduling regular reviews and audits of the Service Management processes.

Best practices:

■ Publish standards and best practices for Service Transition.

■ Provide a framework for establishing consistent processes for assuring and evaluating the service capability and risk profile before and after a release is deployed.

■ Provide supporting systems to automate standard processes in order to reduce resistance to adoption.

■ Ensure there is management understanding of the need for standard ways of working by developing and delivering improvements based on a sound Business Case.

■ Establish the level of management and stakeholder commitment and take action to close any gaps.

■ Continually plan how to improve the buy-in to adopting a common framework and standards.

3.2.4 Maximize re-use of established processes and systems

Policy:

■ Service Transition processes are aligned with the organization's processes and related systems to improve efficiency and effectiveness and where new processes are required, they are developed with re-use in mind.

Principles:

■ Re-use established processes and systems wherever possible.

■ Capture data and information from the original source to reduce errors and aid efficiency.

■ Develop re-usable standard Service Transition models to build up experience and confidence in the Service Transition activities.

■ Implement industry standards and best practices as the basis of standardization to enable integration of deliverables from many suppliers.

Best practices:

■ Integrate the Service Transition processes into the quality management system.

■ Use the organization's programme and project management practices.

■ Use existing communications channels for Service Transition communication.

■ Follow human resources, training, finance and facilities management processes and common practices.

■ Design the Service Transition models that enable easy customization to suit specific circumstances.

■ Structure models such that a consistent approach is repeated for each target service unit or environment with local variation as required.

3.2.5 Align Service Transition plans with the business needs

Policy:

■ Align Service Transition plans and new or changed service with the customer and business organization's requirements in order to maximize value delivered by the change.

Principles:

■ Set customer and user expectations during transition on how the performance and use of the new or changed service can be used to enable business change.

■ Provide information and establish processes to enable business change projects and customers to integrate a release into their business processes and services.

■ Ensure that the service can be used in accordance with the requirements and constraints specified within the service requirements in order to improve customer and stakeholder satisfaction.

■ Communicate and transfer knowledge to the customers, users and stakeholders in order to increase their capability to maximize use of the new or changed service.

■ Monitor and measure the use of the services and underlying applications and technology solutions during deployment and early life support in order to ensure that the service is well established before transition closure.

■ Compare the actual performance of services after a transition against the predicted performance defined in Service Design with the aim of reducing variations in service capability and performance.

Best practices:

■ Adopt programme and project management best practices to plan and manage the resources required to package, build, test and deploy a release into production successfully within the predicted cost, quality and time estimates.

- Provide clear and comprehensive plans that enable the customer and business change projects to align their activities with the Service Transition plans.
- Manage stakeholder commitment and communications.

3.2.6 Establish and maintain relationships with stakeholders

Policy:

- Establish and maintain relationships with customers, customer representatives, users and suppliers throughout Service Transition in order to set their expectations about the new or changed service.

Principles:

- Set stakeholder expectations on how the performance and use of the new or changed service can be used to enable business change.
- Communicate changes to all stakeholders in order to improve their understanding and knowledge of the new or changed service.
- Provide good-quality knowledge and information so that stakeholders can find information about the Service Transition easily, e.g. release and deployment plans, and release documentation.

Best practices:

- Check with stakeholders that the new or changed service can be used in accordance with the requirements and constraints specified within the service requirements.
- Share Service Transition and release plans and any changes with stakeholders.
- Work with business relationship management and service level management to build customer and stakeholder relationships during Service Transition.

3.2.7 Establish effective controls and disciplines

Policy:

- Establish suitable controls and disciplines throughout the service lifecycle to enable the smooth transition of service changes and releases.

Principles:

- Establish and maintain the integrity of all identified service assets and configurations as they evolve through the Service Transition stage.
- Automate audit activities, where beneficial, in order to increase the detection of unauthorized changes and discrepancies in the configurations.

- Clearly define 'who is doing what, when and where' at all handover points to increase accountability for delivery against the plans and processes.
- Define and communicate roles and responsibilities for handover and acceptance through the Service Transition activities (e.g. build, test, release and deployment) to reduce errors resulting from misunderstandings and lack of ownership.
- Establish transaction-based processes for configuration, change and problem management to provide an audit trail and the management information necessary to improve the controls.

Best practices:

- Ensure roles and responsibilities are well defined, maintained and understood by those involved and mapped to any relevant processes for current and foreseen circumstances.
- Assign people to each role and maintain the assignment in the service knowledge management system (SKMS) or Configuration Management system (CMS) to provide visibility of the person responsible for particular activities.
- Implement integrated incident, problem, change, Configuration Management processes with service level management to measure the quality of configuration items throughout the service lifecycle.
- Ensure that the service can be managed, operated and supported in accordance with the requirements and constraints specified within the Service Design by the service provider organization.
- Ensure that only competent staff can implement changes to controlled test environments and production services.
- Perform configuration audits and process audits to identify configuration discrepancies and non-conformance that may impact Service Transitions.

3.2.8 Provide systems for knowledge transfer and decision support

Policy:

- Service Transition develops systems and processes to transfer knowledge for effective operation of the service and enable decisions to be made at the right time by competent decision makers.

Principles:

- Provide quality data, information and knowledge at the right time to the right people to reduce effort spent waiting for decisions and consequent delays.

- Ensure there is adequate training and knowledge transfer to users to reduce the number of training calls that the service desk handles.
- Improve the quality of information and data to improve user and stakeholder satisfaction while optimising the cost of production and maintenance.
- Improve the quality of documentation to reduce the number of incidents and problems caused by poor-quality user documentation, release, deployment, support or operational documentation.
- Improve the quality of release and deployment documentation to reduce the number of incidents and problems caused by poor-quality user documentation, support or operational documentation time between changes being implemented and the documentation being updated.
- Provide easy access to quality information to reduce the time spent searching and finding information, particularly during critical activities such as handling a major incident.
- Establish the definitive source of information and share information across the service lifecycle and with stakeholders in order to maximize the quality of information and reduce the overhead in maintaining information.
- Provide consolidated information to enable change, Release and Deployment Management to expedite effective decisions about promoting a release through the test environments and into production.

Best practices:

- Provide easy access, presentation and reporting tools for the SKMS and CMS in order.
- Provide quality user interfaces and tools to the SKMS and CMS for different people and roles to make decisions at appropriate times.
- Summarize and publish the predicted and unpredicted effects of change, deviations from actual vs predicted capability and performance together with the risk profile.
- Ensure Service Asset and Configuration Management information is accurate to trigger approval and notification transactions for decision making via workflow tools, e.g. changes, acceptance of deliverables.
- Provide knowledge, information and data for deployment, service desk, operations and support teams to resolve incidents and errors.

3.2.9 Plan release and deployment packages

Policy:

- Release packages are planned and designed to be built, tested, delivered, distributed and deployed into the live environment in a manner that provides the agreed levels of traceability, in a cost-effective and efficient way.

Principles:

- A release policy is agreed with the business and all relevant parties.
- Releases are planned well in advance.
- Resource utilization is optimized across Service Transition activities to reduce costs.
- Resources are coordinated during release and deployment.
- Release and distribution mechanisms are planned to ensure the integrity of components during installation, handling, packaging and delivery is maintained.
- Emergency releases are managed in line with the emergency change procedure.
- The risks of backing out or remediating a failed release are assessed and managed.
- The success and failure of the releases packages is measured with the aim of improving effectiveness and efficiency while optimizing costs.

Best practices:

- All updates to releases are recorded in the Configuration Management System.
- Definitive versions of electronic media, including software, are captured in a Definitive Media Library prior to release into the service operations readiness test environment.
- Record the planned release and deployment dates and deliverables with references to related change requests and problems.
- Proven procedures for handling, distribution, delivery of release and deployment packages including verification.
- Pre-requisites and co-requisites for a release are documented and communicated to the relevant parties, e.g. technical requirements for test environment.

3.2.10 Anticipate and manage course corrections

Course corrections

When plotting a long route for a ship or aircraft, assumptions will be made about prevailing winds, weather and other factors, and plans for the journey prepared. Checks along the way – observations based on the actual conditions experienced – will require (usually minor) alterations to ensure the destination is reached.

Successful transition is also a journey – from the 'as is' state within an organization towards the 'as required' state. In the dynamic world within which IT Service Management functions, it is very often the case that factors arise between initial design of a changed or new service and its actual transition. This means the need for 'course corrections' to that Service Transition journey, altering the original Service Design planned course of action to the destination the customer needs to reach.

Policy:

- Train staff to recognize the need for course corrections and empower them to apply necessary variations within prescribed and understood limits.

Principles:

- Build stakeholder expectation that changes to plans are necessary and encouraged.
- Learn from previous course corrections to predict future ones and re-use successful approaches.
- Debrief and propagate knowledge through end-of-transition debriefing sessions and make conclusions available through the service knowledge management system.
- Manage course corrections through appropriate Change Management and baseline procedures.

Best practices:

- Use project management practices and the Change Management process to manage course corrections.
- Document and control changes but without making the process bureaucratic (it must be easier to do it right than to cope with the consequences of doing it wrong).
- Provide information on changes that were applied after the configuration baseline was established.
- Involve stakeholders about changes when appropriate, but manage issues and risks within Service Transition when appropriate.

3.2.11 Proactively manage resources across Service Transitions

Policy:

- Provide and manage shared and specialist resources across Service Transition activities to eliminate delays.

Principles:

- Recognize the resources, skills and knowledge required to deliver Service Transition within the organization.
- Develop a team (including externally sourced resources) capable of successful implementation of the Service Transition strategy, Service Design package and release package.
- Establish dedicated resources to perform critical activities to reduce delays.
- Establish and manage shared resources to improve the effectiveness and efficiency of Service Transition.
- Automate repetitive and error-prone processes to improve the effectiveness and efficiency of key activities, e.g. distribution, build and installation.

Best practices:

- Work with human resources (HR), supplier management etc. to identify, manage and make use of competent and available resources.
- Recognize and use competent and specialist resources outside the core ITSM team to deliver Service Transition.
- Proactively manage shared resources to minimize the impact that delays in one transition have on another transition.
- Measure the impact of using dedicated vs non-dedicated resources on delays, e.g. using operations staff who get diverted to fix major incidents, scheduling issues with test facilities.

3.2.12 Ensure early involvement in the service lifecycle

Policy:

- Establish suitable controls and disciplines to check at the earliest possible stage in the service lifecycle that a new or changed service will be capable of delivering the value required.

Principles:

- Use a range of techniques to maximize fault detection early in the service lifecycle in order to reduce the cost of rectification. (The later in the lifecycle that an error is detected, the higher the cost of rectification.)

- Identify changes that will not deliver the expected benefits and either change the service requirements or stop the change before resources are wasted.

Best practices:

- Involve customers or customer representatives in service acceptance test planning and test design to understand how to validate that the service will add value to the customer's business processes and services.
- Involve users in test planning and design whenever possible. Base testing on how the users actually work with a service – not just how the designers intended it to be used.
- Use previous experience to identify errors in the Service Design.
- Build in – at the earliest possible stage – the ability to check for and to demonstrate that a new or changed service will be capable of delivering the value required of it.
- Use an independent evaluation of the Service Design and internal audits to establish whether the risks of progressing are acceptable.

3.2.13 Assure the quality of the new or changed service

Policy:

- Verify and validate that the proposed changes to the operational services defined in the service and release definitions, service model and Service Design Package can deliver the required service requirements and business benefits.

Principles:

- Service Transition is responsible for assuring that the proposed changes to the operational services can be delivered according to the agreements, specifications and plans within agreed confidence levels.
- Ensure that Service Transition teams understand what the customers and business actually require from a service to improve customer and users' satisfaction.
- Quality assurance and testing practices provide a comprehensive method for assuring the quality and risks of new or changed services.
- Test environments need to reflect the live environment to the greatest degree possible in order to optimize the testing efforts.
- Test design and execution should be managed and delivered independently from the service designer and developer in order to increase the effectiveness of

testing and meet any 'segregation of duty' requirements.

- Perform independent evaluations of the Service Design and the new or changed service to identify the risks that need to be managed and mitigated during build, test, deployment and use of the service – see section 4.6.
- Implement problem and Configuration Management processes across the service lifecycle in order to measure and reduce the known errors caused by implementing releases into production.

Best practices:

- Understand the business's process and priorities – this often requires an understanding of their culture, language, customs and customers.
- Comprehensive stakeholder involvement is important both for effective testing and to build stakeholder confidence, and so should be visible across the stakeholder community.
- Understand the differences between the build, test and production environments in order to manage any differences and improve the ability to predict a service's behaviour.
- Test environments are maintained under Change and Configuration Management, and their continued relevance is considered directly as part of any change.
- Establish the current service baseline and the Service Design baseline prior to evaluation of the change.
- Evaluate the predicted capability, quality and costs of the Service Design taking into account the results of previous experience and stakeholder feedback prior to release and deployment.
- Consider the circumstances that will actually be in place when Service Transition is complete, not just what was expected at the design stage.

3.2.14 Proactively improve quality during Service Transition

Policy:

- Proactively plan and improve the quality of the new or changed service during transition.

Principles:

- Detect and resolve incidents and problems during transition to reduce the likelihood of errors occurring during the operational phase and directly adversely affecting business operations.
- Proactively manage and reduce incidents, problems and errors detected during Service Transition to reduce costs, re-work and the impact on the user's business activities.

■ Align the management of incidents, problems and errors during transition with the production processes in order to measure and manage the impact and cost of errors across the service lifecycle easily.

Best practices:

■ Compare actual vs predicted service capability, performance and costs during pilots and early life support in order to identify any deviations and risks that can be removed prior to Service Transition closure.

■ Perform an independent evaluation of the new or changed service to identify the risk profile and prioritize the risks that need to be mitigated prior to transition closure, e.g. security risks that may impact the warranties.

■ Use the risk profile from the evaluation of the Service Design to develop risk-based tests.

■ Provide and test the diagnostic tools and aids with the service desk, operations and support staff to ensure that, if something goes wrong in testing or live production use, it is relatively simple to obtain key information that helps to diagnose the problem without impacting too much on the user.

■ Encourage cross-fertilization of knowledge between transition and operation stages to improve problem diagnoses and resolution time, e.g. workarounds and fixes.

■ Establish transition incident, problem, error and resolution procedures and measures that reflect those in use in the live environment.

■ Fix known errors and resolve incidents in accordance with their priority for resolution.

■ Document any resolution, e.g. workarounds so that the information can be analysed.

■ Proactively analyse the root cause of high priority and repeat incidents.

■ Record, classify and measure the number and impact of incidents and problems against each release in the test, deployment and production stages in order to identify early opportunities to fix errors.

■ Compare the number and impact of incidents and problems between deployments in order to identify improvements and fix any underlying problems that will improve the user experience for subsequent deployments.

■ Update incident and problem management with workarounds and fixes identified in transition.

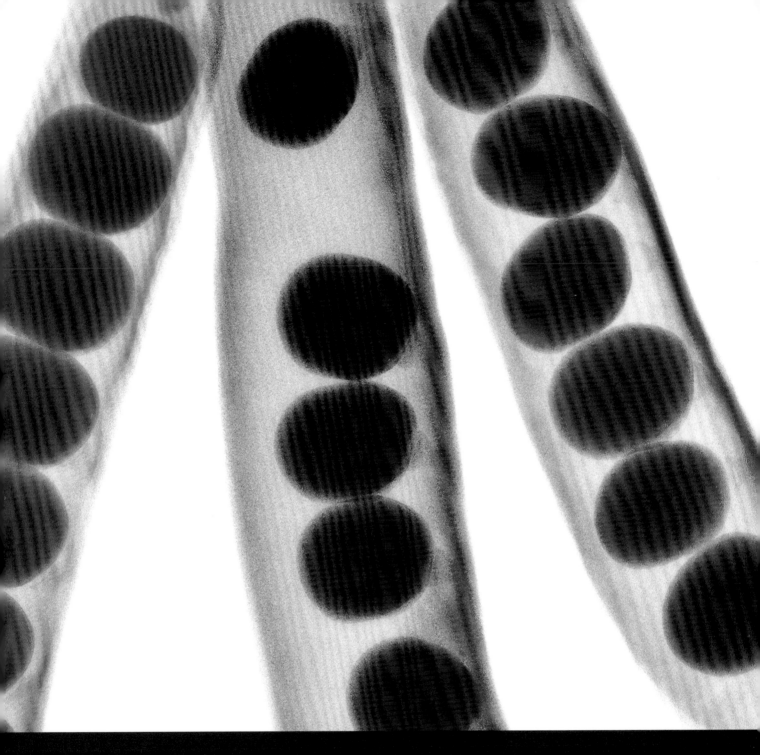

Service Transition processes

4

4 Service Transition processes

This chapter sets out the processes and activities on which effective Service Transition depends. These comprise both lifecycle processes and those almost wholly contained within Service Transition. Each is described in detail, setting out the key elements of that process or activity.

The processes and activities and their relationships are set out in Figure 2.3, and the topics specifically addressed in this chapter are:

■ Transition Planning and Support
■ Change Management
■ Service Asset and Configuration Management
■ Release and Deployment Management
■ Service Validation and Testing
■ Evaluation
■ Knowledge Management.

Some of these processes are used throughout the service lifecycle, but are addressed in this publication since they are central to effective Service Transition.

The other processes and activities are mostly contained within the Service Transition phase of the lifecycle, but also are made use of in other phases, e.g. evaluation of design, and performance testing within operations.

The scope, goals, purpose and vision of Service Transition as a whole are set out in section 2.4.

4.1 TRANSITION PLANNING AND SUPPORT

4.1.1 Purpose, goals and objectives

The purpose of the Transition Planning and Support activities is to:

■ Plan appropriate capacity and resources to package a release, build, release, test, deploy and establish the new or changed service into production
■ Provide support for the Service Transition teams and people
■ Plan the changes required in a manner that ensures the integrity of all identified customer assets, service assets and configurations can be maintained as they evolve through Service Transition
■ Ensure that Service Transition issues, risks and deviations are reported to the appropriate stakeholders and decision makers

■ Coordinate activities across projects, suppliers and service teams where required.

The goals of Transition Planning and Support are to:

■ Plan and coordinate the resources to ensure that the requirements of Service Strategy encoded in Service Design are effectively realized in Service Operations
■ Identify, manage and control the risks of failure and disruption across transition activities.

The objective of Transition Planning and Support is to:

■ Plan and coordinate the resources to establish successfully a new or changed service into production within the predicted cost, quality and time estimates
■ Ensure that all parties adopt the common framework of standard re-usable processes and supporting systems in order to improve the effectiveness and efficiency of the integrated planning and coordination activities
■ Provide clear and comprehensive plans that enable the customer and business change projects to align their activities with the Service Transition plans.

4.1.2 Scope

The scope of the Service Transition Planning and Support activities includes:

■ Incorporating design and operation requirements into the transition plans
■ Managing and operating Transition Planning and Support activities
■ Maintaining and integrating Service Transition plans across the customer, service and contract portfolios
■ Managing Service Transition progress, changes, issues, risks and deviations
■ Quality review of all Service Transition, release and deployment plans
■ Managing and operating the transition processes, supporting systems and tools
■ Communications with customers, users and stakeholders
■ Monitoring and improving Service Transition performance.

4.1.3 Value to business

Effective Transition Planning and Support can significantly improve a service provider's ability to handle high volumes of change and releases across its customer base. An integrated approach to planning improves the alignment of the Service Transition plans with the customer, supplier and business change Project Plans.

4.1.4 Policies, principles and basic concepts

This section sets out basic concepts within that support for effective planning for Service Transition.

Service Design will – in collaboration with customers, external and internal suppliers and other relevant stakeholders – develop the Service Design and document it in a Service Design Package (SDP). The SDP includes the following information that is required by the Service Transition team:

- The applicable service packages (e.g. Core Service Package, Service Level Package)
- The service specifications
- The service models
- The architectural design required to deliver the new or changed Service including constraints
- The definition and design of each release package
- The detailed design of how the service components will be assembled and integrated into a release package
- Release and deployment plans
- The Service Acceptance Criteria.

4.1.4.1 Service Transition policy

Policies that support Service Transition are provided in Chapter 3.

The Change, Configuration and Knowledge Management policies also support Service Transition and further examples of these are provided in sections 4.2, 4.3 and 4.7.

4.1.4.2 Release policy

The release policy should be defined for one or more services and include:

- The unique identification, numbering and naming conventions for different types of release together with a description
- The roles and responsibilities at each stage in the release and deployment process

- The expected frequency for each type of release
- The approach for accepting and grouping changes into a release, e.g. how enhancements are prioritized for inclusion
- The mechanism to automate the build, installation and release distribution processes to improve re-use, repeatability and efficiency
- How the configuration baseline for the release is captured and verified against the actual release contents, e.g. hardware, software, documentation and knowledge
- Exit and entry criteria and authority for acceptance of the release into each Service Transition stage and into the controlled test, training, disaster recovery and production environments
- Criteria and authorization to exit early life support and handover to Service Operations.

A release that consists of many different types of service assets may involve many people, often from different organizations. The typical responsibilities for handover and acceptance of a release should be defined and then they can be modified as required for specific transitions. The main roles and responsibilities at points of handover should be defined to ensure that everyone understands their role and level of authority and those of others involved in the release and deployment process.

An example of a responsibility matrix for an organization that supports client–server applications is shown in Table 4.1. Such a matrix will help to identify gaps and overlaps and typical roles can be planned for the future.

Table 4.1 Example responsibility matrix for release points during Service Transition

	Development	Controlled test	Release to production	Production
Class of object	*Released from*	*Accepted by*	*Authority to release to live*	*Accepted and supported by*
Purchased package	Application development manager	Test manager	Change manager	Operations manager
Customized modules	Application development manager	Test manager	Change manager	Operations manager
Physical database changes	Application development manager	Database administrator	Change manager	Database administrator
Server	Server builder	Server manager	Change manager	Server manager
Desktop build (e.g. a new application)	Desktop development manager	Test manager	Change manager	Desktop support manager
Desktop application (already built and within operational constraints)	Desktop development manager	Desktop support manager	Desktop support manager, change manager	Desktop support manager
Desktop computers	Logistics	Desktop support	Desktop support manager, change manager	Desktop support manager
Desktop service	Service development	Desktop support	Service level management, desktop support manager, change manager	Service level management, desktop support manager
Release/Change authorization	Development manager	Test manager	Release manager, test manager, operations manager, desktop support service, desk user at each site, customer stakeholder, change manager	Service desk users

All releases should have a unique identifier that can be used by Configuration Management and the documentation standards. The types of release should be defined as this helps to set customer and stakeholder expectations about the planned releases. A typical example is:

- **Major releases**, normally containing large areas of new functionality, some of which may eliminate temporary fixes to problems. A major upgrade or release usually supersedes all preceding minor upgrades, releases and emergency fixes.
- **Minor releases**, normally containing small enhancements and fixes, some of which may already have been issued as emergency fixes. A minor upgrade or release usually supersedes all preceding emergency fixes.
- **Emergency releases**, normally containing the corrections to a small number of known errors or sometimes an enhancement to meet a high priority business requirement.

A release policy may say, for example, that only strict 'emergency fixes' will be issued in between formally planned releases of enhancements and non-urgent corrections.

An extract from a release policy is shown in Table 4.2, which shows how different types of release can be defined.

Table 4.2 Extract from a service release policy for a retail organization

SERVICE	Release definition*	Naming/Numbering	Frequency/Occurrence	Release window
Store service	Type A	SS_x	Annual (Feb)	Wednesday 01.00–04.00 hours
	Type B or C	SS_1.x or SS_1.1.x	Quarterly	Not holiday weekends
	Emergency	SS_1.1.1.x	As required	Not 1 September to 31 January
e-store web service	Type A	ESWnnn_x	6 months	01.00–02.00 hours
	Type B and C	ESWnnn_1.x	Monthly	Not holiday weekends
	Emergency	ESWnnn_1.1.x	As required	Not 1 October to 10 January
e-store delivery service	Type A	ESDnnn_x	6 months	01.00–02.00 hours
	Type B	ESDSnnn_1.x	Quarterly	Highest level of authorization required during holiday weekends
	Type C	ESDnnn_1.1.x	Monthly	
	Emergency	ESDnnn_1.1.1.x	As required	

*Release definitions

Type A	Something that impacts the whole system/service
Type B	A release that will impact part of the system, e.g. single sub-system or sub-service
Type C	Correction to a single function
Emergency	A change required to restore or continue service to ensure the Service Level Agreement (SLA) is maintained

4.1.5 Process activities, methods and techniques

4.1.5.1 Transition strategy

The organization should decide the most appropriate approach to Service Transition based on the size and nature of the core and supporting services, the number and frequency of releases required, and any special needs of the users – for example, if a phased roll-out is usually required over an extended period of time.

The Service Transition strategy defines the overall approach to organizing Service Transition and allocating resources. The aspects to consider are:

- Purpose, goals and objectives of Service Transition
- Context, e.g. service customer, contract portfolios
- Scope – inclusions and exclusions
- Applicable standards, agreements, legal, regulatory and contractual requirements:
  - Internal and externals standards
  - Interpretation of legislation, industry guidelines and other externally imposed requirements
  - Agreements and contracts that apply to Service Transition

- Organizations and stakeholders involved in transition:
  - Third parties, strategic partners, suppliers and service providers
  - Customers and users
  - Service Management
  - Service provider
  - Transition organization (see section 6.2)
- Framework for Service Transition:
  - Policies, processes and practices applicable to Service Transition including process service provider interfaces (SPIs)
  - Roles and responsibilities
  - Transition resource planning and estimation
  - Transition preparation and training requirements
  - The release and change authorization
  - Re-using the organization's experience, expertise, tools, knowledge and relevant historical data
  - Shared resources and service to support Service Transition
- Criteria:
  - Entry and exit criteria for each release stage
  - Criteria for stopping or re-starting transition activities

- Success and failure criteria
- Identification of requirements and content of the new or changed service:
  - Services to be transitioned with target locations, customers and organizational units
  - Release definitions
  - Applicable SDP including architectural design
  - Requirements for environments to be used, locations, organizational and technical
  - Planning and management of environments, e.g. commissioning and decommissioning
- People:
  - Assigning roles and responsibilities including approvals
  - Assigning and scheduling training and knowledge transfer
- Approach:
  - Transition model including Service Transition lifecycle stages
  - Plans for managing changes, assets, configurations and knowledge
    - Baseline and evaluation points
    - Configuration audit and verification points
    - Points where RFCs should be raised
    - Use of change windows
  - Transition estimation, resource and cost planning
  - Preparation for Service Transition
  - Evaluation
  - Release packaging, build, deployment and early life support
  - Error handling, correction and control
  - Management and control – recording, progress monitoring and reporting
  - Service performance and measurement system
  - Key performance indicators and improvement targets
- Deliverables from transition activities including mandatory and optional documentation for each stage:
  - Transition plans
  - Change and Configuration Management Plan
  - Release policy, plans and documentation
  - Test plans and reports
  - Build plans and documentation
  - Evaluation plan and report
  - Deployment plans and reports
  - Transition closure report

- Schedule of milestones
- Financial requirements – budgets and funding.

Service Transition lifecycle stages

The SDP should define the lifecycle stages for a Service Transition, e.g.:

- Acquire and test input configuration items (CIs) and components
- Build and test
- Service release test
- Service operational readiness test
- Deployment
- Early life support
- Review and close service transition.

For each stage there will be exit and entry criteria and a list of mandatory deliverables from the stage.

4.1.5.2 Prepare for Service Transition

The Service Transition preparation activities include:

- Review and acceptance of inputs from the other service lifecycle stages
- Review and check the input deliverables, e.g. SDP, Service Acceptance Criteria and evaluation report (see paragraph 4.6.6)
- Identifying, raising and scheduling RFCs
- Checking that the configuration baselines are recorded in Configuration Management before the start of Service Transition (see paragraph 4.3.4.2)
- Checking transition readiness.

The configuration baselines help to fix a point in history that people can reference and apply changes to in a manner that is understandable. Any variance to the proposed service scope, Service Strategy requirements and Service Design baseline must be requested and managed through Change Management.

At a minimum, it should be accepted (by design, transition and stakeholders) that the Service Design and all the release units can be operated and supported within the predicted constraints and environment. The evaluation activity described in section 4.6 performs the evaluation of the SDP and Service Acceptance Criteria and provides a report to Change Management with recommendations on whether the RFC should be authorized.

4.1.5.3 Planning and coordinating Service Transition

Planning an individual Service Transition

The release and deployment activities should be planned in stages as details of the deployment might not be known in detail initially. Each Service Transition plan should be developed from a proven Service Transition model wherever possible. Although Service Design provides the initial plan, the planner will allocate specific resources to the activities and modify the plan to fit in with any new circumstances, e.g. a test specialist may have left the organization.

A Service Transition plan describes the tasks and activities required to release and deploy a release into the test environments and into production, including:

- Work environment and infrastructure for the Service Transition
- Schedule of milestones, handover and delivery dates
- Activities and tasks to be performed
- Staffing, resource requirements, budgets and time-scales at each stage
- Issues and risks to be managed
- Lead times and contingency.

Allocating resources to each activity and factoring in resource availability will enable the Service Transition planner to work out whether the transition can be deployed by the required date. If resources are not available, it may be necessary to review other transition commitments and consider changing priorities. Such changes need to be discussed with change and release management as this may affect other changes that may be dependents or prerequisites of the release.

Integrated planning

Good planning and management are essential to deploy a release across distributed environments and locations into production successfully. An integrated set of transition plans should be maintained that are linked to lower-level plans such as release, build and test plans. These plans should be integrated with the change schedule, release and deployment plans. Establishing good-quality plans at the outset enables Service Transition to manage and coordinate the Service Transition resources, e.g. resource allocation, utilization, budgeting and accounting.

An overarching Service Transition plan should include the milestone activities to acquire the release components, package the release, build, test, deploy, evaluate and proactively improve the service through early life support. It will also include the activities to build and maintain the services and IT infrastructure, systems and environments and the measurement system to support the transition activities.

Adopting programme and project management best practices

It is best practice to manage several releases and deployments as a programme, with each significant deployment run as a project. The actual deployment may be carried out by dedicated staff, as part of broader responsibilities such as operations or through a team brought together for the purpose. Elements of the deployment may be delivered through external suppliers, and suppliers may deliver the bulk of the deployment effort, for example in the implementation of an off-the-shelf system such as an ITSM support tool.

Significant deployments will be complex projects in their own right. The steps to consider in planning include the range of elements comprising that service, e.g. people, application, hardware, software, documentation and knowledge. This means that the deployment will contain sub-deployments for each type of element comprising the service.

Reviewing the plans

The planning role should quality review all Service Transition, release and deployment plans. Wherever possible, lead times should include an element of contingency and be based on experience rather than merely supplier assertion. This applies even more for internal suppliers where there is no formal contract. Lead times will typically vary seasonally and they should be factored into planning, especially for long time-frame transitions, where the lead times may vary between stages of a transition, or between different user locations.

Before starting the release or deployment, the Service Transition planning role should verify the plans and ask appropriate questions such as:

- Are these Service Transition and release plans up to date?
- Have the plans been agreed and authorized by all relevant parties, e.g. customers, users, operations and support staff?
- Do the plans include the release dates and deliverables and refer to related change requests, known errors and problems?
- Have the impacts on costs, organizational, technical and commercial aspects been considered?
- Have the risks to the overall services and operations capability been assessed?

■ Has there been a compatibility check to ensure that the configuration items that are to be released are compatible with each other and with configuration items in the target environments?

■ Have circumstances changed such that the approach needs amending?

■ Were the rules and guidance on how to apply it relevant for current service and release packages?

■ Do the people who need to use it understand and have the requisite skills to use it?

■ Is the service release within the SDP and scope of what the transition model addresses?

■ Has the Service Design altered significantly such that it is no longer appropriate?

■ Have potential changes in business circumstances been identified? See example below.

Anticipating changed business circumstances

A new version of a retail organization's point of sale system was designed and ready for transition to the operational environment. Although the new version offers added features, most improvements related to ease of use, ease of support and maintainability of the software. The transition was originally scheduled for installation in September, but delays in third party suppliers meant the service fails ready for test and subsequent deployment in late November; due for installation two weeks after acceptance testing begins. The initially planned approach of involving 20% of user staff in acceptance trials and store disruption across the user base was no longer appropriate. With the Christmas sales boom imminent, such disruption was not appropriate, and would have been prevented by the annual change freeze. Instead, a longer, slower but less resource-intensive acceptance testing approach was selected with rollout to stores rescheduled for late January.

Where the transition approach does require rethinking and probable alteration, this should be delivered through the formal Change Management process, since the consideration of alternatives and agreement of the revised transition approach must be properly documented. However, for foreseeable scenarios, where the path of action is documented as an accepted reaction to the circumstances, authority to record and proceed with a change may be delegated to Service Transition or other appropriate party for approval, e.g. customer or project. For example, where the Service Transition milestone dates and release dates can be achieved with the same cost and resources with no impact on the service definition.

4.1.6 Provide transition process support

4.1.6.1 Advice

Service Transition should provide support for all stakeholders to understand and be able to follow the Service Transition framework of processes and supporting systems and tools. Although the planning and support team may not have the specialist resources to handle some aspects it is important that they can identify a relevant resource to help projects, e.g. specialists to set up Configuration Management or testing tools.

Projects should implement Service Transition activities and tasks in accordance with applicable Service Transition standards, policies and procedures. However, Project Managers are not always aware of the need to adopt these standards, policies and procedures. When new projects start up the Service Transition and planning and support role should proactively seek opportunities to establish the Service Transition processes into the project quickly – before alternative methods are adopted. Another approach is to work closely with the programme or Project Support and offer support to projects via this route.

4.1.6.2 Administration

The Service Transition Planning and Support role should provide administration for:

■ Managing of Service Transition changes and work orders

■ Managing issues, risks, deviations and waivers

■ Managing support for tools and Service Transition processes

■ Communications to stakeholders – e.g. logistics and deployment plans need to be communicated to all stakeholders

■ Monitoring the Service Transition performance to provide input into Continual Service Improvement.

Changes that affect the agreed baseline configuration items are controlled through Change Management.

Plans and progress should be communicated and made available to relevant stakeholders. The stakeholder list is defined in the service package received from design and Service Transition should establish the continued relevance of that list, and update it as necessary.

4.1.6.3 Progress monitoring and reporting

Service Transition activities require monitoring against the intentions set out in the transition model and plan. Measuring and monitoring the release and deployment will (at the conclusion) establish if the transition is proceeding according to plan.

Maintaining an oversight of the actual transitions against the integrated Service Transition plans, release and change schedules is essential. It includes monitoring the progress of each transition periodically and at milestone or baseline points as well as receiving and chasing updates.

Management reports on the status of each transition will help to identify when there are significant variances from plan, e.g. for project management and the Service Management organization to make decisions and take action.

In many cases the transition plans will require amendment to bring them into line with a reality that has changed since design. This is not synonymous with bad design or error in selecting transition models, but merely a reflection of a dynamic environment.

4.1.7 Triggers, input and output, and inter-process interfaces

The trigger is an authorized RFC for a Service Transition. The inputs are:

- Authorized RFC
- Service Design package
- Release package definition and design specification
- Service Acceptance Criteria (SAC).

Outputs:

- Transition strategy
- Integrated set of Service Transition plans.

4.1.8 Key performance indicators and metrics

Primary key performance indicators (KPIs) for Transition Planning and Support include:

- The number of releases implemented that met the customer's agreed requirements in terms of cost, quality, scope, and release schedule (expressed as a percentage of all releases)
- Reduced variation of actual vs predicted scope, quality, cost and time
- Increased customer and user satisfaction with plans and communications that enable the business to align their activities with the Service Transition plans
- Reduction in number of issues, risks and delays caused by inadequate planning.

Other KPIs for an effective transition and support process include:

- Improved Service Transition success rate through improved scope and integration of the planning activities
- Better management information on the predicted vs actual performance and cost of Service Transition
- Improved efficiency and effectiveness of the processes and supporting systems, tools, knowledge, information and data to enable the transition of new and changed services, e.g. sharing tool licences
- Reduction in time and resource to develop and maintain integrated plans and coordination activities
- Project and service team satisfaction with the Service Transition practices.

4.2 CHANGE MANAGEMENT

Changes arise for a variety of reasons:

- Proactively, e.g. seeking business benefits such as reducing costs or improving services or increasing the ease and effectiveness of support
- Reactively as a means of resolving errors and adapting to changing circumstances.

Changes should be managed to:

- Optimize risk exposure (supporting the risk profile required by the business)
- Minimize the severity of any impact and disruption
- Be successful at the first attempt.

Such an approach will deliver direct benefit to the bottom line for the business by delivering early realization of benefits (or removal of risk), with a saving of money and time.

To make an appropriate response to all requests for change entails a considered approach to assessment of risk and business continuity, change impact, resource requirements, change authorization and especially to the realizable business benefit. This considered approach is essential to maintain the required balance between the need for change and the impact of the change.

This section provides information on the Change Management process and provides guidance that is scalable for:

- Different kinds and sizes of organizations
- Small and large changes required at each lifecycle stage
- Changes with major or minor impact

■ Changes in a required timeframe

■ Different levels of budget or funding available to deliver change.

4.2.1 Purpose, goals and objectives

The purpose of the Change Management process is to ensure that:

■ Standardized methods and procedures are used for efficient and prompt handling of all changes

■ All changes to service assets and configuration items are recorded in the Configuration Management System

■ Overall business risk is optimized.

The goals of Change Management are to:

■ Respond to the customer's changing business requirements while maximizing value and reducing incidents, disruption and re-work

■ Respond to the business and IT requests for change that will align the services with the business needs.

The objective of the Change Management process is to ensure that changes are recorded and then evaluated, authorized, prioritized, planned, tested, implemented, documented and reviewed in a controlled manner.

4.2.2 Scope

Change can be defined in many ways. The definition of a service change is:

> **Service change**
>
> 'The addition, modification or removal of authorized, planned or supported service or service component and its associated documentation.'

The scope of Change Management covers changes to baselined service assets and configuration items across the whole service lifecycle.

Each organization should define the changes that lie outside the scope of their service change process. Typically these might include:

■ Changes with significantly wider impacts than service changes, e.g. departmental organization, policies and business operations – these changes would produce RFCs to generate consequential service changes

■ Changes at an operational level such as repair to printers or other routine service components.

Figure 4.1 shows a typical scope for the service Change Management process for an IT department and how it interfaces with the business and suppliers at strategic, tactical and operational levels. It covers interfaces to internal and external service providers where there are shared assets and configuration items that need to be under Change Management. Service Change Management must interface with business Change Management (to the left in Figure 4.1), and with the supplier's Change Management (to the right in the figure). This may be an external supplier with a formal Change Management system, or with the project change mechanisms within an internal development project.

The Service Portfolio provides a clear definition of all current, planned and retired services. Understanding the Service Portfolio helps all parties involved in the Service Transition to understand the potential impact of the new or changed service on current services and other new or changed services.

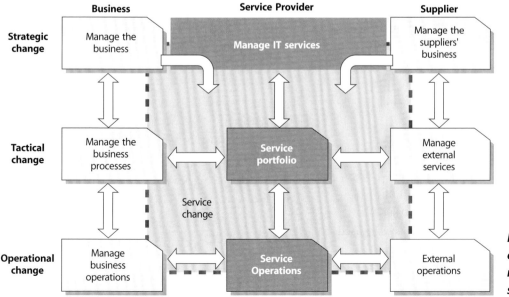

Figure 4.1 Scope of change and release management for services

Strategic changes are brought in via Service Strategy and the business relationship management processes. Changes to a service will be brought in via Service Design, Continual Service Improvement and the service level management process. Corrective change, resolving errors detected in services, will be initiated from Service Operations, and may route via support or external suppliers into a formal RFC.

Exclusions

This chapter does not cover strategic planning for business transformation or organizational change although the interfaces to these processes do need to be managed. Guidance on organizational change is addressed in Chapter 5. Business transformation is the subject of many publications aimed at the general business manager.

4.2.3 Value to business

Reliability and business continuity are essential for the success and survival of any organization. Service and infrastructure changes can have a negative impact on the business through service disruption and delay in identifying business requirements, but Change Management enables the service provider to add value to the business by:

- Prioritizing and responding to business and customer change proposals
- Implementing changes that meet the customers' agreed service requirements while optimizing costs
- Contributing to meet governance, legal, contractual and regulatory requirements
- Reducing failed changes and therefore service disruption, defects and re-work
- Delivering change promptly to meet business timescales
- Tracking changes through the service lifecycle and to the assets of its customers
- Contributing to better estimations of the quality, time and cost of change
- Assessing the risks associated with the transition of services (introduction or disposal)
- Aiding productivity of staff through minimizing disruptions due to high levels of unplanned or 'emergency' change and hence maximising service availability
- Reducing the Mean Time to Restore Service (MTRS), via quicker and more successful implementations of corrective changes
- Liaising with the business change process to identify opportunities for business improvement.

Example of IT service initiated business change

In the retail industry, bar-coding of goods coupled with bar-code readers at the check-out was initially introduced to deliver savings by removing the need to label every item, automating stock control, speeding customer throughput and reducing check-out staff. Suggestions from IT to the business resulted in making use of this facility to power innovative concepts such as Buy One Get One Free and capturing data on each individual's purchasing habits.

The reliance on IT Services and underlying information technology is now so complex that considerable time can be spent on:

- Assessing the impact of business change on IT
- Analysing the impact of a service or IT change on the business
- Notifying affected parties (of what is proposed, planned and implemented)
- Recording and maintaining accurate change, configuration, release and deployment records
- Managing and resolving incidents caused by change
- Identifying the problems that continually arise that require more change
- Introducing the new ideas and technology that cause even more change.

There are therefore considerable cost saving and efficiencies to be gained from well-structured and planned changes and releases.

As there is so much focus today on enterprise risk management, Change Management is a key process that comes under the scrutiny of auditors. The Institute of Internal Auditors, *Global Technology Audit Guide, Change and Patch Management Controls: Critical for Organizational Success*, provides guidance on assessing Change Management capability of an organization. It identifies risk indicators of poor Change Management that apply to business and IT change:

'By managing changes, you manage much of the potential risk that changes can introduce'

The top five risk indicators of poor Change Management are:

- Unauthorized changes (above zero is unacceptable)
- Unplanned outages
- A low change success rate
- A high number of emergency changes
- Delayed project implementations.

The following paragraph is extracted from the guide:

> What do all high-performing IT organizations have in common? They have a culture of Change Management that prevents and deters unauthorized change. They also 'trust but verify' by using independent detective controls to reconcile production changes with authorized changes, and by ruling out change first in the repair cycle during outages. Finally, they also have the lowest mean time to repair (MTTR). Auditors will appreciate that in these high-performing IT organizations, Change Management is not viewed as bureaucratic, but is instead the only safety net preventing them from becoming a low-performer. In other words, IT management owns the controls to achieve its own business objectives, efficiently and effectively.
>
> Achieving a change success rate over 70 percent is possible only with preventive and detective controls.

Note: Mean Time to Restore Service (MTRS) should be used to avoid the ambiguity of Mean Time To Repair (MTTR). Although MTTR is a widely accepted industry term, in some definitions 'repair' includes only repair time but in others includes recovery time. The downtime in MTRS covers all the contributory factors that make the service, component or CI unavailable. MTRS is a measure of how quickly and effectively a service, component or CI can be restored to normal working after a failure and should be calculated using the following formula:

$$MTRS\ (hours) = \frac{Total\ Downtime\ (hours)}{Number\ of\ service\ breaks}$$

4.2.4 Policies, principles and basic concepts

This section sets out basic concepts within Change Management that support its effective execution.

4.2.4.1 Policies

Increasing the success rate of changes and releases requires Executive support for implementing a culture that sets stakeholder expectations about changes and releases and reduces unplanned work.

Pressure will be applied to reduce timescales and meet deadlines; to cut budgets and running costs; and to compromise testing. This must not be done without due diligence to governance and risk. The Service Transition management team will be called on from time to time to make a 'no go' decision and not implement a required change. There must be policies and standards defined which make it clear to the internal and external providers what must be done and what the consequence of non-adherence to policy will be.

Policies that support Change Management include:

- Creating a culture of Change Management across the organization where there is zero tolerance for unauthorized change
- Aligning the service Change Management process with business, project and stakeholder Change Management processes
- Prioritization of change, e.g. innovation vs preventive vs detective vs corrective change
- Establishing accountability and responsibilities for changes through the service lifecycle
- Segregation of duty controls
- Establishing a single focal point for changes in order to minimize the probability of conflicting changes and potential disruption to the production environment
- Preventing people who are not authorized to make a change from having access to the production environment
- Integration with other Service Management processes to establish traceability of change, detect unauthorized change and identify change related incidents
- Change windows – enforcement and authorisation for exceptions
- Performance and risk evaluation of all changes that impact service capability
- Performance measures for the process, e.g. efficiency and effectiveness.

4.2.4.2 Design and planning considerations

The Change Management process should be planned in conjunction with Release and Configuration Management. This helps the service provider to evaluate the impact of the change on the current and planned services and releases.

The requirements and design for the Change Management processes include:

- Requirements, e.g. to comply with relevant legislation, industry codes of practice, standards and organizational practices
- Approach to eliminating unauthorized change
- Identification and classification:
  - Change document identifiers
  - Change document types, change documentation templates and expected content
  - Impact, urgency, priorities

- Organization, roles and responsibilities:
  - Accountabilities and responsibilities of all stakeholders
  - Approach to independent testing and evaluation of change
  - Change authorization – levels of authorization and rules that govern decision making and actions, e.g. escalation
  - Composition of Advisory Boards, e.g. the Change Advisory Board (CAB) and the Emergency CAB (ECAB)
- Stakeholders:
  - Planning of changes and releases to enable stakeholders to make their own preparation and plan their activities
  - Communicating changes, change schedule and release plans
- Grouping and relating changes:
  - Into a release, build or baseline
  - By linking several child RFCs to a master RFC
- Procedures:
  - Change authorization policies, rules and procedures
  - For raising an RFC, including preparation and submission of change proposal
  - How change requests are tracked and managed, i.e. change records
  - How change requests are impact assessed and evaluated promptly
  - Identifying dependencies and incompatibilities between changes
  - For verifying the implementation of a change
  - Overseeing and evaluating deliverables from change and release implementation
  - To review changes regularly to identify trends and improvements, e.g. in the success or failure of changes and releases
- Interfaces to other Service Management processes, e.g. service level management and capacity management for impact assessment and review
- Approach to interfacing Change, Release and Configuration Management with the problem and incident management processes to measure and reduce change-related incidents.
- Configuration Management interfaces:
  - To provide quality information for impact assessment and reporting, e.g. comparison of As-Is to As-Planned configuration
  - To identify high-risk, high-impact CIs
  - To capture CIs, configuration baselines and releases
  - To capture related deliverables, e.g. Acceptance Criteria, test and evaluation reports.

4.2.4.3 Types of change request

A change request is a formal communication seeking an alteration to one or more configuration items. This could take several forms, e.g. 'Request for Change' document, service desk call, Project Initiation Document. Different types of change may require different types of change request. An organization needs to ensure that appropriate procedures and forms are available to cover the anticipated requests. Avoiding a bureaucratic approach to documenting a minor change removes some of the cultural barriers to adopting the Change Management process.

As much use as possible should be made of devolved authorization, both through the standard change procedure (see paragraph 4.2.4.4) and through the authorization of minor changes by Change Management staff.

During the planning of different types of change requests, each must be defined with a unique naming convention, (see paragraph 4.3.5.3). Table 4.3 provides examples of different types of change request across the service lifecycle.

For different change types there are often specific procedures, e.g. for impact assessment and change authorization.

4.2.4.4 Change process models and workflows

Organizations will find it helpful to predefine change process models – and apply them to appropriate changes when they occur. A process model is a way of predefining the steps that should be taken to handle a process (in this case a process for dealing with a particular type of change) in an agreed way. Support tools can then be used to manage the required process. This will ensure that such changes are handled in a predefined path and to predefined timescales.

Changes that require specialized handling could be treated in this way, such as emergency changes that may have different authorization and may be documented retrospectively.

Table 4.3 Example of types of request by service lifecycle stage

Type of change with examples	Documented work procedures	Service Strategy	Service Design	Service Transition	Service Operation	Continual Service Improvement
Request for Change to Service Portfolios – New portfolio line item – To predicted scope, Business Case, baseline – Service pipeline	Service Change Management	✓				
Request for Change to Service or service definition – To existing or planned service attributes – Project change that impacts Service Design, e.g. forecasted warranties – Service improvement	Service Change Management	✓	✓	✓	✓	✓
Project change proposal – Business change – No impact on service or design baseline	Project Change Management procedure		✓	✓		✓
User access request	User access procedure				✓	
Operational activity – Tuning (within specification/constraints) – Re-boot hardware on failure if no impact on other services – Planned maintenance	Local procedure (often pre-authorized – see paragraph 4.2.4.4)				✓	

The change process model includes:

- The steps that should be taken to handle the change including handling issues and unexpected events
- The chronological order these steps should be taken in, with any dependences or co-processing defined
- Responsibilities; who should do what
- Timescales and thresholds for completion of the actions
- Escalation procedures; who should be contacted and when.

These models are usually input to the Change Management support tools in use and the tools then automate the handling, management, reporting and escalation of the process.

4.2.4.5 Standard changes (pre-authorized)

A standard change is a change to a service or infrastructure for which the approach is pre-authorized by Change Management that has an accepted and established procedure to provide a specific change requirement.

Examples might include an upgrade of a PC in order to make use of specific standard and pre-budgeted software, new starters within an organization, or a desktop move for a single user. Other examples include low impact, routine application change to handle seasonal variation.

Approval of each occurrence of a standard change will be granted by the delegated authority for that standard change, e.g. by the budget holding customer for installation of software from an approved list on a PC registered to their organizational unit or by the third party engineer for replacement of a faulty desktop printer.

The crucial elements of a standard change are that:

- There is a defined trigger to initiate the RFC
- The tasks are well known, documented and proven
- Authority is effectively given in advance
- Budgetary approval will typically be preordained or within the control of the change requester
- The risk is usually low and always well understood.

Once the approach to manage standard changes has been agreed, standard change processes and associated change workflows should be developed and communicated. A change model would normally be associated with each standard change to ensure consistency of approach.

Standard changes should be identified early on when building the Change Management process to promote efficiency. Otherwise, a Change Management

implementation can create unnecessarily high levels of administration and resistance to the Change Management process.

All changes, including standard changes, will have details of the change recorded. For some standard changes this may be different in nature from normal change records.

Some standard changes to configuration items may be tracked on the asset or configuration item lifecycle, particularly where there is a comprehensive CMS that provides reports of changes, their current status, the related configuration items and the status of the related CI versions. In these cases the Change and Configuration Management reporting is integrated and Change Management can have 'oversight' of all changes to service CIs and release CIs.

Some standard changes will be triggered by the request fulfilment process and be directly recorded and passed for action by the service desk.

4.2.5 Remediation planning

No change should be approved without having explicitly addressed the question of what to do if it is not successful. Ideally, there will be a back-out plan, which will restore the organization to its initial situation, often through the reloading of a baselined set of CIs, especially software and data. However, not all changes are reversible, in which case an alternative approach to remediation is required. This remediation may require a revisiting of the change itself in the event of failure, or may be so severe that it requires invoking the organization's business continuity plan. Only by considering what remediation options are available before instigating a change, and by establishing that the remediation is viable (e.g. it is successful when tested), can the risk of the proposed change be determined and the appropriate decisions taken.

4.2.6 Process activities, methods and techniques

This section provides approaches to managing service changes effectively by addressing the tasks carried out to achieve and deliver controlled change.

Overall Change Management activities include:

- Planning and controlling changes
- Change and release scheduling
- Communications
- Change decision making and change authorization
- Ensuring there are remediation plans
- Measurement and control

- Management reporting
- Understanding the impact of change
- Continual improvement.

Typical activities in managing individual changes are:

- Create and record the RFC
- Review RFC and change proposal:
  - Filter changes (e.g. incomplete or wrongly routed changes)
- Assess and evaluate the change:
  - Establish the appropriate level of change authority
  - Establish relevant areas of interest (i.e. who should be involved in the CAB)
  - Assess and evaluate the business justification, impact, cost, benefits and risk of changes
  - Request independent evaluation of a change (see 4.2.6.4)
- Authorize the change:
  - Obtain authorization/rejection

- Communicate the decision with all stakeholders, in particular the initiator of the Request for Change
- Plan updates
- Coordinate change implementation
- Review and close change:
  - Collate the change documentation, e.g. baselines and evaluation reports
  - Review the change(s) and change documentation
  - Close the change document when all actions are completed.

Throughout all the process activities listed above and described within this section, information is gathered, recorded in the CMS and reported.

Figure 4.2 shows an example of a change to the service provider's services, applications or infrastructure. Examples of the states of the RFC are shown in italics. Change and configuration information is updated all the way through the activities. Figures 4.3 and 4.4 show the equivalent process flow for some examples of standard change process flows.

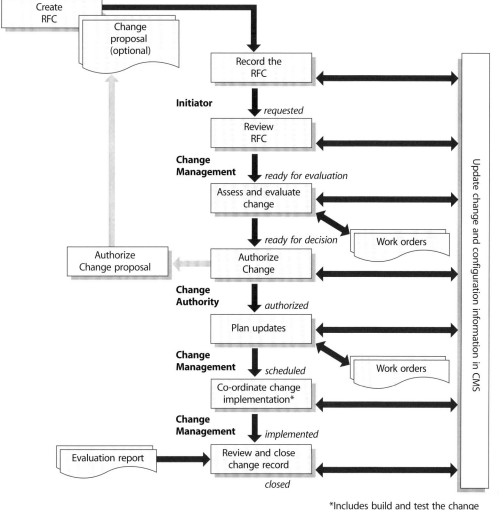

Figure 4.2 Example process flow for a normal change

*Includes build and test the change

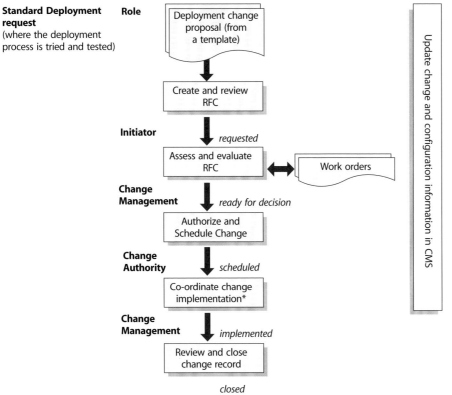

Standard Deployment request
(where the deployment process is tried and tested)

*Includes build and test the change

Figure 4.3 Example process flow for standard deployment request

4.2.6.1 Normal Change Procedure

The text in this section sets out in detail the aspects followed within a Normal Change. The general principles set out apply to all changes, but where normal change procedure can be modified, i.e. for standard or emergency changes, this is set out following the explanation of normal change procedure.

4.2.6.2 Create and record Requests for change

The change is raised by a request from the initiator – the individual or organizational group that requires the change. For example, this may be a business unit that requires additional facilities, or problem management staff instigating an error resolution from many other sources.

For a major change with significant organizational and/or financial implications, a change proposal may be required, which will contain a full description of the change together with a business and financial justification for the proposed change. The change proposal will include sign-off by appropriate levels of business management.

Table 4.4 shows an example of the information recorded for a change; the level of detail depends on the size and impact of the change. Some information is recorded when the document is initiated and some information may be updated as the change document progresses through its lifecycle. Some information is recorded directly on the

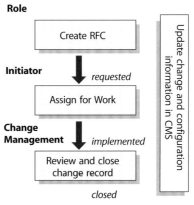

Figure 4.4 Example process flow for standard operational change request

Request for Change form and details of the change and actions may be recorded in other documents and referenced from the RFC, e.g. Business Case, impact assessment report.

Table 4.4 Example of contents of change documentation

Attribute on the change record	RFC	Change proposal (if appropriate)	Related assets/CIs
Unique number	✓		
Trigger (e.g. to purchase order, problem report number, error records, business need, legislation)	✓		
Description	Summary	Full description	
Identity of item(s) to be changed – description of the desired change	Summary	Full description	Service (for enhancement) or CI with errors (corrective changes)
Reason for change, e.g. Business Case	Summary	Full justification	
Effect of not implementing the change (business, technical, financial etc.)	✓		
Configuration items and baseline versions to be changed	✓	Affected baseline/release	Details of CIs in baseline/release
Contact and details of person proposing the change	✓		
Date and time that the change was proposed	✓		
Change category, e.g. minor, significant, major	Proposed		
Predicted timeframe, resources, costs and quality of service	Summary/reference	Full	
Change priority	Proposed		
Risk assessment and risk management plan	Summary/reference	Full	
Back-out or remediation plan	Possibly	Full	
Impact assessment and evaluation – resources and capacity, cost, benefits	Provisional	Initial impact	✓
Would the change require consequential amendment of IT Service Continuity Management (ITSCM) plan, capacity plan, security plan, test plan?	✓		Plans affected
Change decision body	✓		

Table 4.4 Example of contents of change documentation (continued)

Attribute on the change record	RFC	Change proposal (if appropriate)	Related assets/CIs
Decision and recommendations accompanying the decision	✓		
Authorization signature (could be electronic)	✓		
Authorization date and time	✓		
Target baseline or release to incorporate change into	✓		
Target change plan(s) for change to be incorporated into	✓		
Scheduled implementation time (change window, release window or date and time)	✓		
Location/reference to release/implementation plan	✓		
Details of change implementer	✓		
Change implementation details (success/fail/remediation)	✓		✓
Actual implementation date and time	✓		
Review date(s)	✓		
Review results (including cross-reference to new RFC where necessary)	Summary		
Closure	Summary		

The change record holds the full history of the change, incorporating information from the RFC and subsequently recording agreed parameters such as priority and authorization, implementation and review information. There may be many different types of change records used to record different types of change. The documentation should be defined during the process design and planning stage.

Different types of change document will have different sets of attributes to be updated through the lifecycle. This may depend on various factors such as the change process model and change category but it is recommended that the attributes are standardized wherever possible to aid reporting.

Some systems use work orders to progress the change as this enables complete traceability of the change. For example work orders may be issued to individuals or teams to do an impact assessment or to complete work required for a change that is scheduled for a specific time or where the work is to be done quickly.

As an RFC proceeds through its lifecycle, the change document, related records (such as work orders) and related configuration items are updated in the CMS, so that there is visibility of its status. Estimates and actual resources, costs and outcome (success or failure) are recorded to enable management reporting.

Change logging

The procedures for logging and documenting RFCs should be decided. RFCs might be able to be submitted on paper forms, through e-mail or using a web-based interface, for example. Where a computer-based support tool is used, the tool may restrict the format.

All RFCs received should be logged and allocated an identification number (in chronological sequence). Where change requests are submitted in response to a trigger such as a resolution to a problem record (PR), it is important that the reference number of the triggering document is retained to provide traceability.

It is recommended that the logging of RFCs is done by means of an integrated Service Management tool, capable of storing both the data on all assets and CIs and also, importantly, the relationships between them. This will greatly assist when assessing the likely impact of a change to one component of the system on all other components. All actions should be recorded, as they are carried out, within the Change Management log. If this is not possible for any reason, then they should be manually recorded for inclusion at the next possible opportunity.

Procedures will specify the levels of access and who has access to the logging system. While any authorized personnel may create, or add reports of progress to, an RFC (though the support tool should keep Change Management aware of such actions) only Change Management staff will have permission to close an RFC.

4.2.6.3 Review the Request for Change

The procedures should stipulate that, as changes are logged, Change Management should briefly consider each request and filter out any that seem to be:

- Totally impractical
- Repeats of earlier RFCs, accepted, rejected or still under consideration

- Incomplete submissions, e.g. inadequate description, without necessary budgetary approval.

These should be returned to the initiator, together with brief details of the reason for the rejection, and the log should record this fact. A right of appeal against rejection should exist, via normal management channels, and should be incorporated within the procedures.

4.2.6.4 Assess and evaluate the change

The potential impact on the services of failed changes and their impact on service assets and configurations need to be considered. Generic questions (e.g. the 'seven Rs') provide a good starting point.

The seven Rs of Change Management

The following questions must be answered for all changes. Without this information, the impact assessment cannot be completed, and the balance of risk and benefit to the live service will not be understood. This could result in the change not delivering all the possible or expected business benefits or even of it having a detrimental, unexpected effect on the live service.

- Who RAISED the change?
- What is the REASON for the change?
- What is the RETURN required from the change?
- What are the RISKS involved in the change?
- What RESOURCES are required to deliver the change?
- Who is RESPONSIBLE for the build, test and implementation of the change?
- What is the RELATIONSHIP between this change and other changes?

Many organizations develop specific impact assessment forms to prompt the impact assessors about specific types of change. This can help with the learning process, particularly for new services or when implementing a formal impact assessment step for the first time.

Responsibility for evaluating major change should be defined. It is not a best-practice issue because organizations are so diverse in size, structure and complexity that there is not a universal solution appropriate to all organizations. It is, however, recommended that major change is discussed at the outset with all stakeholders in order to arrive at sensible boundaries of responsibility and to improve communications.

Although Change Management is responsible for ensuring that changes are assessed and, if authorized, subsequently developed, tested, implemented and reviewed, clearly final responsibility for the IT service – including changes to it – will rest with the service manager and the service owner. They control the funding available and will have been involved in the change process through direct or delegated membership of the CAB.

When conducting the impact and resource assessment for RFCs referred to them, Change Management, CAB, ECAB or any others (nominated by Change Management or CAB members) who are involved in this process should consider relevant items, including:

■ the impact that the change will make on the customer's business operation

■ the effect on the infrastructure and customer service, as defined in the service requirements baselines, service model, SLA, and on the capacity and performance, reliability and resilience, contingency plans, and security

■ the impact on other services that run on the same infrastructure (or on projects)

■ the impact on non-IT infrastructures within the organization – for example, security, office services, transport, customer help desks

■ the effect of not implementing the change

■ the IT, business and other resources required to implement the change, covering the likely costs, the number and availability of people required, the elapsed time, and any new infrastructure elements required

■ the current change schedule (CS) and projected service outage (PSO)

■ additional ongoing resources required if the change is implemented

■ impact on the continuity plan, capacity plan, security plan, regression test scripts and data and test environment, Service Operations practices.

No change is without risk

Simple changes may seem innocuous but can cause damage out of all apparent proportion to their complexity. There have been several examples in recent years of high profile and expensive business impact caused by the inclusion, exclusion or misplacing of a '.' in software code.

It is best practice to use a risk-based assessment during the impact assessment of a change or set of changes. For example the risk for:

■ An individual change

■ A set of changes implemented together

■ Impacting the timescales of authorized changes on change and release schedules.

Table 4.5 Example of a change impact and risk categorization matrix

Change impact	Change impact/risk categorization matrix	
	High impact Low probability Risk category: 2	High impact High probability Risk category: 1
	Low impact Low probability Risk category: 4	Low impact High probability Risk category: 3
	Probability	

The focus should be on identifying the factors that may disrupt the business, impede the delivery of service warranties or impact corporate objectives and policies. The same disciplines used for corporate risk management or in project management can be adopted and adapted.

Risk categorization

The issue of risk to the business of any change must be considered prior to the authorisation of any change. Many organizations use a simple matrix like the one shown in Table 4.5 to categorize risk, and from this the level of change assessment and authorization required.

The relevant risk is the risk to the business service and changes require thorough assessment, wide communication, and appropriate authorization by the person or persons accountable for that business service. Assessing risk from the business perspective can produce a correct course of action very different from that which would have been chosen from an IT perspective, especially within high-risk industries.

High-risk industry

In one volatile and competitive business environment, the mobile telephone supply business, customers asked IT if they were now able to implement a much-needed change to the business software. The reply was that it could not go forward to the next change window because there was still a 30% risk of failure. Business reaction was to insist on implementation, for in their eyes a 70% chance of success, and the concomitant business advantage, was without any hesitation the right and smart move. Very few of their business initiatives had that high a chance of success.

The point is that the risk and gamble of the business environment (selling mobile telephones) had not been understood within IT, and inappropriate (i.e. IT) rules had been applied.

The dominant risk is the business one and that should have been sought, established, understood and applied by the service provider. Sensibly, of course, this might well be accompanied by documentation of the risk-based decision but nonetheless the need remains to understand the business perspective and act accordingly.

Evaluation of change

Based on the impact and risk assessments, and the potential benefits of the change, each of the assessors should evaluate the information and indicate whether they support approval of the change. All members of the change authority should evaluate the change based on impact, urgency, risk, benefits and costs. Each will indicate whether they support approval and be prepared to argue their case for any alterations that they see as necessary.

Allocation of priorities

Prioritization is used to establish the order in which changes put forward should be considered.

Every RFC will include the originator's assessment of the impact and urgency of the change.

The priority of a change is derived from the agreed impact and urgency. Initial impact and urgency will be suggested by the change initiator but may well be modified in the change authorization process. Risk assessment is of crucial importance at this stage. The CAB will need information on business consequences in order to assess effectively the risk of implementing or rejecting the change.

Impact is based on the beneficial change to the business that will follow from a successful implementation of the change, or on the degree of damage and cost to the business due to the error that the change will correct. The impact may not be expressed in absolute terms but may depend on the probability of an event or circumstance; for example a service may be acceptable at normal throughput levels, but may deteriorate at high usage, which may be triggered by unpredictable external items.

The urgency of the change is based on how long the implementation can afford to be delayed.

Table 4.6 gives examples of change priorities for corrective changes (fixing identified errors that are hurting the business) and for enhancements (that will deliver additional benefits). Other types of change exist, e.g. to enable continuation of existing benefit, but these two are used to illustrate the concept.

Change planning and scheduling

Careful planning of changes will ensure that there is no ambiguity about what tasks are included in the Change Management process, what tasks are included in other

Table 4.6 Change priority examples

Priority	Corrective change	Enhancement change
Immediate Treat as emergency change (see 4.2.6.9)	Putting life at risk Causing significant loss of revenue or the ability to deliver important public services. Immediate action required	Not appropriate for enhancement changes
High To be given highest priority for change building, testing and implementation resources	Severely affecting some key users, or impacting on a large number of users	Meets legislative requirements Responds to short term market opportunities or public requirements Supports new business initiatives that will increase company market position
Medium	No severe impact, but rectification cannot be deferred until the next scheduled release or upgrade	Maintains business viability Supports planned business initiatives
Low	A change is justified and necessary, but can wait until the next scheduled release or upgrade	Improvements in usability of a service Adds new facilities

processes and how processes interface to any suppliers or projects that are providing a change or release.

Many changes may be grouped into one release and may be designed, tested and released together if the amount of changes involved can be handled by the business, the service provider and its customers. However, if many independent changes are grouped into a release then this may create unnecessary dependencies that are difficult to manage. If not enough changes are grouped into a release then the overhead of managing more releases can be time consuming and waste resources (see paragraph 4.4.5.1 on release and deployment planning).

It is recommended very strongly that Change Management schedule changes to meet business rather than IT needs, e.g. avoiding critical business periods.

Pre-agreed and established change and release windows help an organization improve the planning and throughput of changes and releases. For example a release window in a maintenance period of one hour each week may be sufficient to install minor releases only. Major releases may need to be scheduled with the business and stakeholders at a pre-determined time. This approach is particularly relevant in high change environments where a release is a bottleneck or in high availability services where access to the live systems to implement releases is restricted. In many cases, the change or release may need to be adjusted 'on the fly', and so efficient use of release windows will require:

- A list of possible substitutes to make use of the unexpectedly vacant slot
- Empowerment to make and implement release decisions
- Internal metrics that monitor (and reflect and encourage best use of) change and release windows
- A clear understanding of any sequential dependencies and impact on users.

Wherever possible, Change Management should schedule authorized changes into target release or deployment packages and recommend the allocation of resources accordingly.

Change Management coordinates the production and distribution of a change schedule (CS) and projected service outage (PSO). The SC contains details of all the changes authorized for implementation and their proposed implementation dates. The PSO contains details of changes to agreed SLAs and service availability because of the currently planned SC in addition to planned downtime from other causes such as planned maintenance and data backup. These documents are agreed with the relevant customers within the business, with service level management, with the service desk and with availability management. Once agreed, the service desk should communicate any planned additional downtime to the user community at large, using the most effective methods available.

The latest versions of these documents will be available to stakeholders within the organization, preferably contained within a commonly available internet or intranet server. This can usefully be reinforced with a proactive awareness programme where specific impact can be detected.

Assessing remediation

It is important to develop a remediation plan to address a failing change or release long before implementation. Very often, remediation is the last thing to be considered; risks may be assessed, mitigation plans cast in stone. How to get back to the original start point is often ignored or considered only when regression is the last remaining option.

4.2.6.5 Authorizing the change

Formal authorization is obtained for each change from a change authority that may be a role, person or a group of people. The levels of authorization for a particular type of change should be judged by the type, size or risk of the change, e.g. changes in a large enterprise that affect several distributed sites may need to be authorized by a higher-level change authority such as a global CAB or the Board of Directors.

The culture of the organization dictates, to a large extent, the manner in which changes are authorized. Hierarchical structures may well impose many levels of change authorization, while flatter structures may allow a more streamlined approach.

A degree of delegated authority may well exist within an authorization level, e.g. delegating authority to a change manager according to pre-set parameters relating to:

- Anticipated business risk
- Financial implications
- Scope of the change (e.g. internal effects only, within the finance service, specific outsourced services).

An example of a change authorization hierarchy is shown in Figure 4.5.

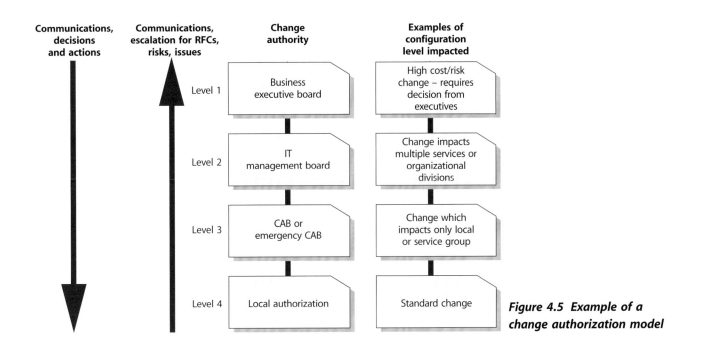

Figure 4.5 Example of a change authorization model

If change assessment at levels 2, 3, or 4 detects higher levels of risk, the authorization request is escalated to the appropriate higher level for the assessed level of risk. The use of delegated authority from higher levels to local levels must be accompanied by trust in the judgement, access to the appropriate information and supported by management. The level at which change is authorized should rest where accountability for accepting risk and remediation exist.

Should disputes arise over change authorization or rejection, there should be a right of appeal to the higher level.

4.2.6.6 Coordinating change implementation

Authorized RFCs should be passed to the relevant technical groups for building of the changes. It is best practice to do this in a formal way that can be tracked, e.g. using work orders. Building of changes is considered in section 4.4.5.3.

Change Management has responsibility for ensuring that changes are implemented as scheduled. This is largely a coordination role as the actual implementation will be the responsibility of others (e.g. hardware technical specialists will implement hardware changes).

Remediation procedures should be prepared and documented in advance, for each authorized change, so that if errors occur during or after implementation, these procedures can be quickly activated with minimum impact on service quality. Authority and responsibility for invoking

remediation is specifically mentioned in change documentation.

Change Management has an oversight role to ensure that all changes that can be are thoroughly tested. In all cases involving changes that have not been fully tested, special care needs to be taken during implementation.

Testing may continue in parallel with early live usage of a service – looking at unusual, unexpected or future situations so that further correcting action can be taken before any detected errors become apparent in live operation.

The implementation of such changes should be scheduled when the least impact on live services is likely. Support staff should be on hand to deal quickly with any incidents that might arise.

4.2.6.7 Review and close change record

On completion of the change, the results should be reported for evaluation to those responsible for managing changes, and then presented as a completed change for stakeholder agreement (including the closing of related incidents, problems or known errors). Clearly, for major changes there will be more customer and stakeholder input throughout the entire process.

A review should also include any incidents arising as a result of the change (if they are known at this stage). If the change is part of a service managed by an external provider, details of any contractual service targets will be required (e.g. no priority 1 incidents during first week after implementation).

A change review (e.g. post-implementation review, PIR) should be carried out to confirm that the change has met its objectives, that the initiator and stakeholders are happy with the results; and that there have been no unexpected side-effects. Lessons learned should be fed back into future changes. Small organizations may opt to use spot checking of changes rather than large-scale PIR; in larger organizations, sampling will have a value when there are many similar changes taking place.

There is a significantly different approach and profile between:

- The review of a service change – immediately visible to the customer and scheduled for discussion at the next service level management review meeting
- An infrastructure change – concerned with how IT delivers rather than what IT delivers, which will be (almost) invisible to the customer.

Change Management must review new or changed services after a predefined period has elapsed. This process will involve CAB members, since change reviews are a standard CAB agenda item. The purpose of such reviews is to establish that:

- The change has had the desired effect and met its objectives
- Users, customers and other stakeholders are content with the results, or to identify any shortcomings
- There are no unexpected or undesirable side-effects to functionality, service levels, warranties, e.g. availability, capacity, security, performance and costs
- The resources used to implement the change were as planned
- The release and deployment plan worked correctly (so include comments from the implementers)
- The change was implemented on time and to cost
- The remediation plan functioned correctly, if needed.

Further details of performing a formal evaluation are provided in Section 4.6. Any problems and discrepancies should be fed back to CAB members (where they have been consulted or where a committee was convened), impact assessors, product authorities and release authorities, so as to improve the processes for the future.

Where a change has not achieved its objectives, Change Management (or the CAB) should decide what follow-up action is required, which could involve raising a revised RFC. If the review is satisfactory or the original change is abandoned (e.g. the circumstances that required the change are no longer current and the requirement disappears) the RFC should be formally closed in the logging system.

4.2.6.8 Change Advisory Board

The Change Advisory Board (CAB) is a body that exists to support the authorization of changes and to assist Change Management in the assessment and prioritization of changes. As and when a CAB is convened, members should be chosen who are capable of ensuring that all changes within the scope of the CAB are adequately assessed from both a business and a technical viewpoint.

The CAB may be asked to consider and recommend the adoption or rejection of changes appropriate for higher-level authorization and then recommendations will be submitted to the appropriate change authority.

To achieve this, the CAB needs to include people with a clear understanding across the whole range of stakeholder needs. The change manager will normally chair the CAB, and potential members include:

- Customer(s)
- User manager(s)
- User group representative(s)
- Applications developers/maintainers
- Specialists/technical consultants
- Services and operations staff, e.g. service desk, test management, ITSCM, security, capacity
- Facilities/office services staff (where changes may affect moves/accommodation and vice versa)
- Contractor's or third parties' representatives, e.g. in outsourcing situations
- Other parties as applicable to specific circumstances (e.g. police if traffic disruptions likely, marketing if public products affected).

It is important to emphasize that the CAB:

- Will be composed according to the changes being considered
- May vary considerably in make-up even across the range of a single meeting
- Should involve suppliers when that would be useful
- Should reflect both users' and customers' views
- Is likely to include the problem manager and service level manager and customer relations staff for at least part of the time.

When the need for emergency change arises, i.e. there may not be time to convene the full CAB, it is necessary to identify a smaller organization with authority to make emergency decisions. This body is the Emergency Change

Advisory Board (ECAB). Change procedures should specify how the composition of the CAB and ECAB will be determined in each instance, based on the criteria listed above and any other criteria that may be appropriate to the business. This is intended to ensure that the composition of the CAB will be flexible, in order to represent business interests properly when major changes are proposed. It will also ensure that the composition of the ECAB will provide the ability, both from a business perspective and from a technical standpoint, to make appropriate decisions in any conceivable eventuality.

A practical tip worth bearing in mind is that the CAB should have stated and agreed evaluation criteria. This will assist in the change assessment activities, acting as a template or framework by which members can assess each change.

CAB meetings

Many organizations are running CABs electronically without frequent face-to-face meetings. There are benefits and problems from such an approach. Much of the assessment and referral activities can be handled electronically via support tools or e-mail. In complex, high-risk or high-impact cases, formal CAB meetings may be necessary.

Handling electronically is more convenient time-wise for CAB members but is also highly inefficient when questions or concerns are raised such that many communications go back and forth. A face-to-face meeting is generally more efficient, but poses scheduling and time conflicts among CAB members as well as significant travel and staff costs for widely dispersed organizations.

Practical experience shows that regular meetings combined with electronic automation is a viable approach for many organizations, and that it can be beneficial to schedule a regular meeting, or when major projects are due to deliver releases. The meetings can then be used to provide a formal review and sign-off of authorized changes, a review of outstanding changes, and, of course, to discuss any impending major changes. Where meetings are appropriate, they should have a standard agenda.

A standard CAB agenda should include:

- Failed changes, unauthorized, backed-out changes, or changes applied without reference to the CAB by incident management, problem management or Change Management
- RFCs to be assessed by CAB members – in structured and priority order
- RFCs that have been assessed by CAB members

- Scheduling of changes and update of change schedule (CS) and PSO
- Change reviews
- The Change Management process, including any amendments made to it during the period under discussion, as well as proposed changes
- Change Management wins/accomplishments for the period under discussion, i.e. a review of the business benefits accrued by way of the Change Management process
- Outstanding changes and changes in progress
- Advance notice of RFCs expected for review at next CAB
- Review of unauthorized changes detected through Configuration Management.

CAB meetings represent a potentially large overhead on the time of members. Therefore all RFCs, together with the SC and PSO, should be circulated in advance, and flexibility allowed to CAB members on whether to attend in person, to send a deputy, or to send any comments. Relevant papers should be circulated in advance to allow CAB members (and others who are required by Change Management or CAB members) to conduct impact and resource assessments.

In some circumstances it will be desirable to table RFCs at one CAB meeting for more detailed explanation or clarification before CAB members take the papers away for consideration, in time for a later meeting. A 'walkthrough' of major changes may be included at a CAB meeting before formal submission of the RFC.

CAB members should come to meetings prepared and empowered to express views and make decisions on behalf of the area they represent in respect of the submitted RFCs, based on prior assessment of the RFCs.

The CAB should be informed of any emergency changes or changes that have been implemented as a workaround to incidents and should be given the opportunity to recommend follow-up action to them.

Note that the CAB is an advisory body only. If the CAB cannot agree to a recommendation, the final decision on whether to authorize changes, and commit to the expense involved, is the responsibility of management (normally the director of IT or the services director, service manager or change manager as their delegated representative). The Change Management authorization plan should specifically name the person(s) authorized to sign off RFCs.

4.2.6.9 Emergency changes

Emergency changes are sometimes required and should be designed carefully and tested before use or the impact of the emergency change may be greater than the original incident. Emergency changes may document some details retrospectively.

The number of emergency changes proposed should be kept to an absolute minimum, because they are generally more disruptive and prone to failure. All changes likely to be required should, in general, be foreseen and planned, bearing in mind the availability of resources to build and test the changes. Nevertheless, occasions will occur when emergency changes are essential and so procedures should be devised to deal with them quickly, without sacrificing normal management controls.

Emergency change is reserved for changes intended to repair an error in an IT service that is negatively impacting the business to a high degree. Changes intended to introduce immediately required business improvements are handled as normal changes, assessed as having the highest urgency.

Emergency change authorization

Defined authorization levels will exist for an emergency change, and the levels of delegated authority must be clearly documented and understood. In an emergency situation it may not be possible to convene a full CAB meeting. Where CAB approval is required, this will be provided by the Emergency CAB (ECAB).

Not all emergency changes will require the ECAB involvement; many may be predictable both in occurrence and resolution and well understood changes available, with authority delegated, e.g. to Operations teams who will action, document and report on the emergency change.

Emergency change building, testing and implementation

Authorized changes are allocated to the relevant technical group for building. Where timescales demand it, Change Management, in collaboration with the appropriate technical manager, ensures that sufficient staff and resources (machine time etc.) are available to do this work. Procedures and agreements – approved and supported by management – must be in place to allow for this. Remediation must also be addressed.

As much testing of the emergency change as is possible should be carried out. Completely untested changes should not be implemented if at all avoidable. Clearly, if a change goes wrong, the cost is usually greater than that

of adequate testing. Consideration should be given to how much it would cost to test all changes fully against the cost of the change failing factored by the anticipated likelihood of its failure.

This means that the less a change is considered likely to fail, the more reasonable it may be to reduce the degree of testing in an emergency. (Remember that there is still merit in testing even after a change has gone live.) When only limited testing is possible – and presuming that parallel development of more robust versions continues alongside the emergency change – then testing should be targeted towards:

- Aspects of the service that will be used immediately (e.g. daily entry features, not end-of-month routines)
- Elements that would cause most short-term inconvenience.

The business should be made aware of associated risks and be responsible for ultimately accepting or rejecting the change based on the information presented.

Change Management will give as much advance warning as possible to the service desk and other stakeholders, and arrange for adequate technical presence to be available, to support Service Operations.

If a Change, once implemented, fails to rectify the urgent outstanding error, there may need to be iterative attempts at fixes. Change Management should take responsibility at this point to ensure that business needs remain the primary concern and that each iteration is controlled in the manner described in this section. Change Management should ensure abortive changes are swiftly backed out.

If too many attempts at an emergency change are abortive, the following questions should be asked:

- Has the error been correctly identified, analysed and diagnosed?
- Has the proposed resolution been adequately tested?
- Has the solution been correctly implemented?

In such circumstances, it may be better to provide a partial service, with some user facilities withdrawn, in order to allow the change to be thoroughly tested or to suspend the service temporarily and then implement the change.

Emergency change documentation

It may not be possible to update all Change Management records at the time that urgent actions are being completed (e.g. during overnight or weekend working). It is, however, essential that temporary records are made during such periods, and that all records are completed retrospectively, at the earliest possible opportunity.

Incident control staff, computer operations and network management staff may have delegated authority to circumvent certain types of incident (e.g. hardware failure) without prior authorization by Change Management. Such circumventions should be limited to actions that do not change the specification of service assets and that do not attempt to correct software errors. The preferred methods for circumventing incidents caused by software errors should be to revert to the previous trusted state or version, as relevant, rather than attempting an unplanned and potentially dangerous change. Change approval is still a prerequisite.

Effectively, the emergency change procedure will follow the normal change procedure except that:

- Approval will be given by the ECAB rather than waiting for a CAB meeting
- Testing may be reduced, or in extreme cases forgone completely, if considered a necessary risk to deliver the change immediately
- Documentation, i.e. updating the change record and configuration data, may be deferred, typically until normal working hours.

4.2.7 Triggers, input and output, and inter-process interfaces

Requests for change can be triggered throughout the service lifecycle and at the interfaces with other organizations, e.g. customers and suppliers. There will also be other stakeholders such as partners that may be involved with the Change Management processes.

Typical examples of types of change that trigger the Change Management process are described below.

Strategic changes

Service strategies require changes to be implemented to achieve specific objectives while minimizing costs and risks. There are no cost-free and risk-free strategic plans or initiatives. There are always costs and risks associated with decisions such as introducing new services, entering new market spaces, and serving new customers. The following are examples of programmes and initiatives that implement strategic changes:

- Legal/regulatory change
- Organizational change
- Policy and standards change
- Change after analysing business, customer and user activity patterns

- Addition of new service to the market space
- Updates to the Service Portfolio, customer portfolio or contract portfolio
- Change of sourcing model
- Technology innovation.

Change to one or more services

Changes to the planned services (in the Service Portfolio) and changes to the services in the service catalogue will trigger the Change Management process. These include changes to:

- Service catalogue
- Service package
- Service definition and characteristics
- Release package
- Capacity and resource requirements
- Service level requirements
- Warranties
- Utilities
- Cost of utilization
- Service assets
- Acceptance Criteria
- Predicted quality of service
- Predicted performance
- Predicted value
- Organizational design
- Stakeholder and communications plans
- Physical change in the environment, e.g. building
- Measurement system
- Plans, e.g. capacity, ITSCM, change, transition, test, release and deployment plans
- Decommission/retire services
- Procedures, manuals, service desk scripts.

Operational change

It is important to know the distinction between different types of requests that will be initiated by users. These types of request will depend on the nature of the organization and services and may include requests such as password reset, access request or request to move an IT asset.

Service Operations staff will also implement corrective and preventative changes, via the standard change procedure, that should be managed through Change Management, e.g. server re-boot, which may impact a shared service.

Changes to deliver continual improvement

When CSI determines that an improvement to a Service is warranted, an RFC should be submitted to Change

Management. Changes such as changes to processes can have an effect on service provision and may also affect other CSI initiatives.

Some strategy and service changes will be initiated by CSI.

4.2.7.1 Inputs

Changes may be submitted as an RFC, often with an associated change proposal that provides the detail of how the change will happen, e.g. approach to implementing a legislative change. The change proposal will be based on a change model and will provide more detail about the specific change proposed. The inputs include:

■ Policy and strategies for change and release
■ Request for Change
■ Change proposal
■ Plans – change, transition, release, deployment, test, evaluation and remediation
■ Current change schedule and PSO
■ Current assets or configuration items, e.g. baseline, service package, release package
■ As-planned configuration baseline
■ Test results, test report and evaluation report.

4.2.7.2 Outputs

Outputs from the process will be:

■ Rejected RFCs
■ Approved RFCs
■ Change to the services, service or infrastructure resulting from approved RFCs
■ New, changed or disposed assets or configuration items, e.g. baseline, service package, release package
■ Change schedule
■ Revised PSO
■ Authorized change plans
■ Change decisions and actions
■ Change documents and records
■ Change Management reports.

4.2.7.3 Interfaces

In order to be able to define clear boundaries, dependencies and rules, change and release management should be integrated with processes used for organizational programmes or projects, supplier management and also integrated with suppliers' processes and procedures. There will be occasions when a proposed change will potentially have a wider impact on other parts of the organization (e.g. facilities or business operations),

or vice versa, and the service change process must interface appropriately with other processes involved.

Integration with business change processes

Where appropriate, the Change Management should be involved with business programme and business project management teams to ensure that change issues, aims, impacts and developments are exchanged and cascaded throughout the organization where applicable. This means that changes to any business or project deliverables that do not impact services or service components may be subject to business or project Change Management procedures rather than the IT service Change Management procedures. However, care must be taken to ensure that changes to service configuration baselines and releases do follow the Change Management process. The Change Management team will, however, be expected to liaise closely with projects to ensure smooth implementation and consistency within the changing management environments.

Programme and project management

Programme and project management must work in partnership to align all the processes and people involved in service change initiatives. The closer they are aligned, the higher the probability that the change effort will be moved forward for as long as it takes to complete. Change Management representatives may attend relevant Project Board meetings.

Sourcing and partnering arrangements should clearly define the level of autonomy a partner may have in effecting change within their service domain without reference to the overall service provider.

A key component is how deeply change processes and tools are embedded into the supplier organization or vice versa and where the release veto takes place. If the supplier has responsibility for the availability of the operational service, conflicts can arise.

Sourcing and partnering

Sourcing and partnering include internal and external vendors and suppliers who are providing a new or existing service to the organization. Effective Change Management practices and principles must be put into place to manage these relationships effectively to ensure smooth delivery of service. Effort also should be put into finding out how well the partners themselves manage change and choose partner and sourcing relationships accordingly.

It is important to ensure that service providers (outsourced or in house) provide the Change Management function and processes that match the needs of the business and customers. Some organizations in outsourcing situations refer RFCs to their suppliers for estimates prior to approval of changes. For further information, refer to the ITIL Service Design publication and guidance on supplier management.

4.2.7.4 Interfaces within Service Management

The Service Management processes may require change and improvements.

Many will also be involved in the impact assessment and implementation of service changes, as discussed below.

Asset and Configuration Management

The Configuration Management System provides reliable, quick and easy access to accurate configuration information to enable stakeholders and staff to assess the impact of proposed changes and to track changes work flow. This information enables the correct asset and service component versions to be released to the appropriate party or into the correct environment. As changes are implemented, the Configuration Management information is updated.

The CMS may also identify related CI/assets that will be affected by the change, but not included in the original request, or in fact similar CI/assets that would benefit from similar change.

An overview of how the change and Configuration Management processes work together for an individual change is shown in Figure 4.6.

Problem Management

Problem Management is another key process as changes are often required to implement workarounds and to fix known errors. Problem Management is one of the major sources of RFCs and also often a major contributor to CAB discussion.

IT Service Continuity

IT Service Continuity has many procedures and plans should be updated via Change Management to ensure that they are accurate, up to date and that stakeholders are aware of changes.

Security Management

Security Management interfaces with Change Management since changes required by security will go via the Change Management process and security will be a key contributor to CAB discussion on many services. Every significant change will be assessed for its potential impact on the security plan.

Capacity and Demand Management

Capacity and Demand Management is a critical aspect of Change Management. Poorly managed demand is a source of costs and risk for service providers because there is always a level of uncertainty associated with the demand for services. Capacity Management has an important role in assessing proposed changes – not only the individual changes but the total impact of changes on service capacity. Changes arising from Capacity Management, including those set out in the capacity plan, will be initiated as RFCs through the change process.

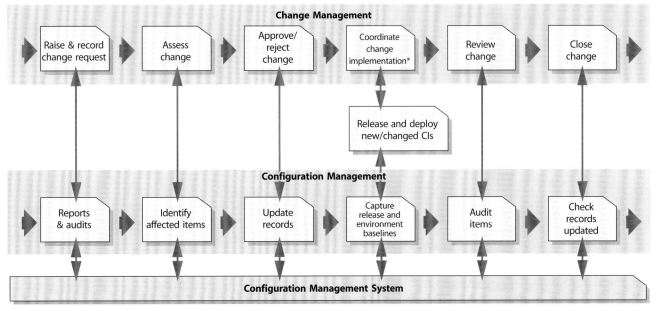

* Includes build and test where applicable

Figure 4.6 Request for Change workflow and key interfaces to Configuration Management

4.2.8 Key performance indicators and metrics

Change Management must ensure that measures have specific meaning. While it is relatively easy to count the number of incidents that eventually generate changes, it is infinitely more valuable to look at the underlying cause of such changes, and to identify trends. Better still to be able to measure the impact of changes and to demonstrate reduced disruption over time because of the introduction of Change Management, and to measure the speed and effectiveness with which the service provider responds to identified business needs.

Measures taken should be linked to business goals wherever practical – and to cost, service availability, and reliability. Any predictions should be compared with actual measurements.

The key performance indicators for Change Management are:

■ The number of changes implemented to services which met the customer's agreed requirements, e.g. quality/cost/time (expressed as a percentage of all changes)

■ The benefits of change expressed as 'value of improvements made' + 'negative impacts prevented or terminated' compared with the costs of the change process

■ Reduction in the number of disruptions to services, defects and re-work caused by inaccurate specification, poor or incomplete impact assessment

■ Reduction in the number of unauthorized changes

■ Reduction in the backlog of change requests

■ Reduction in the number and percentage of unplanned changes and emergency fixes

■ Change success rate (percentage of changes deemed successful at review/number of RFCs approved)

■ Reduction in the number of changes where remediation is invoked

■ Reduction in the number of failed changes

■ Average time to implement based on urgency/priority/change type

■ Incidents attributable to changes

■ Percentage accuracy in change estimate.

Naturally there is other management information required around change and statistics to be gathered and analysed to ensure efficient and effective process, but for organizations with a 'dashboard' reporting approach, these are good metrics to use.

Meaningful measurements are those from which management can make timely and accurate actionable decisions. For example, reporting on the number of changes is meaningless. Reporting on the ratio of changes implemented versus RFCs received provides an efficiency rating. If this rating is low, management can easily see that changes are not being processed in an efficient or effective manner and then take timely action to correct the deficiencies causing this.

4.2.8.1 Examples of the types of measures for change

Some examples of the types of measures used within organizations are listed here; the accrual ones relevant in each different circumstance will vary between organizations and over time, as the change process (and other ITSM elements) mature. Most of the listed measures can be usefully broken down by category, organizational division, geography, supplier, etc.

Output measures

■ Number of disruptions, incidents, problems/errors caused by unsuccessful changes and releases

■ Inaccurate change specifications (e.g. technical, customer, business)

■ Incomplete impact assessment

■ Unauthorized business/customer change by business/IT/customer/user asset or configuration item type, e.g. application data

■ Percentage reduction in time, effort, cost to make changes and releases (e.g. by service, change type, asset type)

■ Service or application re-work caused by inadequate change specification

■ Percentage improvement in predictions for time, quality, cost, risk, resource and commercial impact

■ Percentage improvement in impact analysis and scheduling of changes safely, efficiently and effectively reduces the risk of changes affecting the live environment

■ Percentage reduction in unauthorized changes.

Workloads

■ Frequency of change (by service, business area, etc.)

■ Volume of change.

Process measures

■ People's satisfaction with the speed, clarity, ease of use

■ Number and percentage of changes that follow formal Change Management procedures

- Ratio of planned vs unplanned changes (urgent, emergency)
- Ratio of accepted to rejected change requests
- Number of changes recorded and tracked using automated tools
- Time to execute a change (from initiation through each stage in the lifecycle of a change, ending in completion):
  - By lifecycle stage
  - By service
  - By infrastructure platform
- Staff utilization
- Cost against budget.

4.3 SERVICE ASSET AND CONFIGURATION MANAGEMENT

This section addresses the process of Service Asset and Configuration Management (SACM) within IT Service Management. No organization can be fully efficient or effective unless it manages its assets well, particularly those assets that are vital to the running of the customer's or organization's business. This process manages the service assets in order to support the other Service Management processes.

4.3.1 Purpose, goal and objective

The purpose of SACM is to:

- Identify, control, record, report, audit and verify service assets and configuration items, including versions, baselines, constituent components, their attributes, and relationships
- Account for, manage and protect the integrity of service assets and configuration items (and, where appropriate, those of its customers) through the service lifecycle by ensuring that only authorized components are used and only authorized changes are made
- Protect the integrity of service assets and configuration items (and, where appropriate, those of its customers) through the service lifecycle
- Ensure the integrity of the assets and configurations required to control the services and IT infrastructure by establishing and maintaining an accurate and complete Configuration Management System.

The goals of Configuration Management are to:

- Support the business and customer's control objectives and requirements

- Support efficient and effective Service Management processes by providing accurate configuration information to enable people to make decisions at the right time, e.g. to authorize change and releases, resolve incidents and problems faster.
- Minimize the number of quality and compliance issues caused by improper configuration of services and assets
- Optimize the service assets, IT configurations, capabilities and resources.

The objective is to define and control the components of services and infrastructure and maintain accurate configuration information on the historical, planned and current state of the services and infrastructure.

4.3.2 Scope

Asset Management covers service assets across the whole service lifecycle. It provides a complete inventory of assets and who is responsible for their control. It includes:

- Full lifecycle management of IT and service assets, from the point of acquisition through to disposal
- Maintenance of the asset inventory.

Configuration Management ensures that selected components of a complete service, system or product (the configuration) are identified, baselined and maintained and that changes to them are controlled. It also ensures that releases into controlled environments and operational use are done on the basis of formal approvals. It provides a configuration model of the services, assets and infrastructure by recording the relationships between service assets and configuration items. SACM may cover non-IT assets, work products used to develop the services and configuration items required to support the service that are not formally classified as assets.

The scope covers interfaces to internal and external service providers where there are assets and configuration items that need to be controlled, e.g. shared assets.

4.3.3 Value to business

Optimizing the performance of service assets and configurations improves the overall service performance and optimizes the costs and risks caused by poorly managed assets, e.g. service outages, fines, correct licence fees and failed audits.

SACM provides visibility of accurate representations of a service, release, or environment that enables:

- Better forecasting and planning of changes
- Changes and releases to be assessed, planned and delivered successfully
- Incidents and problems to be resolved within the service level targets
- Service levels and warranties to be delivered
- Better adherence to standards, legal and regulatory obligations (less non-conformances)
- More business opportunities as able to demonstrate control of assets and services
- Changes to be traceable from requirements
- The ability to identify the costs for a service.

4.3.4 Policies, principles and basic concepts

In distributed environments and shared services, individual service components exist within many different services and configuration structures. For example, a person may use a desktop computer that is on the network for a building but may be running a central financial system that is linked to a database on the other side of the world. A change to the network or the financial system may have an impact on this person and his/her business process. In web-based services, there may be data feeds and interfaces from and to services owned by other organizations. Changes at these interfaces need to be managed and it is important to identify the interface such as data feeds and the owner/custodian of these. Changes to any interface items need to be managed through Change Management.

4.3.4.1 Service Asset and Configuration Management policies

The first step is to develop and maintain the SACM policies that set the objectives, scope and principles and critical success factors (CSFs) for what is to be achieved by the process. These policies are often considered with the change and Release and Deployment Management policies as they are closely related. The policies will be based on the organization's business drivers, contractual and Service Management requirements and on compliance to applicable laws, regulations and standards.

Asset policies may be applicable for specific asset types or services, e.g. desktop.

There are significant costs and resources implications to implementing SACM and therefore strategic decisions need to be made about the priorities to be addressed. Many IT service providers focus initially on the basic IT assets (hardware and software) and the services and assets that are business critical or covered by legal and regulatory compliance, e.g. Sarbanes-Oxley, software licensing.

Service Asset and Configuration Management principles

The main policy sets out the framework and key principles against which assets and configurations are developed and maintained. Typical principles include:

- Ensuring that Asset and Configuration Management operations costs and resources are commensurate with the potential risks to the services
- The need to deliver corporate governance requirements, e.g. software asset management, Sarbanes-Oxley
- The need to deliver the capability, resources and service warranties as defined by the service level agreements and contracts
- The requirement for available, reliable and cost-effective services
- The requirement for clear economic and performance criteria for interventions that reduce costs or optimize service delivery, e.g. lower maintenance costs
- The application of whole-life cost appraisal methods
- The transformation from 'find and fix' reactive maintenance to 'predict and prevent' proactive management
- The requirement to maintain adequate asset and configuration information for internal and external stakeholders
- The level of control and requirements for traceability and auditability
- The application of continual improvement methods to optimize the service levels, assets and configurations
- Provision of accurate asset and configuration information for other business and Service Management processes
- Integration of Asset and Configuration Management with other processes
- Migration to a common asset and CMS architecture
- Level of automation to reduce errors and costs.

4.3.4.2 Basic concepts

The configuration model

Configuration Management delivers a model of the services, assets and the infrastructure by recording the relationships between configuration items as shown in Figure 4.7. This enables other processes to access valuable information, e.g.:

- To assess the impact and cause of incidents and problems

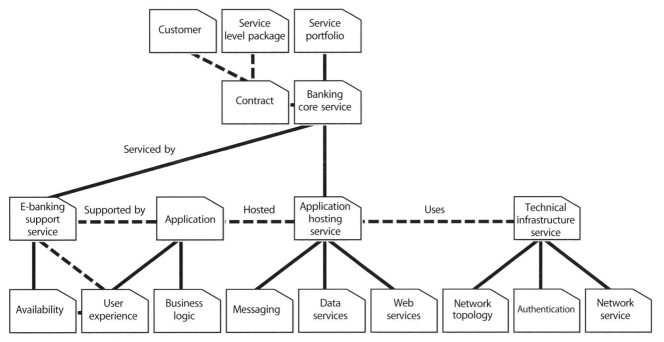

Figure 4.7 Example of a logical configuration model

- To assess the impact of proposed changes
- To plan and design new or changed services
- To plan technology refresh and software upgrades
- To plan release and deployment packages and migrate service assets to different locations and service centres
- To optimize asset utilization and costs, e.g. consolidate data centres, reduce variations and re-use assets.

The real power of Configuration Management's logical model of the services and infrastructure is that it is THE model – a single common representation used by all parts of IT Service Management, and beyond, such as HR, finance, supplier and customers.

> **'Danish clock'**
>
> There is a traditional Danish proverb that runs 'When you have a clock in your house, you know the time – once you get two clocks you are no longer certain.' SACM delivers that one clock for all processes and so glues them together, delivers consistency and helps achieve common purpose. (From Hans Dithmar)

The configuration items and related configuration information can be at varying levels of detail, e.g. an overview of all the services or a detailed level to view the specification for a service component.

Configuration Management should be applied at a more detailed level where the service provider requires tight control, traceability and tight coupling of configuration information through the service lifecycle.

Configuration items

A configuration item (CI) is an asset, service component or other item that is, or will be, under the control of Configuration Management. Configuration items may vary widely in complexity, size and type, ranging from an entire service or system including all hardware, software, documentation and support staff to a single software module or a minor hardware component. Configuration items may be grouped and managed together, e.g. a set of components may be grouped into a release. Configuration items should be selected using established selection criteria, grouped, classified and identified in such a way that they are manageable and traceable throughout the service lifecycle.

There will be a variety of CIs; the following categories may help to identify them.

- **Service lifecycle CIs** such as the Business Case, Service Management Plans, service lifecycle plans, Service Design Package, release and change plans, and test plans. They provide a picture of the service provider's services, how these services will be delivered, what benefits are expected, at what cost, and when they will be realized.
- **Service CIs** such as:
  - Service capability assets: management, organization, processes, knowledge, people
  - Service resource assets: financial capital, systems, applications, information, data, infrastructure and facilities, financial capital, people

- Service model
- Service package
- Release package
- Service acceptance criteria.

- **Organization CIs** – Some documentation will define the characteristics of a CI whereas other documentation will be a CI in its own right and need to be controlled, e.g. the organization's business strategy or other policies that are internal to the organization but independent of the service provider. Regulatory or statutory requirements also form external products that need to be tracked, as do products shared between more than one group.

- **Internal CIs** comprising those delivered by individual projects, including tangible (data centre) and intangible assets such as software that are required to deliver and maintain the service and infrastructure.

- **External CIs** such as external customer requirements and agreements, releases from suppliers or sub-contractors and external services.

- **Interface CIs** that are required to deliver the end-to-end service across a service provider interface (SPI).

4.3.4.3 Configuration Management System

To manage large and complex IT services and infrastructures, Service Asset and Configuration Management requires the use of a supporting system known as the Configuration Management System (CMS).

The CMS holds all the information for CIs within the designated scope. Some of these items will have related specifications or files that contain the contents of the item, e.g. software, document or photograph. For example, a Service CI will include the details such as supplier, cost, purchase date and renewal date for licences and maintenance contracts and the related documentation such as SLAs and underpinning contracts.

The CMS is also used a for wide range of purposes, for example asset data held in the CMS may be made available to external financial Asset Management systems to perform specific Asset Management processes reporting outside of Configuration Management.

The CMS maintains the relationships between all service components and any related incidents, problems, known errors, change and release documentation and may also

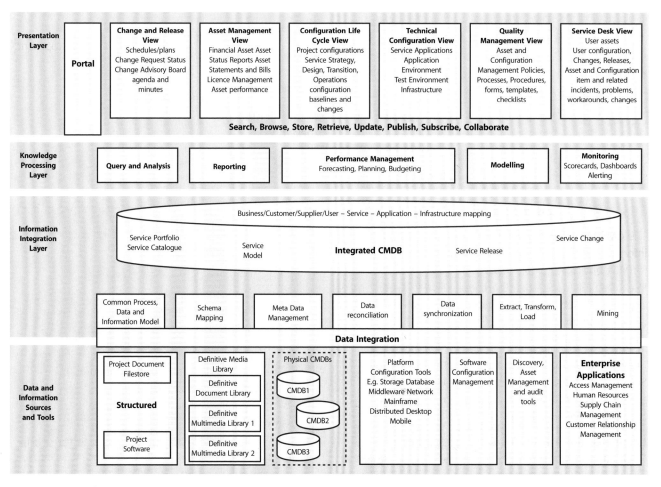

Figure 4.8 Example of a Configuration Management System

contain corporate data about employees, suppliers, locations and business units, customers and users.

Figure 4.8 shows how the CMS covers the data and information layers of the knowledge/information/ knowledge hierarchy explained in section 4.7, Knowledge Management.

At the data level, the CMS may take data from several physical CMDBs, which together constitute a federated CMDB. Other data sources will also plug into the CMS such as the definitive media libraries. The CMS will provide access to data in asset inventories wherever possible rather than duplicating data.

Example of multiple Configuration Management databases

In the commonly encountered partially outsourced service provider, some elements of the Service Management will be outsourced while others will remain in house, and different elements may be outsourced to different external suppliers. For example the network and hardware support may be handled by supplier A, environment and facilities management by supplier B, and multiple applications suppliers and incident management handled internally. The service desk will access information to assist them from the CMS, but that system will derive its data input from discrete repositories – each one a CMDB – owned and maintained by the three parties but working together to supply a single consistent information set.

Configuration information evolves as the service is developed through the service lifecycle. Often there are separate mechanisms for managing different service lifecycle stages as well as different means of managing different applications and platforms.

The CMS typically contains configuration data and information that combined into an integrated set of views for different stakeholders through the service lifecycle as illustrated in Figure 4.8. It therefore needs to be based on appropriate web, reporting and database technologies that provide flexible and powerful visualization and mapping tools, interrogation and reporting facilities.

Many organizations are already using some elements of SACM, often maintaining records in documents, spreadsheets or local databases, and some of these may be used in the overall CMS.

Automated processes to load and update the Configuration Management database should be developed where possible so as to reduce errors and optimize costs. Discovery tools, inventory and audit tools, enterprise

systems and network management tools can be interfaced to the CMS. These tools can be used initially to populate a CMDB, and subsequently to compare the actual 'live' configuration with the information and records stored in the CMS.

Secure libraries and secure stores

A secure library is a collection of software, electronic or document CIs of known type and status. Access to items in a secure library is restricted. Libraries are used for controlling and releasing components throughout the service lifecycle, e.g. in design, building, testing, deployment and operations.

A secure store is a location that warehouses IT assets. It is identified within SACM, e.g. secure stores used for desktop deployment. Secure stores play an important role in the provision of security and continuity – maintaining reliable access to equipment of known quality.

The Definitive Media Library

The Definitive Media Library (DML) is the secure library in which the definitive authorized versions of all media CIs are stored and protected. It stores master copies of versions that have passed quality assurance checks. This library may in reality consist of one or more software libraries or file-storage areas, separate from development, test or live file-store areas. It contains the master copies of all controlled software in an organization. The DML should include definitive copies of purchased software (along with licence documents or information), as well as software developed on site. Master copies of controlled documentation for a system are also stored in the DML in electronic form.

The DML will also include a physical store to hold master copies, e.g. a fireproof safe. Only authorized media should be accepted into the DML, strictly controlled by SACM.

The DML is a foundation for Release and Deployment Management (see section 4.4 on the release and deployment process).

The exact configuration of the DML is defined during the planning activities. The definition includes:

■ Medium, physical location, hardware and software to be used, if kept online – some Configuration Management support tools incorporate document or software libraries, which can be regarded as a logical part of a DML

■ Naming conventions for filestore areas and physical media

■ Environments supported, e.g. test and live environments

- Security arrangements for submitting changes and issuing documentation and software, plus backup and recovery procedures
- The scope of the DML, e.g. source code, object code from controlled builds and associated documentation
- Archive and retention periods
- Capacity plans for the DML and procedures for monitoring growth in size
- Audit procedures
- Procedures to ensure that the DML is protected from erroneous or unauthorized change (e.g. entry and exit criteria for items).

Figure 4.9 shows the relationship between the DML and the CMDB.

Definitive spares

An area should be set aside for the secure storage of definitive hardware spares. These are spare components and assemblies that are maintained at the same level as the comparative systems within the controlled test or live environment. Details of these components, their locations and their respective builds and contents should be comprehensively recorded in the CMS. These can then be used in a controlled manner when needed for additional systems or in the recovery from incidents. Once their (temporary) use has ended, they are returned to the spares store or replacements are obtained.

Configuration baseline

A configuration baseline is the configuration of a service, product or infrastructure that has been formally reviewed and agreed on, that thereafter serves as the basis for further activities and that can be changed only through formal change procedures. It captures the structure, contents and details of a configuration and represents a set of configuration items that are related to each other.

Establishing a baseline provides the ability to:

- Mark a milestone in the development of a service, e.g. Service Design baseline
- Build a service component from a defined set of inputs
- Change or rebuild a specific version at a later date
- Assemble all relevant components in readiness for a change or release
- Provide the basis for a configuration audit and back out, e.g. after a change.

Snapshot

A snapshot of the current state of a configuration item or an environment, e.g. from a discovery tool. This snapshot is recorded in the CMS and remains as a fixed historical record. Sometimes this is referred to a footprint. A snapshot is not necessarily formally reviewed and agreed on – it is just a documentation of a state, which may

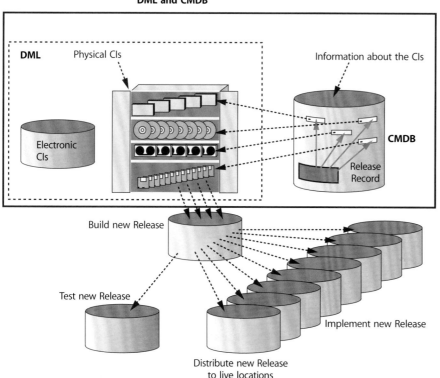

DML and CMDB

Figure 4.9 The relationship between the Definitive Media Library and the Configuration Management Database

contain faults and unauthorized CIs. One example is where a snapshot is established after an installation, perhaps using a discovery tool, and later compared to the original configuration baseline.

The snapshot:

■ Enables problem management to analyse evidence about a situation pertaining at the time incidents actually occurred

■ Facilitates system restore to support security scanning software.

4.3.5 Process activities, methods and techniques

4.3.5.1 Asset and Configuration Management activities

High-level activities for Asset and Configuration Management are shown in an example of an activity model in Figure 4.10.

The activity model illustrated in Figure 4.10 is often used where there are many parties or suppliers and activities

need to be established to obtain the configuration information and data from third parties.

4.3.5.2 Management and planning

There is no standard template for determining the optimum approach for SACM. The management team and Configuration Management should decide what level of Configuration Management is required for the selected service or project that is delivering changes and how this level will be achieved. This is documented in a Configuration Management Plan. Often there will be a Configuration Management Plan for a project, service or groups of services, e.g. network services. These plans define the specific Configuration Management activities within the context of the overarching Service Asset and Configuration Management strategy.

An example of the contents for an Asset or Configuration Management Plan is shown below.

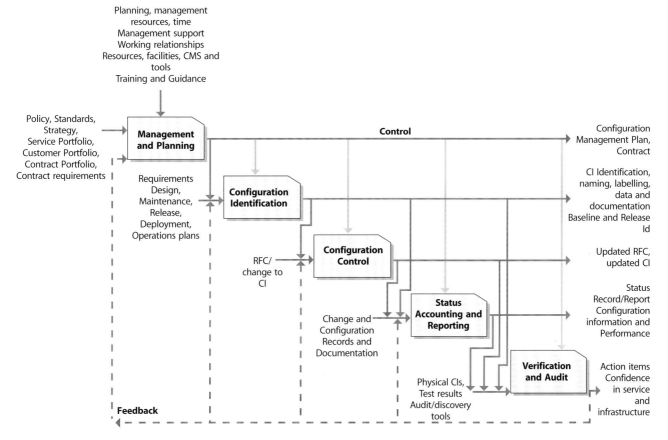

Figure 4.10 Typical Configuration Management activity model

Example of Asset and Configuration Management Plan contents

Context and purpose.

Scope:

- Applicable services
- Environments and infrastructure
- Geographical locations.

Requirements:

- Link to policy, strategy
- Link to business, Service Management and contractual requirements
- Summarize requirements for accountability, traceability, auditability
- Link to requirements for the Configuration Management System (CMS).

Applicable policies and standards:

- Policies
- Industry standards, e.g. ISO/IEC 20000, ISO/IEC 19770-1
- Internal standards relevant to Configuration Management, e.g. hardware standards, desktop standards.

Organization for Configuration Management:

- Roles and responsibilities
- Change and configuration control boards
- Authorization – for establishing baseline, changes and releases.

Asset and Configuration Management System and tools.

Selection and application of processes and procedures to implement Asset and Configuration Management activities, e.g.:

- Configuration identification
- Version management
- Interface management
- Supplier management
- Configuration Change Management
- Release and deployment
- Build management
- Establishing and maintaining configuration baselines
- Maintaining the CMS
- Reviewing the integrity of configurations and the CMS (verification and audit).

Reference implementation plan, e.g. data migration and loading, training and knowledge transfer plan.

Relationship management and interface controls, for example:

- With financial Asset Management
- With projects
- With development and testing
- With customers
- With service provider interfaces (SPI)
- With operations including the service desk.

Relationship management and control of suppliers and sub-contractors.

4.3.5.3 Configuration identification

When planning configuration identification it is important to:

- Define how the classes and types of assets and configuration items are to be selected, grouped, classified and defined by appropriate characteristics, e.g. warranties for a service, to ensure that they are manageable and traceable throughout their lifecycle
- Define the approach to identification, uniquely naming and labelling all the assets or service components of interest across the service lifecycle and the relationships between them
- Define the roles and responsibilities of the owner or custodian for configuration item type at each stage of its lifecycle, e.g. the service owner for a service package or release at each stage of the service lifecycle.

The configuration identification process activities are to:

- Define and document criteria for selecting configuration items and the components that compose them
- Select the configuration items and the components that compose them based on documented criteria
- Assign unique identifiers to configuration items
- Specify the relevant attributes of each configuration item
- Specify when each configuration item is placed under Configuration Management
- Identify the owner responsible for each configuration item.

Configuration structures and the selection of configuration items

The configuration model should describe the relationship and position of CIs in each structure. There should be service configuration structures that identify all the components in a particular service (e.g. the retail service).

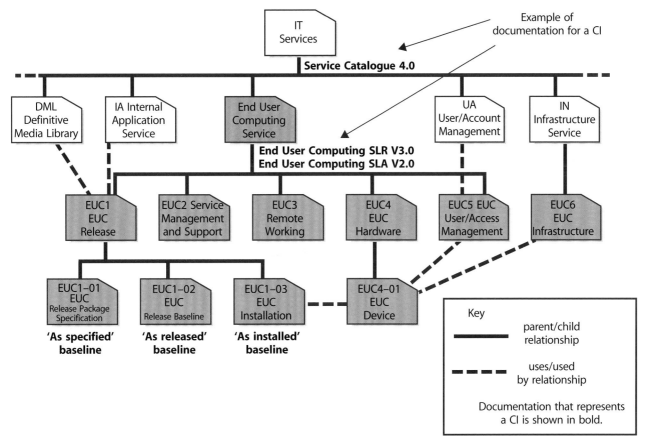

Figure 4.11 (a) Example configuration breakdown for an end-user computing service

An important part of Configuration Management is deciding the level at which control is to be exercised, with top-level CIs broken down into components which are themselves CIs, and so on.

CIs should be selected by applying a top down approach, considering if it is sensible to break down a CI into component CIs. A CI can exist as part of any number of different CIs or CI groups at the same time. For instance, a database product may be used by many applications. Usage links to re-usable and common components of the service should be defined – for instance, a configuration structure for a retail service will use infrastructure CIs such as servers, network and software CIs. The ability to have multiple views through different configuration structures improves accessibility, impact analysis and reporting.

Configuration Management of work products and service components from the service lifecycle may be performed at several levels of granularity. The items placed under Configuration Management will typically include service bundles, service packages, service components, release packages and products that are delivered to the customer, designated internal work products, acquired services, products, tools, systems and other items that are used in

creating and describing the configurations required to design, transition and operate the service.

Figure 4.11 (a) and (b) gives an example in schematic representation of how a CI structure for an end-user computing service and a Managed Virtual System might be broken down.

Choosing the right CI level is a matter of achieving a balance between information availability, the right level of control, and the resources and effort needed to support it. Information at a low CI level may not be valuable – for example, although a keyboard is usually exchanged independently, the organization sees it as a consumable, so does not store data about it. CI information is valuable only if it facilitates the management of change, the control of incidents and problems, or the control of assets that can be independently moved, copied or changed.

Factors that influence recording level of configuration items

The factors that affect choice of lowest CI level are not just financial. As mentioned above most organizations do not store data on keyboards, because they consider them consumables, to be thrown away when not working, as one would a broken pen. However, some organizations find it

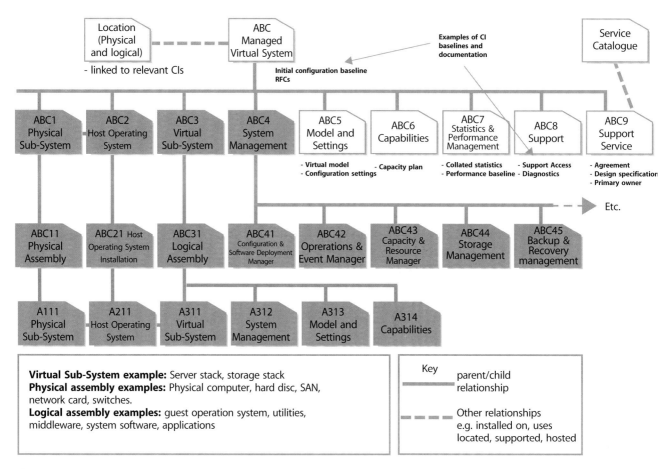

Figure 4.11 (b) Example configuration breakdown for a Managed Virtual System

worth retaining data on keyboards – for example in the United Nations, which supports many different languages within its office building, recording the specific language keyboard used is an important factor in speedy incident resolution when keyboards fail, i.e. they know which kind of replacement keyboard to send to any given user.

The organization should plan to review the CI level regularly – to confirm (or otherwise) that information down to a low level is still valuable and useful, and that the handling of changes and problems and the management of assets are not deficient because the CMDB does not go down to a sufficiently low level.

Each asset and CI needs to be uniquely identified, whether it is generated inside or outside the organization. The identification should also differentiate between successive versions and should enable the items under control to be unambiguously traceable to their specifications or equivalent, documented descriptions. Configuration descriptions and data should conform, where possible, to service, product or technology standards. Configuration data should permit forward and backward traceability to other baselined configuration states, where required.

Naming configuration items

Naming conventions should be established and applied to the identification of CIs, configuration documents and changes, as well as to baselines, builds, releases and assemblies.

Individual CIs should be uniquely identifiable by means of the identifier and version. The version identifies an updated instance of what can be regarded as the same CI. More than one version of a CI can coexist at any given time. The naming conventions should be unique and take into account the existing corporate or supplier naming/numbering structures. The naming conventions or information management system should include the management of:

■ Hierarchical relationships between CIs within a configuration structure
■ Hierarchical or subordinate relationships in each CI
■ Relationships between CIs and their associated documents
■ Relationships between CIs and changes
■ Relationships between CIs, incidents, problems and known errors.

Configuration Management should arrange for a naming convention to be established for all documents, e.g. RFCs. Document templates are a good method for standardizing configuration documentation. Without templates there are often far too many documents generated with overlapping content that can make executing changes extremely difficult.

Each type of template and form should be uniquely identifiable with a version number. A typical method of identification is <Form type>_nnnn where nnnn is a sequentially assigned number for each new instance of the form.

When the naming convention is being planned, it is very important that sufficient account is taken of possible future growth. Identifiers should be relatively short, but meaningful, and should follow existing conventions wherever possible. For hardware, if the CI naming conventions are not based on suppliers' device names and models, a mechanism should be set up to relate Configuration Management and suppliers' identifiers to each other, for example, for the convenience of procurement staff and hardware engineers. Standard terminology and abbreviations should be used throughout the organization as far as possible (e.g. NYC rather than sometimes NY or N York). Failure to do so will result in an inability to match common incidents, problems etc. Attributes that might change should never be used as a part of CI naming.

Labelling configuration items

All physical device CIs should be labelled with the configuration identifier so that they can be easily identified. Plans should be made to label CIs and to maintain the accuracy of their labels.

Items need to be distinguished by unique, durable identification, e.g. labels or markings that follow relevant standards where appropriate. Physical non-removable asset tags (labels) should be attached to all hardware CIs; cables/lines should be clearly labelled at each end and at any inspection points. It is advisable to use a standard format and colour for all such labels, because this makes it easier for users to identify and quote from them, for instance when telephoning the service desk to report a fault. Barcode-readable labels improve the efficiency of physical audits. A standard policy on labelling hardware is similarly beneficial at the service desk, e.g. if all hardware is labelled in the bottom left-hand corner of the left side, it is much quicker and easier to explain to the user where they will find the required information.

Attributes for configuration items

Attributes describe the characteristics of a CI that are valuable to record and which will support SACM and the ITSM processes it supports.

The SACM plan references the configuration information and data architecture. This includes the attributes to be recorded for each type of asset or CI. Typical attributes include:

- Unique identifier
- CI type
- Name/description
- Version (e.g. file, build, baseline, release)
- Location
- Supply date
- Licence details, e.g. expiry date
- Owner/custodian
- Status
- Supplier/source
- Related document masters
- Related software masters
- Historical data, e.g. audit trail
- Relationship type
- Applicable SLA.

These attributes will define specific functional and physical characteristics of each type of asset and CI, e.g. size or capacity, together with any documentation or specifications.

Defining configuration documentation

The characteristics of a CI are often contained in documents. For example, the service definition, requirements specification and service level agreement for a service describe the characteristics of a Service CI. Many organizations specify mandatory and optional documents that describe a CI and use document templates to ensure consistent information is entered. Table 4.7 is a RACI (Responsible, Accountable, Consulted, Informed) chart, which illustrates the types of documentation of service assets or configuration items that are the responsibility of different service lifecycle stages and typical documentation.

Collecting CI attribute data can facilitate use/re-use/reference to existing documents, data, files, records, spreadsheets etc. This will help users implementing this to determine a good approach to collecting data.

Table 4.7 Configuration documentation for assets and responsibilities through the service lifecycle

Service lifecycle stage	Examples of service lifecycle assets and CIs impacted	Service Strategy	Service Design	Service Transition	Service Operation	Continual Service Improvement
Service Strategy	Portfolios – service contract, customer Service Strategy requirements Service lifecycle model	A	C	C	R	C
Service Design	Service package (including SLA) Service Design package, e.g. service model, contract, supplier's Service Management Plan, process interface definition, customer engagement plan Release policy Release package definition	I	A	C	R	C
Service Transition	Service Transition model Test plan Controlled environments Build/installation plan Build specification Release plan Deployment plan CMS SKMS Release package Release baseline Release documentation Evaluation report Test report	I	C	A	R	C
Service Operations	Service Operations model Service support model Service desk User assets User documentation Operations documentation Support documentation	I	C	C	A/R	R
Continual Service Improvement	CSI model Service improvement plan Service reporting process	A/C	A/C	A/C	R	A

R=Responsible, A=Accountable, C=Consulted, I=Informed

Relationships

Relationships describe how the configuration items work together to deliver the services. These relationships are held in the CMS – this is the major difference between what is recorded in a CMS and what is held in an asset register.

The relationships between CIs are maintained so as to provide dependency information. For example:

- A CI is a part of another CI, e.g. a software module is part of a program; a server is part of a site infrastructure – this is a 'parent–child' relationship.
- A CI is connected to another CI, e.g. a desktop computer is connected to a LAN.
- A CI uses another CI, e.g. a program uses a module from another program; a business service uses an infrastructure server.
- A CI is installed on another, e.g. MS Project is installed on a desktop PC.

Although a 'child' CI should be 'owned' by one 'parent' CI, it can be 'used by' any number of other CIs. If a standard desktop build is supplied and installed on all PCs within a division or location, then that build, including all the software CIs included, will be a CI that is linked by a relationship to the PCs. The software included will be 'part of' the build. This can considerably reduce the number of relationships that are needed, compared with when individual software CIs relationships are used.

Relationships are also the mechanism for associating RFCs, incident records, problem records, known errors and release records with the services and IT infrastructure CIs to which they refer. All these relationships should be included in the CMS. RFCs and change and release records will identify the CIs affected.

Some of these relationships were shown in Figure 4.11. For example, EUC is the parent CI of EUC1 to EUC5 and EUC1 is in turn the parent of three CIs, EUC1_01 to EUC1_03, shown as the next level in the hierarchy. EUC1 uses the DML and Internal Application (IA) service.

Relationships may be one-to-one, one-to-many and many-to-one. Placing portfolios under the control of the CMS provides a good example. The combination of Service Portfolios and customer portfolios generates the contract portfolio. In other words, every item in the contract portfolio is mapped to at least one item in the Service Portfolio and at least one item in the customer portfolio.

Types of configuration item

Components should be classified into asset or CI types because this helps to identify and document what is in use, the status of the items and where they are located. Typical CI types include service, hardware, software, documentation and staff.

Identification of media libraries

Physical and electronic media libraries should be uniquely identified and recorded in the CMS with the following information:

- Contents, location and medium of each library
- Conditions for entering an item, including the minimum status compatible with the contents of the library
- How to protect the libraries from malicious and accidental harm and deterioration, together with effective recovery procedures
- Conditions and access controls for groups or types of person registering, reading, updating, copying, removing and deleting CIs
- Scope of applicability, e.g. applicable from environment 'system test' through to 'operation'.

Identification of configuration baselines

Configuration baselines should be established by formal agreement at specific points in time and used as departure points for the formal control of a configuration. Configuration baselines plus approved changes to those baselines together constitute the currently approved configuration. Specific examples of baselines that may be identified include:

- A particular 'standard' CI needed when buying many items of the same type (e.g. desktop computer) over a protracted period; if some are to include additional components (e.g. a DVD writer), this could correspond to 'baseline plus'; if all future desktop computers are to have features then a new baseline is created
- An application release and its associated documentation.

Several baselines corresponding to different stages in the life of a 'baselined item' can exist at any given time – for example, the baseline for an application release that is currently live, the one that was last live and has now been archived, the one that will next be installed (subject to change under Configuration Management control), and one or more under test. Furthermore, if, for instance, new software is being introduced gradually regionally, more than one version of a baseline could be 'live' at the same time. It is therefore best to refer to each by a unique version number, rather than 'live', 'next' or 'old'.

By consolidating the evolving configuration states of configuration items to form documented baselines at designated points or times the Configuration Management will be more effective and efficient. Each baseline is a mutually consistent set of CIs that can be declared at key milestones. An example of a baseline is an approved description of a service that includes internally consistent versions of requirements, requirement traceability matrices, design, specific service components and user documentation.

Each baseline forms a frame of reference for the service lifecycle as a whole. Baselines provide the basis for assessing progress and undertaking further work that is internally self-consistent and stable. For example, the Service Portfolio and the Business Case for a Service should present a consistent and clear definition of what the service package is intending to deliver. This may form the 'scope baseline' for the service(s) and give internal and external parties a clear basis for subsequent analysis and development. An example of the baseline points is shown in Figure 4.12.

Baselines are added to the CMS as they are developed. Changes to baselines and the release of work products built from the CMS are systematically controlled and monitored via the configuration control, Change

Management and configuration auditing functions of SACM. In configuration identification, define and record the rationale for each baseline and associated authorizations required to approve the configuration baseline data.

As a Service progresses through the service lifecycle, each baseline provides progressively greater levels of detail regarding the eventual outputs to be delivered. Furthermore, this hierarchy of baselines enables the final outputs to be traced back to the original requirements.

It needs to be kept in mind that earlier baselines may not be totally up to date with changes that have been made later, e.g. 'course corrections' to requirements documentation may be reflected in the release documentation.

Identification of release unit

'Release unit' describes the portion of the service or infrastructure that is normally released together in accordance with an organization's release policy. The unit may vary, depending on the type(s) or item(s) of software and hardware.

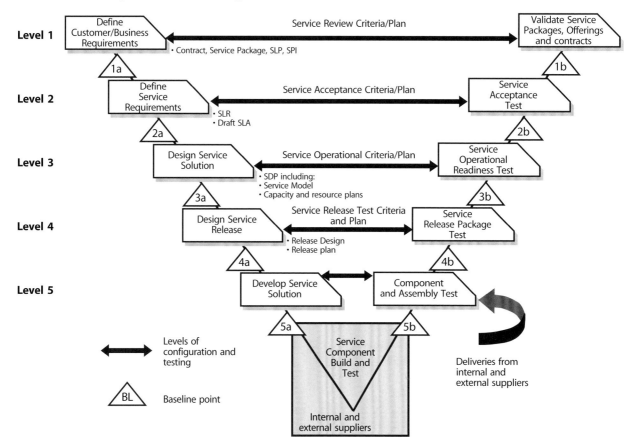

Figure 4.12 Example of service lifecycle configuration levels and baseline points, represented by the numbered triangles

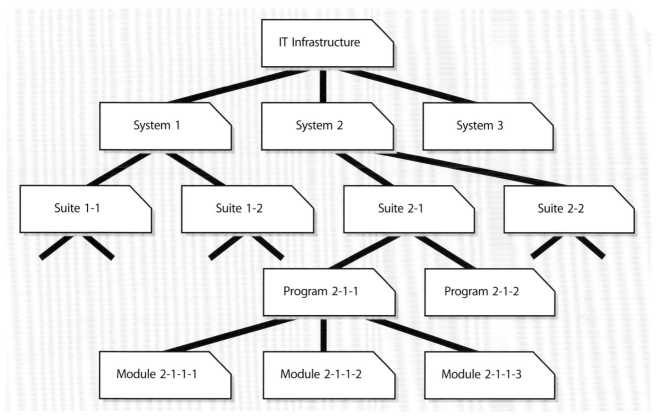

Figure 4.13 Simplified example of an IT infrastructure

Figure 4.13 gives a simplified example showing an IT infrastructure made up of systems, which are in turn made up of suites, comprising programs, which are made up of modules.

Release information is recorded within the CMS, supporting the release and deployment process. Releases are uniquely identified according to a scheme defined in the release policy. The release identification includes a reference to the CI that it represents and a version number that will often have two or three parts. Example release names are:

■ Major releases: Payroll_System v.1, v.2, v.3 etc.
■ Minor releases: Payroll_System v.1.1, v.1.2, v.1.3 etc.
■ Emergency fix releases: Payroll_System v.1.1.1, v.1.1.2, v.1.1.3 etc.

4.3.5.4 Configuration control

Configuration control ensures that there are adequate control mechanisms over CIs while maintaining a record of changes to CIs, versions, location and custodianship/ownership. Without control of the physical or electronic assets and components, the configuration data and information there will be a mismatch with the physical world.

No CI should be added, modified, replaced or removed without an appropriate controlling documentation or procedure being followed. Policies and procedures need to be in place that cover:

■ Licence control, to ensure that the correct number of people are using licences and that there is no unlicensed use and no wastage
■ Change Management
■ Version control of service asset, software and hardware versions, images/builds and releases
■ Access control, e.g. to facilities, storage areas and CMS
■ Build control, including the use of build specification from the CMS to perform a build
■ Promotion, migration of electronic data and information
■ Taking a configuration baseline of assets or CIs before performing a release (into system, acceptance test and production) in a manner that can be used for subsequent checking against actual deployment
■ Deployment control including distribution
■ Installation
■ Maintaining the integrity of the DML.

Often there are many procedures that can change a CI. These should be reviewed and aligned with the CI types where possible as standardization prevents errors. During the planning stage it is important to design an effective configuration control model and implement this in a way that staff can easily locate and use the associated training products and procedures.

If many Configuration Management tools are used there is often a control plan for each tool that is aligned with the overall configuration control model.

Control should be passed from the project or supplier to the service provider at the scheduled time with accurate configuration information, documentation and records. A comprehensive checklist covering the service provider information requirements, Supplier information and organizational information required can be made and signed off. Provisions for conducting SACM need to be established in supplier agreements. Methods to ensure that the configuration data is complete and consistent should be established and maintained. Such a method may include baseline on transition, defined audit policies and audit intervals. It is important that the need for this information and control method is established as early as possible during the development lifecycle and incorporated as a deliverable of the new or changed service.

4.3.5.5 Status accounting and reporting

Each asset or CI will have one or more discrete states through which it can progress. The significance of each state should be defined in terms of what use can be made of the asset or CI in that state. There will typically be a range of states relevant to the individual asset or CIs.

A simple example of a lifecycle is:

- Development or draft – denoting that the CI is under development and that no particular reliance should be placed on it
- Approved – meaning that the CI may be used as a basis for further work
- Withdrawn – meaning withdrawn from use, either because the CI is no longer fit for purpose or because there is no further use for it.

The way CIs move from one state to another should be defined, e.g. an application release may be registered, accepted, installed or withdrawn. An example of a lifecycle for a package application release is shown in Figure 4.14. This will include defining the type of review and approval required and the authority level necessary to give that approval. In Figure 4.12 the role that can promote the CI from Accepted to Installed is 'release management'. At each lifecycle status change the CMS should be updated with the reason, date-time stamp and person that did the status change. The planning activities should also establish any attributes that should be updated at each state.

Configuration status accounting and reporting is concerned with ensuring that all configuration data and documentation is recorded as each asset or CI progresses through its lifecycle. It provides the status of the configuration of a service and its environment as the configuration evolves through the service lifecycle.

Status reporting provides the current and historical data concerned with each CI that in turn enables tracking of changes to CIs and their records, i.e. tracking the status as a CI changes from one state to another, e.g. 'development', 'test', 'live' or 'withdrawn'.

The organization should perform configuration status accounting and reporting activities throughout the lifecycle of the service in order to support and enable an efficient Configuration Management process. Typical activities include:

- Maintaining configuration records through the service lifecycle and archiving them according to agreements, relevant legislation or best industry practice, standards, e.g. ISO 9001, Quality Management System
- Managing the recording, retrieval and consolidation of the current configuration status and the status of all preceding configurations to confirm information correctness, timeliness, integrity and security
- Making the status of items under Configuration Management available throughout the lifecycle, e.g. to ensure appropriate access, change, build and release controls are followed, e.g. build specifications
- Recording changes to CIs from receipt to disposal

Application Release

Figure 4.14 Example of asset and configuration item lifecycle

■ Ensuring that changes to configuration baselines are properly documented. This can be achieved by consolidating the evolving configuration states of configuration items to form documented baselines at designated times or under defined circumstances.

Records

During the configuration identification and control activities, configuration status records will be created. These records allow for visibility and traceability and for the efficient management of the evolving configuration. They typically include details of:

■ Service configuration information (such as identification number, title, effective dates, version, status, change history and its inclusion in any baseline)

■ The service or product configuration (such as design or build status)

■ The status of release of new configuration information

■ Changes implemented and in progress

■ Capturing the results from quality assurance tests to update the configuration records.

The evolving service configuration information should be recorded in a manner that identifies the cross-references and interrelationships necessary to provide the required reports.

Service asset and configuration reports

Reports of varying types will be needed for Configuration Management purposes. Such reports may cover individual configuration items, a complete service or the full Service Portfolio. Typical reports include:

■ A list of product configuration information included in a specific configuration baseline

■ A list of configuration items and their configuration baselines

■ Details of the current revision status and change history

■ Status reports on changes, waivers and deviations

■ Details of the status of delivered and maintained products concerning part and traceability numbers

■ Revision status

■ Report on unauthorized usage of hardware and software

■ Unauthorized CIs detected

■ Variations from CMS to physical audit reports.

Status reports of assets for a business unit or software licence holdings are often required by financial management for budgeting, accounting and charging.

4.3.5.6 Verification and audit

The activities include a series of reviews or audits to:

■ Ensure there is conformity between the documented baselines (e.g. agreements, interface control documents) and the actual business environment to which they refer

■ Verify the physical existence of CIs in the organization or in the DML and spares stores, the functional and operational characteristics of CIs and to check that the records in the CMS match the physical infrastructure

■ Check that release and configuration documentation is present before making a release.

Before a major release or change, an audit of a specific configuration may be required to ensure that the customer's environment matches the CMS. Before acceptance into the live environment, new releases, builds, equipment and standards should be verified against the contracted or specified requirements. There should be a test certificate that proves that the functional requirements of a new or updated CI have been verified, or some other relevant document (e.g. RFC).

Plans should be made for regular configuration audits to check that the CMDB and related configuration information is consistent with the physical state of all CIs, and vice versa. Physical configuration audits should be carried out to verify that the 'as-built' configuration of a CI conforms to its 'as-planned' configuration and its associated documents. Interrogation facilities are required to check that the CMDB and the physical state of CIs are consistent.

These audits should verify that correct and authorized versions of CIs exist, and that only such CIs exist, and are in use in the operational environment. From the outset, any ad-hoc tools, test equipment, personal computers and other unregistered items should either be removed or registered through formal Configuration Management. Registration or removal will be via the Change Management process and has to prevent the authorization of non-acceptable CIs or the removal of CIs that may be supporting business processes. Unregistered and unauthorized items that are discovered during configuration audits should be investigated, and corrective action taken to address possible issues with procedures and the behaviour of personnel. All exceptions are logged and reported.

Configuration audits check in addition that change and release records have been properly authorized by Change Management and that implemented changes are as authorized. Configuration audits should be considered at the following times:

■ Shortly after changes to the CMS
■ Before and after changes to the IT services or infrastructure
■ Before a release or installation to ensure that the environment is as expected
■ Following recovery from disasters and after a 'return to normal' (this audit should be included in contingency plans)
■ At planned intervals
■ At random intervals
■ In response to the detection of any unauthorized CIs.

Automated audit tools enable regular checks to be made at regular intervals, e.g. weekly. For example, desktop audit tools compare the build of an individual's desktop to the master build that was installed. If exceptions are found, some organizations return the build to its original state.

A rolling programme of configuration audits can help use resources more effectively. The service desk and support groups will check that CIs brought to their attention, e.g. the software that a caller is using, are as recorded in the CMS. Any deviations are reported to Configuration Management for investigation.

If there is a high incidence of unauthorized CIs detected, the frequency of configuration audits should be increased, certainly for those parts of the services or IT infrastructure affected by this problem. Note that unauthorized installations are discouraged when the Configuration Management team is seen to be in control and to carry out regular and frequent audits. If an epidemic of unauthorized CIs is detected, selective or general configuration audits should be initiated to determine the scale of the problem, to put matters right, and to discourage a proliferation of unauthorized CIs. Publicity will help to reduce further occurrences. Service Design and Service Operations staff need to be notified and involved in the investigation of unauthorized CIs.

4.3.6 Triggers, input and output, and inter-process interfaces

Updates to asset and configuration information are triggered by change requests, purchase orders, acquisitions and service requests.

4.3.6.1 Process relationships

By its very nature – as the single virtual repository of configuration data and information for IT Service Management – SACM supports and interfaces with every other process and activity to some degree. Some of the more noteworthy interfaces are:

■ Change Management – identifying the impact of proposed changes
■ Financial management – capturing key financial information such as cost, depreciation methods, owner and user (for budgeting and cost allocation), maintenance and repair costs
■ ITSCM – awareness of assets the business services depend on, control of key spares and software
■ Incident/problem/error – providing and maintaining key diagnostic information; maintenance and provision of data to the service desk
■ Availability management in detection of points of failure.

The relationship with change and release and deployment is synergistic, with these processes benefiting greatly from a single coordinated planning approach. Configuration control is synonymous with change control – understanding and capturing updates to the infrastructure and services.

4.3.7 Information management

Backup copies of the CMS should be taken regularly and securely stored. It is advisable for one copy to be stored at a remote location for use in the event of a disaster. The frequency of copying and the retention policy will depend on the size and volatility of the IT infrastructure and the CMS. Certain tools may allow selective copying of CI records that are new or have been changed.

The CMS contains information on backup copies of CIs. It will also contain historical records of CIs and CI versions that are archived, and possibly also of deleted CIs or CI versions. The amount of historical information to be retained depends on its usefulness to the organization. The retention policy on historical CI records should be regularly reviewed, and changed if necessary. If the cost to the organization of retaining CI information is greater than the current or potential value, do not retain it, taking note of relevant regulatory and statutory requirements in relation to retention of records.

Typically, the CMS should contain records only for items that are physically available or could be easily created using procedures known to, and under the control of, Configuration Management. When Configuration

Management has been operating for a period of time, regular housekeeping should be carried out to ensure that redundant CI records are systematically archived.

4.3.8 Key performance indicators and metrics

As with all processes the performance of SACM should be monitored, reported on and action taken to improve it.

SACM is the central support process facilitating the exchange of information with other processes and as such has few customer facing measures. However, as an underlying engine to other processes in the lifecycle, SACM must be measured for its contribution to these parts of the lifecycle and the overall KPIs that affect the customer directly.

In order to optimize the cost and performance of the service assets and configurations the following measures are applicable:

- Percentage improvement in maintenance scheduling over the life of an asset (not too much, not too late)

- Degree of alignment between provided maintenance and business support

- Assets identified as the cause of service failures

- Improved speed for incident management to identify faulty CIs and restore service

- Impact of incidents and errors affecting particular CI types, e.g. from particular suppliers or development groups, for use in improving the IT services

- Percentage re-use and redistribution of under-utilized resources and assets

- Degree of alignment of insurance premiums with business needs

- Ratio of used licences against paid for licences (should be close to 100%)

- Average cost per user for licences (i.e. more effective charging options achieved)

- Achieved accuracy in budgets and charges for the assets utilized by each customer or business unit

- Percentage reduction in business impact of outages and incidents caused by poor Asset and Configuration Management

- Improved audit compliance.

Other measures include:

- Increased quality and accuracy of asset and configuration information

- Fewer errors caused by people working with out-of-date information

- Shorter audits as quality asset and configuration information is easily accessible

- Reduction in the use of unauthorized hardware and software, non-standard and variant builds that increase complexity, support costs and risk to the business services

- Reduction in the average time and cost of diagnosing and resolving incidents and problems (by type)

- Improvement in time to identify poor-performing and poor-quality assets

- Occasions when the 'configuration' is not as authorized

- Changes that were not completed successfully or caused errors because of poor impact assessment, incorrect data in the CMS, or poor version control

- Exceptions reported during configuration audits

- Value of IT components detected in use

- Reduction in risks due to early identification of unauthorized change.

4.3.9 Challenges, critical success factors and risks

Challenges to SACM include:

- Persuading technical support staff to adopt a checking in/out policy – this can be perceived as being a hindrance to a fast and responsive support service; if the positives of such a system are not conveyed adequately then staff may be inclined to try and circumvent it; even then, resistance can still occur; placing this as an objective within their annual appraisal is one way to help enforce the policy

- Attracting and justifying funding for SACM, since it is typically out of sight to the customer units empowered with funding control; in practice it is typically funded as an 'invisible' element of Change Management and other ITSM process with more business visibility

- An attitude of 'just collecting data because it is possible to do'; this leads SACM into a data overload which is impossible, or at least disproportionately expensive, to maintain

- Lack of commitment and support from management who do not understand the key role it must play supporting other processes.

Critical success factors include:

- Focusing on establishing valid justification for collecting and maintaining data at the agreed level of detail

- Demonstrating a top-down approach – focused on identifying service CIs and subsequently the CIs that support those services, thereby allowing a rapid and clear demonstration of potential points of failure for any given service

- Setting a justified level of accuracy, i.e. the correlation between the logical model within SACM and the 'real world'

- Making use of enabling technology to automate the CMS practices and enforce SACM policies.

Risks to successful SACM include:

- The temptation to consider it technically focused, rather than service and business focused, since technical competence is essential to its successful delivery

- Degradation of the accuracy of configuration information over time that can cause errors and be difficult and costly to correct

- The CMS becomes out of date due to the movement of hardware assets by non-authorized staff; half-yearly physical audits should be conducted with discrepancies highlighted and investigated; managers should be informed of inconsistencies in their areas.

4.4 RELEASE AND DEPLOYMENT MANAGEMENT

Release and Deployment Management aims to build, test and deliver the capability to provide the services specified by Service Design and that will accomplish the stakeholders' requirements and deliver the intended objectives.

4.4.1 Purpose, goal and objective

The purpose of Release and Deployment Management is to:

- Define and agree release and deployment plans with customers and stakeholders

- Ensure that each release package consists of a set of related assets and service components that are compatible with each other

- Ensure that integrity of a release package and its constituent components is maintained throughout the transition activities and recorded accurately in the CMS

- Ensure that all release and deployment packages can be tracked, installed, tested, verified, and/or uninstalled or backed out if appropriate

- Ensure that organization and stakeholder change is managed during the release and deployment activities (see section 5).

- Record and manage deviations, risks, issues related to the new or changed service and take necessary corrective action

- Ensure that there is knowledge transfer to enable the customers and users to optimize their use of the service to support their business activities

- Ensure that skills and knowledge are transferred to operations and support staff to enable them to effectively and efficiently deliver, support and maintain the service according to required warranties and service levels.

The goal of Release and Deployment Management is to deploy releases into production and establish effective use of the service in order to deliver value to the customer and be able to handover to service operations.

The objective of Release and Deployment Management is to ensure that:

- There are clear and comprehensive release and deployment plans that enable the customer and business change projects to align their activities with these plans

- A release package can be built, installed, tested and deployed efficiently to a deployment group or target environment successfully and on schedule

- A new or changed service and its enabling systems, technology and organization are capable of delivering the agreed service requirements, i.e. utilities, warranties and service levels

- There is minimal unpredicted impact on the production services, operations and support organization

- Customers, users and Service Management staff are satisfied with the Service Transition practices and outputs, e.g. user documentation and training.

4.4.2 Scope

The scope of Release and Deployment Management includes the processes, systems and functions to package, build, test and deploy a release into production and establish the service specified in the Service Design package before final handover to service operations.

4.4.3 Value to business

Effective Release and Deployment Management enables the service provider to add value to the business by:

- Delivering change, faster and at optimum cost and minimized risk

- Assuring that customers and users can use the new or changed service in a way that supports the business goals

- Improving consistency in implementation approach across the business change, service teams, suppliers and customers

- Contributing to meeting auditable requirements for traceability through Service Transition.

Well-planned and implemented release and deployment will make a significant difference to an organization's service costs. A poorly designed release or deployment will, at best, force IT personnel to spend significant amounts of time troubleshooting problems and managing complexity. At worst, it can cripple the environment and degrade the live services.

4.4.4 Policies, principles and basic concepts

4.4.4.1 Release unit and identification

A 'release unit' describes the portion of a service or IT infrastructure that is normally released together according to the organization's release policy. The unit may vary, depending on the type(s) or item(s) of service asset or service component such as software and hardware. Figure 4.15 gives a simplified example showing an IT service made up of systems and service assets, which are in turn made up of service components.

The general aim is to decide the most appropriate release-unit level for each service asset or component. An organization may, for example, decide that the release unit for business critical applications is the complete application in order to ensure that testing is comprehensive. The same organization may decide

that a more appropriate release unit for a website is at the page level.

The following factors should be taken into account when deciding the appropriate level for release units:

- The ease and amount of change necessary to release and deploy a release unit

- The amount of resources and time needed to build, test, distribute and implement a release unit

- The complexity of interfaces between the proposed unit and the rest of the services and IT infrastructure

- The storage available in the build, test, distribution and live environments.

Releases should be uniquely identified according to a scheme defined in the release policy as discussed in section 4.1.4.2. The release identification should include a reference to the CIs that it represents and a version number that will often have two or three parts, e.g. emergency fix releases: Payroll_System v.1.1.1, v.1.1.2, v.1.1.3.

4.4.4.2 Release design options and considerations

Service Design will define the approach to transitioning from the current service to the new or changed service or service offering. The SDP defines the service and solution design components to be transitioned to deliver the required service package(s) and service level package(s).

Common options for release and deployment that are considered in Service Design are discussed below. The selected option will have a significant impact on the release and deployment resources as well as the business outcomes. It is important to understand the patterns of

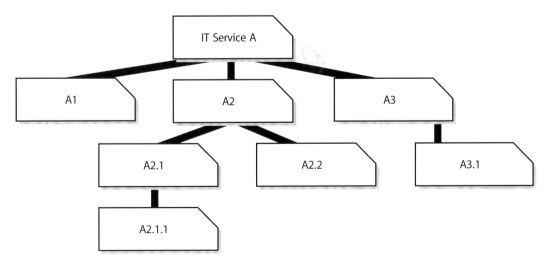

Figure 4.15 Simplified example of release units for an IT service

business activity (PBA) and user profiles when planning and designing the releases.

'Big bang' vs phased

Options for deploying new releases to multiple locations are illustrated in Figure 4.16 and described below:

■ 'Big bang' option – the new or changed service is deployed to all user areas in one operation. This will often be used when introducing an application change and consistency of service across the organization is considered important.

■ Phased approach – the service is deployed to a part of the user base initially, and then this operation is repeated for subsequent parts of the user base via a scheduled rollout plan. This will be the case in many scenarios such as in retail organizations for new services being introduced into the stores' environment in manageable phases.

Figure 4.16 also illustrates a possible sequence of events over time as follows:

■ There is an initial launch of the 'Release 1' of the system to three workstations (1–3).

■ Two further workstations (4+5) are then added at the same time.

■ 'Release 2' of the system is then rolled out in a 'big bang' approach to all workstations (1–5) at once.

■ Two further workstations (6+7) are then added, in another step.

■ There is a phased implementation of the upgrade to 'Release 3' of the system, initially upgrading only three workstations (1–3) and then the remaining four (4–7).

■ A further workstation (8) is then added to the system.

Variations of the phased approach include:

■ Portions of the service are delivered to the live environment in phases, but all end users are affected simultaneously (e.g. incremental changes to a shared application).

■ Each release is deployed gradually across the total population of end users (e.g. one geographical location at a time).

■ Different types of service element are deployed in separate phases, e.g. hardware changes are first, followed by user training and then by the new or changed software.

■ A combination of all of these approaches is usually adopted, and the plans may deliberately allow for variations in the light of actual deployment experience.

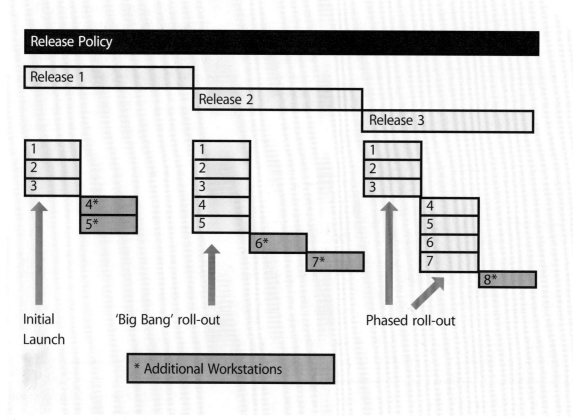

Figure 4.16 Options for 'big bang' and phased rollout

In the type of phased implementation illustrated above, it is only possible to employ this approach if the service has been designed to allow new and old versions to coexist. If this is not possible then the only alternative is to upgrade all affected parts together in a 'big bang' implementation. For elements such as documentation, for skilled staff this is rarely a problem; for many instances of hardware and software it is possible. For other transitions, such as those involving major network changes, it can be virtually impossible to achieve.

Figure 4.17 illustrates phased deployment to a number of different geographical locations. It assumes that new versions will work alongside the previous one. The example used assumes that new functionality is implemented first in the head office of the organization, then in a pilot branch and finally in the remaining branches. If there are a very large number of locations to deal with, it may still take a long time to implement the initial system or upgrades in all branches, thus increasing the likelihood of needing to support even more versions of the system in the live environment concurrently.

Push and pull

A push approach is used where the service component is deployed from the centre and pushed out to the target locations. In terms of service deployment, delivering updated service components to all users – either in big-bang or phased form – constitutes 'push', since the new or changed service is delivered into the users' environment at a time not of their choosing.

A pull approach is used for software releases where the software is made available in a central location but users are free to pull the software down to their own location at a time of their choosing or when a user workstation restarts. The use of 'pull' updating a release over the internet has made this concept significantly more pervasive. A good example is virus signature updates, which are typically pulled down to update PCs and servers when it best suits the customer; however at times of extreme virus risk this may be overridden by a release that is pushed to all known users.

In order to deploy via 'push' approach, the data on all user locations must be available. Pull approaches do not rest so heavily on accurate configuration data and they can trigger an update to user records. This may be through new users appearing and requesting downloads or expected users not doing so, triggering investigation into their continued existence. As some users will never 'pull' a release it may be appropriate to allow a 'pull' within a specified time limit and if this is exceeded a push will be forced, e.g. for an anti-virus update.

Automation vs manual

Whether by automation or other means, the mechanisms to release and deploy the correctly configured service components should be established in the release design phase and tested in the build and test stages.

Automation will help to ensure repeatability and consistency. The time required to provide a well-designed and efficient automated mechanism may not always be available or viable. If a manual mechanism is used it is important to monitor and measure the impact of many repeated manual activities as they are likely to be inefficient and error-prone. Too many manual activities will slow down the release team and create resource or capacity issues that affect the service levels.

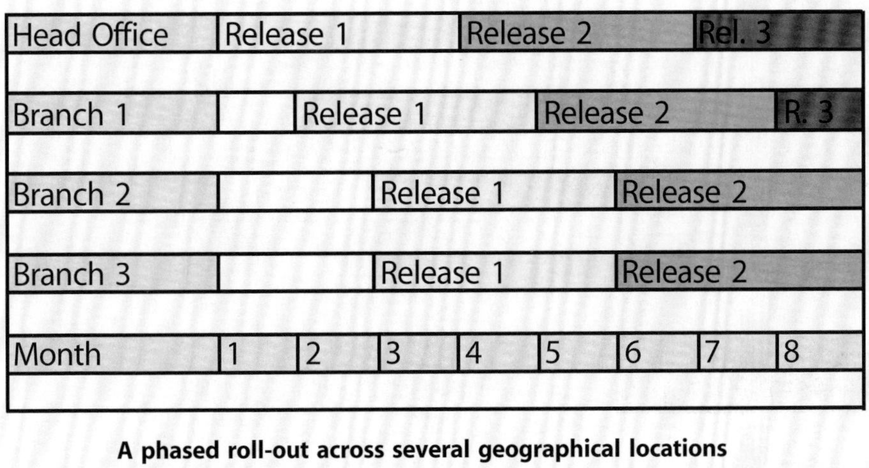

Head Office	Release 1		Release 2		Rel. 3		
Branch 1		Release 1		Release 2		R. 3	
Branch 2		Release 1		Release 2			
Branch 3		Release 1		Release 2			
Month	1	2	3	4	5	6	7	8

A phased roll-out across several geographical locations

Figure 4.17 Phased deployment across geographical locations

Many of the release and deployment activities are capable of a degree of automation. For example:

- Discovery tools aid release planning.
- Discovery and installation software can check whether the required prerequisites and co-requisites are in place before installation of new or changed software components.
- Automated builds can significantly reduce build and recovery times that in turn can resolve scheduling conflicts and delays.
- Automated configuration baseline procedures save time and reduce errors in capturing the status of configurations and releases during build, test and deployment.
- Automatic comparisons of the actual 'live' configuration with the expected configuration or CMS help to identify issues at the earliest opportunity that could cause incidents and delays during deployment.
- Automated processes to load and update data to the CMS help to ensure the records are accurate and complete.
- Installation procedures automatically update user and licence information in the CMS.

Designing release and release packages

Figure 4.18 provides an example of how the architectural elements of a service may be changed from the current baseline to the new baseline with releases at each level. The architecture will be different in some organizations

but is provided in this section to give a context for release and deployment activities. The release and deployment teams need to understand the relevant architecture in order to be able to plan, package, build and test a release to support the new or changed service. This helps to prioritize the release and deployment activities and manage dependencies, e.g. the technology infrastructure needs to be ready with operations staff ready to support it with new or changed procedures before an application is installed.

Figure 4.18 also shows how the service architectural elements depend on the Service Portfolio that defines the service offerings and service packages. Dependent services will need to be built and tested in Service Transition. For example an IT financial service may be dependent on several internal support services and an external service. For more details about the structure of services, see the Service Strategy and Service Design publications.

There are normally dependencies between particular versions of service components required for the service to operate. For example a new version of an application may require an upgrade to the operating system and one or other of these two changes could require a hardware change, e.g. a faster processor or more memory. In some cases, the release package may consist of a set of documentation and procedures. These could be deployed via a manual update or through an automatic publishing mechanism, e.g. to the SKMS/website.

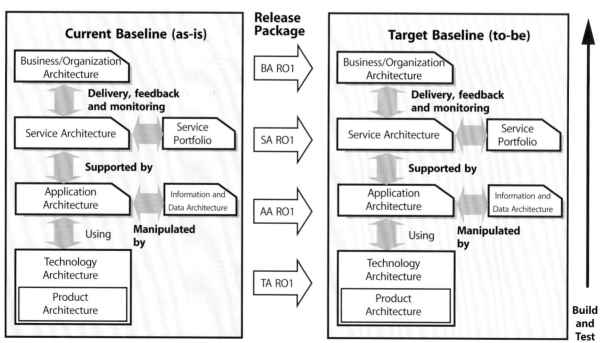

Figure 4.18 Architecture elements to be built and tested

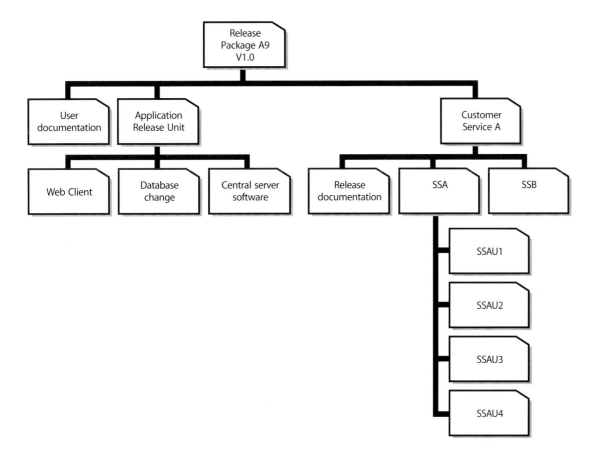

Figure 4.19 Example of a release package

A release package may be a single release unit or a structured set of release units such as the one shown in Figure 4.19.

The example in Figure 4.19 shows an application with its user documentation and a release unit for each technology platform. On the right there is the customer service asset that is supported by two supporting services – SSA for the infrastructure service and SSB for the application service. These release units will contain information about the service, its utilities and warranties and release documentation. Often there will be different ways of designing a release package and consideration needs to be given to establishing the most appropriate method for the identifiable circumstances, stakeholders and possibilities.

Where possible, release packages should be designed so that some release units can be removed if they cause issues in testing.

Valuable release windows

A UK government department is especially well placed to make full use of all available release windows. They work in a secure financial, low risk environment, with carefully planned changes scheduled well in advance and allocated to pre-arranged release windows, which are scheduled several months apart. Because of their careful and longer term planning, when a change proves unsuitable for release, i.e. tests are failed, alternative, quality-assured changes are usually available – prepared and tested but lower in business priority and so targeted at later releases. These can be accelerated to make use of the unexpected vacancy created by the test failure. The test and build process also allows elements of later scheduled releases to be slotted in for release, or successful components of the failed release to be implemented, even though the full products is not ready. This allows subsequent fuller release to be a 'smaller' product, therefore allowing further additional changes to be scheduled alongside them in later release windows.

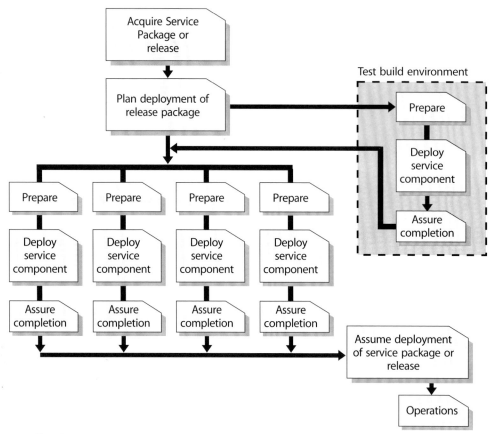

Figure 4.20 Coordinating the deployment of service components

Any significant new or changed service or service offering will require the deployment stage to consider the full range of elements comprising that service – infrastructure, hardware, software, applications, documentation, knowledge etc. Effectively this means the deployment will contain sub-deployments for elements comprising the service, as illustrated in Figure 4.20. The combination, relationship and interdependencies of these components will require careful and considered planning. Significant deployments will be complex projects in their own right.

To understand the deployment options a high level assessment of the deployment units, locations and environments may be required, for example:

■ Assessment baseline – this is a snapshot of the relevant environment, services and infrastructure, including 'softer' elements such as skills level and ⌐des where applicable, should be taken as a first

 〜mponents – this may include deciding
 break down a major deployment into
〜 there will be different ways of
 ⌐down and consideration needs to
 ⌐lishing the most appropriate method

for all the identifiable circumstances, stakeholders and possibilities.

■ Determine the appropriate deployment approach for each.

4.4.4.3 Release and deployment models

A service may be deployed into the production environment in a number of ways. Service Design will select the most suitable release and deployment models that include the approach, mechanisms, processes, procedures and resources required to build and deploy the release on time and within budget.

The release methods during the early build and test stages may differ significantly from live operations so plan ahead to ensure that appropriate release methods are adopted at the right time.

Release and deployment models define:

■ Release structure – the overall structure for building a release package and the target environments

■ The exit and entry criteria including mandatory and optional deliverables and documentation for each stage

- Controlled environments required to build and test the release for each release level; there will be multiple logical and physical environments through the Service Transition stage mapped to different physical environments available to the transition team
- The roles and responsibilities for each configuration item at each release level
- The release promotion and configuration baseline model
- Template release and deployment schedules
- Supporting systems, tools and procedures for documenting and tracking all release and deployment activities
- The handover activities and responsibilities for executing the handover and acceptance for each stage of release and deployment.

Considerations in designing the release and deployment model include activities to:

- Verify that a release complies with the SDP, architecture and related standards
- Ensure the integrity of hardware and software is protected during installation, handling, packaging and delivery
- Use standard release and deployment procedures and tools
- Automate the delivery, distribution, installation, build and configuration audit procedures where appropriate to reduce costly manual steps
- Manage and deploy/re-deploy/remove/retire software licences
- Package and build the release package so that it can be backed out or remediated if required
- Use Configuration Management procedures, the CMS and DML to manage and control components during the build and deployment activities, e.g. to verify the prerequisites, co-requisites and post-installation requests
- Document the release and deployment steps
- Document the deployment group or target environment that will receive the release
- Issue service notifications.

4.4.5 Process activities, methods and techniques

4.4.5.1 Planning

Release and deployment plans

Plans for release and deployment will be linked into the overall Service Transition plan and adopt the selected release and deployment model. The approach is to derive a sound set of guidelines for the release into production and subsequent deployment that can be scaled from small organizations to large multinationals. Although smaller organizations will have less complex environments, the disciplines detailed here are still relevant. Even within a single organization, the release and deployment plans need to be scalable since the extent of their scale of impact on the organization will vary, perhaps from impacting only one small specialist team in one location through to multinational impact on all users when introducing new desktop equipment and services, or transferring services to different suppliers.

Release and deployment plans should be authorized through Change Management. They should define the:

- Scope and content of the release
- Risk assessment and risk profile for the release
- Organizations and stakeholders affected by the release
- Stakeholders that approved the change request for the release and/or deployment
- Team responsible for the release
- Approach to working with stakeholders and deployment groups to determine the:
  - Delivery and deployment strategy
  - Resources for the release and deployment
  - Amount of change that can be absorbed.

Pass/fail criteria

Service Transition is responsible for planning the pass/fail situations. At a minimum these should be defined for each authorization point through the release and deployment stage. It is important to publish these criteria to relevant stakeholders well in advance to set expectations correctly. An example of a pass situation before build and test is:

- All tests are completed successfully; the evaluation report and RFC for build and test are signed off.

Examples of fail situations include:

- Insufficient resources to pass to the next stage. For example, an automated build is not possible and so the resource requirement becomes error-prone, too onerous and expensive; testing identifies that there will not be enough money to deliver the proposed design in the operations phase.
- Service Operation does not have capabilities to offer particular service attributes.
- Service Design does not conform to the service operation standards for technologies, protocols, regulations, etc.

- The service cannot be delivered within the boundaries of the design constraints.
- Service acceptance criteria are not met.
- Mandatory documents are not signed off.
- SKMS and CMS are not updated, perhaps due to a process that is manually intensive.
- The incidents, problems and risks are higher than predicted, e.g. by over 5%.

Build and test prior to production

Build and test planning establishes the approach to building, testing and maintaining the controlled environments prior to production. The activities include:

- Developing build plans from the SDP, design specifications and environment configuration requirements
- Establishing the logistics, lead times and build times to set up the environments
- Testing the build and related procedures
- Scheduling the build and test activities
- Assigning resources, roles and responsibilities to perform key activities, e.g.:
  - Security procedures and checks
  - Technical support
  - Preparing build and test environments
  - Managing test databases and test data
  - Software asset and licence management

- Configuration Management – configuration audit, build and baseline management
- Defining and agreeing the build exit and entry criteria.

Figure 4.21 provides an example of a model that can be used to represent the different configuration levels to be built and tested to deliver a service capability. The left-hand side represents the specification of the service requirements down to the detailed Service Design. The right-hand side focuses on the validation and test activities that are performed against the specifications defined on the left-hand side. At each stage on the left-hand side, there is direct involvement by the equivalent party on the right-hand side. It shows that service validation and acceptance test planning should start with the definition of the service requirements. For example, customers who sign off the agreed service requirements will also sign off the service Acceptance Criteria and test plan.

The V-model approach is traditionally associated with the waterfall lifecycle, but is, in fact, just as applicable to other lifecycles, including iterative lifecycles, such as prototyping, RAD approaches. Within each cycle of the iterative development, the V-model concepts of establishing acceptance requirements against the requirements and design can apply, with each iterative design being considered for the degree of integrity and competence that would justify release to the customer for trial and assessment.

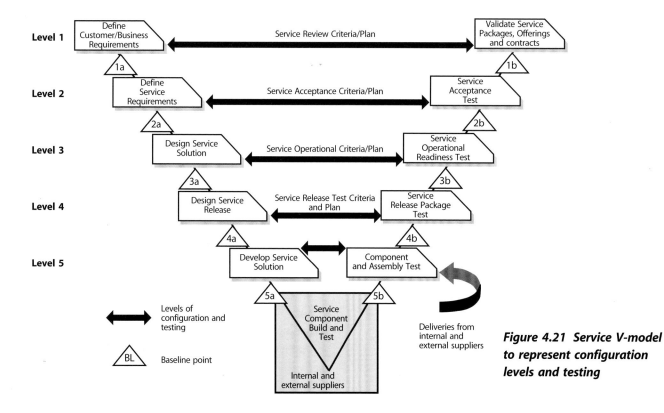

Figure 4.21 Service V-model to represent configuration levels and testing

Table 4.8 Levels of configuration for build and testing

Level	Requirements and design	Build/deliverable	Validation and testing
Level 1 Customer/business needs	Structured definition of contract requirements	Customer contract (based on Service Portfolio, SLP)	**Service test and evaluation** Determines whether a service can enable the users and customers to use the service to support their business needs (is fit for purpose and fit for use).
Level 2 Service requirements	Service requirement specifications and SAC, traceable back to the contract requirements	Service capability and resources to deliver against the SLA and service requirements	**Service test** Test the Service Acceptance Criteria are met. Includes validation of service performance against the service level requirements and SLA in pilots, deployment and early life support.
Level 3 Service solution	SDP, Service model, service environments	Solution/system required to deliver the service capability; includes the Service Management and Service Operations systems and capabilities	**Service operational readiness test** To evaluate the integration and operation of the service capability and resources. It verifies that the target deployment organization and people are prepared to deploy and operate the new or changed service in the live environment, e.g. deployment team, Service Operations, customers, users and other stakeholders. Tests include scenario-based testing such as simulation and service rehearsal.
Level 4 Service release		Release package	**Service release test** A test that the service components can be integrated correctly and that the release can be installed, built and tested in the target environments. Service release testing includes non-functional testing that can be performed at this level.
Level 5 Component and assemblies	Component and assembly test specification	Component or assembly of components	**Component and assembly test** Test that a service component or assembly of components matches its detailed specification. Components or assemblies are tested in isolation, with a view to their delivering as specified, in terms of inputs generating expected outputs. Evidence of component quality or testing earlier in the chain may be obtained for test evidence, from both internal and external suppliers.

Further details on validation, testing and service evaluation are provided in sections 4.5 and 4.6. The test strategy defines the overall approach to validation and testing. It includes the organization of validation and testing activities and resources and can apply to the whole organization, a set of services or an individual service.

Typical levels of configuration for build and testing are shown in Table 4.8.

Various controlled environments will need to be built or made available for the different types and levels of testing as well as to support other transition activities such as training. Existing deployment processes and procedures can be used to build the controlled test environments. The environments will need to be secure to ensure there is no unauthorized access and that any segregation of duty requirements are met. The types of environments, both logical and physical, required during release and deployment include:

■ Build environments – used to compile or assemble the release package or service assets

■ Unit test environment – used for verifying the functionality, performance, recovery and usability characteristics of an individual service component, e.g. online procedure

■ Assembly test environment – used for verifying the functionality, performance, recovery and usability characteristics of an assembly of service components

■ Integration environment – for building and integrating service components

■ System test environment – used for testing all aspects of the integrated service architecture, including the application and technical infrastructure; substantial user acceptance testing is executed in this environment

■ Service release test environment – used to install, build and test a release package in a controlled environment; this is often combined with the system test environment

■ Service Operations readiness test environment – for testing the service and service unit capabilities before promotion into live; may include the Service Management acceptance test, some operational acceptance tests and user acceptance tests of the end-to-end service

■ Business simulation environments

■ Service Management simulation environments

■ Training environments – sometimes this may include an established test database that can be used as a safe and realistic training environment

■ Pilot environments, including conference room pilots

■ Backup and recovery environments, e.g. disaster recovery.

Planning pilots

Pilots are useful for testing the service with a small part of the user base before rolling it out to the whole service community. It is important to determining the appropriate scope of a pilot (how much of the service is to be included in the pilot, size of department or user base). This is a key step in establishing the pilot effort. If the scope is too small then insufficient functionality and implementation variations will be trialled and the likelihood of significant errors not being discovered until full rollout is higher. If the scope is too large it will not deliver the speed and flexibility that deliver the benefits, but will effectively be a first rollout.

A pilot can be used to establish the viability of most, if not all, aspects of the service. But this will only happen if all stakeholders are actively involved in the pilot and use the service as it would be done in a full rollout.

The pilot should include steps to collect feedback on the effectiveness of the deployment plan. This can include:

■ Surveying views and satisfaction from:
  ● End users
  ● Customers
  ● Suppliers
  ● Service desk and other support staff

■ Network management

■ Data and Knowledge Management – statistics on use and effectiveness

■ Analysing statistics from service desk calls, suppliers, capacity and availability.

Commitment to support the pilot is required from all involved parties. Obtaining that commitment can be a challenge since pilots typically will represent additional work for those users involved over and above their day jobs. Collaboration from suppliers and support staff (who may have to be supporting two versions of a service in parallel, or deliver a small separate unit dedicated to supporting the pilot) must also be obtained.

Planning should accommodate rolling back a pilot before the full rollout of an authorized new service. New services tend to be piloted with test equipment and this needs to be rolled back to its original state. In addition, users who were part of the pilot should be working with the same components of a service as other users after the full rollout, not the setup put in place for the pilot. This simplifies, day-to-day operations in IT Service Management.

Although a pilot is often thought of as one trial in the production environment before rolling a service out across the full customer and user environment, there may be justification for a range of pilots, e.g. a pilot for deployment to each geographical region. Many considerations are relevant, with the best solution for a given circumstance being a balance between benefit and cost. Factors include:

■ **Speed and cost** – A single pilot will be cheaper and faster than multiple pilots, and is the obvious choice for a homogeneous organization where a single pilot will encounter (almost) all eventualities and so provide a high degree of confidence that a successful pilot would be followed by a successful roll-out across the wider organization.

■ **Diverse organization** – In an organization with a range of circumstances across the user base, or with multiple operating environments, a matching range of pilots may be sensible, with a trial in each of the areas. These can be managed in parallel, with simultaneous trialling in each environment, which reduces elapsed time but increases management overhead and complexity. Alternatively, by running the pilots serially, lessons learned in one environment may be usefully applied to the subsequent ones, since even in diverse organization there is likely to be significant common ground, e.g. within the actual service components. Examples of significant diversity include:

- Different training methods needed for different groups
- Technology
- Language or culture
- Network capability.

- **Trialling options** – Where alternative solutions are possible for a major rollout, it may be worth trying each of the options in a separate pilot (preferably in closely matched areas to make comparisons meaningful). Armed with the results from each pilot, a decision as to the approach for the main rollout can be taken based on solid empirical evidence.

- **Political considerations** – Internal or external political issues may mean that a specific group or groups needs to be involved – or not involved – in a pilot for a new or changed service.

Example of need for multiple piloting

A government organization delivers desktop IT services to all their staff – in corporate headquarters (HQ) and in locations throughout the world. When new or significant changes are to be rolled out, typically three parallel pilots are carried out to test the three levels of communication and support technology they have identified:

- Those in HQ on direct network connection and with local dedicated support staff
- Those in larger locations with reliable high-speed connection and semi-specialized local IT administrators
- Those in smaller locations with unreliable communications and no trained local support.

Experience has shown that the three groups have different implementation and support issues and that the pilots in all three types of customer are worth the extra costs and complications.

Planning release packaging and build

Planning the release packaging and build activities includes the activities to develop the mechanisms, plans or procedures for the following:

- Verifying the entry/exit criteria
- Managing stakeholder change and communications by:
  - Obtaining and maintaining the list of contacts and their details

- Communicating the proposed changes, the expected benefits and how the change affects the organization and staff
- Training people and transferring knowledge
- Establishing the Services and service assets, e.g. agreements and contracts are in place
- Agreeing schedules:
  - Agreeing the delivery schedules and handling any changes/delays
  - Finalising the logistics and delivery procedures and checklists
  - Scheduling and allocating controlled transition environments, facilities and tools for: i) acquisition of service assets and components, and ii) release packaging, building and testing
- Developing procedures and mechanisms using available Configuration Management, release, content/electronic publishing and other tools to:
  - Build, copy, promote, distribute, audit, install and activate a release
  - Manage software licences, digital rights and Intellectual Property Rights (IPR)
- Converting systems and users from the current applications and technology to the new or changed service, e.g. migrate or reformat application data and information
- Developing the Service Management capability and resources for:
  - Conducting site surveys
  - Updating service information, e.g. service catalogue, release documentation
  - Building and preparing the management systems and other operational systems, e.g. systems and event management, measurement systems
  - Operating and handling the predicted capacity required for support
  - Operating the controlled environments including procedures to scale up capacity if required
  - Documenting and providing the information to be created and/or updated during transition, e.g. remediation plans to be issued and published
  - Installing the new or changed service ready for activation
  - Transferring/transitioning a service or service team or organization
  - Decommissioning and/or disposing of service assets and components
  - Retiring services

■ Assessing the readiness of a target deployment group (customers, users and Service Operations staff) to take a release

■ Defining and agreeing the exit criteria.

Deployment planning

There are many planning considerations that need to be considered. Planners should be able to answer the questions included in Table 4.9.

Logistics and delivery planning

Once the overall deployment approach is understood, develop the logistics and delivery plans. These plans deal with aspects such as:

■ How and when release units and service components will be delivered

■ What the typical lead times are; what happens if there is a delay

■ How to track progress of the delivery and obtain confirmation of delivery

■ Availability of secure storage where required

■ Managing customs and other implications of international distribution.

As well as the delivery aspects, there are typically consequential logistics to be dealt with, e.g. decommissioning and disposing of redundant items, including software and licences, hardware, skills, computer and staff accommodation, support contracts (utility supply, maintenance, cleaners etc.). There may also be a need for temporary equipment (e.g. swing equipment) or throwaway software that is required for the transition.

If the transition plans call for any parallel running of services or equipment, this is particularly taxing from a logistics perspective, since double facilities are likely to be required for a short time.

Once the logistics and delivery plans have been determined, they need to be communicated to all stakeholders, including formal notification to those consulted in deriving the plan.

Delivery is not sufficient; successful logistics requires that the components arrive and perform as required. Therefore deployment planning for all despatched items – hardware,

Table 4.9 Questions to be answered when planning deployment

Deployment question	Examples
What needs to be deployed?	Do you have a good understanding of the service and release that is being deployed? What are the components that make up the release package? What are the business drivers for the deployment? Is it required to meet a critical business need?
Who are the users?	Which users are affected by the deployment? What language do they use? Do they need any special training?
Are there location dependencies?	Are there any holidays, shut-downs or other interruptions to normal business at this location? What level of detail needs to be recorded, e.g. building, floor, room?
Where are the users?	Are all the users and systems local to the deployment, or are some remote, and how will this affect the logistics?
Who else needs to be prepared well in advance?	Do the service desk and support staff need training? Are there any access issues to be solved – security or physical?
When does the deployment need to be completed?	Does the deployment need to be completed by a certain date and time or can it be completed by following a flexible schedule?
Why is the deployment happening?	Is the deployment needed to fix a problem or is it required for some new functionality that has been requested, and do the users understand what is coming?
What are the critical success factors and exit criteria?	How will you know that the deployment has been successful? Who will authorize the deployment? How will you know when the deployment is finished?
What is the current capability of the service provider?	What are the current services, processes and Service Management capability – capacity, financial aspects, current systems and infrastructure?

software, documentation, and training – will address how components are tracked and documented on delivery. This should include:

- Checking against a definitive list of required service assets and components' unique IDs and versions
- A delivery note detailing the components to be delivered, including unique IDs, versions and quantities
- What there should be (contents list to check against)
- What needs to be there to meet it, in terms of equipment, prerequisites and co-requisites
- How to ensure it is correct/working – what tools, parameters, feedback mechanisms, Acceptance Criteria need to be applied?
- Metrics for monitoring and determining success of the release deployment effort.

Financial/commercial planning

Financial and commercial aspects will need to be specifically checked before the deployment and activities added to the deployment plans where necessary. For example:

- **Working capital** – Are sufficient funds available to deliver the customer expectations, e.g. to fund initial changes to gain emotional acceptance during the deployment?
- **Contracts and licenses** – Have all necessary contract and licence transfers been arranged?
- **Funding** – Is funding available for the supporting systems to manage the service, e.g. CMS and related licences?
- **Intellectual property** – Has the full range of IP, its ongoing ownership and usage has been addressed, including:
  - Software developed by one of the parties
  - Documentation such as user manuals?

4.4.5.2 Preparation for build, test and deployment

Before authorizing the build and test stage, the Service Design and the release design must be validated against the requirement for the new or changed service offering. This should result in constructive feedback on the Service Design. Record, track and measure any risks and issues against the services, service assets and CIs within the service package, SLP, SDP or release package. Prioritize the issues and actions to ensure they can be resolved in a timely manner. Finally, produce a validation report and associated results ready for service evaluation.

An independent evaluation of the service and release design uses the validation report and results (see 4.6.5). This evaluation checks that the change to the services or service offering will deliver the predicted outcomes, i.e. the service expected by the user or customer. If there are issues, an interim evaluation report is prepared. This report lists the deviations from the SDP, a risk profile and recommendations for Change Management. If there are deviations in the service level requirements then the service package, SLP or SAC may be changed (via Change Management) and action should be taken to modify the proposed service release and related changes. Successful completion of the evaluation of the Service Design baseline ensures that service release build and test starts with a stable, baselined and approved design.

For some releases the Service Transition Manager may need to assign individuals or establish a team of competent people to execute the plans. If individuals are not dedicated there is risk that they may be diverted to work on other projects. Such risks need to be mitigated as they are often the cause of delays.

On most occasions, the introduction of a technology-enabled service requires training for the release, deployment, build and test teams. The training needs of these groups will be at different levels. Recognition of the different skill sets, capabilities and competencies within the various groups is a useful prerequisite in identifying the necessary training. In specifying the training programme, the number of people that require training needs to be determined, and the way the knowledge can be provided needs to be considered. While the need for training differs from release to release, the impact of training can be significant. For example if support staff are spread around many locations, specific training, automated mechanisms, such as e-learning or computer-based training (CBT) solutions over the internet or intranet, may become an attractive proposition.

Examples of training needs include:

- Interpreting the Service Design documentation and plans
- Use of support tools, e.g. for central release staff
- Changes in health and safety requirements
- Changes in security policies and procedures
- Technical training
- Service Management and process training, e.g. new build procedure for new configuration item type.

4.4.5.3 Build and test

During the build and test stages, the common services and infrastructure need to be managed carefully since they can significantly affect the build and test of a technology enabled service and its underlying technology infrastructure. Key aspects that need to be managed during the activities to build and test a service or service offering are:

■ Usage of the build and test environments
■ Standardization and integration aspects
■ Management of the configurations:
  ● During the build and test activities, e.g. version control, baseline management, control of inputs and outputs from a build or test stage
  ● Recording the complete record of the build so that it can be rebuilt if required
  ● Maintaining evidence of testing, e.g. test results and test report
  ● Controlling access rights to physical and technology components, e.g. setting parameters
  ● Checking that security requirements are met
  ● Verification activities, e.g. prerequisites are met before a build or test begins
  ● Managing environmental issues, e.g. space, cooling, power, fire precautions, accessibility and safety measures
  ● Preparing and controlling the service release ready for promotion to the next environment
  ● Promoting or handing over the service release to the next stage or team.

Configuration baselines of the controlled environments and the release package before and after an installation, build or deployment are recorded in the CMS to provide a restore point. The configuration information also needs to be updated to reflect the receipt and implementation of a release unit or the complete release package to a deployment group or target environment. The definitive version of the release package (approved in service release test) must be placed in the DML even where the release package consists only of documentation for a hardware upgrade. The release package must always be taken from the DML to deploy to the Service Operations readiness, service acceptance and live environments.

Release and build documentation

Procedures, templates and guidance should be used to enable the release team to take service assets and products from internal and external suppliers and build an integrated release package efficiently and effectively.

Procedures and documents for purchasing, distributing, installing, moving and controlling assets and components that are relevant to acquiring, building and testing a release include:

■ Contract and agreements (e.g. for ordering new equipment or software)
■ Purchase requests and ordering
■ Request fulfilment
■ Goods inwards and delivery
■ Health and safety guidelines
■ Security policies and procedures
■ Leasing agreements
■ Intellectual property rights/digital rights
■ Support agreements
■ Procedures for:
  ● Managing service and infrastructure configurations
  ● Distributing and installing software
  ● Distributing, translating and converting data and information
  ● Delivering, installing and moving equipment
  ● Cleansing data and media
  ● Disposing of documentation, media and equipment
  ● Building, commissioning and decommissioning test environments, infrastructures and facilities
  ● Publishing knowledge, information and data
  ● Validation and testing
  ● Change Management
■ Service Asset and Configuration Management
■ Acceptance and authorization
■ Documenting licence agreements and licence headings together with 'proof of licence'.

'Proof of licence' is what a court will accept as proof of a legal entity having a licence. Each software manufacturer in general states the requirements for their proof of licence, so no hard and fast rules can be given here. As a general principle, proof of licence requires some form of evidence directly from the software manufacturer. There is a spectrum of types of evidence for having a proof of licence. Typical examples include:

■ Printed licence confirmation documents from software manufacturers (with security features)
■ Electronic licence confirmation documents from software manufacturers held on controlled-access websites

■ Certificates of authenticity (COAs), which are typically engraved, or with other security features. These may be loose pieces of paper, pieces of paper pasted onto manual covers, labels glued onto equipment, labels printed or glued on retail boxes.

The proposed solution should be documented to enable knowledge gathered during the build and test stages to be handed over to the Service Operations and Continual Service Improvement to be retained for future releases. It is important that the information is ordered and maintained in a systematic manner as during the build and test activities updates to the documentation will be required. The documentation includes:

■ Roles and responsibilities
■ Process descriptions and procedures
■ Support and operations manuals, service desk scripts etc.
■ Communications, training and knowledge transfer deliverables
■ User manuals with work instructions
■ Service information
■ Business context and marketing information
■ Service catalogue, SLA and supporting documentation:
  ● Hardware and software information
  ● Logical and physical architectural overview
  ● Detailed technical descriptions and references
■ Technical information
■ Service Management and operations plans
■ Business continuity planning details
■ Index of documentation for the service and release – baselined.

Acquire and test input configuration items and components

Configuration items and components (e.g. services, service assets) are acquired from projects, suppliers, partners and development groups. To prevent the acquisition of unknown and potentially risky components for a build it is essential to use CIs that have achieved a certain quality level or components from a catalogue of standard components that have been previously assessed, tested and authorized for use in specific conditions. Otherwise a change will need to be raised to assess the component and either incorporate it into the standards catalogue or accept it as a one-off exception for this release.

The acquisition activities include:

■ Interfacing with procurement processes to acquire the components (or with internal production departments if supplied in-house)

■ Capturing and recording:
  ● New or updated service assets and CIs through SACM
  ● Receipt of components
  ● Delivery, change and release documentation from the supplier
■ Checking, monitoring and reporting the quality of incoming CIs and service components
■ Ensuring that proof of licence can be demonstrated where required
■ Initiating action if quality is different from expectation, and assess the likely impact of this on the transition
■ Updating status of configuration items in SACM, e.g. to indicate that they are ready to be released into the next stage or rejected.

Verification activities to check the components destined for a release package or build include:

■ Establishing that all items are bona fide, and have genuinely been ordered or commissioned
■ Standard labelling and naming conventions have been applied as specified in the design specifications for the CIs and service components
■ Recording externally acquired items and checking these against their delivery and release documentation
■ Checking that:
  ● Developed products and service components have successfully passed appropriate documented quality reviews
  ● All software is as expected and no malicious additions are included (e.g. software items that could contain viruses)
  ● All amendments to previous versions or configuration baselines have been authorized by Change Management and no other amendments have been included – this may require a configuration audit and comparison facilities to check against the desired configuration
  ● All definitive items have been added to the DML and correctly recorded in the CMS
  ● Rejection/return of components is adequately controlled and documented.

Issues, non-conformance, known errors and deviations reports about the quality of service components and any risks should be passed to the relevant stakeholders, e.g. quality assurance, CSI, Service Design.

Release packaging

Build management procedures, methodologies, tools and checklists should be applied to ensure that the release package is built in a standard, controlled and reproducible way in line with the solution design defined in the Service Design Package. As a release package progresses towards production it may need to be rebuilt. For example: if a newer version of a CI or component needs to be incorporated quickly to fix errors; if the documentation needs to be updated.

The key activities to build a release package are:

■ Assemble and integrate the release components in a controlled manner to ensure a reproducible process.
■ Create the build and release documentation including:
  ● Build, installation and test plans, procedures and scripts
  ● Details of how to monitor and check the quality of the release and how to recognize and react to problems
  ● The automated or manual processes and procedures required to distribute, deploy and install the release into the target environment (or remove it as necessary)
  ● Procedures to back out release units or remediate a change should a release fail
  ● Procedures for tracking and managing software licences and digital rights.
■ Install and verify the release package.
■ Baseline the contents of the release package.
■ Send a service notification to inform relevant parties that the release package is available for installation and use.

If testing of a release package is successful, the release and the contents of the release package are placed under the control of Configuration Management, baselined and verified against the release design and release package definition. From this point all changes to the release package are managed through Change Management, e.g. to fix an error in testing. If at any step the testing of a release package does not complete successfully, reassessment and rescheduling of the release is managed through Change Management.

Build and manage the test environments
Effective build and test environment management is essential to ensure that the builds and tests are executed in a repeatable and manageable manner. Inadequate control of these environments means that unplanned changes can compromise the testing activities and/or cause significant re-work. Dedicated build environments should be established for assembling and building the components for controlled test and deployment environments.

Preparation of the test environments includes building, changing or enhancing the test environments ready to receive the release.

An IT service is, on most occasions, built from a number of technology resources or management assets. In the build phase, these different blocks, often from different suppliers, are installed and configured together to create the solution as designed. Standardization facilitates the integration of the different building blocks to provide a working solution and service.

Automating the installation of systems and application software onto servers and workstations reduces the dependencies on people and streamlines the procedures. Depending on the release and deployment plans, the installation may be performed in advance (for example, if equipment is being replaced) or it may have to occur in situ in the live environment.

The physical infrastructure elements, together with the environment in which they will operate, need to be tested appropriately. Part of the testing may be to test the replication of the infrastructure solution from one environment to another. This gives a better guarantee that the rollout to the production environment will be successful.

Test environments must be actively maintained and protected using Service Management best practices. For any significant change to a service, the question should be asked (as it is for the continued relevance of continuity and capacity plans): 'If this change goes ahead, will there need to be a consequential change to the test data?' During the build and test activities, operations and support teams need to be kept fully informed and involved as the solution is built to facilitate a structured transfer from the project to the operations team.

4.4.5.4 Service testing and pilots
The testing activities are coordinated through test management, which plans and controls the testing execution that is described in section 4.5. Testing aims to build confidence in the service capability prior to final acceptance during pilot or early life support. It will be based on the test strategy and model for the service being changed.

The test criteria reflect the anticipated conditions in which the service is expected to operate and deliver benefit. However, these surrounding circumstances may change, and in many modern situations such change is almost inevitable and often unpredictable. These changes and their impact on service testing and acceptance must be observed, understood and documented. Their consequences need to be expressed in terms of changed Acceptance Criteria and updates to the service package, including the SLP. This will need the collaboration and input of the business, customers and other affected stakeholders, which may well include suppliers and operations. The Service Designer will be involved in making any amendments since this knowledge may assist in building in additional and relevant flexibility to designs of future new or changed services.

An example of tests that can be executed during release and deployment is shown in Figure 4.22. Further details of these tests are described in section 4.5 on validation and testing. In practice, the test types overlap the different levels of testing to provide a full range of testing across the service life.

A service release test checks that the service components can be integrated correctly and that the release can be installed, built and tested in the target environment.

Service Operations readiness testing ensures that a service and its underlying application and technology infrastructure can be transferred into the production environment in a controlled manner. It provides a level of confidence that the new or changed service will provide the level of service specified in the service requirements and service level requirements. However, it is too early to finalize the SLA at this point. The SLA is finalized in the pilot or more usually in early life support before the Service Transition is closed. The service operational readiness test aims to:

■ Determine whether a service and its underlying service assets can be released into the production environment, the first time and for subsequent deployments

■ Ensure that the business processes, customers, users and service provider interfaces (SPIs) are capable of using the service properly

■ Ensure that the service teams are capable of operating the service and using the Service Management systems properly.

Tests that are conducted as part of service operational readiness test include:

■ **Deployment readiness test** – to ensure that the deployment processes, procedures and systems can

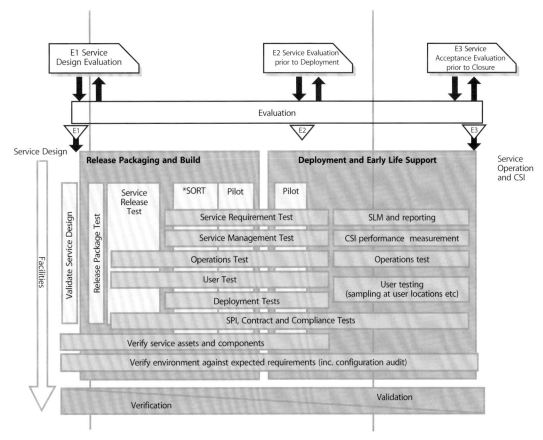

*Service Operational Readiness Test

Figure 4.22 Example of service testing through Service Transition

deploy, install, commission and decommission the release package and resultant new or changed service in the production/deployment environment

- **Service Management test** – to ensure that the service performance can be measured, monitored and reported in production
- **Service Operations test** – to ensure that the service teams will be able to operate the service in production
- **Service level test** – to ensure that the new or changed service will deliver the service level requirements
- **User test** – to ensure that users can access and use the new or changed service, e.g. they have access to the updated service catalogue and contact details for the service desk
- **Service provider interface test** – to ensure that interfaces to the service are working
- **Deployment verification test** – to ensure that the service capability has been correctly deployed for each target deployment group or environment.

Service rehearsals

One testing method is to simulate as much of the service as possible in a service rehearsal (sometimes referred to as 'model office'). A service rehearsal is a simulation of as much of the service as possible in an extensive and widely participatory practice session. It is the ultimate stage of internal testing, the last stage before any public live running. This is like a 'dress rehearsal' of a play, setting out all the elements – costume, lighting etc. – in a last private run-through of the performance. It can deliver significant benefits by establishing errors and unworkable procedures before they impact the business in live operation. However, they are complex, time consuming and relatively expensive to prepare, deliver and document. A careful and deliberate balance is therefore required between the anticipated costs and the risk damage profile that they could prevent.

A service rehearsal takes place just before deployment of the service; if held too early there is a significant chance that the environment, technology, people and legislation into which the service is being released will change and invalidate the results. If too close to the declared release date any issues found will not be addressed before the service goes live.

The objectives of the service rehearsal include:

- Confirmation that all stakeholders have been identified and are committed to operating or using the service –

if not this will be evidenced through lack of players for roles within the service rehearsal
- Ensure that all stakeholders have processes and procedures in place and are ready to receive process and resolve incidents, problems and changes relating to the new or changed service
- Testing the effectiveness of 'mistake-proofing' included within the service procedures. (Mistake proofing, often referred to by the Japanese term 'Poca Yoke', is about introducing advance warnings of user mistakes or bad practice and where possible introducing steps in the procedures to prevent these mistakes – such as electrical switch interlocks, and check-sum digits in data entry.) While testing can check how a service reacts for predicted user error, the service rehearsal will encourage unforeseen behaviour and establish how that behaviour affects the service's ability to deliver the required benefits.

The service rehearsal requires adequate representation from all stakeholders, with commitment to providing staff for – typically – a full day rehearsal for a new or significantly changed service. It is often beneficial to involve 'ordinary' representatives of the stakeholder community, not those with previous experience or knowledge of the service. Typical mistakes will be more likely to come from typical users – those who have been involved in design and development will find it impossible to 'unlearn' and will be coloured by their expectations of service behaviour.

The focus of a service rehearsal is typically on one day of actual rehearsal, but successful delivery of a service rehearsal involves more stages, including preparation and analysis, mirroring the Plan–Do–Check–Act cycle. Typical stages for a service rehearsal would include the following activities.

Plan – prepare for the day

Request for a service rehearsal – the project or service implementation teams consider that a service rehearsal would be appropriate and trigger the process with a request.

Tasks include the following:

- Appoint a rehearsal manager who gathers all relevant information.
- Identify key and secondary processes.
- Identify all stakeholders and their contact information.
- Produce initial rehearsal guide – the script to be followed.
- Establish and document typical examples of incidents, service requests, capacity and availability issues and

other events that will need to be handled when the service is live.

- Produce documentation to allow the simulation, processing, tracking and analysis of the expected scenarios.
- Identify all stakeholders, supplier and service provider personnel who need to be involved and ensure their commitment, through direct funding, internal commitment etc.
- Create detailed scripts – in collaboration with customer or account manager.
- Invite all stakeholders to planning and preparation meetings and briefings (could be by documentation, e-mail, Webinars etc. if physical briefings are not practicable.)

Do – deliver the rehearsal

Hold meetings to:

- Introduce the objectives, documents, involvement, recording etc.
- Walkthrough the scenarios and scripts to establish authenticity of the approach at a detailed level
- Carry out the rehearsal, i.e. let the players deliver the script and observe the processing of key events and elements, e.g. follow an incident through from occurrence to loggings, diagnosis, resolution, recovery and closure.

Check – document the day

Tasks include:

- Analysing and evaluating the results of the rehearsal and determining the implications
- Producing a written test report on the rehearsal, with recommendations, e.g. re-work the service before deployment
- Recording identified errors, issues and risks.

Act – take action following the rehearsal

Considering the results from the rehearsal, the options will be:

- Declare service to have passed without serious concern.
- OR consider that the service is not suitable for progressing at this stage and refer back to Service Design and/or Service Transition for re-work and rescheduling. (It may occasionally be that service rehearsal shows that the actual environment within which the service is expected to function is different enough from expectation to prevent acceptable behaviour from the service in reality – this might require rethink and revision at the Service Strategy and/or business process level.)
- Review and close the service rehearsal, providing improvement ideas to CSI, SD and ST management as appropriate.

Pilots

Pursuing the theatrical analogy seen in service rehearsal, if the service rehearsal is the 'dress rehearsal' – the last practice before being seen by the public   then the pilot is the 'off Broadway' run of a play. It is done for real and in public, but for a small audience only and with the expectation of further (hopefully minor) polishing of the performance, script, scenery and effects. Conducting a pilot is easier to control as it is deployed to a smaller environment/user base.

A pilot sets out to detect if any elements of the service do not deliver as required and to identify gaps/issues in Service Management that put the service and/or the customer's business and assets at risk. It does not need to cover all service and system functionality, but will focus on the areas of risk and perform enough of the service to determine if it will work sufficiently well in deployment. It aims to ensure that the service capability supports delivery of the service requirements and service level requirements. As far as possible it should check that the service utilities are fit for purpose and the warranties are fit for use.

Establish clear objectives for the pilot implementation such as:

- To establish metrics and provide confidence that the predicted performance and service levels will be met
- To evaluate the actual benefits and costs achieved during the pilot against the Business Case
- To create acceptance of new processes and ways of working within the user base, service provider and suppliers
- To identify, assess and mitigate some of the risks associated with a full deployment.

As there are likely to be design changes and improvements that need to be built into the release before full deployment, it is important to agree how these will be funded up front. It is also important to ensure that there is a common understanding about how the pilot implementation will be signed off.

During the pilot the release and deployment team should:

- Be ready to invoke contingency/recovery procedures
- Involve key people that will be involved in the full deployment

- Ensure that people involved in the pilot are trained and that they understand their new/changed role and responsibilities
- Document necessary operational and support procedures, information and training material that can not be adequately simulated in a test environment
- Establish the viability of training and support documentation and modify where necessary
- Establish customer, user and stakeholder interaction with the service in real-time situations, e.g. with real business decisions being made
- Capture appropriate metrics in order to compare to the service performance model
- Establish additional criteria that may need to be met before full deployment starts
- Determine the likely level of service support and Service Management resources that will be required and resolve any issues
- Discover and fix issues and errors early and fix many of them before final deployment. This includes the less critical minor irritations and eccentricities of a service that would not necessarily cause non-acceptance but do significantly reduce the emotional acceptance of the service among the user community
- Document improvements and where appropriate incorporate them into plans for full deployment.

When the release has been in use for a sufficient period during a pilot it is important to check that the service is capable of delivering the requirements of the customer, user and the Service Design as well as the predicted outcomes (although not all these will be realized at this point).

If the pilot is of sufficient length, it may be appropriate to conduct an independent evaluation to compare the actual vs predicted service capability and performance (specified in the Service Design) on behalf of the stakeholders, users and customers. This evaluation includes a risk assessment on whether the service will continue to deliver the service requirements, e.g. service levels and warranties.

The outputs from a successfully delivered service pilot will include:

- New or changed service and capability that have been tested and evaluated
- Pilot test report and results
- A report generated by the evaluation function, which is passed to Change Management and which comprises: an updated risk profile, deviations report, recommendation
- Key stakeholder agreement that the release is ready for a full deployment
- Demonstrated benefits of the service (within agreed tolerance levels)
- Confirmation that the deployment team has tested the deployment process and accepts the cost model, deployment model and metrics to be used for monitoring during deployment and early life support
- Target deployment groups in different geographical locations accepting the service release and committing to the deployment plans, particularly groups with different cultures and languages.

4.4.5.5 Plan and prepare for deployment

The planning and preparation activities prepare the deployment group for deployment. This is an opportunity to prepare the organization and people for organizational change; see section 5.2. The overall approach to planning the deployment is described in release and deployment planning (see paragraph 4.4.5.1). During the actual deployment stage the detailed implementation plan is developed. This includes assigning individuals to specific activities. For example a specific individual may be assigned to deliver training for a training activity on the deployment plan.

The entry criteria for planning and preparing a target deployment group or environment include:

- Deployment stakeholders are sufficiently confident in the service release to deploy the release, own their aspects of deployment and they are committed to the deployment (see section 5.2).
- Senior management, customers, the business and service provider teams accept the deployment costs, management, organization and people implications of the release as well as any organization, function and process changes.

An example of the deployment activities that apply to the deployment for a target group is shown in Figure 4.23.

Preparing for deployment includes assessing each deployment group's readiness to receive and implement a release package, identifying gaps that need to be filled and planning the activities required to deploy, transfer or decommission/retire services or service assets. It will also include transferring a service or a service unit as well as move and disposal activities.

Assessment

Although the deployment assessment should be conducted early, it should be revisited periodically. The results of this assessment are fed into detailed implementation planning for the target deployment group.

The readiness assessment for a deployment group identifies:

■ Issues and risks in delivering the current services that may affect the deployment. The kinds of risk include:
  ● Lack of dedicated internal resources and external supplier resources
  ● Lack of training, skills and awareness
  ● Unplanned or late change in requirements
■ Anticipated impacts, e.g. on the organizational structure, environment for the new or changed services, direct customers and users, partners, suppliers
■ Gaps that need to be filled.

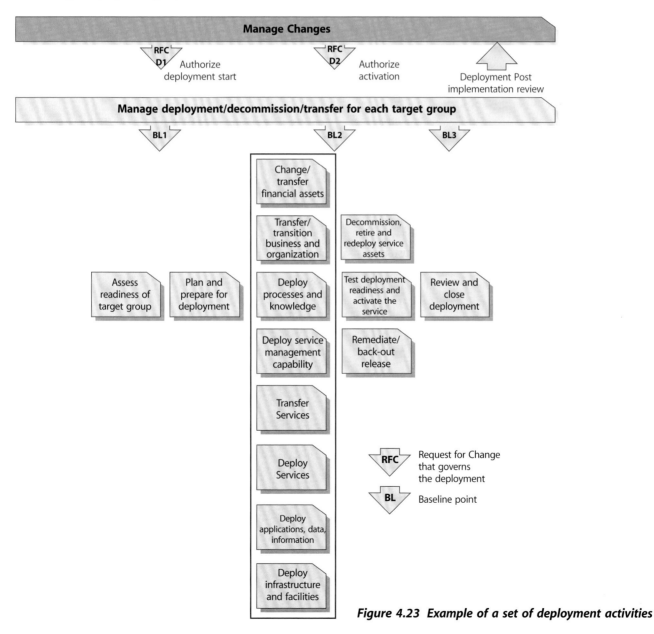

Figure 4.23 Example of a set of deployment activities

The aspects to assess include:

- Financial aspects and assets:
  - Current and required working capital
  - Establishing new or changed contracts, licences, IPR and digital rights
- Issues and risks in delivering the current services that may affect the deployment
- Applicable health, safety, security and environmental regulations, supplier and procurement aspects
- Current capability of the business customers and users to use and gain value from the new or changed service
- Current service, service capability and resources used including:
  - Service structure
  - Service dynamics
  - Service metrics and reports, including warranties and service levels achieved
- Current Service Management capability and resources:
  - Differences from the prerequisites for deployment, e.g. inadequate licensing arrangements, network bandwidth
  - Current operations and support resources, e.g. tools, people
  - Support resources and workloads as there may be a significant increase in the number of incidents per user that can stretch the resources for managing incidents, problems and fixes
  - Performance reports and improvement plans
  - Ability to predict and track the actual incident and problem volumes during deployment; this may require updating asset or user records with the date and time of installation or deployment to enable trend analysis
- Identifying requirements to tailor the new or changed service or underlying solution, e.g. processes, procedures, work instructions
- Organizational readiness:
  - Role, resource and skills gap analysis
  - Training needs analysis
  - Ability to assign competent individuals to the required roles
  - Motivation and empowerment – does the current organization and culture encourage the application of the required skills? Is there the right leadership and commitment?
  - Assess the readiness of customers, users, service provider staff and other stakeholders such as suppliers, partners

- Aspects relating to applications, information and data:
  - Access to application, information and data
  - Accessing secret, restricted or confidential documents and data
  - Knowledge and experience in using the application – users and support staff
- Infrastructure and facilities:
  - Difficult access, e.g. located high up in a building without appropriate lifting equipment (elevator or crane, etc.); city centre with restricted parking; remote locations
  - Intermediate and final storage and stores for definitive hardware and media
  - IT equipment space and capacity requirements such as:
    - size and equipment footprints
    - power requirements and circuit-breaker ratings
    - uninterruptible power supply (UPS) and generator loadings
    - temperature and humidity requirements
    - heat outputs and air-conditioning requirements
    - door clearance and engineering access requirements
    - cabling requirements
  - Electromagnetic interference (EMI) and radio frequency interference (RFI) requirements
  - Air quality requirements
  - Weight and false floor loadings
  - Network considerations
  - Equipment health, safety, security and environmental requirements.

Develop plans and prepare for deployment

Planning for a specific deployment includes assigning specific resources to perform deployment and early life support activities. While developing these plans, identify and assess risks specific to this deployment group by using the service model to identify business and service critical assets that have the highest risk of causing disruption. The activities include:

- Risk mitigation plans
- Developing transfer/transition, upgrade, conversion, disposal, retirement plans
- Logistics and delivery planning:
  - The service assets and components for deployment, establishing how and when they will be delivered, and confirmation that delivery has been successfully achieved and recorded

- Site preparation in accordance with applicable health, safety, security and environmental regulations and requirements
- Tailoring processes, procedures and knowledge, e.g. language translation, time frame adjustments
- Knowledge transfer and training stakeholders in how to use, benefit, manage, support and operate the new or changed service:
  - Identify essential and potential recipients of training (such as customer, users, ITSM, service desk, support, operations, deployment teams, projects)
  - Update of service desk with knowledge of the target deployment group and their environment
- Communicating to the people involved:
  - About the changes and the expected benefits
  - How the change affects the organization and staff
- Making any changes in emergency of continuity plans and procedures
- Mobilizing the Service Operations and support organization
- Mobilizing users to be ready to use the service
- Additional activities identified from the assessment.

The next step is to verify the detailed deployment plans, perform any deployment readiness tests and raise an RFC to be authorized through the Change Management process. The service is then ready for deployment.

4.4.5.6 Perform transfer, deployment and retirement

The following activities provide an example of the different aspects that will be performed in the order specified on the deployment plan.

Transfer financial assets

Changes and transfers of financial assets need to be completed as part of deployment. This will include but is not constrained by the following:

- Any changes in supplier financial agreements and charges
- Purchase or transfer of annual support and maintenance costs including systems to manage the service, e.g. CMS
- New licence costs and renewals
- Annual disaster recovery contracts with third parties
- Provision or transfer of working capital
- Transfer of intellectual property.

Transfer/transition business and organization

Transfer of a business unit, service or service unit will involve change to the organization itself. The subject of organizational change is addressed in Chapter 5. Activities that need to be performed include:

- Finalize organization structure, roles and responsibilities.
- Communicate change in organization, roles and responsibilities.
- Ensure that people adapt to and adopt new practices. This requires good communication of the consequences and requirements of the deployed service, e.g. best use of resources to deliver the message; understanding personal and group concerns; and ensuring messages to diverse and related groups are consistent and appropriate.
- Engender, at the very least, acceptance and preferably active support of the changes imposed on people.
- Ensure that people understand the continuity plans and procedures.

When the change includes a transfer of service provider, e.g. new outsourcing, insourcing, change of outsourced provider, then some specific elements need to be considered, e.g. organizational change, quick wins to avoid confusion and higher staff turnaround.

Competent people with the right skills are required to perform the deployment, operate and manage the new or changed service in the business, customer and service provider organization. The related activities include:

- Recruit staff with appropriate skills. Rather than developing new skills for existing staff, it may be more efficient to recruit new staff who already have the required skills. This may be in addition to existing staff, or may require the replacement of some staff with inappropriate skills, with more relevant staff for the revised circumstances of the new service.
- Identify existing people (e.g. staff, suppliers, users) with appropriate skills, moving or re-allocating people as necessary. For the skills required to actually deploy the new or changed service, temporary secondment, or even overtime, may be the most efficient approach.
- Consider outsource/contract resources to provide the required skills. This is similar to seconding internal staff, but in this case buying the temporarily required skills from external providers where they already exist. If skills are needed longer term, a requirement to pass those skills on to permanent (or longer term) staff can be useful.

- Provide training. Manage the training logistics, coordination, setup, communications, registration, delivery and evaluation activities including users and Service Operations teams.
- Execute the knowledge transfer plan and track progress to completion.
- Evaluate competence of new and changed staff and other people.

Deploy processes and materials

Deploy or publish the processes and materials ready for people involved in the business and service organization change, e.g. users and Service Operations teams that need to execute the new or changed processes. The materials may include policies, processes, procedures, manuals, overviews, training products, organizational change products etc.

Training people to use new processes and procedures can take time, particularly for a global deployment to thousands of people.

Deploy Service Management capability

Deploy new or changed processes, systems and tools to the service provider teams responsible for Service Management activities. Check that everyone is competent and confident to operate, maintain and manage the service in accordance with the service model and processes. Remove or archive redundant services and assets, e.g. processes, procedures and tools.

During deployment monitor the service against the service model and performance standards as far as possible.

Transfer service

Transferring a service will also involve organizational change described earlier in this section. The issues around transferring a service and the activities that need to be performed include:

- Reviewing the service performance, issues and risks, by performing some service tests and a service evaluation prior to the transfer
- Configuration auditing of service assets and configurations
- Finalizing service catalogue (add or remove the service) and related information
- Sending a service notification to communicate the change to relevant stakeholders.

When the change includes a transfer of service provider, e.g. new outsourcing, insourcing, change of outsourced provider, then some specific elements need to be considered that include:

- Managing contract changes
- Managing changes to existing agreements
- Updating contract details and information in the SKMS
- Transferring ownership of service assets and configuration items, remembering to update the CMS.

Deploy service

Deploy the service release and carry out the activities to distribute and install the service, supporting services, applications, data, information, infrastructure and facilities. These will include:

- Distributing and delivering the service and service components at the correct location and time
- Building, installing and configuring the services and service components with any converted or new data and information
- Testing the system and services according to the installation and acceptance tests and producing the installation and test reports
- Recording any incidents, unexpected events, issues or deviations from the plans
- Correcting any deviations that are outside the design limitations and constraints.

Decommissioning and service retirement

Some specific aspects need to be considered for decommissioning and retiring services and service assets. For example the procedures for retiring, transferring (e.g. to another budget holder) or redeploying service assets need to take into account any security, confidentiality, licensing, environmental or other contractual requirements. This includes:

- Removing deployed copies of software and data from retired hardware; failure to do this may result in licence contravention or in staff using unsupported software
- Identifying licences and other assets which can be redeployed; software being retired from use in one area may well remain in active use elsewhere
- Disposing of equipment according to environmental policies and procedures

- Moving assets that can be redeployed to secure storage areas if required. If the assets being retired are remaining in use elsewhere, especially for hardware, the released assets may serve a useful role as spare equipment to be retained in asset stores for speedy redeployment in the event of failures.

Records of retirement, transfer and disposal should be maintained and used to update other information such as licence information.

Remove redundant assets

A comprehensive understanding of the assets used by a retired service needs to be gained and managed. With a full understanding any redundant assets can be identified and removed, therefore potentially saving licence fees, liberating capacity and preventing accidental use. Failure to develop and properly perform these activities can result in:

- Wasted disk space and licences
- Overpayment of licence and maintenance fees
- Removal of assets associated with the redundant service but also used by other services, therefore causing incidents within those services, e.g. common software components and network elements.

As part of the clean-up activities it is important to delete or archive redundant data, information and records related to the previous service or products. The full scope and scale of a service or service asset needs to be considered, and this should extend to the following areas:

- Support contracts with third party suppliers, as changes in likely usage may require renegotiation of contracts.
- In-house second/third level support staff with specialist knowledge may no longer require that knowledge. This may require re-assessment of their role, level of payment, retention etc. and opportunities for redeployment may be identified.
- Service desk workload may be affected.
- Records within the knowledge base relating to the decommissioned components may need to be archived and deleted.

4.4.5.7 Verify deployment

When the deployment activities are complete, it is important to verify that users, Service Operations, other staff and stakeholders are capable of using or operating the service. The tests should specifically verify that:

- The service, service assets and service capability/resources are in place, e.g. by performing an audit such as a configuration audit of the deployed baseline against the as-planned baseline
- Updates to documentation and information are completed, e.g. service catalogue, contracts, agreements, contact details
- Communications, orientation and learning materials are ready to distribute to stakeholders, Service Operations and users
- All roles are assigned to individuals/organizations
- People and other resources are prepared to operate and use the new or changed service or service capability in normal, emergency and disaster situations
- People have access to the information necessary to use, operate or support the service
- The measurement and reporting systems are established to measure performance of the service and underlying resources.

This is a good point to gather feedback on the deployment process to feed into future improvements, e.g. using satisfaction surveys.

Report any issues and incidents and take corrective actions as necessary.

Successful confirmation of the deployment verification triggers the initiation and launch of early life support for the deployment group.

4.4.5.8 Early life support

Early life support (ELS) provides the opportunity to transition the new or changed service to Service Operations in a controlled manner and establish the new service capability and resources. An example of the ELS activities is shown in Figure 4.24.

In Service Design, the stakeholders will have agreed the entry and exit criteria from early life support but it may be necessary to finalize the performance targets and exit criteria early in this stage. This can help to understand the deployment verification process and set customer and stakeholder expectations about the handover of the service to Service Operations.

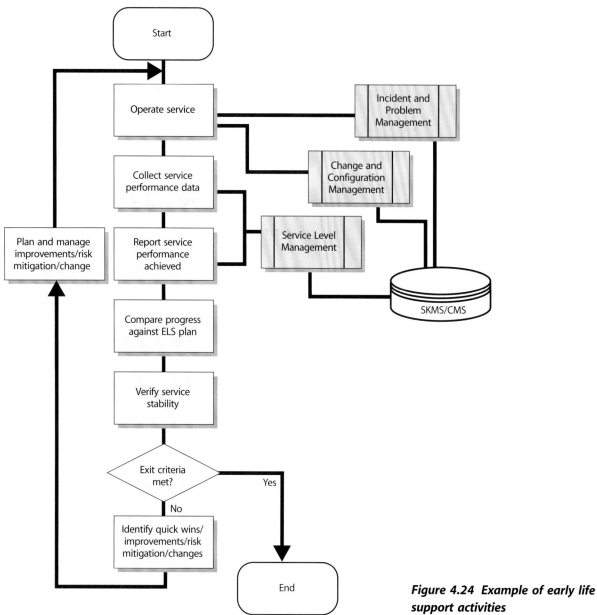

Figure 4.24 Example of early life support activities

ELS provides appropriate resources to resolve operational and support issues quickly, centrally and locally, to ensure that the users can use the service to support their business activities without unwarranted disruption. The deployment teams should analyse where users and support resources will experience issues and problems, perhaps based on previous experience; for example, clarification about:

- Role assignments, roles and responsibilities
- Financial and funding arrangements
- Procurement and request fulfilment
- Security policies and procedures
- Raising incidents and change requests
- Escalation procedures
- Complaints procedure

- Using diagnostics tools and aids
- Software licensing rules.

During ELS, the deployment team implements improvements and resolves problems that help to stabilize the service. The Continual Service Improvement publication provides relevant information on measurement and service improvements. The deployment resources will gradually back out from providing the additional support as the users and service teams become familiar with the changes and the incidents and risks reduce.

Metrics for the target deployment group or environment measure service performance, performance of the Service Management and operations processes and teams and the number of incidents and problems by type. The deployment team's aim is to stabilize the service for the

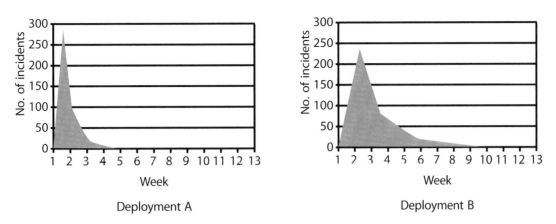

Figure 4.25 Illustration of the benefits of targeted early life support

target deployment group or environment as quickly and effectively as possible. An example of a deployment performance graph is shown in Figure 4.25.

Variation in performance between different deployment groups and service units should be analysed and lessons learned from one deployment used to improve subsequent deployments.

The example shown in Figure 4.25 shows the number of incidents for two branches of a retail organization that have the same number of users and the same deployment schedule. In deployment A the incident levels have reduced faster. On further investigation the Service Transition manager discovered that the team responsible for Deployment A was more competent at training users and transferring knowledge to the service desk so that they could help users to be more effective more quickly.

During ELS, the deployment team should ensure that the documentation and knowledge base are updated with additional diagnostics, known errors, workarounds and frequently asked questions. The team should also resolve any knowledge transfer or training gaps.

At agreed milestones in early life support, it is important to assess the issues and risks, particularly those that impact the handover schedule and costs. Service Transition monitors the performance of the new or changed service in early life support until the exit criteria are achieved. These include when:

■ Users can use the service effectively and efficiently for their business activities

■ Service owners and process owners are committed to manage and operate the service in accordance with the service model, performance standards and processes

■ Service delivery is managed and controlled across any service provider interfaces

■ Consistent progress is being made towards delivering the expected benefits and value at each milestone in early life support

■ Service levels and service performance standards are being consistently achieved without unexpected variation before formal handover to Service Operations

■ SLAs are finalized and signed off by senior management and customers

■ Unexpected variations in the performance of the service and customer assets such as changes in residual risks are monitored, reported and managed appropriately

■ Checking that training and knowledge transfer activities are completed by obtaining positive confirmation from the target audience. This may be in the form of competency tests

■ The service release, the SLA, other agreements and any contractual deliverables are signed off.

4.4.5.9 Review and close a deployment

When reviewing a deployment the following activities should be included:

■ Capture experiences and feedback on customer, user and service provider satisfaction with the deployment, e.g. through feedback surveys.

■ Highlight quality criteria that were not met.

■ Check that any actions, necessary fixes and changes are complete.

■ Review open changes and ensure that funding and responsibility for open changes are agreed before handover.

■ Review performance targets and achievements, including resource use and capacity such as user accesses, transactions and data volumes.

- Make sure there are no capability, resource, capacity or performance issues at the end of the deployment.
- Check that any problems, known errors and workarounds are documented and accepted by the customers/business and/or suppliers.
- Review the Risk Log and identify those that impact Service Operations and support. Address risks or agree action such as moving the risks to the Service Transition Risk Log.
- Check that redundant assets have been removed.
- Check that the service is ready for transition from early life support into Service Operations.

Each deployment should consider whether any relevant issues have been detected that should be passed through to CSI, such as:

- Feedback on the deployment model and plan
- Errors in procedures detected
- 'Near misses' where things could have gone wrong in foreseeable circumstances or where intervention was required
- Incorrect data or information in relevant records
- Incident and problems caused by deployment
- Problems with updating records.

Deployment is completed with a handover of the support for the deployment group or target environment to Service Operations.

A post implementation review of a deployment is conducted through Change Management.

4.4.5.10 Review and close Service Transition

In order to finalize that a Service Transition is completed, there should be a formal review carried out that is appropriate to the scale and magnitude of the change. A review of the Service Transition should include:

- Checking that all transition activities completed, e.g. documentation and information is captured, updated, secured, archived
- Checking that accurate metrics were captured.

Independent evaluation of the service release uses the outputs from deployment. This evaluation checks the actual performance and outcomes of the new or changed service against the predicted performance and outcomes, i.e. the service expected by the user or customer. An evaluation report (see 4.6.6) is prepared that lists the deviations from the SP/SLP/SDP, a risk profile and recommendations for Change Management. If there are deviations in the service level requirements then the service package, SLP or SAC may need to change (via

Change Management, in agreement with the customer representative and other stakeholders). Successful completion of the evaluation ensures that the service can be formally closed and handed over to Service Operations and CSI.

A transition report should be produced that summarizes the outcomes. As part of producing such a report a post transition workshop could be held involving all parties as a 'lessons learned' exercise. Lessons learned and improvements are fed into Change Management for a post implementation review and into Continual Service Improvement for future transitions.

4.4.6 Triggers, input and output, and inter-process interfaces

The release process commences with receipt of an approved RFC to deploy a production-ready release package. Deployment commences with receipt of an approved RFC to deploy a release package to a target deployment group or environment, e.g. business unit, customer group and/or service unit.

The inputs are:

- Authorized RFC
- Service package, SLP
- SDP, including service model and SAC
- IT service continuity plan and related business continuity plan
- Service Management and operations plans and standards
- Technology and procurement standards and catalogues
- Acquired service assets and components and their documentation
- Build models and plans
- Environment requirements and specifications for build, test, release, training, disaster recovery, pilot and deployment
- Release policy and release design from Service Design
- Release and deployment models including template plans
- Exit and entry criteria for each stage of release and deployment.

The outputs are:

- Release and deployment plan
- Completed RFCs for the release and deployment activities
- Service notification
- Updated service catalogue with the relevant information about the new or changed service

- New tested service capability and environment including SLA, other agreements and contracts, changed organization, competent and motivated people, established business and Service Management processes, installed applications, converted databases, technology infrastructure, products and facilities
- New or changed Service Management documentation
- Service package that defines the requirements from the business/customer for the service
- SLP that defines the service level requirements, e.g. hours of service, business critical services, data and periods, service level targets
- SLA, underpinning OLAs and contracts
- Service model that describes the structure and dynamics of how the service is operated and managed
- New or changed service reports
- Tested continuity plans
- Complete and accurate configuration item list with an audit trail for the CIs in the release package and also the new or changed service and infrastructure configurations
- Service capacity plan that is aligned to the relevant business plans
- Deployment ready release package (baselined) – for future deployments
- Service Transition Report.

Deployment is completed with a handover of the new or changed service to operations on successful completion of the post implementation review of the deployment conducted within Change Management.

4.4.7 Information management

Throughout the deployment process, appropriate records will be created and maintained. As configuration items are successfully deployed, the CMS will be updated with information such as:

- New or changed configuration items
- Relationships between requirements and test cases
- Installation/build plans
- Logistics and delivery plans
- Validation and test plans, evidence and reports
- New or changed locations and users
- Status updates (e.g. from allocated to live)
- Change in ownership of assets
- Licence holding.

Other data and information will also be captured and recorded within the broader service knowledge management system. This could include:

- Deployment information, history of the deployment itself, who was involved, timings etc.
- Training records, typically held by HR in many organizations, but relating to ITSM staff the responsibility for their update will logically rest with ITSM also.
- Access rules and levels
- Known errors. Typically a new or changed service will be introduced with identified errors, which while not according to the original Service Design specification are nonetheless minor enough in nature to be acceptable in live operation. These may well be under active investigation and resolution by the service builders, or may be considered acceptable. In either case the errors will be deployed into the live error database as an element of the deployment of the live service. This information will be available through the SKMS to the service desk who will then be able to link incidents reported against these known errors.

As part of the clean-up activities it is important to delete or archive redundant records related to the previous service or products.

4.4.8 Key performance indicators and metrics

4.4.8.1 Customers or business

Indicators include:

- Variance from service performance required by customers (minimal and reducing)
- Number of incidents against the service (low and reducing)
- Increased customer and user satisfaction with the services delivered
- Decreased customer dissatisfaction – service issues resulting from poorly tested or untested services increases the negative perception on the service provider organization as a whole.

4.4.8.2 Service providers

Indicators include:

- Reduced resources and costs to diagnose and fix incidents and problems in deployment and production
- Increased adoption of the Service Transition common framework of standards, re-usable processes and supporting documentation
- Reduced discrepancies in configuration audits compared with the real world.

4.4.9 Challenges, critical success factors and risks

Challenges for release and deployment include:

- Developing standard performance measures and measurement methods across projects and suppliers
- Dealing with projects and suppliers where estimated delivery dates are inaccurate and there are delays in scheduling Service Transition activities
- Understanding the different stakeholder perspectives that underpin effective risk management for the change impact assessment and test activities
- Building a thorough understanding of risks that have impacted or may impact successful Service Transition of services and releases
- Encouraging a risk management culture where people share information and take a pragmatic and measured approach to risk.

Critical success factors include:

- The new or changed service capability and resources are built in the target environment or deployment group.
- The new or changed service has been tested against the Service Design.
- The service capability has been proved in a pilot deployment.
- Re-usable test models are developed that can be used for regression testing in future releases.

Risks to successful release and deployment include:

- Poorly defined scope and understanding of dependencies in earlier lifecycle stages leading to scope creep during release and deployment
- Using staff that are not dedicated to release and deployment activities, especially if the effort is a significant amount of their time
- Management:
  - Management incompetence
  - Inadequate corporate policies, e.g. security, software licensing
  - Inadequate adoption of management practices
  - Poor leadership
- Finances:
  - Shortage of finances
  - Delays move deployment into different financial year
  - Lack of clarity on funding for changes/fixes during transition
- Controls:

- Lack of definition of the required controls leads to poorly evaluated and unauthorized changes, adversely affecting release and deployment plans
  - Difficulty tracking and managing software licences, e.g. due to complexity
  - Unexpected or changes in regulatory controls or licensing requirements
- Management of organizational change
  - Unclear expectations/objectives from customers, users, suppliers and other stakeholders
  - Cultural differences/misunderstandings
  - Human factors
  - With suppliers/partners
  - Poor communication
  - Organizational change impacts employee morale
  - People issues with infringement of personal data protection criteria
  - Personality clashes
  - Key personnel who have inadequate authority to fulfil their roles
  - Poor staff recruitment and selection procedures
  - Lack of clarity over roles and responsibilities
  - Vested interests creating conflict and compromising quality
  - Individual or group interests are given unwarranted priority
- Poor commitment and decision making
- Failure to obtain appropriate approval at the right time
- Indecision or late decision making
- Lack of operational support
- Inadequate or inaccurate information
- Health and safety compromised
- The time allowed for release and deployment – will it make or break the project?
- Suppliers/sourcing/partnering relationships during transition:
  - Failure of suppliers to meet contractual requirements; this could be in terms of quality, quantity, timescales or their own exposure to risk
  - Delays in contract negotiation
  - Organizational change impacts employee morale, employee and supplier performance
  - Data protection impacts data sharing
  - Shrinking resource pool from disaffected employees
- Governance issues:
  - Senior management commitment is missing in one or other of the organizations

- The supplier management function is not mature or is non-existent
- Changes in work practices and procedures adversely affect one or other of the organizations
- Inadequate 'back-out' or 'contingency' plan if sourcing/partnering fails
- Application/technical infrastructure risks:
  - Inadequate design
  - Professional negligence
  - Human error/incompetence
  - Infrastructure failure
  - Differences/dependencies in infrastructure/applications
  - Increased dismantling/decommissioning costs
  - Safety being compromised
  - Performance failure (people or equipment)
  - Breaches in physical security/information security
  - Unforeseen barriers or constraints due to infrastructure.

4.5 SERVICE VALIDATION AND TESTING

The underlying concept to which Service Testing and Validation contributes is quality assurance – establishing that the Service Design and release will deliver a new or changed service or service offering that is fit for purpose and fit for use. Testing is a vital area within Service Management and has often been the unseen underlying cause of what was taken to be inefficient Service Management processes. If services are not tested sufficiently then their introduction into the operational environment will bring a rise in:

- Incidents, since failures in service elements and mismatches between what was wanted and what was delivered impact on business support
- Service desk calls for clarification, since services that are not functioning as intended are inherently less intuitive causing a higher support requirement
- Problems and errors that are harder to diagnose in the live environment
- Costs, since errors are more expensive to fix in production than if found in testing
- Services that are not used effectively by the users to deliver the desired value.

4.5.1 Purpose, goal and objectives

The purpose of the Service Validation and Testing process is to:

- Plan and implement a structured validation and test process that provides objective evidence that the new or changed service will support the customer's business and stakeholder requirements, including the agreed service levels
- Quality assure a release, its constituent service components, the resultant service and service capability delivered by a release
- Identify, assess and address issues, errors and risks throughout Service Transition.

The goal of Service Validation and Testing is to assure that a service will provide value to customers and their business.

The objectives of Service Validation and Testing are to:

- Provide confidence that a release will create a new or changed service or service offerings that deliver the expected outcomes and value for the customers within the projected costs, capacity and constraints
- Validate that a service is 'fit for purpose' – it will deliver the required performance with desired constraints removed
- Assure a service is 'fit for use' – it meets certain specifications under the specified terms and conditions of use
- Confirm that the customer and stakeholder requirements for the new or changed service are correctly defined and remedy any errors or variances early in the service lifecycle as this is considerably cheaper than fixing errors in production.

4.5.2 Scope

The service provider takes responsibility for delivering, operating and/or maintaining customer or service assets at specified levels of warranty, under a service agreement. Service Validation and Testing can be applied throughout the service lifecycle to quality assure any aspect of a service and the service providers' capability, resources and capacity to deliver a service and/or service release successfully. In order to validate and test an end-to-end service the interfaces to suppliers, customers and partners are important. Service provider interface definitions define the boundaries of the service to be tested, e.g. process interfaces and organizational interfaces.

Testing is equally applicable to in-house or developed services, hardware, software or knowledge-based services. It includes the testing of new or changed services or service components and examines the behaviour of these in the target business unit, service unit, deployment group or environment. This environment could have aspects outside the control of the service provider, e.g. public networks, user skill levels or customer assets.

Testing directly supports the release and deployment process by ensuring that appropriate levels of testing are performed during the release, build and deployment activities. It evaluates the detailed service models to ensure that they are fit for purpose and fit for use before being authorized to enter Service Operations, through the service catalogue. The output from testing is used by the evaluation process to provide the information on whether the service is independently judged to be delivering the service performance with an acceptable risk profile.

4.5.3 Value to business

Service failures can harm the service provider's business and the customer's assets and result in outcomes such as loss of reputation, loss of money, loss of time, injury and death. The key value to the business and customers from Service Testing and Validation is in terms of the established degree of confidence that a new or changed service will deliver the value and outcomes required of it and understanding the risks.

Successful testing depends on all parties understanding that it cannot give, indeed should not give, any guarantees but provides a measured degree of confidence. The required degree of confidence varies depending on the customer's business requirements and pressures of an organization.

4.5.4 Policies, principles and basic concepts

4.5.4.1 Inputs from Service Design

A service is defined by a service package that comprises one or more service level packages (SLPs) and re-usable components, many of which themselves are services, e.g. supporting services. The service package defines the service utilities and warranties that are delivered through the correct functioning of the particular set of identified service assets. An SLP provides a definitive level of utility or warranty from the perspective of outcomes, assets and patterns of business activity (PBA) of customers. It is therefore a key input to test planning and design.

The design of a service is related to the context in which a service will be used (the categories of customer asset). The attributes of a service characterize the form and function of the service from a utilization perspective.

These attributes should be traceable to the predicted business outcomes that provide the utility from the service. Some attributes are more important than others for different sets of users and customers, e.g. basic, performance and excitement attributes. A well-designed service provides a combination of these to deliver an appropriate level of utility for the customer.

The Service Design Package defines the agreed requirements of the service, expressed in terms of the service model and Service Operations plan that provide key input to test planning and design. Service models are described further in the Service Strategy publication.

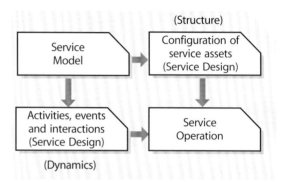

Figure 4.26 Service models describe the structure and dynamics of a service

The service model (Figure 4.26) describes the structure and dynamics of a service that will be delivered by Service Operations, through the Service Operations plan. Service Transition evaluates these during the validation and test stages.

Structure is defined in terms of particular core and supporting services and the service assets needed and the patterns in which they are configured. As the new or changed service is designed, developed and built, the service assets are tested and verified against the requirements and design specifications: is the service asset built correctly?

For example, the design for managed storage services must have input on how customer assets such as business applications utilize the storage, the way in which storage adds value to the applications, and what costs and risks the customer would like to avoid. The information on risks is of particular importance to service testing as this will influence the test coverage and prioritization.

Service models also describe the dynamics of creating value. Activities, flow of resources, coordination, and interactions describe the dynamics (see Figure 4.27). This includes the cooperation and communication between

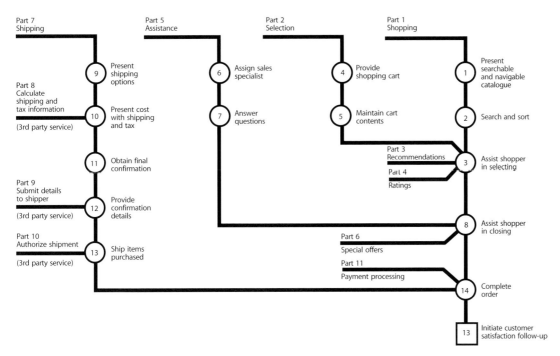

Figure 4.27 Dynamics of a service model

service users and service agents such as service provider staff, processes or systems that the user interacts with, e.g. a self-service menu. The dynamics of a service include patterns of business activity, demand patterns, exceptions and variations.

Service Design uses process maps, workflow diagrams, queuing models, and activity patterns to define the service

models. As Service Transition evaluates the detailed service models to ensure they are fit for purpose and fit for use it is important to have access to these models to develop the test models and plans.

The Service Design package defines a set of design constraints (Figure 4.28) against which the service release and new or changed service will be developed and built.

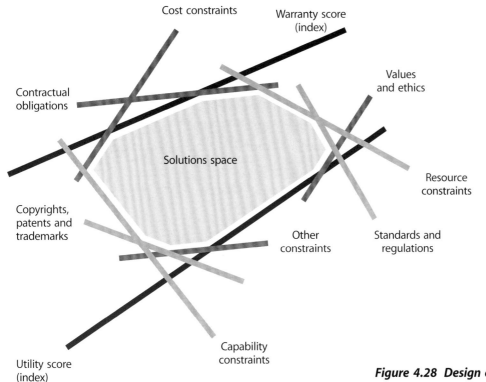

Figure 4.28 Design constraints of a service

Validation and testing should test the service at the boundaries to check that the design constraints are correctly defined and particularly if there is a design improvement to add or remove a constraint.

4.5.4.2 Service quality and assurance

Service assurance is delivered though verification and validation, which in turn are delivered through testing (trying something out in conditions that represent the final live situation – a test environment) and by observation or review against a standard or specification.

Validation confirms, through the provision of objective evidence, that the requirements for a specific intended use or application have been fulfilled. Validation in a lifecycle context is the set of activities ensuring and gaining confidence that a system or service is able to accomplish its intended use, goals and objectives.

The validation of the service requirements and the related service Acceptance Criteria begins from the time that the service requirements are defined. There will be increasing levels of service validation testing performed as a service release progresses through the service lifecycle.

Verification is confirmation, through the provision of objective evidence, that specified requirements have been fulfilled, e.g. a service asset meets its specification.

Early in the service lifecycle, validation confirms that the customer needs, contracts and service attributes, specified in the service package, are translated correctly into the Service Design as service level requirements and constraints, e.g. capacity and demand limitations. Later in the service lifecycle tests are performed to assess whether the actual service delivers the required levels of service, utilities and warranties. The warranty is an assurance that a product or service will be provided or will meet certain specifications. Value is created for customers if the utilities

are fit for purpose and the warranties are fit for use (Figure 4.29). This is the focus of service validation.

4.5.4.3 Policies

Policies that drive and support Service Validation and Testing include service quality policy, risk policy, Service Transition policy, release policy and Change Management policy.

Service quality policy

Senior leadership will define the meaning of service quality. Service Strategy discusses the quality perspectives that a service provider needs to consider. In addition to service level metrics, service quality takes into account the positive impact of the service (utility) and the certainty of impact warranty. The Service Strategy publication outlines four quality perspectives:

- Level of excellence
- Value for money
- Conformance to specifications
- Meeting or exceeding expectations.

One or more, if not all four, perspectives are usually required to guide the measurement and control of Service Management processes. The dominant perspective will influence how services are measured and controlled, which in turn will influence how services are designed and operated. Understanding the quality perspective will influence the Service Design and the approach to validation and testing.

Risk policy

Different customer segments, organizations, business units and service units have different attitudes to risk. Where an organization is an enthusiastic taker of business risk, testing will be looking to establish a lower degree of confidence than a safety critical or regulated organization might seek. The risk policy will influence control required

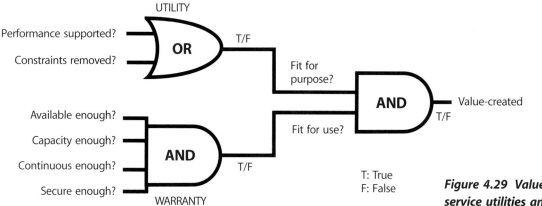

Figure 4.29 Value creation from service utilities and warranties

through Service Transition including the degree and level of validation and testing of service level requirements, utility and warranty, i.e. availability risks, security risks, continuity risks and capacity risks.

Service Transition policy

See Chapter 3.

Release policy

The type and frequency of releases will influence the testing approach. Frequent releases such as once-a-day drive requirements for re-usable test models and automated testing.

Change Management policy

The use of change windows can influence the testing that needs to be considered. For example if there is a policy of 'substituting' a release package late in the change schedule or if the scheduled release package is delayed then additional testing may be required to test this combination if there are dependencies.

The testing policy will reflect the requirements from Service Strategy. Examples of policy statements include:

- Test library and re-use policy. The nature of IT Service Management is repetitive, and benefits greatly from re-use. The service test management role within an organization should take responsibility for creating, cataloguing and maintaining a library of test models, test cases, test scripts and test data that can be re-used. Projects and service teams need to be motivated and incentivized to create re-usable test assets and re-use test assets.
- Integrate testing into the project and service lifecycle. This helps to detect and remove functional and non-functional defects as soon as possible and reduces the incidents in production.
- Adopt a risk-based testing approach aimed at reducing risk to the service and the customer's business.
- Engage with customers, stakeholders, users and service teams throughout the project and service lifecycle to enhance their testing skills and capture feedback on the quality of services and service assets.
- Establish test measurements and monitoring systems to improve the efficiency and effectiveness of Service Validation and Testing Continual Service Improvement.
- Automate using automated testing tools and systems, particularly for:
  - Complex systems and services, such as geographically distributed services, large-scale infrastructures and business critical applications

- Where time to change is critical, e.g. if there are tight deadlines and a tendency to squeeze testing windows.

4.5.4.4 Test strategy

A test strategy defines the overall approach to organizing testing and allocating testing resources. It can apply to the whole organization, a set of services or an individual service. Any test strategy needs to be developed with appropriate stakeholders to ensure there is sufficient buy-in to the approach.

Early in the lifecycle the service validation and test role needs to work with Service Design and service evaluation to plan and design the test approach using information from the service package, SLPs, SDP and the interim evaluation report. The activities will include:

- Translating the Service Design into test requirements and test models, e.g. understanding combinations of service assets required to deliver a service as well as the constraints that define the context, approach and boundaries to be tested
- Establishing the best approach to optimize the test coverage given the risk profile and change impact and resource assessment
- Translating the service Acceptance Criteria into entry and exit criteria at each level of testing to define the acceptable level of margin for errors at each level
- Translating risks and issues from the impact, resource and risk assessment on the related RFC for the SDP/service release into test requirements.

It is also vital to work with Project Managers to ensure that:

- Appropriate test activities and resources are included in Project Plans
- Specialist testing resources (people, tools, licences) are allocated if required
- The project understands the mandatory and optional testing deliverables
- The testing activities are managed, monitored and controlled.

The aspects to consider and document in developing the test strategy and related plans are shown below. Some of the information may also be specified in the Service Transition plan or other test plans and it is important to structure the plans so that there is minimal duplication.

Test strategy contents

- Purpose, goals and objectives of service testing
- Context

- Applicable standards, legal and regulatory requirements
- Applicable contracts and agreements:
  - Service Management policies, processes and standards
  - Policies, processes and practices applicable to testing
- Scope and organizations:
  - Service provider teams
  - Test organization
  - Third parties, strategic partners, suppliers
  - Business units/locations
  - Customers and users
- Test process:
  - Test management and control – recording, progress monitoring and reporting
  - Test planning and estimation, including cost estimates for service planning, resources, scheduling
  - Test preparation, e.g. site/environment preparation, installation prerequisites
  - Test activities – planning, performing and documenting test cases and results
- Test metrics and improvement
- Identification of items to be tested:
  - Service package
  - Service level package
  - SDP – service model (structure and dynamics), solution architecture design
- Service Operation plan
- Service Management Plans:
  - Critical elements where business priorities and risk assessment suggest testing should concentrate
  - Business units, service units, locations where the tests will be performed
- Service provider interfaces
- Approach:
  - Selecting the test model
  - Test levels
  - Test approaches, e.g. regression testing, modelling, simulation
  - Degree of independence for performing, analysing and evaluating tests
  - Re-use – experience, expertise, knowledge and historical data
  - Timing, e.g. focus on testing individual service assets early vs testing later when the whole service is built

- Developing and re-using test designs, tools, scripts and data
- Error and change handling and control
- Measurement system
- Criteria:
  - Pass/fail criteria
  - Entry and exit criteria for each test stage
  - For stopping or re-starting testing activities
- People requirements:
  - Roles and responsibilities including approval/rejection (these may be at different levels, e.g. rejecting an expensive and long running project typically requires higher authority than accepting it as planned)
  - Assigning and scheduling training and knowledge transfer
  - Stakeholders – service provider, suppliers, customer, user involvement
- Environment requirements:
  - Test environments to be used, locations, organizational, technical
  - Requirements for each test environment
  - Planning and commissioning of test environment
- Deliverables:
  - Mandatory and optional documentation
  - Test plans
  - Test specifications – test design, test case, test procedure
  - Test results and reports
  - Validation and qualification report
  - Test summary reports.

4.5.4.5 Test models

A test model includes a test plan, what is to be tested and the test scripts that define how each element will be tested. A test model ensures that testing is executed consistently in a repeatable way that is effective and efficient. The test scripts define the release test conditions, associated expected results and test cycles.

To ensure that the process is repeatable, test models need to be well structured in a way that:

- Provides traceability back to the requirement or design criteria
- Enables auditability through test execution, evaluation and reporting
- Ensures the test elements can be maintained and changed.

Examples of test models are illustrated in Table 4.10.

Table 4.10 Examples of service test models

Test model	Objective/target deliverable	Test conditions based on
Service contract test model	To validate that the customer can use the service to deliver a value proposition.	Contract requirements. Fit for purpose, fit for User criteria.
Service requirements test model	To validate that the service provider can/has delivered the service required and expected by the customer.	Service requirements and Service Acceptance Criteria.
Service level test model	To ensure that the service provider can deliver the service level requirements, and service level requirements can be met in the production environment, e.g. testing the response and fix time, availability, product delivery times, support services.	Service level requirements, SLA, OLA.
Service test model	To ensure that the service provider is capable of delivering, operating and managing the new or changed service using the 'as-designed' service model that includes the resource model, cost model, integrated process model, capacity and performance model etc.	Service model.
Operations test model	To ensure that the Service Operations teams can operate and support the new or changed service/service component including the service desk, IT operations, application management, technical management. It includes local IT support staff and business representatives responsible for IT service support and operations. There may be different models at different release/test levels, e.g. technology infrastructure, applications.	Service model, Service Operations standards, processes and plans.
Deployment release test model	To verify that the deployment team, tools and procedures can deploy the release package into a target deployment group or environment within the estimated timeframe. To ensure that the release package contains all the service components required for deployment, e.g. by performing a configuration audit.	Release and deployment design and plan.
Deployment installation test model	To test that the deployment team, tools and procedures can install the release package into a target environment within the estimated timeframe.	Release and deployment design and plan.
Deployment verification test model	To test that a deployment has completed successfully and that all service assets and configurations are in place as planned and meet their quality criteria.	Tests and audits of 'actual' service assets and configurations.

As the Service Design phase progresses, the tester can use the emerging Service Design and release plan to determine the specific requirements, validation and test conditions, cases and mechanisms to be tested. An example is shown in Table 4.11.

Table 4.11 Service requirements, 1: improve user accessibility and usability

Validation reference	Validation condition	Test levels	Test case	Mechanism
1.1	20% improvement in user survey rating	1	M020	Survey
1.2	20% reduction in user complaints	1	M023	Process metrics
1.3	20% increase in use of self service channel	2	M123	Usage statistics
1.4	Help function available on front page of self service point application	3	T235	Functional test
1.5	Web pages comply with web accessibility standards	4 (Application)	T201	Usability test
1.6	10% increase in public self service points	4/5 Technical infrastructure	T234	Installation statistics
1.7	Public self-service points comply with standard IS1223	4/5 Technical infrastructure	T234	Compliance test

4.5.4.6 Validation and testing perspectives

Effective validation and testing focuses on whether the service will deliver as required. This is based on the perspective of those who will use, deliver, deploy, manage and operate the service. The test entry and exit criteria are developed as the Service Design Package is developed. These will cover all aspects of the service provision from different perspectives including:

- Service Design – functional, management and operational
- Technology design
- Process design
- Measurement design
- Documentation
- Skills and knowledge.

Service acceptance testing starts with the verification of the service requirements. For example, customers, customer representatives and other stakeholders who sign off the agreed service requirements will also sign off the service Acceptance Criteria and service acceptance test plan. The stakeholders include:

- Business customers/customer representatives
- Users of the service within the customer's business who will use the new or changed service to assist them in delivering their work objectives and deliver service and/or product to their customers
- Suppliers
- Service provider/service unit.

Business users and customer perspective

The business involvement in acceptance testing is central to its success, and is included in the Service Design package, enabling adequate resource planning.

From the business's perspective this is important in order to:

- Have a defined and agreed means for measuring the acceptability of the service including interfaces with the service provider, e.g. how errors or queries are communicated via a single point of contact, monitoring progress and closure of change requests and incidents
- Understand and make available the appropriate level and capability of resource to undertake service acceptance.

From the service provider's perspective the business involvement is important to:

- Keep the business involved during build and testing of the service to avoid any surprises when service acceptance takes place
- Ensure the overall quality of the service delivered into acceptance is robust, since this starts to set business perceptions about the quality, reliability and usability of the system, even before it goes live
- Deliver and maintain solid and robust acceptance test facilities in line with business requirements

■ Understand where the acceptance test fits into any overall business service or product development testing activity.

Even when in live operation, a service is not 'emotionally' accepted by customer and user until they become familiar and content with it. The full benefit of a service will not be realized until that emotional acceptance has been achieved.

Emotional (non) acceptance

Southern US Steel Mill implemented a new order manufacturing service. It was commissioned, designed and delivered by an outside vendor. The service delivered was innovative and fully met the agreed criteria. The end result was that the company sued the vendor citing that the service was not usable because factory personnel (due to lack of training) did not know how to use the system and therefore emotionally did not accept it.

Testing is a situation where 'use cases', focusing on the usable results from a service can be a valuable aid to effective assessment of a service's usefulness to the business.

User testing – application, system, service

Testing is comprised of tests to determine whether the service meets the functional and quality requirements of the end users (customers) by executing defined business processes in an environment that, as closely as possible, simulates the live operational environment. This will include changes to the system or business process. Full details of the scope and coverage will be defined in the user test and user acceptance test (UAT) plans. The end users will test the functional requirements, establishing to the customer's agreed degree of confidence that the service will deliver as they require. They will also perform tests of the Service Management activities that they are involved with, e.g. ability to contact and use the service desk, response to diagnostics scripts, incident management, request fulfilment, change request management.

A key practice is to make sure that business users participating in testing have their expectations clearly set and realize that this is a test and to expect that some things may not go well. There is a risk that they may form an opinion too early about the quality of the service being tested and word may spread that the quality of the service is poor and should not be used.

Operations and service improvement perspective

Steps must be taken to ensure that IT staff requirements have been delivered before deployment of the service.

Operations staff will use the service acceptance step to ensure that appropriate:

■ Technological facilities are in place to deliver the new or changed service

■ Staff skills, knowledge and resource are available to support the service after go-live

■ Supporting processes and resources are in place, e.g. service desk, second/third line support, including third party contracts, capacity and availability monitoring and alerting

■ Business and IT continuity has been considered

■ Access is available to documentation and SKMS.

Continual Service Improvement will also inherit the new or changed service into the scope of their improvement programme, and should satisfy themselves that they have sufficient understanding of its objectives and characteristics.

4.5.4.7 Levels of testing and test models

Testing is related directly to the building of service assets and products so that each one has an associated acceptance test and activity to ensure it meets requirements. This involves testing individual service assets and components before they are used in the new or changed service.

Each service model and associated service deliverable is supported by its own re-usable test model that can be used for regression testing during the deployment of a specific release as well as for regression testing in future releases. Test models help with building quality early into the service lifecycle rather than waiting for results from tests on a release at the end.

Levels of build and testing are described in the release and deployment section (paragraph 4.4.5.3). The levels of testing that are to be performed are defined by the selected test model.

Using a model such as the V-model (Figure 4.30) builds in Service Validation and Testing early in the service lifecycle. It provides a framework to organize the levels of configuration items to be managed through the lifecycle and the associated validation and testing activities both within and across stages.

The level of test is derived from the way a system is designed and built up. This is known as a V-model, which maps the types of test to each stage of development. The V-model provides one example of how the Service Transition levels of testing can be matched to corresponding stages of service requirements and design.

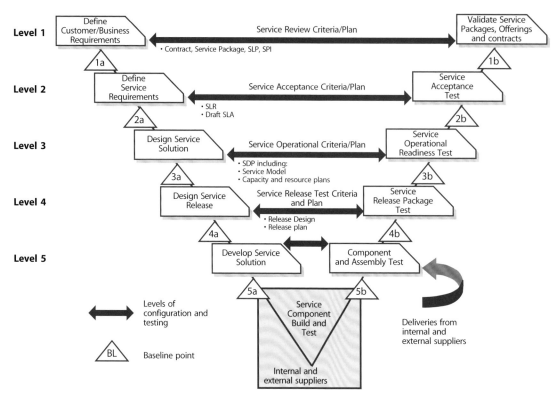

Figure 4.30 Example of service V-model

The left-hand side represents the specification of the service requirements down to the detailed Service Design. The right-hand side focuses on the validation activities that are performed against the specifications defined on the left-hand side. At each stage on the left-hand side, there is direct involvement by the equivalent party on the right-hand side. It shows that service validation and acceptance test planning should start with the definition of the service requirements. For example, customers who sign off the agreed service requirements will also sign off the service Acceptance Criteria and test plan.

4.5.4.8 Testing approaches and techniques

There are many approaches that can be combined to conduct validation activities and tests, depending on the constraints. Different approaches can be combined to the requirements for different types of service, service model, risk profile, skill levels, test objectives and levels of testing. Examples include:

- Document review
- Modelling and measuring – suitable for testing the service model and Service Operations plan
- Risk-based approach that focuses on areas of greatest risk, e.g. business critical services, risks identified in change impact analysis and/or service evaluation

- Standards compliance approach, e.g. international or national standards or industry specific standards
- Experience-based approach, e.g. using subject matter experts in the business, service or technical arenas to provide guidance on test coverage
- Approach based on an organization's lifecycle methods, e.g. waterfall, agile
- Simulation
- Scenario testing
- Role playing
- Prototyping
- Laboratory testing
- Regression testing
- Joint walkthrough/workshops
- Dress/service rehearsal
- Conference room pilot
- Live pilot.

In order to optimize the testing resources, test activities must be allocated against service importance, anticipated business impact and risk. Business impact analyses carried out during design for business and service continuity management and availability purposes are often very relevant to establishing testing priorities and schedules and should be available, subject to confidentiality and security concerns.

4.5.4.9 Design considerations

Service test design aims to develop test models and test cases that measure the correct things in order to establish whether the service will meet its intended use within the specified constraints. It is important to avoid focusing too much on the lower level components that are often easier to test and measure. Adopting a structured approach to scoping and designing the tests helps to ensure that priority is given to testing the right things. Test models must be well structured and repeatable to facilitate auditability and maintainability.

The service is designed in response to the agreed business and service requirements and testing aims to identify if these have been achieved. Service validation and test designs consider potential changes in circumstances and are flexible enough to be changed. They may need to be changed after failures in early service tests identify a change in the environment or circumstances and therefore a change on the testing approach.

Design considerations are applicable for service test models, test cases and test scripts and include:

- Business/Organization:
  - Alignment with business services, processes and procedures
  - Business dependencies, priorities, criticality and impact
  - Business cycles and seasonal variations
  - Business transaction levels
  - The numbers and types of users and anticipated future growth
  - Possible requirements due to new facilities and functionality
  - Business scenarios to test the end to end service
- Service architecture and performance:
  - Service Portfolio/structure of the services, e.g. core service, supporting and underpinning supplier services
  - Options for testing different type of service assets, utilities and warranty, e.g. availability, security, continuity
  - Service level requirements and service level targets
  - Service transaction levels
  - Constraints
  - Performance and volume predictions
  - Monitoring, modelling and measurement system, e.g. is there a need for significant simulation to recreate peak business periods? Will the new or changed service interface with existing monitoring and management tools?

- Service release test environment requirements
- Service Management:
  - Service Management models, e.g. capacity, cost, performance models
  - Service Operations model
  - Service support model
  - Changes in requirements for Service Management information
  - Changes in volumes of service users and transactions
- Application information and data:
  - Validating that the application works with the information/databases and technical infrastructure
  - Functionality testing to test the behaviour of the infrastructure solution and verify: i) no conflicts in versions of software, hardware or network components; and ii) common infrastructure services used according to the design
  - Access rights set correctly
- Technical infrastructure:
  - Physical assets – do they meet their specifications?
  - Technical resource capacity, e.g. storage, processing power, power, network bandwidth
  - Spares – are sufficient spares available or ordered and scheduled for delivery? Are hardware/software settings recorded and correct?

Aspects that generally need to be considered in designing service tests include:

- **Finance** – Is the agreed budget adequate, has spending exceeded budget, have costs altered (e.g. software licence and maintenance charge increases)?
- **Documentation** – Is all necessary documentation available or scheduled for production, is it practicable (sufficiently intuitive for the intended audience, available in all required languages), in correct formats such as checklists, service desk scripts?
- **Supplier** of the service, service asset, component – What are the internal or external interfaces?
- **Build** – Can the service, service asset or component be built into a release package and test environments?
- **Testable** – Is it testable with the resources, time and facilities available or obtainable?
- **Traceability** – What traceability is there back to the requirements?
- **Where and when** could testing take place? Are there unusual conditions under which a service might need to run that should be tested?
- **Remediation** – What plans are there to remediate or back out a release through the environments?

Awareness of current technological environments for different types of business, customer, staff and user is essential to maintaining a valid test environment. The design of the test environments must consider the current and anticipated live environment when the service is due for operational handover and for the period of its expected operation. In practice, for most organizations, looking more than six to nine months into the business or technological future is about the practical limit. In some sectors, however, much longer lead times require the need to predict further into the future, even to the extent of restricting technological innovation in the interests of thorough and expansive testing – examples are military systems, NASA and other safety critical environments.

Designing the management and maintenance of test data needs to address relevant issues such as:

■ Separation of test data from any live data, including steps to ensure that test data cannot be mistaken for live data when being used, and vice versa (there are many real-life examples of live data being copied and used as test data and being the basis for business decisions e.g. desktop icons pointing at the wrong database)

■ Data protection regulations – when live data is used to generate a test database; if information can be traced to individuals it may well be covered by data protection legislation, which for example may forbid its transportation between countries

■ Backup of test data, and restoration to a known baseline to enable repeatable testing; this also applies to initiation conditions for hardware tests that should be baselined

■ Volatility of test data and test environments, processes and procedures, which should be in place to quickly build and tear down the test environment for a variety of testing needs and so care must be taken to ensure that testing activities for one group do not compromise testing activities for another group

■ Balancing cost and benefit – as test environments populated with relevant data are expensive to build and to maintain, so the benefits in terms of risk reduction to the business services must be balanced against the cost of provision. Also, how closely the test environment matches live production is a key consideration that needs to be weighed balancing cost with risk.

4.5.4.10 Types of testing

The following types of test are used to verify that the service meets the user and customer requirements as well as the service provider's requirements for managing, operating and supporting the service. Care must be taken to establish the full range of likely users, and then to test all the aspects of the service, including support and reporting.

Functional testing will depend on the type of service and channel of delivery. Functional testing is covered in many testing standards and best practices (see Further information).

Service testing will include many non-functional tests. These tests can be conducted at several test levels to help build up confidence in the service release. They include:

■ Usability testing
■ Accessibility testing
■ Process and procedure testing
■ Knowledge transfer and competence testing
■ Performance, capacity and resilience testing
■ Volume, stress, load and scalability testing
■ Availability testing
■ Backup and recovery testing
■ Coherency testing
■ Compatibility testing
■ Documentation testing
■ Regulatory and compliance testing
■ Security testing
■ Logistics, deployability and migration testing
■ Coexistence and compatibility testing
■ Remediation, continuity and recovery testing
■ Configuration, build and installability testing
■ Operability and maintainability testing.

There are several types of testing from different perspectives, which are described below.

Service requirements and structure testing – service provider, users and customers

Validation of the service attributes against the contract, service package and service model includes evaluating the integration or 'fit' of the utilities across the core and supporting services and service assets to ensure there is complete coverage and no conflicts.

	Asset 1	Asset 2	Asset 3	Asset 4	Utility	Warranty 1	Warranty 2	Warranty 3	Warranty 4
	TC1				U1	TC1	TC1/TC2	TC1	
		TC2	TC3/TC4		U2		TC2		TC3/TC4
	TC3	TC2/TC3			U3		TC2		
			TC5		U4		TC2/TC5		
		TC3/TC4			U5		TC2/TC5		
				TC1	U6		TC1/TC2		TC1

TCn = Test case identifier

Figure 4.31 Designing tests to cover range of service assets, utilities and warranties

Figure 4.31 shows a matrix of service utility to service warranty and the service assets that support each utility. This matrix is one that can be used to design the service tests to ensure that the service structure and test design coverage is appropriate. Service tests cases are designed to test the service requirements in terms of utility, capacity, resource utilization, finance and risks. For example approaches to testing the risk of service failure include performance, stress, usability and security testing.

Service level testing testing – service level managers, operations managers and customers

Validate that the service provider can deliver the service level requirements, e.g. testing the response and fix time, availability, product delivery times and support services.

The performance from a service asset should deliver the utility or service expected. This is not necessarily that the asset can deliver what it should be capable of in its own right. For example a car's factory specification may assert that it is capable of 150kph, but for most customers delivering 100kph will fully meet the requirement.

Warranty and assurance tests – fit for use testing

As discussed earlier in this section, the customers see the service delivered in terms of warranties against the utilities that add value to their assets in order to deliver the expected business support. For any service, the warranties are expressed in measurable terms that enable tests to be designed to establish that the warranty can be delivered (within the agreed degree of confidence). The degree of detail may vary considerably, but will always reflect the agreement established during Service Design. In all cases the warranty will be described, and should be measurable, in terms of the customer's business and the potential effects on it of success or failure of the service to meet that warranty.

The following tests are used to provide confidence that the warranties can be delivered, i.e. the service is fit for use:

■ **Availability** is the most elementary aspect of assuring value to customers. It assures the customer that services will be available for use under agreed terms and conditions. Services are expected to be made available to designated users only within specified areas, locations and time schedules.

- **Capacity** is an aspect of service warranty that assures the customer that a service will support a specified level of business activity or demand at a specified level of service quality. Customers can make changes to their utilization of services while being assured that their business processes and systems will be adequately supported by the service. Capacity management is a critical aspect of Service Management because it has a direct impact on the availability of services. The capacity available to support services also has an impact of the level of service continuity committed or delivered. Effective management of service capacity can therefore have first-order and second-order effects on service warranty.

- **Continuity** is the level of assurance provided to customers that the service will continue to support the business through major failures or disruptive events. The service provider undertakes to maintain service assets that will provide a sufficient level of contingency and responsiveness. Specialized systems and processes will kick in to ensure that the service levels received by the customer's assets do not fall below a predefined level. Assurance is also provided that normal service levels will be restored within a predefined time limit to limit the overall impact of a failure or event. The effectiveness of service continuity is measured in terms of disturbance to the productive state of customer assets.

- **Security** assures that the utilization of services by customers will be secure. This means that customer assets within the scope of service delivery and support will not be exposed to certain security risks. Service providers undertake to implement general and service-level controls that will ensure that the value provided to customers is complete and not eroded by any avoidable costs and risks. Service security covers the following aspects of reducing risks:
  - Authorized and accountable usage of services as specified by customer
  - Protection of customers' assets from unauthorized or malicious access
  - Security zones between customer assets and service assets
  - Plays a supporting role to the other three aspects of service warranty
  - When effective has a positive impact on those aspects.

  Service security inherits all the general properties of the security of physical and human assets, as well as intangibles such as data, information, coordination and communication.

Usability – users and maintainers

Usability testing is likely to be of increasing importance as more services become widely used as a part of everyday life and ordinary business usage. Focusing on the intuitiveness of a service can significantly increase the efficiency and reduce the unit costs of both using and supporting a service.

User accessibility testing considers the restricted abilities of actual or potential users of a new or changed service and is commonly used for testing web services. Care must be taken to establish the types of likely users, e.g. hearing impaired users may be able to operate a PC-based service but would not be supported by a telephone-only-based service-desk support system. This testing might focus on usability for:

- Disabled users, e.g. visually or hearing impaired
- Sensory restricted users, e.g. colour-blind
- Users working in second language or based in a different culture.

Contract and regulation testing

Audits and tests are conducted to check that the criteria in contracts have been accepted before acceptance of the end-to-end service. Service providers may have a contractual requirement to comply with the requirements of ISO/IEC 20000 or other standards and they would need to ensure that the relevant clauses of the standard are met during implementation of a new or changed service and release.

Regulatory acceptance testing is required in some industries such as defence, financial services and pharmaceuticals.

Compliance testing

Testing is conducted to check compliance against internal regulations and existing commitments of the organization, e.g. fraud checks.

Service Management testing

The service models will dictate the approach to testing the integrated Service Management processes. ISO/IEC 20000 covers the minimum requirements for each process to be compliant with the standard and maintenance of the process interrelationships.

Examples of Service Management manageability tests are shown in Table 4.12.

Table 4.12 Examples of Service Management manageability tests

Service Management functions	Examples of design phase manageability checks	Examples of build phase manageability checks	Examples of deployment phase manageability checks	Examples of operating manageability checks	Examples of early life support and CSI manageability checks
Configuration Management	Are the designers aware of the corporate standards used for Configuration Management? How does the design meet organizational standards for acceptable configurations? Does the design support the concept of version control? Is the design created in a way that allows for the logical breakdown of the service into configuration items (CIs)?	Have the developers built the service, application and infrastructure to conform to the corporate standards that are used for Configuration Management? Does the service use only standard supporting systems and tools that are considered acceptable? Does the service include support for version, build, baseline and release control and management? Have the developers built in the chosen CI structure to the service, application and infrastructure?	Does the service deployment update the CMS at each stage of the rollout? Is the deployment team using an updated inventory to complete the plan and the deployment?	Can the operations team gain access to the CMS so that they can confirm the service they are managing is the correct version and configured correctly? Are the operating instructions under version and build control similar to those used for the application builds?	As the service is reviewed within the optimize phase, is the CMS used to assist with the review? Are Configuration Management personnel involved in the optimization process, including providing advice in the use of and updating the inventory?
Change Management	Does the Service Design cope with change? Do the designers understand the Change Management process used by the organization?	Have the service assets and components been built and tested against the corporate Change Management process? Has the emergency change process been tested? Is the impact assessment procedure for the CI type clearly defined and has it been tested?	Are the corporate Change Management process and standards used during deployment?	Is the operations team involved in the Change Management process; is it part of the sign-off and verification process? Does a member of the operations team attend the Change Management meetings?	As modifications are identified within this phase, does the team use the Change Management system to coordinate the changes? Does the optimization team understand the Change Management process?

Table 4.12 Examples of Service Management manageability tests (continued)

Service Management functions	Examples of design phase manageability checks	Examples of build phase manageability checks	Examples of deployment phase manageability checks	Examples of operating manageability checks	Examples of early life support and CSI manageability checks
Release and Deployment Management	Do the service designers understand the standards and tools used for releasing and deploying services? How will the design ensure that the new or changed service can be deployed into the environment in a simple and efficient way?	Has the service, application and infrastructure been built and tested in ways that ensure it can be released into the environment in a simple and efficient way?	Is the service being deployed in a manner that minimizes risks, such as a phased deployment? Has a remediation/back-out option been included in the release package or process for the service and its constituent components?	Does the release and deployment process ensure that deployment information is available to the operations teams? Do the Service Operations teams have access to release and information even before the service or application is deployed into the live environment?	Do members of the CSI team understand the release process, and are they using this for planning the deployment of improvements? Is Release and Deployment Management involved in providing advice to the assessment process?
Security management	How does the design ensure that the service is designed with security in the forefront?	Is the build process following security best practice for this activity?	Can the service be deployed in a manner that meets organizational security standards and requirements?	Does the service support the ongoing and periodic checks that security management needs to complete while the service is in operational use?	
Incident management	Does the design facilitate simple creation of incidents when something goes wrong? Is the design compatible with the organizational incident management system? Does the design accommodate automatic logging and detection of incidents?	Is a simple creation-of-incidents process, for when something goes wrong, built into services and tested (e.g. notification from applications)? Has the compatibility with the organizational incident management system been tested?	Does the deployment use the incident management system for reporting issues and problems? Do the members of the deployment team have access to the incident management system so that they can record incidents and also view incidents that relate to the deployment?	Does the operations team have access to the incident management system and can it update information within this system? Does the operations team understand its responsibilities in dealing with incidents? Is the operations team provided with reports on how well it deals with incidents, and does it act on these?	Do members of the CSI team have access to the incident management system so that they can record incidents and also view incidents that may be addressed in optimization?

Table 4.12 Examples of Service Management manageability tests (continued)

Service Management functions	Examples of design phase manageability checks	Examples of build phase manageability checks	Examples of deployment phase manageability checks	Examples of operating manageability checks	Examples of early life support and CSI manageability checks
Problem management	How does the design facilitate the methods used for root cause analysis used within the organization?	Has the method of providing information to facilitate root cause analysis and problem management been tested?	Has a problem manager been appointed for this deployment and does the deployment team know who it is?	Does the operations team contribute to the problem management process, ideally by assisting with and facilitating root cause analysis? Does the operations team meet problem management staff regularly? Does the operations team see the weekly/ monthly problem management report?	Is the optimization process being provided with information by problem management to incorporate into the assessment process?
Capacity management	Are the designers aware of the approach to capacity management used within the organization? How to measure operations and performance? Is modelling being used to ensure that the design meets capacity needs?	Has the service been built and tested to ensure that it meets the capacity requirements? Has the capacity information provided by the service been tested and verified? Are stress and volume characteristics built into the services and constituent applications?	Is capacity management involved in the deployment process so that it can monitor the capacity of the resources involved in the deployment?	Is capacity management information being monitored and reported on as this service is used, and is this information provided to capacity management?	Is capacity management feeding information into the optimization process?
Availability management	Does the design address the availability requirements of the service? Has the service been designed to fit in with backup and recovery capabilities of the organization?	How has the service been built to address the availability requirements, and how has this been tested? What testing has been done to ensure that the service meets the backup and recovery capabilities of the organization? What happens when the service and underlying applications are under stress?	Is availability management monitoring the availability of the service, the applications being deployed and the rest of the technology infrastructure to ensure that the deployment is not affecting availability? How is the ability to back up and recover the service during deployment being dealt with?	How is the service's availability being measured, and is this information being fed back to the availability management function within the IT organization?	Does the assessment use the availability information to complete the proposal of modifications that are needed for the service? Is any improvement required in the service's ability to be backed up and recovered?

Table 4.12 Examples of Service Management manageability tests (continued)

Service Management functions	Examples of design phase manageability checks	Examples of build phase manageability checks	Examples of deployment phase manageability checks	Examples of operating manageability checks	Examples of early life support and CSI manageability checks
Service continuity management	How does the design meet the service continuity requirements of the organization? Will the design meet the needs of the business recovery process following a disaster?	Has the service been built to support the business recovery process following a disaster, and how has this been tested?	Will any changes be required to the business recovery process following a disaster if one should occur during or after the deployment of this service?	Is the business recovery process for the service tested regularly by operations?	What optimization is required in the business recovery process to meet the business needs?
Service level management	How does the design meet the SLA requirements of the organization?	Does the service meet the SLA and performance requirements, and has this been tested?	Is service level management aware of the deployment of this service? Does this service have an initial SLA for the deployment phase? Does the service affect the SLA requirements during deployment?	Is the SLA visible and understood by the operations team so that it appreciates how its running of the service affects the delivery of the SLA? Does operations see the weekly/monthly service level report?	Is service level management information available for inclusion in the optimization process?
Financial management	Does the design meet the financial requirements for this service? How does the design ensure that the final new or changed service will meet return of investment expectations?	Has the service been built to deliver financial information, and how is this being tested?	Is management accounting being done during the deployment so that the total cost of deployment can be included within the cost of ownership?	Does operations provide input into the financial information about the service? For example, if a service requires an operator to perform additional tasks at night, is this recorded?	Is financial information available to be included in the assessment process?

Operational tests – systems, services

There will be many operational tests depending on the type of service. Typical tests include:

- **Load and stress** – These tests establish if the new or changed service will perform to the required levels on the capacity likely to be available. The capacity elements may include any anticipated bottlenecks within the infrastructure that might be expected to restrict performance, including:
  - Load and throughput
  - Behaviour at the upper limits of system capability
  - Network bandwidth
  - Data storage
  - Processing power or live memory

- Service desk resources – people and technology such as telephone lines and logging
- Available software licences/concurrent seats
- Support staff – both numbers and skills
- Training facilities, classrooms, trainers, CBT licences etc.
- Overnight batch processing timings, including backup tasks.

- **Security** – All services should be considered for their potential impact on relevant security concerns, and subsequently tested for their actual likely impact on security. Any service that has an anticipated security impact or exposes an anticipated security risk will have been assessed at design stage, and the requirement for security involvement built into the service package. Organizations should make reference to and may wish to seek compliance with ISO 27000 where security is a significant concern to their services.

■ **Recoverability** – Every significant change will have been assessed for the question 'If this change is made, will the Disaster Recovery (DR) plan need to be changed accordingly'. Notwithstanding that consideration earlier in the lifecycle, it is appropriate to test that the new or changed service is catered for within the existing (or amended with the changed) DR plan. Typically, concerns identified during testing should be addressed to the service continuity team and considered as active elements for future DR tests.

Regression testing

Regression testing means 'repeating a test already run successfully, and comparing the new results with the earlier valid results'. On each iteration of true regression testing, all existing, validated tests are run, and the new results are compared with the already-achieved standards. Regression testing ensures that a new or changed service does not introduce errors into aspects of the services or IT infrastructure that previously worked without error. Simple examples of the type of error that can be detected are software contention issues, hardware and network incompatibility. Regression testing also applies to other elements such as Service Management process testing and measurement. In reality it is the integrated concept of service testing – assessing whether the service will deliver the business benefit – that makes regression testing so very important in modern organizations, and will make it ever more important.

4.5.5 Process activities, methods and techniques

The testing process is shown schematically in Figure 4.32. The test activities are not undertaken in a sequence. Several activities may be done in parallel, e.g. test execution begins before all the test design is complete. The activities are described below.

1. Validation and test management

Test management includes the planning, control and reporting of activities through the test stages of Service Transition. These activities include:

■ Planning the test resources
■ Prioritizing and scheduling what is to be tested and when
■ Management of incidents, problems, errors, non-conformances, risks and issues
■ Checking that incoming known errors and their documentation are processed
■ Monitoring progress and collating feedback from validation and test activities
■ Management of incidents, problems, errors, non-conformances, risks and issues discovered during transition
■ Consequential changes, to reduce errors going into production
■ Capturing configuration baseline
■ Test metrics collection, analysis, reporting and management.

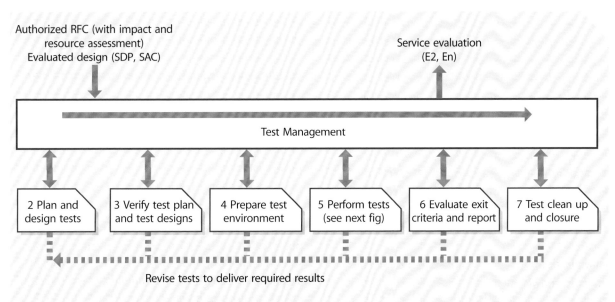

Figure 4.32 Example of a validation and testing process

Test management includes managing issues, mitigating risks and implementing changes identified from the testing activities as these can impose delays and create dependencies that need to be proactively managed.

Test metrics are used to measure the test process and manage and control the testing activities. They enable the test manager to determine the progress of testing, the earned value and the outstanding testing, and this helps the test manager to estimate when testing will be completed. Good metrics provide information for management decisions that are required for prioritization, scheduling and risk management. They also provide useful information for estimating and scheduling for future releases.

2. Plan and design test

Test planning and design activities start early in the service lifecycle and include:

- Resourcing
- Hardware, networking, staff numbers and skills etc. capacity
- Business/customer resources required, e.g. components or raw materials for production control services, cash for ATM services
- Supporting services including access, security, catering, communications
- Schedule of milestones, handover and delivery dates
- Agreed time for consideration of reports and other deliverables
- Point and time of delivery and acceptance
- Financial requirements – budgets and funding.

3. Verify test plan and test design

Verify the test plans and test design to ensure that:

- The test model delivers adequate and appropriate test coverage for the risk profile of the service
- The test model covers the key integration aspects and interfaces, e.g. at the SPIs
- That the test scripts are accurate and complete.

4. Prepare test environment

Prepare the test environment by using the services of the build and test environment resource and also use the release and deployment processes to prepare the test environment where possible; see paragraph 4.4.5.2. Capture a configuration baseline of the initial test environment.

5. Perform tests

Carry out the tests using manual or automated techniques and procedures. Testers must record their findings during the tests. If a test fails, the reasons for failure must be fully documented. Testing should continue according to the test plans and scripts, if at all possible. When part of a test fails, the incident or issues should be resolved or documented (e.g. as a known error) and the appropriate re-tests should be performed by the same tester.

An example of the test execution activities is shown in Figure 4.33. The deliverables from testing are:

- Actual results showing proof of testing with cross-references to the test model, test cycles and conditions
- Problems, errors, issues, non-conformances and risks remaining to be resolved
- Resolved problems/known errors and related changes
- Sign-off.

6. Evaluate exit criteria and report

The actual results are compared to the expected results. The results may be interpreted in terms of pass/fail; risk to the business/service provider; or if there is a change in a projected value, e.g. higher cost to deliver intended benefits.

To produce the report, gather the test metrics and summarize the results of the tests. Examples of exit criteria are:

- The service, with its underlying applications and technology infrastructure, enables the business users to perform all aspects of function as defined.
- The service meets the quality requirements.
- Configuration baselines are captured into the CMS.

7. Test clean up and closure

Ensure that the test environments are cleaned up or initialized. Review the testing approach and identify improvements to input to design/build, buy/build decision parameters and future testing policy/procedures.

4.5.6 Trigger, input and outputs, and inter-process interfaces

4.5.6.1 Trigger

The trigger for testing is a scheduled activity on a release plan, test plan or quality assurance plan.

4.5.6.2 Inputs

The key inputs to the process are:

- **The service package** – This comprises a core service package and re-usable components, many of which themselves are services, e.g. supporting service. It defines the service's utilities and warranties that are

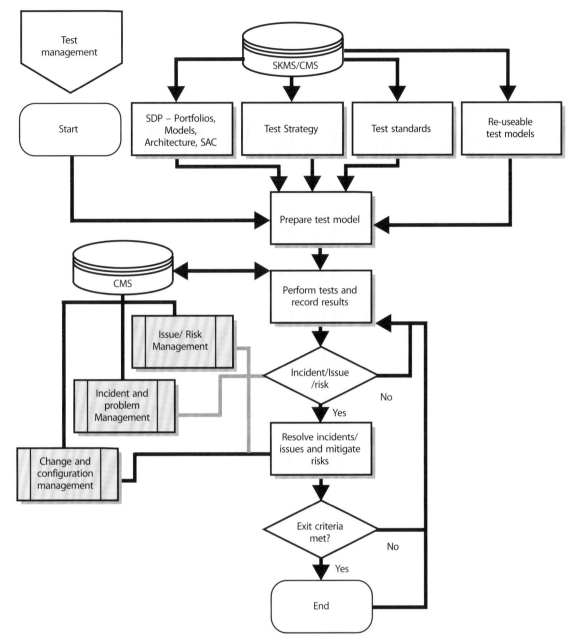

Figure 4.33 Example of perform test activities

delivered through the correct functioning of the particular set of identified service assets. It maps the demand patterns for service and user profiles to SLPs.

■ **SLP** – One or more SLPs that provided a definitive level of utility or warranty from the perspective of outcomes, assets, patterns of business activity of customers (PBA).

■ **Service provider interface definitions** – These define the interfaces to be tested at the boundaries of the service being delivered, e.g. process interfaces, organizational interfaces.

■ **The Service Design package** – This defines the agreed requirements of the service, expressed in terms of the service model and Service Operations plan. It includes:

● Operation models (including support resources, escalation procedures and critical situation handling procedures)

● Capacity/resource model and plans – combined with performance and availability aspects

● Financial/economic/cost models (with TCO, TCU)

● Service Management model (e.g. integrated process model as in ISO/IEC 20000)

● Design and interface specifications.

- **Release and deployment plans** – These define the order that release units will be deployed, built and installed.
- **Acceptance Criteria** – These exist at all levels at which testing and acceptance are foreseen.
- **RFCs** – These instigate required changes to the environment within which the service functions or will function.

4.5.6.3 Outputs

The direct output from testing is the report delivered to service evaluation (see section 4.6). This sets out:

- Configuration baseline of the testing environment
- Testing carried out (including options chosen and constraints encountered)
- Results from those tests
- Analysis of the results, e.g. comparison of actual results with expected results, risks identified during testing activities.

After the service has been in use for a reasonable time there should be sufficient data to perform an evaluation of the actual vs predicted service capability and performance. If the evaluation is successful, an evaluation report is sent to Change Management with a recommendation to promote the service release out of early life support and into normal operation.

Other outputs include:

- Updated data, information and knowledge to be added to the service knowledge management system, e.g. errors and workarounds, testing techniques, analysis methods
- Test incidents, problems and error records
- Improvement ideas for Continual Service Improvement to address potential improvements in any area that impacts on testing:
  - To the testing process itself
  - To the nature and documentation of the Service Design outputs
- Third party relationships, suppliers of equipment or services, partners (co-suppliers to end customers), users and customers or other stakeholders.

4.5.6.4 Interfaces to other lifecycle stages

Testing supports all of the release and deployment steps within Service Transition.

Although this chapter focuses on the application of testing within the Service Transition phase, the test strategy will ensure that the testing process works with all stages of the lifecycle:

- Working with Service Design to ensure that designs are inherently testable and providing positive support in achieving this; examples range from including self-monitoring within hardware and software, through the re-use of previously tested and known service elements through to ensuring rights of access to third party suppliers to carry out inspection and observation on delivered service elements easily
- Working closely with CSI to feed failure information and improvement ideas resulting from testing exercises
- Service Operation will use maintenance tests to ensure the continued efficacy of services; these tests will require maintenance to cope with innovation and change in environmental circumstances
- Service Strategy should accommodate testing in terms of adequate funding, resource, profile etc.

4.5.7 Information management

The nature of IT Service Management is repetitive, and this ability to benefit from re-use is recognized in the suggested use of transition models. Testing benefits greatly from re-use and to this end it is sensible to create and maintain a library of relevant tests and an updated and maintained data set for applying and performing tests. The test management group within an organization should take responsibility for creating, cataloguing and maintaining test scripts, test cases and test data that can be re-used.

Similarly, the use of automated testing tools (Computer Aided Software Testing – CAST) is becoming ever more central to effective testing in complex software environments. Equivalently standard and automated hardware testing approaches are fast and effective.

Test data

However well a test has been designed, it relies on the relevance of the data used to run it. This clearly applies strongly to software testing, but equivalent concerns relate to the environments within which hardware, documentation etc. is tested. Testing electrical equipment in a protected environment, with smoothed power supply and dust, temperature and humidity control will not be a valuable test if the equipment will be used in a normal office.

Test environments

Test environments must be actively maintained and protected. For any significant change to a service, the question should be asked (as for continued relevance of the continuity and capacity plans, should the change be accepted and implemented): 'If this change goes ahead, will there need to be a consequential impact to the test data?' If so, it may involve updating test data as part of the change, and the dependency of a service, or service element, on test data or test environment will be evident from the SKMS, via records and relationships held within the CMS. Outcomes from this question include:

■ Consequential updating of the test data

■ A new separate set of data or new test environment, since the original is still required for other services

■ Redundancy of the test data or environment – since the change will allow testing within another existing test environment, with or without modification to that data/environment (this may in fact be the justification behind a perfective change – to reduce testing costs)

■ Acceptance that a lower level of testing will be accepted since the test data/environment cannot be updated to deliver equivalent test coverage for the changed service.

Maintenance of test data should be an active exercise and should address relevant issues including:

■ Separation from any live data, and steps to ensure that it cannot be mistaken for live data when being used, and vice versa (there are many real-life examples of live data being copied and used as test data and being the basis for business decisions)

■ Data protection regulations – when live data is used to generate a test database, if information can be traced to individuals it may well be covered by data protection legislation that, for example, may forbid its transportation between countries

■ Backup of test data, and restoration to a known baseline for enabling repeatable testing; this also applies to initiation conditions for hardware tests that should be baselined.

An established test database can also be used as a safe and realistic training environment for a service.

4.5.8 Key performance indicators and metrics

4.5.8.1 Primary (of value to the business/customers)

The business will judge testing performance as a component of the Service Design and transition stages of the service lifecycle. Specifically, the effectiveness of testing in delivering to the business can be judged through:

■ Early validation that the service will deliver the predicted value that enables early correction

■ Reduction in the impact of incidents and errors in live that are attributable to newly transitioned services

■ More effective use of resource and involvement from the customer/business

■ Reduced delays in testing that impact the business

■ Increased mutual understanding of the new or changed service

■ Clear understanding of roles and responsibilities associated with the new or changed service between the customers, users and service provider

■ Cost and resources required from user and customer involvement (e.g. user acceptance testing).

The business will also be concerned with the economy of the testing process – in terms of:

■ Test planning, preparation, execution rates

■ Incident, problem, event rates

■ Issue and risk rate

■ Problem resolution rate

■ Resolution effectiveness rate

■ Stage containment – analysis by service lifecycle stage

■ Repair effort percentage

■ Problems and changes by service asset or CI type

■ Late changes by service lifecycle stage

■ Inspection effectiveness percentage

■ Residual risk percentage

■ Inspection and testing return on investment (ROI)

■ Cost of unplanned and unbudgeted overtime to the business

■ Cost of fixing errors in live operation compared to fixing errors early in the lifecycle (e.g. the costs can be £10 to fix an error in Service Design and £10,000 to fix the error if it reaches production)

■ Operational cost improvements associated with reducing errors in new or changed services.

4.5.8.2 Secondary (internal)

The testing function and process itself must strive to be effective and efficient, and so measures of its effectiveness and costs need to be taken. These include:

■ Effort and cost to set up a testing environment

■ Effort required to find defects – i.e. number of defects (by significance, type, category etc.) compared with testing resource applied

■ Reduction of repeat errors – feedback from testing ensures that corrective action within design and transition (through CSI) prevents mistakes from being repeated in subsequent releases or services

- Reduced error/defect rate in later testing stages or production
- Re-use of testing data
- Percentage incidents linked to errors detected during testing and released into live
- Percentage errors at each lifecycle stage
- Number and percentage of errors that could have been discovered in testing
- Testing incidents found as percentage of incidents occurring in live operations
- Percentage of faults found in earlier assessment stages – since remedial costs accelerate steeply for correction in later stages of transition
- Number of known errors documented in earlier testing phases.

Testing is about measuring the ability of a service to perform as required in a simulated (or occasionally the actual) environment, and so to that extent is focused on measurement. Care must be taken to try and separate out the measures that actually relate to the testing process from the number of errors introduced into services and systems. Careless measurement can appear to improve testing effectiveness although the development practices are worse – it is simply easier to find defects when there are lots of them. The point here is that testing is actually a stage of the design, build, release and deployment processes and the important measure is the overall one – about delivering services that deliver benefits and fail less often.

4.5.9 Challenges, critical success factors and risks

Still the most frequent challenges to effective testing are based on lack of respect and understanding for the role of testing. Traditionally testing has been starved of funding, and this results in:

- Inability to maintain test environment and test data that matches the live environment
- Insufficient staff, skills and testing tools to deliver adequate testing coverage
- Projects overrunning and allocated testing time frames being squeezed to restore project go-live dates but at the cost of quality
- Developing standard performance measures and measurement methods across projects and suppliers

- Projects and suppliers estimating delivery dates inaccurately and causing delays in scheduling Service Transition activities.

Critical success factors include:

- Understanding the different stakeholder perspectives that underpin effective risk management for the change impact assessment and test activities
- Building a thorough understanding of risks that have impacted or may impact successful Service Transition of services and releases
- Encouraging a risk management culture where people share information and take a pragmatic and measured approach to risk.
- Quality is built into every stage of the service lifecycle using a structured framework such as the V-model
- Issues are identified early in the service lifecycle
- Testing provides evidence that the service assets and configurations have been built and implemented correctly in addition to the service delivering what the customer needs
- Re-usable test models are developed that can be used for regression testing in future releases

Risks to successful Service Validation and Testing include:

- Unclear expectations/objectives
- Lack of understanding of the risks means that testing is not targeted at critical elements that need to be well controlled and therefore tested
- Resource shortages (e.g. users, support staff) introduce delays and have an impact on other Service Transitions.

4.6 EVALUATION

Evaluation is a generic process that considers whether the performance of something is acceptable, value for money etc. – and whether it will be proceeded with, accepted into use, paid for, etc.

4.6.1 Purpose, goal and objective

The purpose of evaluation is to provide a consistent and standardized means of determining the performance of a service change in the context of existing and proposed services and IT infrastructure. The actual performance of a change is assessed against its predicted performance and any deviations between the two are understood and managed.

The goal of evaluation is to set stakeholder expectations correctly and provide effective and accurate information to Change Management to make sure changes that adversely affect service capability and introduce risk are not transitioned unchecked.

The objective is to:

- Evaluate the intended effects of a service change and as much of the unintended effects as is reasonably practical given capacity, resource and organizational constraints
- Provide good quality outputs from the evaluation process so that Change Management can expedite an effective decision about whether a service change is to be approved or not.

4.6.2 Scope

Specifically in this section we consider the evaluation of new or changed services defined by Service Design, during deployment and before final transition to service operations. The importance of evaluating the actual performance of any service change against its anticipated performance is an important source of information to service providers to help ensure that expectations set are realistic and to identify that if there are any reasons that production performance does not meet what was expected.

4.6.3 Value to business

Evaluation is, by its very nature, concerned with value. Specifically effective evaluation will establish the use made of resources in terms of delivered benefit and this information will allow a more accurate focus on value in future service development and Change Management. There is a great deal of intelligence that Continual Service Improvement can take from evaluation to analyse future improvements to the process of change and the predictions and measurement of service change performance.

4.6.4 Policies, principles and basic concepts

Policies

The following policies apply to the evaluation process:

- Service Designs or service changes will be evaluated before being transitioned.
- Any deviation between predicted and actual performance will be managed by the customer or customer representative by accepting the change even though actual performance is different to what was predicted; rejecting the change; or requiring a new change to be implemented with revised predicted performance agreed in advance. No other outcomes of evaluation are allowed.
- An evaluation shall not be performed without a customer engagement package.

Principles

The following principles shall guide the execution evaluation process:

- As far as is reasonably practical, the unintended as well as the intended effects of a change need to be identified and their consequences understood and considered.
- A service change will be fairly, consistently, openly and, wherever possible, objectively evaluated.

Basic concepts

The evaluation process uses the Plan–Do–Check–Act (PDCA) model to ensure consistency across all evaluations.

4.6.5 Process activities, methods and techniques

4.6.5.1 Service evaluation terms

The key terms shown in Table 4.13 apply to the service evaluation process.

Table 4.13 Key terms that apply to the service evaluation process

Term	Function/Means
Service change	A change to an existing service or the introduction of a new service; the service change arrives into service evaluation and qualification in the form of a Request for Change (RFC) from Change Management
Service Design package	Defines the service and provides a plan of service changes for the next period (e.g. the next 12 months). Of particular interest to service evaluation is the Acceptance Criteria and the predicted performance of a service with respect to a service change
Performance	The utilities and warranties of a service
Performance model	A representation of the performance of a service
Predicted performance	The expected performance of a service following a service change
Actual performance	The performance achieved following a service change
Deviations report	The difference between predicted and actual performance
Risk	A function of the likelihood and negative impact of a service not performing as expected
Countermeasures	The mitigation that is implemented to reduce risk
Test plan and results	The test plan is a response to an impact assessment of the proposed service change. Typically the plan will specify how the change will be tested; what records will result from testing and where they will be stored; who will approve the change; and how it will be ensured that the change and the service(s) it affects will remain stable over time. The test plan may include a qualification plan and a validation plan if the change affects a regulated environment. The results represent the actual performance following implementation of the change
Residual risk	The remaining risk after countermeasures have been deployed
Service capability	The ability of a service to perform as required
Capacity	An organization's ability to maintain service capability under any predefined circumstances
Constraint	Limits on an organization's capacity
Resource	The normal requirements of an organization to maintain service capability
Evaluation plan	The outcome of the evaluation planning exercise
Evaluation report	A report generated by the evaluation function, which is passed to Change Management and which comprises: ■ A risk profile ■ A deviations report ■ A recommendation ■ A qualification statement.

4.6.5.2 Evaluation process

Figure 4.34 shows the evaluation process with inputs and outputs.

4.6.5.3 Evaluation plan

Evaluation of a change should be carried out from a number of different perspectives to ensure any unintended effects of a change are understood as well as the intended effects.

Generally speaking we would expect the intended effects of a change to be beneficial. The unintended effects are harder to predict, often not seen even after the service

change is implemented, and frequently ignored. Additionally, they will not always be beneficial, for example in terms of impact on other services, impact on customers and users of the service, and network overloading.

Intended effects of a change should match the Acceptance Criteria. Unintended effects are often not seen until pilot stage or even once in production; they are difficult to measure and very often not beneficial to the business.

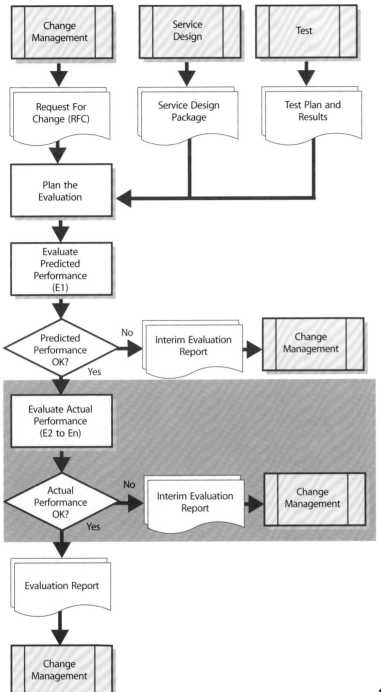

Figure 4.34 Evaluation process

4.6.5.4 Understanding the intended effect of a change

The details of the service change, customer requirements and Service Design package should be carefully analysed to understand fully the purpose of the change and the expected benefit from implementing it. Examples might include: reduce cost of running the service; increase service performance; reduce resources required to operate the service; or improve service capability.

The change documentation should make clear what the intended effect of the change will be and specific measures that should be used to determine effectiveness of that change. If they are in any way unclear or ambiguous the evaluation should cease and a recommendation not to proceed should be forwarded to Change Management.

Even some deliberately designed changes may be detrimental to some elements of the service. For example, the introduction of SOX-compliant procedures, which, while delivering the benefit of legal compliance, introduce extra work steps and costs.

4.6.5.5 Understanding the unintended effect of a change

In addition to the expected effects on the service and broader organization there are likely to be additional effects which were not expected or planned for. These effects must also be surfaced and considered if the full impact of a service change is to be understood. One of the most effective ways of identifying such effects is by discussion with all stakeholders. Not just customers, but also users of the service, those who maintain it, those who fund it etc. Care should be taken in presenting the details of the change to ensure stakeholders fully understand the implications and can therefore provide accurate feedback.

4.6.5.6 Factors for considering the effect of a service change

Table 4.14 shows the factors to be included when considering the effect of a service change.

4.6.5.7 Evaluation of predicted performance

Using customer requirements (including Acceptance Criteria), the predicted performance and the performance model, a risk assessment is carried out. If the risk assessment suggests that predicted performance may create unacceptable risks from the change or not meet the Acceptance Criteria, an interim evaluation report is sent to alert Change Management.

The interim evaluation report includes the outcome of the risk assessment and/or the outcome of the predicted performance versus Acceptance Criteria, together with a recommendation to reject the service change in its current form.

Evaluation activities cease at this point pending a decision from Change Management.

4.6.5.8 Evaluation of actual performance

Once the service change has been implemented a report on actual performance is received from operations. Using customer requirements (including Acceptance Criteria), the actual performance and the performance model, a risk assessment is carried out. Again if the risk assessment suggests that actual performance is creating unacceptable risks, an interim evaluation report is sent to Change Management.

The interim evaluation report includes the outcome of the risk assessment and/or the outcome of the actual performance versus Acceptance Criteria, together with a recommendation to remediate the service change.

Evaluation activities cease at this point pending a decision from Change Management.

4.6.5.9 Risk management

There are two steps in risk management: risk assessment and mitigation. Risk assessment is concerned with analysing threats and weaknesses that have been or would be introduced as a result of a service change.

Table 4.14 Factors for considering the effects of a service change

Factor	Evaluation of Service Design
S – Service provider capability	The ability of a service provider or service unit to perform as required.
T – Tolerance	The ability or capacity of a service to absorb the service change or release.
O – Organizational setting	The ability of an organization to accept the proposed change. For example, is appropriate access available for the implementation team? Have all existing services that would be affected by the change been updated to ensure smooth transition?
R – Resources	The availability of appropriately skilled and knowledgeable people, sufficient finances, infrastructure, applications and other resources necessary to run the service following transition.
M – Modelling and measurement	The extent to which the predictions of behaviour generated from the model match the actual behaviour of the new or changed service.
P – People	The people within a system and the effect of change on them.
U – Use	Will the service be fit for use? The ability to deliver the warranties, e.g. continuously available, is there enough capacity, will it be secure enough?
P – Purpose	Will the new or changed service be fit for purpose? Can the required performance be supported? Will the constraints be removed as planned?

A risk occurs when a threat can exploit a weakness. The likelihood of threats exploiting a weakness and the impact if they do, are the fundamental factors in determining risk.

The risk management formula is simple but very powerful:

Risk = Likelihood x Impact

Obviously, the introduction of new threats and weaknesses increases the likelihood of a threat exploiting a weakness. Placing greater dependence on a service or component increases the impact if an existing threat exploits an existing weakness within the service. These are just a couple of examples of how risk may increase as a result of a service change.

It is a clear requirement that a proposed service change must assess the existing risks within a service and the predicted risks following implementation of the change.

If the risk level has increased then the second stage of risk management is used to mitigate the risk. In the examples given above mitigation may include steps to eliminate a threat or weakness and using disaster recovery and backup techniques to increase the resilience of a service on which the organization has become more dependent.

Following mitigation the risk level is re-assessed and compared with the original. This second assessment and any subsequent assessments are in effect determining residual risk – the risk that remains after mitigation. Assessment of residual risk and associated mitigation continues to cycle until risk is managed down to an acceptable level.

The guiding principle here is that either the initial risk assessment or any residual risk level is equal to or less than the original risk prior to the service change. If this is not the case then evaluation will recommend rejection of proposed service change, or back out of an implemented service change.

The approach to risk representation recommended here takes a fundamentally different approach. Building on the work of Drake (2005a, 2005b) this approach recognizes that risks almost always grow exponentially over time if left unmanaged, and that a risk that will not cause a loss probably is not worth worrying about too much.

It is therefore proposed that a stronger risk representation is as shown in Figure 4.35. Principally, this representation is intended to promote debate and agreement by stakeholders: is the risk positioned correctly in terms of time and potential or actual loss; could mitigation have been deployed later (e.g. more economically); should it have been deployed earlier (e.g. better protection); etc.

Deviations – predicted vs actual performance

Once the service change passes the evaluation of predicted performance and actual performance, essentially as standalone evaluations, a comparison of the two is carried out. To have reached this point it will have been determined that predicted performance and actual performance are acceptable, and that there are no unacceptable risks. The output of this activity is a deviations report. For each factor in Table 4.14 the report states the extent of any deviation between predicted and actual performance.

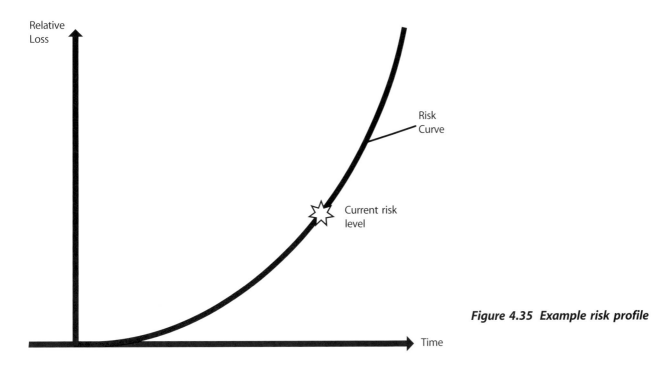

Figure 4.35 Example risk profile

Test plan and results

The testing function provides the means for determining the actual performance of the service following implementation of a service change. Test provides the service evaluation function with the test plan and a report on the results of any testing. The actual results are also made available to service evaluation. These are evaluated and used as described in paragraph 4.6.5.8.

In some circumstances it is necessary to provide a statement of qualification and/or validation status following a change. This takes place in regulated environments such as pharmaceuticals and defence.

The context for these activities is shown in Figure 4.36.

The inputs to these activities are the qualification plan and results and/or validation plan and results. The evaluation process ensures that the results meet the requirements of the plans. A qualification and/or validation statement is provided as output.

4.6.6 Evaluation report

The evaluation report contains the following sections.

Risk profile

A representation of the residual risk left after a change has been implemented and after countermeasures have been applied.

Deviations report

The difference between predicted and actual performance following the implementation of a change.

A qualification statement (if appropriate)

Following review of qualification test results and the qualification plan, a statement of whether or not the change has left the service in a state whereby it could not be qualified.

A validation statement (if appropriate)

Following review of validation test results and the validation plan, a statement of whether or not the change has left the service in a state whereby it could not be validated.

A recommendation

Based on the other factors within the evaluation report, a recommendation to Change Management to accept or reject the change:

■ Review and close transition
■ Knowledge Management.

4.6.7 Triggers, inputs and outputs and inter-process interfaces

Triggers:

■ Request for Evaluation from Service Transition manager or Change Management
■ Activity on Project Plan.

Inputs:

■ Service package
■ SDP and SAC
■ Test results and report.

Outputs:

■ Evaluation report for Change Management.

4.6.8 Information management

■ Service Portfolio
■ Service package
■ SDP, SAC
■ Test results and report
■ Evaluation report.

Figure 4.36 Context for qualification and validation activities

4.6.9 Key performance indicators and metrics

The customer/business KPIs are:

- Variance from service performance required by customers (minimal and reducing)
- Number of incidents against the service (low and reducing).

The internal KPIs include:

- Number of failed designs that have been transitioned (zero)
- Cycle time to perform an evaluation (low and reducing).

4.6.9.1 Challenges

Challenges include:

- Developing standard performance measures and measurement methods across projects and suppliers
- Projects and suppliers estimating delivery dates inaccurately and causing delays in scheduling evaluation activities
- Understanding the different stakeholder perspectives that underpin effective risk management for the evaluation activities
- Understanding, and being able to assess, the balance between managing risk and taking risks as it affects the overall strategy of the organization and service delivery
- Measuring and demonstrating less variation in predictions during and after transition
- Taking a pragmatic and measured approach to risk
- Communicating the organization's attitude to risk and approach to risk management effectively during risk evaluation
- Building a thorough understanding of risks that have impacted or may impact successful Service Transition of services and releases
- Encouraging a risk management culture where people share information.

4.7 KNOWLEDGE MANAGEMENT

The ability to deliver a quality service or process rests to a significant extent on the ability of those involved to respond to circumstances – and that in turn rests heavily on their understanding of the situation, the options and the consequences and benefits, i.e. their knowledge of the situation they are, or may find themselves, in.

That knowledge within the Service Transition domain might include:

- Identity of stakeholders
- Acceptable risk levels and performance expectations
- Available resource and timescales.

The quality and relevance of the knowledge rests in turn on the accessibility, quality and continued relevance of the underpinning data and information available to service staff.

4.7.1 Purpose, goal and objective

The purpose of Knowledge Management is to ensure that the right information is delivered to the appropriate place or competent person at the right time to enable informed decision.

The goal of Knowledge Management is to enable organizations to improve the quality of management decision making by ensuring that reliable and secure information and data is available throughout the service lifecycle.

The objectives of Knowledge Management include:

- Enabling the service provider to be more efficient and improve quality of service, increase satisfaction and reduce the cost of service
- Ensuring staff have a clear and common understanding of the value that their services provide to customers and the ways in which benefits are realized from the use of those services
- Ensuring that, at a given time and location, service provider staff have adequate information on:
  - Who is currently using their services
  - The current states of consumption
  - Service delivery constraints
  - Difficulties faced by the customer in fully realizing the benefits expected from the service.

4.7.2 Scope

Knowledge Management is a whole lifecycle-wide process in that it is relevant to all lifecycle sectors and hence is referenced throughout ITIL from the perspective of each publication. It is dealt with to some degree within other ITIL publications but this chapter sets out the basic concept, from a Service Transition focus.

4.7.2.1 Inclusions

Knowledge Management includes oversight of the management of knowledge, the information and data from which that knowledge derives.

4.7.2.2 Exclusions

Detailed attention to the capturing, maintenance and use of asset and configuration data is set out in Section 4.2.

4.7.3 Value to business

Knowledge Management is especially significant within Service Transition since relevant and appropriate knowledge is one of the key service elements being transitioned. Examples where successful transition rests on appropriate Knowledge Management include:

■ User, service desk, support staff and supplier understanding of the new or changed service, including knowledge of errors signed off before deployment, to facilitate their roles within that service

■ Awareness of the use of the service, and the discontinuation of previous versions

■ Establishment of the acceptable risk and confidence levels associated with the transition, e.g. measuring, understanding and acting correctly on results of testing and other assurance results.

Effective Knowledge Management is a powerful asset for people in all roles across all stages of the service lifecycle. It is an excellent method for individuals and teams to share data, information and knowledge about all facets of an IT service. The creation of a single system for Knowledge Management is recommended.

Specific application to Service Transition domain can be illustrated through considering the following examples:

■ Blurring of the concept of intellectual property and information when engaged in sourcing and partnering, therefore new approaches to controlling 'knowledge' must be addressed and managed during Service Transition

■ Knowledge transfer often being a crucial factor in facilitating effective transition of new or changed services and essential to operational readiness

■ Training of users, support staff, suppliers and other stakeholders in new or changed services

■ Recording of errors, faults, workarounds etc. detected and documented during the Service Transition phase

■ Capturing of implementation and testing information

■ Re-using previously developed and quality assured testing, training and documentation

■ Compliance with legislative requirements, e.g. SOX, and conformance to standards such as ISO 9000 and ISO/IEC 20000

■ Assisting decisions on whether to accept or proceed with items and services by delivering all available relevant information (and omitting unnecessary and confusing information) to key decision makers.

4.7.4 Policies, principles and basic concepts

4.7.4.1 The Data-to-Information-to-Knowledge-to-Wisdom structure

Knowledge Management is typically displayed within the Data-to-Information-to-Knowledge-to-Wisdom (DIKW) structure. The use of these terms is set out below.

Data is a set of discrete facts about events. Most organizations capture significant amounts of data in highly structured databases such as Service Management and Configuration Management tools/systems and databases.

The key Knowledge Management activities around data are the ability to:

■ Capture accurate data

■ Analyse, synthesize, and then transform the data into information

■ Identify relevant data and concentrate resources on its capture.

Information comes from providing context to data. Information is typically stored in semi-structured content such as documents, e-mail, and multimedia.

The key Knowledge Management activity around information is managing the content in a way that makes it easy to capture, query, find, re-use and learn from experiences so that mistakes are not repeated and work is not duplicated.

Knowledge is composed of the tacit experiences, ideas, insights, values and judgements of individuals. People gain knowledge both from their own and from their peers' expertise, as well as from the analysis of information (and data). Through the synthesis of these elements, new knowledge is created.

Knowledge is dynamic and context based. Knowledge puts information into an 'ease of use' form, which can facilitate decision making. In Service Transition this knowledge is not solely based on the transition in progress, but is gathered from experience of previous transitions, awareness of recent and anticipated changes and other areas that experienced staff will have been unconsciously collecting for some time.

Wisdom gives the ultimate discernment of the material and having the application and contextual awareness to provide a strong common sense judgement.

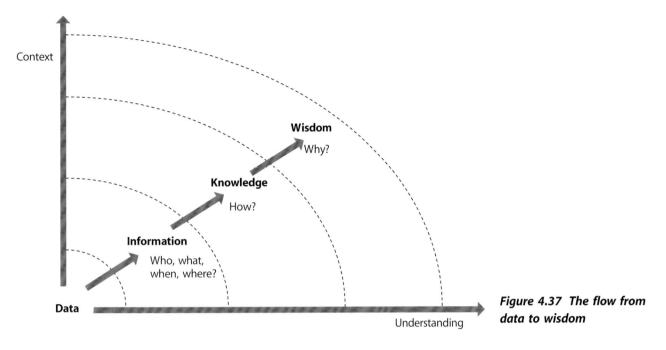

Figure 4.37 The flow from data to wisdom

This is shown in Figure 4.37.

4.7.4.2 The service knowledge management system

Specifically within IT Service Management, Knowledge Management will be focused within the Service Knowledge Management System (SKMS) concerned, as its name implies, with knowledge. Underpinning this knowledge will be a considerable quantity of data, which will be held in a central logical repository or Configuration Management System (CMS) and Configuration Management Database (CMDB). However, clearly the SKMS is a broader concept that covers a much wider base of knowledge, for example:

■ The experience of staff
■ Records of peripheral matters, e.g. weather, user numbers and behaviour, organization's performance figures
■ Suppliers' and partners' requirements, abilities and expectations
■ Typical and anticipated user skill levels.

Figure 4.38 is a very simplified illustration of the relationship of the three levels, with data being gathered within the CMDB, and feeding through the CMS into the SKMS and supporting the informed decision making process.

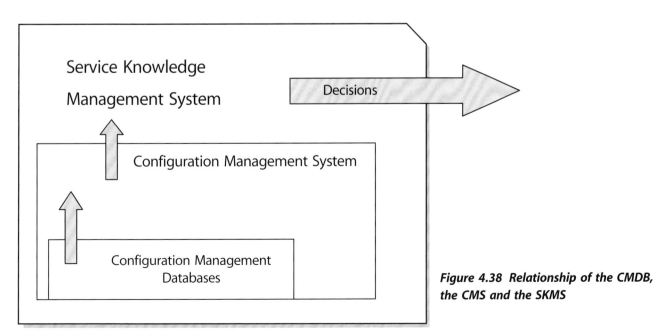

Figure 4.38 Relationship of the CMDB, the CMS and the SKMS

4.7.5 Process activities, methods and techniques

4.7.5.1 Knowledge Management strategy

An overall strategy for Knowledge Management is required. Where there is an organizational approach to Knowledge Management, initiatives within Service Transition, IT Service Management or other groupings should be designed to fit within the overall organizational approach.

In the absence of an organizational Knowledge Management approach, appropriate steps to establish Knowledge Management within Service Transition or within IT Service Management will be required. But even in this case developments should always be established with a view to as wide as practicable a span of Knowledge Management – covering direct IT staff, users, third party support and others likely to contribute or make beneficial use of the knowledge.

The strategy – either in place in the wider organization or being developed – will address:

- The governance model
- Organizational changes underway and planned and consequential changes in roles and responsibilities
- Establishing roles and responsibilities and ongoing funding
- Policies, processes, procedures and methods for Knowledge Management
- Technology and other resource requirements
- Performance measures.

Knowledge identification capture and maintenance

Specifically the strategy will identify and plan for the capture of relevant knowledge and the consequential information and data that will support it. The steps to delivering this include:

- Assisting an organization to identify knowledge that will be useful
- Designing a systematic process for organizing, distilling, storing and presenting information in a way that improves people's comprehension in a relevant area
- Accumulating knowledge through processes and workflow
- Generating new knowledge
- Accessing valuable knowledge from outside sources
- Capturing external knowledge and adapting it – data, information and knowledge from diverse sources such as databases, websites, employees, suppliers and partners.

4.7.5.2 Knowledge transfer

During the service lifecycle an organization needs to focus on retrieving, sharing and utilizing their knowledge through problem solving, dynamic learning, strategic planning and decision making. To achieve this, knowledge needs to be transferred to other parts of the organization at specific points in the lifecycle. Many of the Service Management processes will link into this, for example allowing the service desk to have optimum knowledge and understanding at the point for any Service Transition into support. They will be reliant on information sourced from release management such as known errors going into production but which are not show stoppers for the release schedule, or known error scripts from any of the technical support teams. Links with HR, facilities and other supporting services need to be established, maintained and utilized.

The challenge is often the practical problem of getting a knowledge package from one part of the organization to other parts of the organization. It is more than just sending an e-mail! Knowledge transfer is more complex; more accurately it is the activity through which one unit (e.g. a group, department or division) is affected by the experience of another. Its form must be applicable for those using it, and achieve a positive rating of 'ease of use'. The transfer of knowledge can be observed through changes in the knowledge or performance of recipients, at an individual or unit level.

An analysis of the knowledge gap (if any) within the organization should be undertaken. The gap will need to be researched and established by direct investigation of staff's understanding of the knowledge requirements for them to deliver their responsibilities compared with their actual observed knowledge. This can be a difficult task to deliver objectively and, rather than risk resentment or suspicion, it is often worth seeking skilled and experienced support to build this. The output from the knowledge gap exercise will form the basis for a communications improvement plan which will enable planning and measurement of success in communication of knowledge.

Traditionally knowledge transfer has been based on formal classroom training and documentation. In many cases the initial training is provided to a representative from a work group who is then required to cascade the knowledge to their working colleagues. Other techniques are often appropriate and form useful tools in the Service Transition armoury. Techniques worth considering include the following.

Learning styles

Different people learn in different ways, and the best method of transferring and maintaining knowledge within the Service Management and user community will need to be established. Learning styles vary with age, culture, attitude and personality. IT staff can be usefully reminded, especially where they are supporting users in a different working style, e.g. graphics design, performers, sales teams, that merely because a knowledge transfer mechanism works for them, it may not be appropriate for their current user base.

For many some element of 'hands-on' experience is a positive support for learning, and simulation exercises can be a useful consideration, or supervised experience and experimentation.

Knowledge visualization

This aims to improve the transfer of knowledge by using computer and non-computer-based visuals such as diagrams, images, photographs and storyboards. It focuses on the transfer of knowledge between people and aims to transfer insights, experiences, attitudes, values, expectations, perspectives, opinions and predictions by using various complementary visualizations. Dynamic forms of visualization such as educational animation have the potential to enhance understandings of systems that change over time. For example this can be particularly useful during a hardware refresh when the location of a component may change on an item, although the functionality does not alter.

Driving behaviour

Knowledge transfer aims to ensure that staff are able to decide on the correct actions to deliver their tasks in any foreseeable circumstances. For predictable and consistent tasks, the procedure can be incorporated within software tools that the staff use within those tasks. These procedures then drive behaviour in the accepted way. Change process models (see Figure 4.2) and service desk scripts are excellent examples. This includes the ability to recognize when the laid down practices are or might be inappropriate, e.g. in unexpected circumstances, when staff will either move away from the laid down rules when they do not deliver as required or else will escalate the situation.

Seminars, Webinars and advertising

Formally launching a new or changed service can create an 'event' that enhances the transfer of knowledge. Technology-based events such as Webinars offer the ability to deliver a high profile knowledge delivery mechanism with the ability to retain it online and deliver

it subsequently to other locations and new staff. Internet and intranet portals can deliver equivalent messages in an ongoing fashion and allow discussion forums to question and develop knowledge.

Journals and newsletters

Regular communicating channels, once established, are useful in allowing knowledge to be transferred in smaller units – incrementally rather than 'big bang' can be easier to absorb and retain. They also allow for progressive training and adaptation to circumstance and time periods. Crucially these techniques can be made entertaining and targeted at specific groupings.

Aimed at the audience

A stock control system was introduced with staff in the warehouses directly inputting and working with the new system. Initially all documentation was formal and written in semi-technical terms and the staff taught how to use the system via traditional training and coaching. Once the system had settled in a monthly newsletter was planned to keep staff aware of changes, improvements, hints, tips etc. The first versions were, again, formal and addressed the required information only. It quickly became clear that the required knowledge was not in place within the staff. Success followed when the updates evolved into a genuine newsletter – among competitions, holiday snaps, humorous and even satirical articles the required user knowledge was transferred much more successfully. The lesson was that by targeting communications accurately at a known and understood audience, and making the experience pleasant, the required knowledge transfers along with the rest. And as a bonus the staff contributed entertaining articles and hints and tips they had evolved.

4.7.5.3 Data and information management

Knowledge rests on the management of the information and data that underpins it. To be efficient this process requires an understanding of some key process inputs such as how the data and information will be used:

- What knowledge is necessary based on what decisions must be made
- What conditions need to be monitored (changing external and internal circumstances, ranging from end-user demand, legal requirements through to weather forecasts)
- What data is available (what could be captured), as well as rejecting possible data capture as infeasible; this input may trigger justification for expenditure or changes in working practices designed to facilitate the capture of relevant data that would otherwise not be available

- The cost of capturing and maintaining data, and the value that data is likely to bring, bearing in mind the negative impact of data overload on effective knowledge transfer
- Applicable policies, legislation, standards and other requirements
- Intellectual property rights and copyright issues.

Successful data and information management will deliver:

- Conformance with legal and other requirements, e.g. company policy, codes of professional conduct
- Defined forms of data and information in a fashion that is easily usable by the organization
- Data and information that is current, complete and valid
- Data and information disposed of as required
- Data and information to the people who need it when they need it.

Establishing data and information requirements

The following activities should be planned and implemented in accordance with applicable organization policies and procedures with respect to the data and information management process. This plan and design is the responsibility of Service Strategy and Service Design.

Often, data and information is collected with no clear understanding of how it will be used and this can be costly. Efficiency and effectiveness are delivered by establishing the requirements for information. Sensible considerations, within the constraints determined as described above, might include:

- Establishing the designated data and information items, their content and form, together with the reason, e.g. technical, project, organizational, Service Management process, agreement, operations and information; data is costly to collect and often even more expensive to maintain, and so should be collected only when needed
- Encouraging the use of common and uniform content and format requirements to facilitate better and faster understanding of the content and help with consistent management of the data and information resources
- Establishing the requirements for data protection, privacy, security, ownership, agreement restrictions, rights of access, intellectual property and patents with the relevant stakeholder
- Defining who needs access to what data and information as well as when they access it, including the relative importance of it at different times. For example access to payroll information might be

considered more important in the day before payroll is run than at other times of the month
- Considering any changes to the Knowledge Management process through Change Management.

Define the information architecture

In order to make effective use of data, in terms of delivering the required knowledge, a relevant architecture matched to the organizational situation and the knowledge requirements is essential. This in turn rests on:

- Creating and regularly updating a Service Management information model that enables the creation, use and sharing of information that is flexible, timely and cost-effective
- Defining systems that optimize the use of the information while maintaining data and information integrity
- Adopting data classification schemes that are in use across the organization, and if necessary negotiating changes to enable them to deliver within the Service Management area; where such organization-wide (or supply chain or industry sector) schemes do not exist, data classification schemes derived for use within Service Management should be designed with the intention of their being applicable across the organization to facilitate support for future organization-wide Knowledge Management.

An example of a knowledge, information and data architecture is shown in Figure 4.39.

Establishing data and information management procedures

When the requirements and architecture have been set up, data and information management to support Knowledge Management can be established. The key steps required involve setting up mechanisms to:

- Identify the service lifecycle data and information to be collected
- Define the procedure required to maintain the data and information and make it available to those requiring it
- Store and retrieve
- Establish authority and responsibility for all required items of information
- Define and publicize rights, obligations and commitments regarding the retention of, transmission of and access to information and data items based on applicable requirements and protecting its security, integrity and consistency

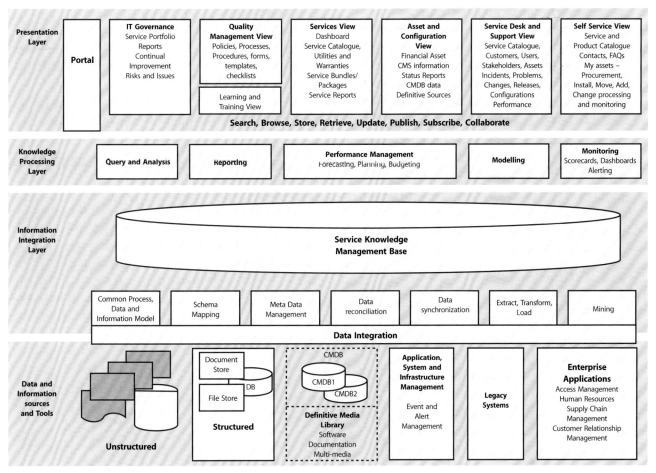

Figure 4.39 Service knowledge management system

- Establish adequate backup and recovery of data and information; this should address reinstating the ability to make constructive use of information, not just the re-establishment of a database
- Identify the requirements to review, in the light of changing technology, organizational requirements, evolving policy and legislation (and if necessary to adapt to) changes in:
  - information system infrastructure in the light of evolving hardware and software technology
  - security, service continuity, storage and capacity
- Deal with collection and retention requirements.

When the procedures are designed, promulgated and accepted the organization can:

- Implement mechanisms to capture, store and retrieve the identified data from the relevant sources
- Manage the data and information storage and movement, especially in line with appropriate legislation.

- Archive designated information, in accordance with the data and information management plan including safely disposing of unwanted, invalid or unverifiable information according to the organization policy.

Evaluation and improvement

As with all processes, the capture and usage of data and information to support Knowledge Management and decision making requires attention to ongoing improvement, and the service improvement plan will take as relevant input:

- Measurement of the use made of the data and information management–data transactions
- Evaluation of the usefulness of the data and information – identified by relevance of reports produced
- Identification of any data or information or registered users that no longer seem relevant to the organization's knowledge requirements.

4.7.5.4 Using the service knowledge management system

Providing services to customers across time zones, work cycles, and geographies requires good knowledge sharing across all locations and time periods of Service Operations. A service provider must first establish a service knowledge management system that can be shared, updated and used by its operating entities, partners, and customers. Figure 4.39 shows an example of the architecture for such a system.

Implementation of a service knowledge management system helps reduce the costs of maintaining and managing the services, both by increasing the efficiency of operational management procedures and by reducing the risks that arise from the lack of proper mechanisms.

All training and knowledge material needs to be aligned to the business perspective. Materials that can be included are:

■ The business language and terminology and how IT terminology is translated
■ The business processes and where IT underpins them
■ Any SLAs, and supporting agreements and contracts that would change as a result of the new Service Transition – this is especially important for the service desk analysts whose target at support transition will be to sustain service; if classifications are accurate this will facilitate the whole process.

For those in the Service Transition process a good way of consolidating understanding is to either spend time in the development areas, taking part in some of the testing processes, or to spend time in the business at the receiving end of the Service Transition to understand the process from the business perspective.

Case study

Current situation An organization analysed that at least 75% of the cost of delivering support comes from resolving customer issues. It was using point technologies such as a service desk workflow tool, search engines, scripting tools or simple knowledge bases. These systems generally focused parts of the resolution process and they were not very effective. This contributed to dissatisfied customers, resulted in an ineffective service desk and caused integration issues for IT.

Solution A comprehensive SKMS was implemented to help to address these obstacles by combining intelligent search and Knowledge Management with Service Management and business process support, authoring workflows and comprehensive self-service facilities.

The SKMS was supported by the problem management and Change Management process.

The experience of end users who come to the website for help was dramatically improved. Instead of an empty search box followed by no results or far too many, the application leads the user through a structured set of steps. Based on the specifics of the incident or request and the customer, web screens will guide users to specific answers, follow-up questions, escalation options, opportunities to drill down or just highly relevant search results. The following improvements were achieved:

■ Increased agent productivity
■ Reduced aversion to web self-service
■ Fewer escalations.

Over time the web workflows were tuned to deliver more and more optimized experiences. Good experiences helped to add value to the product and services and this resulted in greater loyalty that in turn increased profits.

Conclusion A wealth of information exists in most organizations that is not initially thought to contribute to the decision process, but, when used as supplemental to traditional configuration data, can bring the lessons of history into sharp focus. Often this information is in an informal fashion. Marketing, sales, customer and staff information is a commonly overlooked source of valuable trend data that, along with traditional configuration, can paint a larger, more meaningful picture of the landscape and uncover the right 'course corrections' to bring a Service Transition or operational support for a service back on track and keep an organization travelling towards its objectives. Without this clear picture, the effectiveness diminishes and efficiency will decay. By recognizing that this is in place, organizations can more easily justify the resource costs of establishing and maintaining the data, processes, knowledge and skills needed to make it as effective as possible and maximize the benefits.

Useful materials include:

■ Process maps to understand all the integrated activities

■ Any known error logs and the workarounds – again particularly important for the service desk

■ Business and other public calendars.

Technology for service desks and customer service needs to make it easier for customers, users and service desk agents. Some minimal progress has been made with generic Knowledge Management tools and there are significant developments in the Service Management industry to develop mature, process-oriented business applications supported by comprehensive knowledge bases. Examples of potential benefits are:

■ **Agent efficiency** – The largest component of ROI from Knowledge Management is reduced incident handling time and increased agent productivity.

■ **Self-service** – A comprehensive SKMS provides the customer with knowledge directly on the support website. The cost of self-service is an order of magnitude lower than assisted service.

4.7.6 Triggers, inputs and outputs and inter-process interfaces

Crucial to Knowledge Management is the need to ensure that the benefits of Knowledge Management are understood and enthusiastically embraced within the whole organization. Specifically, effective Knowledge Management depends on the committed support and delivery by most, if not all, of those working in and around IT Service Management.

Service Operations

Errors within the service detected during transition will be recorded and analysed and the knowledge about their existence, consequences and workarounds will be made available to Service Operations in an easy to use fashion.

Operations staff

■ Front-line incident management staff, on service desk and second-line support, are the point of capture for much of the everyday IT Service Management data. If these staff do not understand the importance of their role then Knowledge Management will not be effective. Traditionally support analysts have been reluctant to record their actions fully, feeling that this can undermine their position within the organization – allowing issues to be resolved without them. Changing this to an attitude of appreciating the benefits – to individuals and the organization – of widely re-usable

knowledge is the key to successful Knowledge Management.

■ Problem management staff will be key users of collected knowledge and typically responsible for the normalization of data capture by means of developing and maintaining scripts supporting data capture within incident management.

Transition staff

Service Transition staff capture data of relevance through all lifecycle phases and so need to be aware of the importance of collecting it accurately and completely. Service Transition staff capture data and information:

■ Relevant to adaptability and accessibility of the service as designed, to be fed back, via CSI, to Service Design

■ 'Course corrections' and other adaptations to the design required during transition. Awareness and understanding of these will make subsequent transitions easier.

4.7.7 Key performance indicators and metrics

A strong Business Case is critical for effective Knowledge Management and it is important that the measures of success are visible to all levels involved in the implementation.

Typical measures for an IT service provider's contribution are:

■ Successful implementation and early life operation of new and changed services with few knowledge-related errors

■ Increased responsiveness to changing business demands, e.g. higher percentage of queries and question solved via single access to internet/intranet through use of search and index systems such as Google

■ Improved accessibility and management of standards and policies

■ Knowledge dissemination

■ Reduced time and effort required to support and maintain services

■ Reduced time to find information for diagnosis and fixing incidents and problems

■ Reduced dependency on personnel for knowledge.

4.7.7.1 Evaluation and improvement

Although hard to measure the value of knowledge, it is nonetheless important to determine the value to the organization in order to ensure the case for expenditure and support of Knowledge Management is maintainable. The costs associated with Knowledge Management can then be measured and compared against that value.

4.7.7.2 Indicators relevant to business/customers

Knowledge Management is an enabling process and so demonstration of its effectiveness needs to be inferred from indirect measurement. Elements of the service quality that will be positively influenced by good Knowledge Management might include:

■ Reduction in the 'user error' category of errors due to targeted knowledge transfer, coupled with cheaper user training costs

■ Lower incident, problem and error resolution times influenced by better targeted support staff training and by a relevant, maintained and accessible knowledge base containing workarounds

■ Enhanced customer experiences such as:
  ● Quicker resolution of a query
  ● The ability to solve issues directly without external support
  ● Less transfer of issues to other people and resolution at lower staff levels

■ Reduced time for transition and duration of early life support.

Measuring benefit from knowledge transfer

The value of improved knowledge transfer during Service Transition through improved Knowledge Management can be measured via the increased effectiveness of staff using and supporting the new or changed service. This (effectively the steepness of the learning curve) in turn can be measured through:

■ Incidents and lost time categorized as 'lack of user knowledge'

■ Average diagnosis and repair time for faults fixed in-house

■ Incidents related to new or changed services fixed by reference to knowledge base.

Although not every element of the above can be directly attributable to Knowledge Management, the trends in these measures will be influenced by the quality of Knowledge Management, as shown by the example in Figure 4.40.

Clearly, the performance of the support groups post transition will be a determining factor of the quality of the knowledge transfer, typically delivered via training; however, it is more proactive to check understanding before arriving at this point. After each piece of training

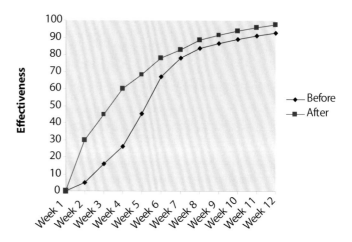

Figure 4.40 Contribution of knowledge to effectiveness of support staff

activity there should be a feedback mechanism to check understanding and quality of delivery. This could be in the form of a post course questionnaire, or even a test to confirm understanding.

4.7.7.3 Measures directly relevant to the service provider

Indications of the effectiveness of the Knowledge Management process itself include:

■ Usage of the knowledge base, measured by:
  ● Number of accesses to the SKMS
  ● Average time taken to find materials

■ Errors reported by staff or detected at audit (none probably means no one was using it)

■ Involvement of staff in discussion/query/answer forums providing support through knowledge sharing and capture of that shared knowledge

■ Degree of re-use of material in documentation such as procedures, test design and service desk scripts

■ Satisfaction with training courses, newsletters, web briefings etc.

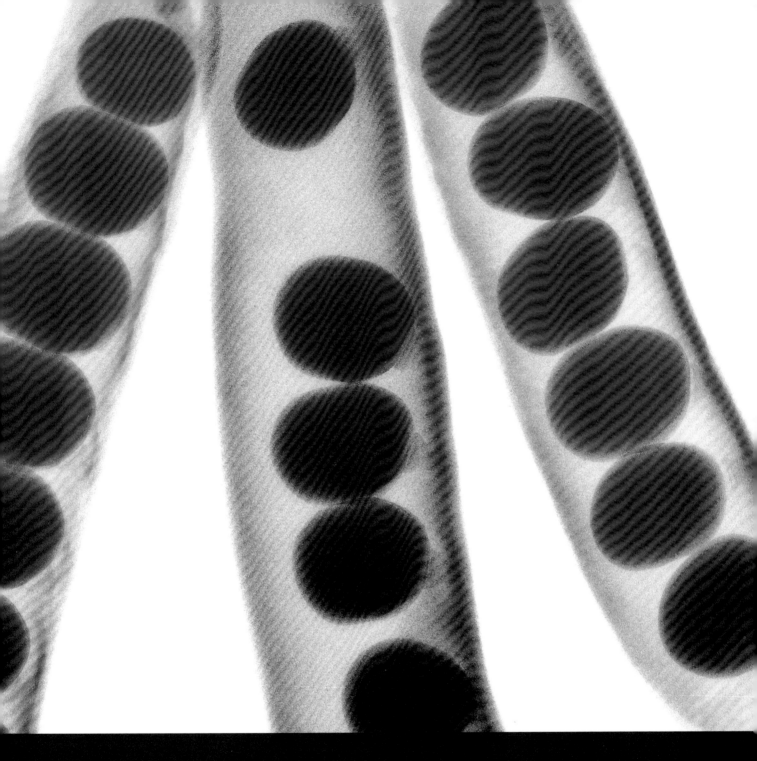

Service Transition common operation activities

5 Service Transition common operation activities

As well as the processes discussed in Chapter 4, Service Transition supports and is supported by other activities. This chapter deals with those elements that are an essential part of, or a strong contributor towards, Service Transition. The chapter addresses two specific activities that are important to Service Transition:

■ **Organizational and stakeholder change** – Reflecting the holistic nature of change that Service Transition must be based on, organizations do not transform their IT service by only changing the IT services. Modern innovations mean that the organization itself will also inevitably change to make use of the new and changed services available.

■ **Communications** – One of the major traditional weaknesses in Service Transition has been the inability to deliver sufficient prompt understanding of the implications, benefits and usage of IT services.

5.1 MANAGING COMMUNICATIONS AND COMMITMENT

Communication is central to any Service Transition change process. The greater the change, the greater the need for clear communication about the reasons and rationale behind it, the benefits expected, the plans for its implementation and its proposed effects. Communications need to be targeted at the right audience and clearly communicate the messages and benefits consistently. If total honesty is not possible, admit this and explain why it is not possible, e.g. for security reasons. Understanding people's commitment is important before planning the communications.

5.1.1 Communications during Service Transition

Typically many people are affected by a service change and consequently sufficient stakeholder buy-in is required to carry the transition forward successfully. It is important to establish an individual's stage within the 'emotional cycle' to understand the method of approach. It is important to identify:

■ Those who are already in support of the transition, and on whom it is not sensible to spend time right now since they do not need conversion; they will be picked up at the 'acceptance' stage

■ Those who are strongly opposed, and who would be unlikely to respond positively to persuasion. It is not constructive to spend time on these people since effort is most likely to be unrewarded at the moment.

The best use of time is to concentrate on those people who are between the two extremes, e.g. stakeholders capable of understanding and welcoming the transition. Although this seems obvious, it is common for people to spend too much time talking to those who are sympathetic to an idea, since this is easier and delivers the positive feedback that people tend to require to feed their confidence and job satisfaction. At this stage the Service Transition team needs to be intuitive to its audience.

The Service Transition team will soon become familiar with the need to change attitudes and the operation of converting culture. For them it is a routine task, holding no threat. It can be hard to remember that, for those affected by the change, it is not a usual situation and they will be worried and a shared understanding will help greatly.

> **Example: Emergency room syndrome**
> A hospital doctor, working in the emergency room will be used to seeing typical patients presenting typical symptoms. Thus, at 3 a.m., the doctor, possibly after very long hours and while grabbing some well-deserved rest, is called to see a patient who is, in their mind, just yet another middle-aged man with severe chest pains. Although routine and unexciting to the doctor, nonetheless a good doctor will remember that it is the first time this particular man has nearly died from a heart attack. The doctor will not let their familiarity with the situation and their lack of enthusiasm be evident. Instead, they will match their manner to that of the patient and treat the situation with the urgency and importance the customer expects.

It is important the Service Transition team members are capable of understanding the impact of their work on others, and therefore tailoring their own approach to the stakeholder audience. Ultimately, the Service Transition team's goal is to build enthusiasm and commitment to the change, while ensuring that all stakeholders are clear about how the changes will impact themselves, and what will be expected of them in the coming months. Clear two-way communication channels will help employees feel their feedback and ideas are valued.

Stakeholder management can consume significant amounts of labour, with up to 50% of staff effort often consumed by this task during significant organizational change periods.

5.1.2 Communication planning

After establishing the strategies that will promote positive change enablers, and having understood the level of commitment within the organization, Service Transition must ensure that there is a detailed communications plan that will target information where it will be most effective.

When announcing information during a Service Transition change, the following considerations should be made for each statement you need to communicate:

■ How should the information be delivered? All at once or divided into segments and released over a period of time? If it is going to be released in segments, then what are the components and what is the sequence of timing for the communication message delivery?

■ How should the information be delivered? (See paragraph 4.7.5.2.) What tone and style should the message be conveyed in – upbeat, cautious, optimistic?

■ What actions could be taken before the communication that will increase the understanding and the acceptance of the information given?

■ How and when will groups be involved during the cascading of the communication information to other levels in the organization?

■ Are the communications successful in overcoming the particular communication barriers on this Service Transition (e.g. cultural differences, the added structure of large teams, the additional requirements associated with geographically dispersed personnel)?

■ Is there consideration to address the communication needs of other stakeholders in the project (e.g. decision makers, opinion leaders, system users, internal and external regulatory bodies, and any other persons impacted by the implementation of the new Service Transition)?

Figure 5.1 shows an overview of the key elements for consideration when planning for effective communication.

To ensure that a communication strategy is effective, surveys and measures should be determined for regular monitoring. This will take the form of feedback from those people that have had any communication. It should also include how people are feeling on their 'change cycle' to establish that the target is right. At this point there may

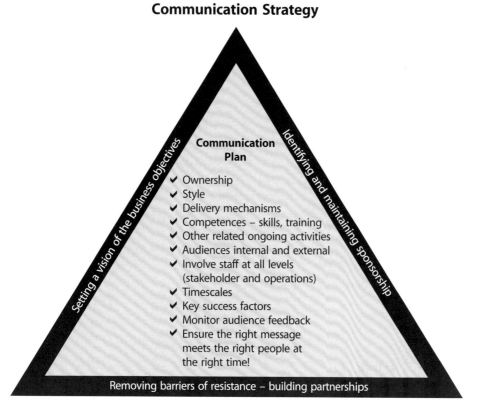

Communication Strategy

Setting a vision of the business objectives

Identifying and maintaining sponsorship

Communication Plan

✔ Ownership
✔ Style
✔ Delivery mechanisms
✔ Competences – skills, training
✔ Other related ongoing activities
✔ Audiences internal and external
✔ Involve staff at all levels (stakeholder and operations)
✔ Timescales
✔ Key success factors
✔ Monitor audience feedback
✔ Ensure the right message meets the right people at the right time!

Removing barriers of resistance – building partnerships

Figure 5.1 Example of communications strategy and plan contents

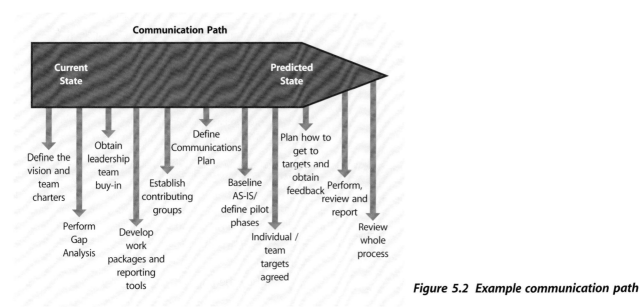

Figure 5.2 Example communication path

be individuals that are identified that should have more personal contact from the Service Transition Team in order for them to achieve an acceptable state.

To obtain an appreciation of the sequence of events, a communication path diagram such as the one shown in Figure 5.2 helps the planning of the communication process.

5.1.3 Methods of communication

Using multiple communication means will help understanding of the overall message. Common media types include:

- Large workshops – to deliver a clear and consistent message to the target audience on the overall Service Transition approach; this will generally be at the start of any communication strategy in order to build understanding, ownership and even excitement across the teams

- Organization newsletter – to reinforce any messages already delivered; however, care needs to be taken that this approach is used as reinforcement rather than as the first time that employees may have seen the communication cascade

- Training sessions – as part of the Service Transition, roles or processes will be likely to change; this requires targeted training, which should be planned giving sufficient time for employees to get to grips with any new ways of working

- Team meetings – giving support to team leaders from the Service Transition team, who will ensure at their own weekly meetings that they can reinforce any messages; it is at this lower level meeting that the

questions that employees have may be better understood, as people will feel within their own comfort zone as they are used to this method of communication with colleagues they work with daily

- Face to face – key stakeholders to make time to visit staff in their work environment (floor walks), to set a positive example of the support by senior management, and allow employees to ask questions pertinent to themselves

- Q&A feedback postings – boards or mail boxes where employees can raise anonymous questions and receive feedback on any concerns they may have

- Corporate intranet

- Reinforcement memos – consistent memos from the senior stakeholder reinforcing key information, or giving an update on the implementation activities, will keep the Service Transition alive for those people not perhaps actually involved at all stages

- Posters/roadmaps – good-quality colourful communications at the end of office floors showing implementation activities, progress or general updates; these are a positive way of keeping communications alive and delivering a consistent message

- Pay advice notes – key communication attached to payslips to ensure a practical 100% communication update

- 'Z-cards'/encapsulated reference cards – small credit-card-sized documents holding key information and expected to be carried by staff in their wallets or purses.

Example: The service desk

It is important to understand the dynamics of the service desk operation. Generally this group of staff will be doing shift working, with hours covering early mornings, evenings and weekends. They also tend to be one of the largest groups within the support operation, so it is particularly important that they get a consistent message during communication about the change. Some of the communication means that would be appropriate for this audience could be as follows.

Taking selected key people from the service desk such as the shift leaders, and team leaders to hear the large workshop brief. This will ensure that a large enough group have heard the full brief, and they will then be in a position to debrief their smaller teams. Members of the Service Transition team could then attend the individual team meetings to support the team leader as they conduct the debrief, and answer any questions. Using reinforcement memos, this ensures that the service desk staff feel that they are being communicated to by the senior stakeholder rather than being left out. It will also help at the point that they are about to take over any support from the Service Transition changes. This is also a cost-effective means of keeping a large group of people up to date and engaged in the process.

Models help to communicate what people should expect for each service or each type of change. Figure 5.3 is an example of a change model used to transition services from an organization to a commercial service provider. This is an example of a total organizational change where there will be changes in management, processes and staffing, although many staff may transfer into the new service provider organization. Having access to a set of service, change and transition models in a form that is easy to communicate will help to set expectations during the Service Transition.

5.1.4 Motivation and the importance of communication

People need to be kept up to date with the progress of change, good or bad, if they are to be motivated to make it happen. Hackman and Oldham (1980) described the state of affairs when people try to do well, because they find the work satisfying, as internal motivation. The concept is defined in Table 5.1.

People will be mobilized and engaged if they can see progress. Short-term wins should be communicated and progress celebrated.

Service Transition

Plan Service Transition	Perform (Do)	Review (Check)	Close (Act)
❏ Business Case ❏ Service Transition Statement of Work ❏ Service Management plan ❏ Organisation models ❏ Service Transition team charters ❏ Management Sponsors ❏ Team and skill assessment ❏ Change Management process initiated ❏ Profile and awareness assessment on cultural values ❏ Joint verification plan ❏ Communications plan ❏ Reviewed legal / contract / commercial bases ❏ Risk management strategy	❏ Perform Service Transition Kick Off ❏ Initiate Communications Plan ❏ Initiate Service Transition processes and work flow ❏ Initiate Supplier / Partner activity and reporting ❏ Manage customer relationships ❏ Initiate legal / contract management ❏ Assess, review and manage risks ❏ Establish quality management checks for all processes during service transition	❏ Evaluate quality and act upon discrepancies ❏ Perform regular customer and team reviews involved in service transition ❏ Refine service transition processes and solutions based on SLAs etc and communicate ❏ Maintain the management of change in all areas ❏ Test escalation processes ❏ Ensure transition is within scope and cost models ❏ Maintain risk management throughout	❏ Review organizational and cultural changes ❏ Validate SLAs are met ❏ Perform customer and team reviews for feedback and lessons learnt ❏ Produce post-implementation review report for change management ❏ Sign off contract and cost models ❏ Obtain business sign off for Service Transition ❏ Define plan for ongoing Continual Service Improvement

Figure 5.3 Example of Service Transition steps for outsourcing

Table 5.1 Job characteristics that motivate people

The essential characteristics of the job	What the worker gets from them	The result if all these job characteristics are present
Feedback from the job	Knowledge of the actual results of work activities	High internal work motivation
Autonomy	Experienced responsibility for outcomes of work	
Skill variety Task identity Task significance	Experienced meaningfulness of the work	

5.2 MANAGING ORGANIZATION AND STAKEHOLDER CHANGE

Service Transition's basic role is, on the basis of agreed design, to implement a new or changed service, effectively making the organization different than it was before. For a change of any significance, this is delivering an organizational change, ranging from moving a few staff to work from new premises through to major alterations in the nature of business working, e.g. from face-to-face retail to web-based trading.

Change is an inevitable and important part of organizational development and growth. Change can occur in incremental phases or suddenly, affecting some or all of an organization, its people and its culture. Without change, progress does not happen.

Organizational change efforts fail or fall short of their goals because changes and transitions are not led, managed and monitored efficiently across the organization and throughout the change process. These gaps in key organizational activities often result in resistance, dissatisfaction and increased costs. Change is never easy; it usually takes longer than planned and creates barriers and resistance along the way. Effective leaders and managers understand the change process and plan and lead accordingly. Major negative impact can come from losing staff – disillusioned people leaving – which brings risks to the organization, e.g. loss of knowledge and lack of handover.

This section provides more detail about the involvement of Service Transition in managing organizational change. It includes assurance of the organization change products from Service Design, stakeholder management and communications and approaches to cope with change during transition.

5.2.1 The emotional cycle of change

What creates confusion and chaos in organizations more than change not managed well or not managed at all? Research shows that many change efforts fail, fall short of their goals or result in organizational dissatisfaction and inefficiency.

The research on Change Management strongly suggests that without the support of people, change will not happen. Business managers and change agents must understand the emotional impact that change has on people and how to manage it accordingly. Much research has been done on the emotional impact of change.

What this means is that failure to consider organizational change and how it affects people is a significant factor in causing transitions to fail. In order to facilitate the acceptance of change, it is important to understand the 'emotional stages' that a person needs to get through before acceptance. This is illustrated in Figure 5.4.

For all significant changes, individuals will go through this process. At first they enter into a degree of shock, before going into avoidance. This will often manifest itself in increased efficiency while the situation is denied. This is usually a rapid stage, at which point performance drops as people choose to 'shoot the messenger' and blame the change initiators and Service Transition team, followed by self-blame as insecurity and the threat of the situation is felt. Performance is now at its lowest. It follows that the quicker the Service Transition team can get individuals through the cycle, the shorter the timescales before acceptance and optimum performance. One can use the experience of those within the affected area to understand concerns, and the nature of resistance in order to communicate at the appropriate stages. This may often take considerable personal time of the Service Transition team, to listen to people's concerns, but ultimately will get individuals engaged and performing in as short a time as possible.

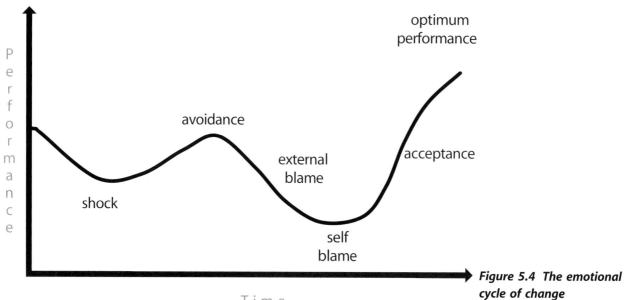

Figure 5.4 The emotional cycle of change

Appropriate communication through these stages of transition will drive the energy of individuals from low to high, obtaining involvement and generating a more positive attitude as the change takes place. As emphasized, this is a pattern followed by individuals, and different people will pass through these typical phases at different speeds, so understanding where individuals are on this curve and supporting and progressing them can be a significant resource commitment for Service Transition.

5.2.1.1 Effective management of change

There are five important ingredients of change: necessity, vision, plan, resources and competence. They are discussed separately in this chapter. If there is no necessity established, there is lot of resistance from the people; if there is no vision, there is confusion among the employees; if there is no plan, there is chaos in the activities and transition; if there are no/fewer resources, there is a frustration among the employees; and if there is no competence, there is a fear of failure among the employees. Therefore it is extremely important to pay adequate attention and establish management commitment to take adequate care of these requirements of the change.

5.2.2 Organization, roles and responsibilities

Managing change and transition is the responsibility of the managers and Executives involved in that change. They must have an awareness that change has to be managed, that people have to be communicated with openly and honestly and that resistance has to be sought out, listened to and responded to appropriately. This is especially the case if a change is on a scale that is significant enough to affect the organization as a whole. The Management Board and Executive must ensure that there are adequate connections and controls throughout the organization to alert them to any barriers and to facilitate the transition to its goal.

A clear, strategic vision coming from the Management Board and/or Executive is imperative to drive and maintain the change.

5.2.3 Service Transition's role in organizational change

Organizational change is always a challenge. Factors that drive successful change initiatives at the organization level include:

■ Leadership for the change
■ Organization adoption
■ Governance process
■ Organization capabilities
■ Business and service performance measures
■ A strong communication process with regular opportunity for staff feedback.

Although Service Transition is not accountable for the overall management of business and technical change the Service Transition process owner or manager is a key stakeholder and needs to be proactive in reporting issues and risks to the change leaders, e.g. when the volume of changes may impact Service Operation's ability to keep the services running.

Organizational adoption is a subset of Change Management practice. It typically happens at two levels: individual and organizational. It is important to understand the culture of the organizations and the people involved. This will often be quite diverse across different cultures, business units, geographies and including:

■ Business culture – this may be different depending on the industry, geography, etc.
■ Culture of customer organization(s)
■ Culture of service provider/IT organization
■ Culture of supplier organization(s)
■ Individual personalities, especially of senior managers and change champions.

Cultural and organization assessment and change design are the responsibility of strategy and design. However, most significant Service Transitions will have an effect on working practices and so require a change in the behaviour and attitudes of many teams and stakeholder groups. Understanding the organizational change elements of a transition is therefore vital. The assessment of the likely risks and success is an important element of the transition as a whole. Service Transition will be involved early in the lifecycle to ensure that these aspects are assessed and incorporated into the design and build of the organizational change.

Service Transition must be actively involved in changing the mindsets of people across the lifecycle to ensure they are ready to play their role in Service Transition. These people will include:

■ Service Transition staff
■ Customers
■ Users
■ Service Operations staff
■ Suppliers
■ Key stakeholders.

Service Transition will focus on simple messages at any one time to ensure there is consistency in the implementation of the changes. For example, Service Transition would be interested in helping people to:

■ Understand the need for knowledge and effective knowledge transfer
■ Understand the importance of making decisions at the right speed/within the appropriate time
■ Understand the need to complete and review configuration baselines in a timely manner
■ Apply more effective risk assessment and management methods for Service Transition

■ Follow the deadlines for submitting changes and releases.

Service Design will perform the assessment of the capability and capacity of the IT organization to transition the new or changed services. Service Transition has a quality assurance role to check that the organization and stakeholders are ready for the change and it will raise any issues and risks related to organizational change that are identified, e.g. during testing, pilots, deployment and early life support.

Service Transition is also responsible for ensuring that the organizational change happens according to the plans, that the change is still relevant in current circumstances and that the organizational change delivers the predicted organization, capabilities and resources. This will involve checking that changes are being adopted, e.g. that a critical mass of customers, users and Service Operations staff accept the change and make a personal commitment to implementing it. Anecdotal evidence suggests that once a 'critical mass' of around 70% of affected people have accepted the change into their normal way of working the change can safely be held as established behaviour. If the adoption rate is lower then a significant chance exists that an organization might revert to the 'old ways'. The actual figure will be greatly influence by the degree of staff involvement with a particular change, e.g. a few key staff can deliver a disproportionately major influence for acceptance or rejection.

Achieving successful Service Transition requires organized, competent and well-motivated people to build, test, deploy and operate the service. Successful Service Transitions rely on changing the organization and people and it is important to focus on such aspects as competency assessment and development, recruiting, skills development, knowledge transfer, team building, process improvements and resource deployment. If there is a gap in capability then Service Transition will provide input into the relevant party, e.g. project management, Service Design, Continual Service Improvement.

5.2.3.1 Understanding the organizational culture

For successful Service Transition, an organization needs to determine the underlying values and drivers that enable effective management of change. Each organization and combination of organizations is different so the Service Transition approach to change is determined, in part, by the culture and so may vary across the organization.

Organizational culture is the whole of the ideas, corporate values, beliefs, practices, and expectations about behaviour and daily customs that are shared by the employees in an organization. Culture can support an implementation or it can be the source of resistance.

When performing Service Transition activities it is important to gain an understanding of the type of culture currently existing in the organization and how this is likely to be affected by any proposed changes. Conversely, it is equally important to understand the effect current culture may have as a 'barrier' to realizing change. Examples of key questions to be posed to help identify culture are shown in Table 5.2. These questions are useful when reviewing the Service Strategy and Service Design deliverables.

5.2.4 Strategy and design for managing organizational change

As discussed in the Service Strategy publication, an organization's age and size affect its structure.

During a Service Transition, changes in roles, processes and relationships must be made or problems will arise. Understanding the different phases of development of the stakeholder organizations helps Service Transition manage the stakeholders and users better.

Table 5.2 Understanding the culture of the parties involved

Cultural aspect	Question
Language	Is there a common language or shared language(s)? Does the language inhibit and reinforce boundaries or facilitate effective change and knowledge transfer? Is the organizational language style mostly formal or informal?
Change	Does the organization appear to resist change or is it constantly evolving?
Communication	What are the preferred modes of communication? What is the content and style of internal communications? Where does official and unofficial communication happen? Are communication channels open and democratic or closed and hierarchical? How is knowledge and experience shared? Are rumours/gossip prevalent?
Knowledge flow	How do people describe the way knowledge and information is transferred around the organization? How easy is it to find what you need to know, when you need it? How easy is it to find the right person with the right experience?
Communities	Are there identifiable 'communities' within the organization? Is there a community leader, e.g. problem management community leader? What is the structure and function of these communities?
Networks	Are an individual's networks well developed, on the whole? What kind of information is exchanged by these people?
Working environment	Does the working environment create the right conditions for knowledge transfer and integrated working, e.g. close proximity physically and/or electronic tools? How are desks configured? How are communal areas used?
History	How does the organization see its own history? Is it valued and used or quickly forgotten? How does the organization value past experiences, e.g. do people still refer back to their old company after a merger?
Meetings	Are meetings seen as productive? How are they managed? Are they effective? Does everyone feel safe to speak? How is opinion or criticism handled? How is output captured or taken forward?
Rewards and motivations	How are individuals/teams rewarded or recognized for sharing knowledge/information and experience? What motivates people in the organization? What else might be blocking engagement of an individual/team, e.g. other major change, major incident handling?
Time	What are individuals', teams' and the organizational attitudes to time, e.g. busy or relaxed; punctual, rigid and unchanging or flexible?

5.2.5 Planning and implementing organizational change

Often plans and designs for managing change are not balanced and the organization and people side of change are omitted (one well-known illustration of this is the McKinsey 7S model). Within IT departments Project Managers often focus on the technical activities rather than the changes required for the organization or individuals. It is important that Project Plans are reviewed to ensure that the organizational change activities are included.

In order to manage organization change it is important that the stakeholders and teams understand what is required and can answer these questions:

- What are the business and organizational strategic drivers, personalities and policy changes?
- What problems does the proposed change solve?
- What will the new or changed service deliver?
- What does the new or changed service look like?
- How do current objectives need to be modified?
- What are the objectives of the change as defined by management, and how will success be judged throughout the levels of the organization?
- What are the processes, templates, decision points and systems to be used and what level of reporting data is required for the decisions to be made?
- Who will be involved and who previously involved will no longer be?
- Who will be affected within and outside the organization?
- What are the constraints – type, range and flexibility – time slots, equipment, staff and supplier availability?
- What is the planned timescale?
- Who or what can help in planning the implementation?
- What skills and measures should be considered?
- How will 'normal' life be affected?
- What will the consequential changes be, e.g. to business methods?

As part of quality assurance and implementation, the stakeholders and IT teams can be sampled to understand and clarify their expectations about these aspects.

5.2.6 Organizational change products

The change in the organization from the current state to a new state can require a combination of elements to be changed in order to fully realize the organization transformation. The required service is defined in the Service Design package. The following work-products are typical outputs from Service Strategy and Service Design that assist with managing organizational change during Service Transition:

- Stakeholder map
- Current organization and capability assessment
- Current and required competency model and competency assessments
- Constraints (including organization, capability, resources)
- Service Management process model
- Policies, processes and procedures
- Roles and responsibility definitions, e.g. a RACI (Responsible, Accountable, Consulted, Informed) matrix
- Relationship management
- Communication Plan
- Supplier framework, especially where multiple suppliers are involved.

An example of a RACI matrix for managing change during the service lifecycle that supports Service Transition activities is shown in Table 5.3. In many instances on the chart the 'R' for responsibility appears in more than one column. This is indicative of the hierarchical nature of the responsibility, with strategic, tactical and operational responsibilities being required and thus spreading across more than a single column. In these instances the left-hand occurrences are more managerial, the ones to the right focusing on delivery.

Service Transition will check that organizational change products and services are fit for purpose. For large-scale changes, such as mergers and acquisitions and outsourcing, this will include validation of the approach to:

- Career development – Are succession plans being built? Do individuals have an understanding of their progression prospects?
- Performance evaluation at organization, team and individual level – Are regular reviews conducted? Is the documentation formal, and is there demonstration of a consistent approach?

Table 5.3 Example of RACI matrix for managing change

Role Responsibility	Change sponsor, e.g. business and IT leaders	Change enabler, e.g. process owners, service owners	Change agent, e.g. team leader instructing change	Change target, e.g. individual performing the change
Articulate a vision for the business and service change in their domain	A/R	A/R	C	I
Recognize and handle resistance to change	A/R	A	A	C
Initiate change, understand the levers for change and the obstacles	A/R	A/R	C	C
Manage change and input to change plan	A/R	A/R	C	C
Input to design of target organization or structure, etc.	A/R	A/R	C	
Set up a system for communicating change	A/R	A/R	C	
Steer change	A/R	A	A	C
Mobilize the organization	A/R	C	C	C
Mobilize their department, unit, team	A/R	A/R	C	
Lead workshops and group analysis of the current processes	A/R	A/R		
Run effective meetings	A/R	A/R	A/R	A/R
Solve problems in groups	A/R	A/R	A/R	

- Rewards and compensation – Is there a net benefit to people affected by the change?
- Recruitment and selection – Where there is any shortfall in any roles required, is there a fair and consistent process to selection, including the process of internal movement as well as selection from the external market?

Typical work-products that the Service Transition team depends on are shown in Table 5.4.

Table 5.4 Example of organization work-products from the build stage

Organization model
New or changed organizational structure
Career development structure
Reward and compensation structure
Performance evaluation structure
Performance measurement structure
Competency model detailed design
Competency list
Competency/activity matrix
Target job, role, staffing and competence requirements matrix
Job definition and design
Role definitions and descriptions
Staffing plan
Individual
Individual assessment
Competency assessment (including role and skill assessment)
Performance assessment
Performance enhancement needs assessment
Learning needs assessment
Education and training
Learning approach
Learning test approach
Performance enhancement design
Learning definition and design
Course definition
Performance enhancement support design
Performance enhancement support plan

Table 5.5 Organizational role and skills assessment checklist

Check	Evidence
Is there an assessment of the number of staff required and their current skill levels?	Plan
Is there a documented vision/strategy to address any risks in each area (e.g. resource shortfalls – start hiring actions, sub-contract or outsource the whole area)?	Vision/strategy
Have the generic roles and interactions throughout the Service Transition been reviewed?	Roles and responsibilities interaction matrix
Are the specific roles and measures defined?	Performance measures by role
Have the skills for each area, i.e. content, application, technical and business, been defined?	Skills requirements for each area
Is there an assessment of the organization's personnel against the requirements?	Assessment report
Have personnel from areas in the organization other than the areas covered by the Service Transition been considered?	Assessment report
Have the requirements for both development and maintenance that support the business needs been considered?	Requirements
Has the level of risk that relates to the support available for certain areas been documented? Also the areas that cannot be supported and the assumptions that apply to the analysis?	Risk assessment report

5.2.7 Assessing organizational readiness for change

The checklist presented in Table 5.5 can be used to assess the role and skill requirements during Service Transition.

5.2.8 Monitoring progress of organizational change

To enable a Service Transition programme to be effective and successful, regular checks/surveys should be performed throughout many different levels of the organization. Table 5.6 shows a feedback survey that could be used on both the individual and teams involved.

Table 5.6 Example of a feedback survey

Aspect	Response
Service Transition meetings are properly managed and run effectively.	
I have a clear idea of what is expected of me during this Service Transition.	
I am confident that I can successfully accomplish the assigned Service Transition work.	
My manager encourages me to exchange ideas about how to work better and/or improve the current processes.	
My manager is willing to listen to my concerns and ideas and pursue them on my behalf.	
The Service Transition communication methods, frequency and content meet my needs.	
The atmosphere during the Service Transition is friendly and helpful and open.	
There is sufficient effort being made to get and evaluate the opinions and thinking of all members of the Service Transition team.	
I clearly understand the operational needs of this Service Transition.	
The work that I am responsible for will meet the Service Transition and operational needs of the business users.	
The job requirements allow me to balance my workload and personal life.	
I believe real actions and Service Transition management consideration will result from my feedback captured from surveys.	

The results of any survey should be useful in determining the progress made through Service Transition. This will include the status of employee commitment and any areas for improvement. This will also serve as a useful tool at various milestones within the transition journey. Employees will feel that their opinions count at a critical time as they go into the Service Transition programme. This is where positive engagement of the new processes can be increased by 'taking the majority with you'.

Monitoring is, of course, only the first part of a series of actions. The responses obtained must be analysed and understood. Where required, issues should be addressed and fixed as soon as possible. Respondents to the survey must be kept informed of changes that result from their feedback. Only in this way can staff have confidence that their feedback matters and achieves improvements.

Often improvements will be identified in the post implementation review of the service change and can feed into Continual Service Improvement.

5.2.9 Dealing with the organization and people in sourcing changes

A change in sourcing of IT services is one of the most significant, and often most traumatic, kinds of organizational change. Several different impacts and effects on staff will need to be considered, planned and prepared for.

Employee shock

One of the biggest changes that will be caused by sourcing is 'employee shock'. As described in the retained organization section, many staff functions will evolve into more generic concerns such as project management and negotiation management. There will also be a morale issue caused by transition of staff replaced by the sourcing function. These perceptions need to be addressed early on, at the beginning of the initiative, so that the employees are completely aware of what is about to happen. Lack of communication and secretive behaviour only promotes suspicion and can lead to negative and disruptive attitudes. Sourcing is best done in an open atmosphere where all the options are clear and identified.

Business change

Another major change is the way business is conducted. Sharing 'everything' with a sourcing vendor may lead to distrust if it is not presented in the correct terms. Care must be taken to ensure that information is passed to the sourcing vendor on a 'need to know' basis. This will keep the relationship professional.

Location change

The location of the sourcing can also present issues and risks during Service Transition. Typical sourcing locations are presented below and each represents a difference from where the service was provided before sourcing:

- Local sourcing exists in the same geographical area
- Global (multi-shore) sourcing chooses the best solution non-dependent on geographical location
- Near-shore sourcing borders the client location offering same language, time zones and culture
- Off-shore sourcing is located in one specific geographical location
- Combinations are becoming common with different functions, or aspects of functions, delivered in different fashions, e.g. 9–5 service desk delivered locally but out-of-hours service supported from off-shore.

The cultural and organizational issues relating to the change in location need to be addressed for a successful Service Transition.

Linking of sourcing activities throughout the organization

In planning a Service Transition to another organization, the sourcing strategy is mapped across the organization. This is where the budget is tied to the financial group, services are tied to the service delivery group, security considerations are tied to the security group etc.

Each group that is linked to the sourcing initiative must make provisions for interaction with the sourcing vendor so that the sourcing operation will continue to run smoothly. It is important to obtain commitment from key people, and commitment planning techniques can be used (see previous section). The links should be tested during each phase of the transition process to verify that the link is working and providing the correct transaction between the business and the sourcing vendor.

For example, if the business wants to update the security software on the systems that the sourcing vendor is using to run the business's financial information, the security group should have an established contact with the vendor to convey this need.

If the vendor needs to increase the business specific skill level of a new employee, they should have an established contact to the training department of the business and/or specialist experts within the organization.

Every aspect of the sourcing operation as it pertains to the business it supports must be linked to the appropriate area/group within the business. These links need to be identified and established early on or the sourcing relationship will not be efficient and will have many bottlenecks that will affect productivity. Service Transition will need to test these links as early as possible.

5.2.10 Methods, practices and techniques

5.2.10.1 Hints and tips on managing change

There is a tendency for senior Executives to skip the need for organizational change by dictating what behaviours should be done and sacking people to get the message across. Typically it works in the short term, but then falls apart after the key Executive leaves or moves on to something else.

Table 5.7 provides useful advice on the dos and don'ts of managing change.

5.2.10.2 J. P. Kotter's 'Eight steps to transforming your organization'

J. P. Kotter's 'Eight steps to transforming your organization', shown in Table 5.8, is a well-proven approach to managing transformation. This is a useful method to use to identify gaps in plans for managing organizational change.

Table 5.7 Tips for managing change

Do	Don't
■ Establish a baseline and vision	■ Try to micro-manage everything
■ Develop a communication strategy and check that communications are understood	■ Put minor changes through bureaucratic processes
■ Identify impact on other services, processes, systems and people not involved in Service Transition	■ Forget the agreed degree of exposure to risk – in many circumstances the business is taking commercial risks as a deliberate policy, but IT and others stand to undermine the business justifications and policies by trying to remove risk from their component of a business change
■ Identify impact on customers/users and other stakeholders	
■ Be able to articulate and communicate why are we making this change	
■ Identify new skills/knowledge required	■ Focus solely on the IT – all components of a service must be transitioned
■ Consider development requirements and how these requirements will be addressed – training, coaching, mentoring	■ Forget the people
■ Promote the right culture	■ Over-complicate things – they are harder for people to understand
■ Promote organizational discipline	■ Ignore the after effects of failed changes on people
■ Integrate HR support	■ Neglect the costs of transition
■ Put the right people in the right role/job	■ Succumb to inertia – instead re-assess validity and relevance of the service or change
■ Help people to manage stress	■ Pretend that there will be no losers.
■ Encourage people to think that the situation can be improved – it generally can be	
■ Provide easy access to information about the change	
■ Ensure new or changed documentation/instructions are concise and understandable for the target audience.	

Table 5.8. J. P. Kotter's 'Eight steps to transforming your organization'

Leading change: eight Steps	Core challenge	Desired behaviour
1. Establish a sense of urgency	Get people 'out of the bunker' and ready to move.	People start telling each other, 'Let's go, we need to change things!'
2. Create a guiding coalition	Get the right people in place with the trust, emotional commitment and teamwork to guide the difficult change process.	A group powerful enough to guide large changes influences others to accept change, and one that works well together.
3. Develop a vision and strategy	Get the guiding team to create the right vision and strategies to guide action in all of the remaining stages of change. This requires moving beyond number crunching to address the creative and emotional components of vision.	The guiding team develops the right vision and strategy for the change effort.
4. Communicate the change vision (and, communicate it over and over again)	Get as many people as possible acting to make the vision a reality.	People begin to buy in to the change and this shows in their behaviour.
5. Empower broad-based action	Remove key obstacles that stop people from acting on the vision.	More people feel able to act, and do act, on the vision.
6. Create short-term wins	Produce enough short-term (quick) wins fast enough to energize the change helpers, enlighten the pessimists, defuse the cynics and build momentum for the effort	Momentum builds as people try to fulfil the vision, while fewer and fewer resist change.
7. Consolidate gains and produce more change	Continue with wave after wave of change, not stopping until the vision is a reality – no matter how big the obstacles.	People remain energized and motivated to push change forward until the vision is fulfilled – fully realized.
8. Anchor new approaches in the culture	Create a supporting structure that provides roots for the new ways of operating.	New and winning behaviour continues despite the pull of tradition, turnover of change leaders, etc.

Further detail on J. P. Kotter's 'Eight steps to transforming your organization' is described in the Continual Service Improvement publication. These are iterative stages, and at each communication event, people's understanding needs to be checked.

5.2.10.3 Organizational change strategies

Service Transition will be interested in the proposed strategies to manage organizational change. These can be used to assess the approach from Service Design and to manage change during Service Transition and identify issues and risks relating to organizational change.

Kotter and Schlesinger (1979) suggested the following strategies that work well in practice:

■ **Education and commitment** – The sooner managers give people information about the change and the implications for them, the more successful the implementation of change is likely to be. Education and commitment begin in the early planning activities. The discussions generated around the pros and cons of the plan will help to dispel scepticism about the need for change and forge strong alliances that can be used as a change agent.

■ **Participation and involvement** – Allowing people to participate in the change normally overcomes resistance. On its own it is not enough; it must be used in conjunction with a policy of education and commitment, so that people understand the need for change, and effective monitoring and review for managers to be able to assess the impact of change on the Service Transition programme. It is not unusual for people to revert to familiar working practices, even though they support the changes. 'Change fatigue' is a well-recognized concept that can be expected at some stage and should be monitored.

■ **Facilitation and support** – Managers should be ready to respond positively when fears and anxieties about the change are expressed. Talking through the issues and performing a skills gap analysis may be sufficient, but at other times training in the new processes will be necessary, preferably prior to implementation. The manager should constantly promote the benefits of the change, reminding people of the objectives, and communicating a clear vision of what the organization will look like in the future and how employees' contribution is valuable in making that happen. Some expressed resistance can be positive because it shows that the employees are involved and can likely be moved through the cycle (Figure 5.4) to a point of acceptance. Employees who show no visible emotion are the ones who need extra attention to identify the hidden issues and deal with them, otherwise secretive and subversive activities may result.

■ **Negotiation and agreement** – Change is easier to implement if you have agreement; gaining agreement suggests negotiation, so managers should be prepared to negotiate, formally if necessary. The relative cost of gaining agreement should be set against the importance of the change. Service Transition has a major role ensuring such agreement is gained after each service lifecycle stage. Involvement with unions and HR will be needed, especially if negative impact on individuals is expected.

■ **Manipulation and co-option** – It is sometimes necessary to strike deals with those who oppose change, either by making them privy to restricted information or by 'buying-off', i.e. giving them extra rewards (financial or otherwise) to gain their participation. This approach should be used with the caveat that it is likely to cause problems later on. It is often used when the service provider changes and there is a risk to the operational services if key staff with irreplaceable knowledge and experience leave.

■ **Explicit and implicit coercion** – There are occasions when coercion is the appropriate tactic. It will come with associated costs, similar to the directive approach of 'act now explain later'. Coercion may well run counter to the values and beliefs of your organization and, by inference, to individuals working in it. Strong leadership is needed if using this strategy, together with a full knowledge of the situation and the possible problems that will be caused.

Other methods that managers commonly use are:

■ Rewarding desirable behaviour, while at the same time ignoring or discouraging inappropriate behaviour that is detrimental to the Service Transition programme.

■ Treating 'hurting' systems by identifying what it is that the people, whose commitment you need, dislike about the current system and put it right. Managers can do this for individuals or encourage them to identify their own solutions.

■ Exposing the issues in a sensitive manner. People are likely to take a stance against the change if they are made to feel that their worries are insignificant or they are being backed into a corner. Holding an informal, open meeting at which no minutes are taken, where all the issues are discussed, in order to gain a greater understanding of one another's viewpoint on the services to date and the transition plan, will help to avoid entrenched attitudes.

■ Being a role model for the change. Managers should behave in ways that are congruent with the expected outcome, reinforcing the vision of the change. Their enthusiasm can be infectious, acting as a positive agent for change.

■ Using peer group pressure to persuade people that the change is good for the organization. Managers need to identify those individuals who command respect among their peers and gain their support. The Pareto Principle of 80:20 is an effective measure – once 80% of the people will let change happen (or even make change happen) you can move on to the next phase; the other 20% will follow.

■ Encouraging the sharing of positive changes and celebrating success. Allowing others to see it really does work will encourage them to embrace the change.

5.2.10.4 Techniques to overcome individuals' resistance to change

Rosabeth Moss Kanter identified ten reasons why people would resist change, and optional strategies that will promote positive change enablers. These can be useful for Service Transition staff to understand when involved in managing stakeholder change to overcome issues from individuals during transition. The ten reasons are:

■ **Loss of control** – When you move people from a process with which they are familiar to one they know little about, they will experience a feeling of losing control. This can be overcome by involving them in the decision making, even allowing them to make decisions for themselves. It is essential to inform people of what choices they have – even if they are extremely limited. Managers should anticipate who is likely to oppose the changes and decide how to win them over. A detailed explanation of the business benefit and the return on investment (ROI) will strike a sense of urgency and awareness to how the new Service Transition will support the business needs.

■ **Excessive personal uncertainty** – The first question most people will ask is 'What is this going to mean for my job?' This can be answered effectively by explaining the need for, and implication of, the change at both a business and a personal level, including the often difficult issue of estimating how long the period of uncertainty will last. Honesty is the best policy.

■ **Avoid surprises** – People like to be given the opportunity to think through the implications of change to/for them; springing new ideas on them will create scepticism.

■ **The difference effect** – People build identities around many facets of their work – their role, the job, the building, the corporate name – it gives them a sense of tradition. Managers should only change what they must, keeping familiar symbols wherever possible.

■ **Loss of face** – People dislike moving from a position of competence to one of incompetence, which can often happen when new processes, systems and ways of working are introduced. Managers can alleviate this problem by acknowledging the person's competence under the old regime and letting them participate in deciding the change process. This can also be done by allowing a joint responsibility for personal objective setting. This will generate early engagement as the change transitions.

■ **Fear around competence** – Some people will believe that they cannot adopt the new ways of working – 'You can't teach an old dog new tricks!' The solution is to give them the training/coaching they need before the new system is implemented, allowing them to have practice runs before the system goes live so that they prove their competence to themselves, thereby creating enhanced levels of confidence. This can have the added bonus of increasing their desire for change, and personal responsibility to their own career development.

■ **Ripples** – The unexpected effect of an action taken in one area on another. Managers would be naïve to think that planned change is trouble free; sometimes it is impossible to predict accurately the effect one change will have on another part of the organization. During the planning phase people should be encouraged to think widely and divergently, considering unlikely as well as likely possibilities when attempting to predict outcomes; this catastrophe planning can help to minimize the ripple effect.

■ **Increase in workload** – Change frequently results in more work. If this is the reality, it should be acknowledged and rewarded if possible.

■ **Past resentments** – If the proposed change is associated with an individual or organization about which the person has a grievance they will resist the change. Allowing them to air their resentments, managers will have the opportunity to remove or repair them.

■ **Real threats** – There are times when change is going to have a negative impact on the individual, and they are justified in resisting. Pretending it is going to be all right does not help; managers need to act first and act fast by talking with them as soon as possible, and involving them in the solution.

5.3 STAKEHOLDER MANAGEMENT

Stakeholder management is a crucial success factor in Service Transition. The new or changed service must support and deliver stakeholder requirements to be considered successful and their active involvement will increase the likelihood of delivering as required. Failure to properly identify all stakeholder groups makes it almost inevitable that many of those affected will be unaware of proposed changes and unable to register their concerns and wishes, nor will they be able to be supportive if they are not included.

5.3.1 Stakeholder management strategy

The stakeholder management strategy from Service Design sets out:

■ Who the stakeholders are

■ What their interests and influences are likely to be

■ How the project or programme will engage with them

■ What information will be communicated

■ How feedback will be processed.

Figure 5.5 Potential stakeholders

It is helpful for Service Transition if stakeholders are listed under categories such as 'users/beneficiaries' or 'providers'. Each category can then be broken down further if necessary. Categories should be recognizable groups rather than abstract ones; for example, 'employees based in one geographical location' are a readily identifiable group, whereas 'members of the public who support human rights' are not. Some categories may identify the same individuals, but it is often useful to differentiate

between stakeholders 'wearing different hats', such as those shown in Figure 5.5.

5.3.2 Stakeholder map and analysis

Stakeholders inevitably have different interest areas in the overall change; for example, some will be concerned with how the change will affect their working environment; others will want to influence changes in the way customers are handled. A stakeholder matrix (see Figure 5.6) is a useful way of mapping the various stakeholders against their interests in the Service Transition, its activities and outcomes. Service Transition should work with Service Design to ensure that there is an accurate and relevant stakeholder map or equivalent.

Examples of those who may be affected are:

■ Sponsors of the service change, e.g. technology refresh

■ Those affected by the service change or Service Transition

■ Suppliers of goods or services into the service bundle or service package

■ Service Management teams involved in the new or changed service

■ Customers or consumers who will be affected by the Service Transition or the new or changed service

■ Relationship management staff

■ Internal and/or external audit

■ Information security

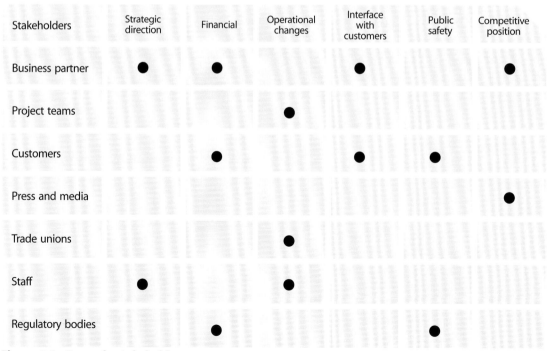

Figure 5.6 Example stakeholder map

- Fraud unit
- Risk management
- Shareholders, management and staff of the organization
- Labour groups/trade unions
- Political or regulatory bodies
- The wider community, such as the general public
- Project and programme management teams delivering the projects within the overall service lifecycle.

A stakeholder analysis helps to ensure that there is sufficient understanding of the stakeholder requirements and the stakeholder's interest in, and impact on, the change. Stakeholders' positions (in terms of influence and impact) may be rational and justifiable, or emotional and unfounded. However, they must all be taken into account since, by definition, stakeholders can affect the change process and hence the Service Transition.

There is often a re-usable element of the stakeholder map and analysis. For example, where many projects are delivering into a shared service and infrastructure, the stakeholders may be the same: including the business sponsor, the Service Operations manager, the head of Service Management and the members of the Change Advisory Board.

The stakeholder analysis helps to ensure that communication channels are targeted appropriately and that messages, media and levels of detail reflect the needs of the relevant stakeholders. The communications channels may need to accommodate stakeholders who cannot be engaged directly with the Service Transition. In many cases, working through partners, industry groups, regulatory bodies, etc. may be required. Often one larger communication approach, covering all areas, can help deliver a consistent and stronger message than by operating at functional level.

One technique for analysing stakeholders is to consider each stakeholder in terms of their importance to Service Transition and the potential impact of the change on them and 'plot' them on a matrix (see Figure 5.7). This will guide the activities that Service Transition should adopt. For example, a business sponsor will have a 'high' status of importance to the overall service change, and, depending on the scale and opportunities for any return on their investment, the impact of the new or changed service may be 'low', 'medium' or 'high'.

Stakeholders may move up or down the matrix as the service package progresses through the lifecycle, so it is important to revisit the stakeholder analysis work particularly during the detailed planning for Service Transition. Responsible stakeholders can and should enhance and even alter the course of the Service Transition.

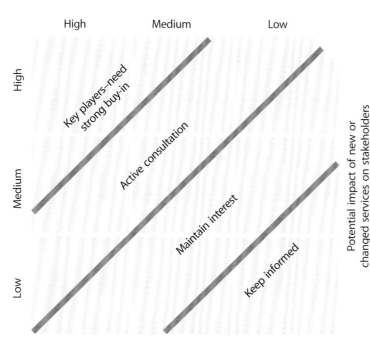

Figure 5.7 Power impact matrix

5.3.2.1 Stakeholder changes

During the service lifecycle, stakeholders may come and go. Key stakeholders, such as the change sponsors, should (hopefully!) remain constant throughout. But sufficient records and documentation will be maintained to enable effective handover in the event individuals are replaced; sufficient is adjudged in accordance with business risk and cost.

Some stakeholders will be able to participate in advisory or assurance roles; others will be important in assessing the realization of the benefits; others will have an audit perspective.

5.3.3 Changes in stakeholder commitment

Figure 5.8 is an example commitment plan. It shows the current commitment level of individuals and groups, and how that commitment must change if the transition is to be successful.

Each individual is rated with an 'O' to indicate their current position and an 'X' to indicate the degree of commitment needed from them. Sometimes they need to step back, e.g. the departing director of customer in this table would need to hand over the leadership role.

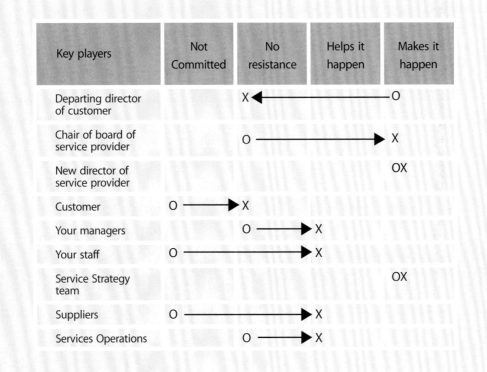

Figure 5.8 Example commitment planning chart

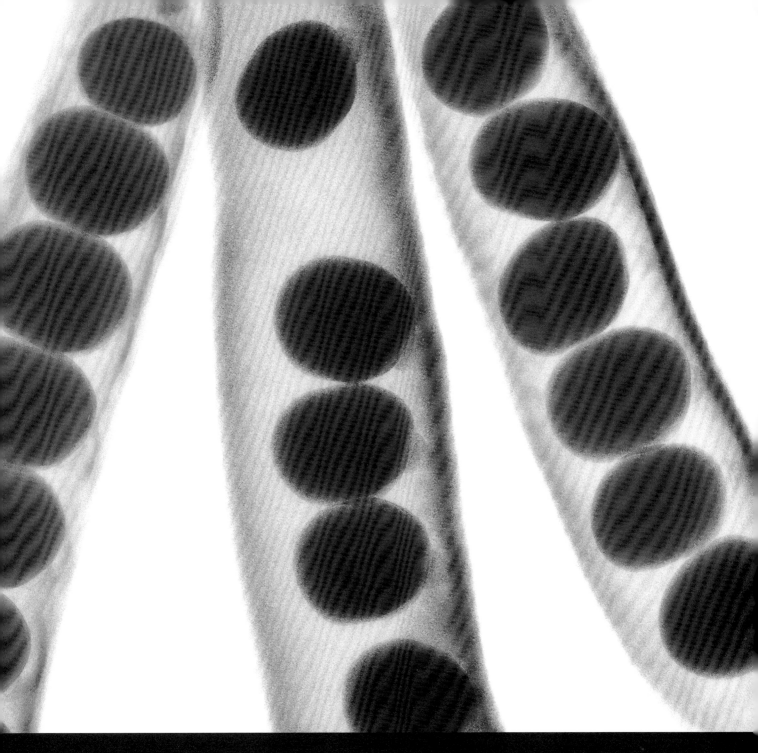

Organizing for Service Transition

6

6 Organizing for Service Transition

A characteristic of a process is that all related activities need not necessarily be limited to one specific organizational unit. SACM, for example, can be conducted in departments such as Service Operation, application management, network management, systems development and non-IT departments like procurement. Since processes and their activities run through a whole organization, the activities should be mapped to the existing IT departments or sections and coordinated by process managers. Once detailed procedures and work instructions have been developed, an organization will then map its staff to the activities of the process. Clear definitions of accountability and responsibility are critical success factors for any process implementation. Without this, roles and responsibilities within the new or changed process can be confusing, and individuals might revert to how the activities were handled before the new or changed procedures were put in place.

6.1 GENERIC ROLES

Responsibility for each process and service must be allocated for effective delivery of that service or process. All staff involved in process and service delivery need to understand these roles and to be aware of where that responsibility lies. These owner roles are not necessarily a person dedicated for each process or service. The two key roles, process owner and service owner, are set out below.

6.1.1 Process owner role

The process owner is responsible for ensuring that all activities defined within the process are undertaken and is responsible for:

- Defining the process strategy
- Assisting with process design
- Ensuring that appropriate process documentation is available and current
- Defining appropriate policies and standards to be employed throughout the process
- Periodically auditing the process to ensure compliance to policy and standards
- Periodically reviewing the process strategy to ensure that it is still appropriate and change as required
- Communicating process information or changes as appropriate to ensure awareness
- Providing process resources to support activities required throughout the Service Management lifecycle

- Ensuring process technicians have the required knowledge and the required technical and business understanding to deliver the process, and understand their role in the process
- Reviewing opportunities for process enhancements and for improving the efficiency and effectiveness of the process
- Addressing issues with the running of the process
- Providing input to the ongoing service improvement plan.

6.1.2 Service owner role

The service owner is responsible to the customer for the initiation, transition and ongoing maintenance and support of a particular service.

The service owner has the following responsibilities:

- To act as prime customer contact for all service-related enquiries and issues
- To ensure that the ongoing service delivery and support meet agreed customer requirements
- To identify opportunities for service improvements, discuss with the customer and raise the RFC for assessment if appropriate
- To liaise with the appropriate process owners throughout the Service Management lifecycle
- To solicit required data, statistics and reports for analysis and to facilitate effective service monitoring and performance
- To be accountable to the IT director or Service Management director for the delivery of the service.

6.2 ORGANIZATIONAL CONTEXT FOR TRANSITIONING A SERVICE

Other organizational units and third parties need to have clearly defined interface and handover points with Service Transition to ensure the delivery of the defined deliverables within the agreed schedule.

Programmes, projects, Service Design and suppliers are responsible for the delivery of service assets and components in accordance with the requirements of the Service Design, SLAs and contracts in addition to initiating any changes that affect a service release or deployment.

Service Transition will acquire changes, service assets and components from these parties. An example Service

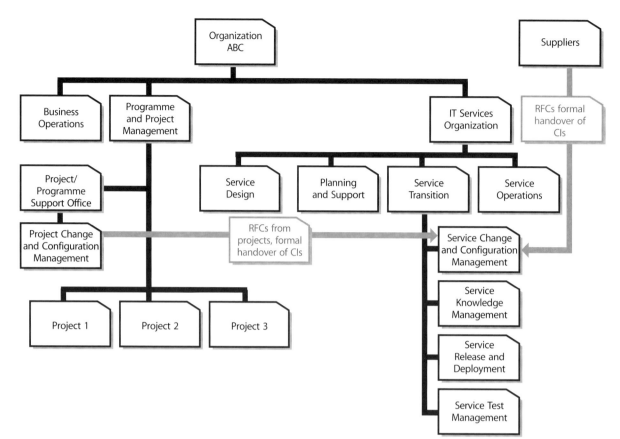

Figure 6.1 Example of Service Transition organization and its interfaces

Transition organization is illustrated in Figure 6.1 in addition to other teams within the IT services organization.

As shown above, there are interfaces to projects and business operations that need to be clearly defined. It is essential that throughout the Service Management lifecycle there is clear interaction and understanding of responsibility by all that neither element can work in isolation. It is critical that projects have a clear understanding of Service Design, transition and operations requirements and objective of delivery, and vice versa.

Often projects and programmes will work in isolation from Service Transition and operations, believing that they have no part to play in the ongoing service delivery. Similarly, transition and operations can ignore ongoing project activity; working on the basis that they will only be concerned about it once it is 'their turn' to deal with it. This is a very short-sighted approach and one that should be removed.

Cooperation, understanding and mutual respect are critical to ensuring that new, changed and ongoing delivery of services to the customer are optimized.

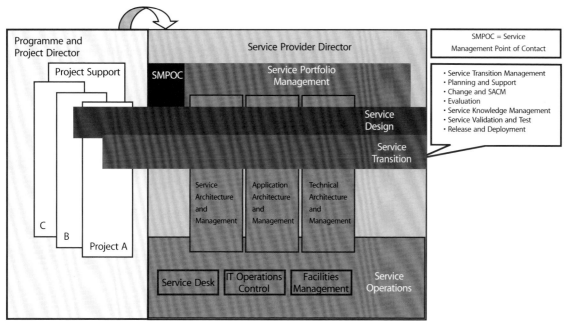

Figure 6.2 Organizational interfaces for a Service Transition

Figure 6.2 illustrates the required interaction between programmes, projects and Service Management elements.

During the release and deployment there will be interactions with the business, customers and users and these responsibilities are defined in this section.

6.3 ORGANIZATION MODELS TO SUPPORT SERVICE TRANSITION

Many people and processes are involved in Service Transition. Some of the key organization requirements that support the application of ITIL best practices for Service Transition are described in this section.

6.3.1 Management of Service Transition

Service Transition requires active management, with recognition of its key role in delivering effective IT services within an organization. One key element of this recognition is the allocation of the role of Service Transition manager.

An example of a function or organizational structure for Service Transition is shown in Figure 6.3.

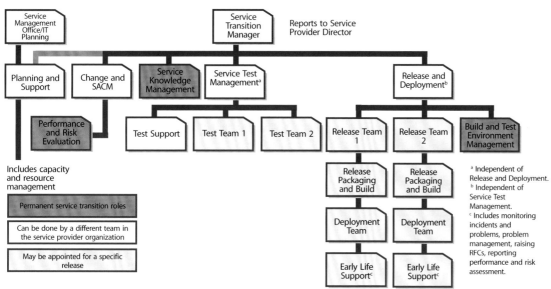

Figure 6.3 Example of an organization for Service Transition

6.3.2 Service Transition roles and responsibilities

The specific roles and responsibilities covered within this section relate primarily to Service Transition, although they will be used to some extent by other processes within the Service Management lifecycle. These are:

- Service Transition management
- Planning and support
- Service Asset and Configuration Management and Change Management
- Performance and risk evaluation
- Service Knowledge Management
- Service test management
- Release and deployment
- Release packaging and build
- Deployment
- Early life support
- Build and test environment management.

Depending on the size of the organization and the scope of the service being transitioned, some of these roles will be combined and performed by one individual. However, service test management and physical testing must always be performed by resources independent of other functions or processes.

It is essential to recognize that all staff involved in Service Transition are responsible for:

- Identifying and raising risks and issues, which may directly relate to their process area or may be something that they observe elsewhere within or outside of Service Transition
- Being constantly aware of and understanding the business context in which they are working and understanding the customer's business needs of the services they are providing
- Being fully aware of projects under way and the expected service delivery of those projects, including potential impact on their area of responsibility
- Ensuring that they follow the published standards for documentation, change, asset and Configuration Management and Knowledge Management processes as well the incident and problem management processes. Where standards do not exist, raising this as a risk at the earliest opportunity.

6.3.2.1 *The Service Transition manager*

The Service Transition manager has day-to-day management and control of the Service Transition teams and their activities. The prime responsibilities for this role are:

- Overall planning and management of Service Transition delivery including Continual Service Improvement
- Managing and coordinating the Service Transition functions
- Budgeting and accounting for Service Transition team activities and resources
- Acting as the prime interface for senior management in terms of Service Transition planning and reporting
- Making a final recommendation to the business and IT regarding the decisions to release and deploy into production
- Ensuring all organizational policies and procedures are followed throughout transition
- Ensuring the final delivery meets the agreed customer and stakeholder requirements specified in the Service Design.

6.3.2.2 *Planning and support*

Planning and support may not be a direct responsibility of the Service Transition manager, as in some organizations this function may be consolidated into an overall Service Management office/IT planning responsibility. Regardless of where this function sits, the role must still be performed.

This function provides support for the Service Transition teams and people. The activities include:

- Defining the requirements, processes and tools for Transition Planning and Support
- Maintaining and integrating lower level plans to establish overall integrated transition plans, including planned vs actuals
- Maintaining and monitoring progress on Service Transition changes, issues, risks and deviations including tracking progress on actions and mitigation of risks
- Maintaining records on and providing management information on resource use, project/Service Transition progress, budgeted and actual spend
- Managing and coordinating requests for resources
- Coordinating Service Transition activities across projects, suppliers and service teams where appropriate
- Publishing Service Transition performance statistics and identifying key areas for improvement
- Undertaking formal quality reviews of the Service Transition, release and deployment plans and agreed

transition activities in accordance with the quality management plan

■ Managing support for tools and Service Transition processes

■ Communicating with stakeholders.

6.3.2.3 Service Asset and Configuration Management and Change Management roles

Service Design is responsible for designing the baselines appropriate for the service and identifying the relevant assets and CIs with input from the business change manager(s) and others who have responsibilities for delivering services and maintaining business continuity.

During the first stages of a project the programme or project office may be responsible for administering the Configuration Management process, maintaining copies of relevant documentation concerning the CIs, and controlling the release of CIs following appropriate approvals. At defined release points for a service and service package, the programme or project office will pass responsibility to Service Transition who will take responsibility for Configuration Management of the CI documentation.

Responsibilities for reviewing and approving assets and CIs across the service lifecycle and during deployment need to be defined and allocated to individuals with appropriate skills and authority.

Role specifications for the Change Management, Service Asset and Configuration Management teams need to be developed. Typical roles include:

■ Service asset manager

■ Configuration manager

■ Configuration analyst

■ Configuration administrator/librarian

■ CMS/tools administrator

■ Change manager.

Assign the configuration manager and other key roles as early as possible, because assigned individuals can then be involved in the implementation. For some operational activities Configuration Management will require staff who will adopt a diligent approach and pay due attention to detail.

The service asset manager

The service asset manager has the following responsibilities:

■ Works to the overall objectives agreed with the IT services manager; implements the organization's service Asset Management policy and standards

■ Evaluates existing Asset Management systems and the design, implementation and management of new/improved systems for efficiency and effectiveness, including estimating and planning the work and resources involved, and monitoring and reporting on progress against plan

■ Agrees scope of the Asset Management processes, function, the items that are to be controlled, and the information that is to be recorded; develops Asset Management standards, Asset Management plans and procedures

■ Mounts an awareness campaign to win support for new Asset Management procedures; ensures that changes to the Asset Management methods and processes are properly approved and communicated to staff before being implemented; plans, publicizes and oversees implementation of new Asset Management systems

■ Arranges recruitment and training of staff

■ Manages the evaluation of proprietary Asset Management tools and recommends those that best meet the organization's budget, resource, timescale and technical requirements

■ Manages the Asset Management plan, principles and processes and their implementation

■ Agrees assets to be uniquely identified with naming conventions; ensures that staff comply with identification standards for object types, environments, processes, lifecycles, documentation, versions, formats, baselines, releases and templates

■ Proposes and/or agrees interfaces with Change Management, problem management, network management, release management, computer operations, logistics, finance and administration functions

■ Plans population of the asset DB; manages the asset DB, central libraries and tools; ensures regular housekeeping of the asset DB

■ Provides reports, including management reports (indicating suggested action to deal with current or foreseen shortcomings), impact analysis reports and asset status reports

■ Initiates actions needed to secure funds to enhance the infrastructure and staffing levels in order to cope with growth and change

■ Assists auditors to audit the activities of the Asset Management team for compliance with laid-down procedures; ensures corrective action is carried out.

The configuration manager

The configuration manager has the following responsibilities:

- Works to the overall objectives agreed with the IT services manager; implements the organization's Configuration Management policy and standards
- Evaluates existing Configuration Management Systems and the design, implementation and management of new/improved systems for efficiency and effectiveness, including estimating and planning the work and resources involved, and monitoring and reporting on progress against plan
- Agrees scope of the Configuration Management processes, function, the items that are to be controlled, and the information that is to be recorded; develops Configuration Management standards, Configuration Management Plans and procedures
- Mounts an awareness campaign to win support for new Configuration Management procedures; ensures that changes to the Configuration Management methods and processes are properly approved and communicated to staff before being implemented; plans, publicizes and oversees implementation of new Configuration Management Systems
- Arranges recruitment and training of staff
- Manages the evaluation of proprietary Configuration Management tools and recommends those that best meet the organization's budget, resource, timescale and technical requirements
- Manages the Configuration Management Plan, principles and processes and their implementation
- Agrees CIs to be uniquely identified with naming conventions; ensures that staff comply with identification standards for object types, environments, processes, lifecycles, documentation, versions, formats, baselines, releases and templates
- Proposes and/or agrees interfaces with Change Management, problem management, network management, release management, computer operations, logistics, finance and administration functions
- Plans population of the CMS; manages CMS, central libraries, tools, common codes and data; ensures regular housekeeping of the CMS
- Provides reports, including management reports (indicating suggested action to deal with current or foreseen shortcomings), impact analysis reports and configuration status reports

- Initiates actions needed to secure funds to enhance the infrastructure and staffing levels in order to cope with growth and change
- Assists auditors to audit the activities of the Configuration Management team for compliance with laid-down procedures; ensures corrective action is carried out.

The configuration analyst

The configuration analyst has the following responsibilities:

- Proposes scope of the Asset and Configuration Management processes, function, the items that are to be controlled, and the information that is to be recorded; develops Asset and Configuration Management standards, plans and procedures
- Trains Asset and Configuration Management specialists and other staff in Asset and Configuration Management principles, processes and procedures
- Supports the creation of the Asset and Configuration Management Plans and principles and their implementation
- Creates Asset and Configuration Management processes and procedures, which includes CI registration procedures; access controls and privileges; ensures that the correct roles and responsibilities are defined in the Asset and Configuration Management Plans and procedures
- Proposes and agrees with the asset and configuration manager CIs to be uniquely identified with naming conventions; ensures that developers and configuration system users comply with identification standards for object types, environments, processes, lifecycles, documentation, versions, formats, baselines, releases and templates
- Liaises with the configuration administrator/librarian on population of the asset and CMS; manages asset and CMS, central libraries, common codes and data; ensures regular housekeeping of the asset and CMS
- Uses or provides the asset and CMS to facilitate impact assessment for RFCs and to ensure that implemented changes are as authorized; creates change records, configuration baselines, and package release records in order to specify the effect on CIs of an authorized change; ensures any changes to change authorization records are themselves subject to Change Management procedures; ensures that the asset and CMS is updated when a change is implemented
- Uses the asset and CMS to help identify other CIs affected by a fault that is affecting a CI

- Performs configuration audits to check that the physical IT inventory is consistent with the asset and CMS and initiates any necessary corrective action
- Creates and populates project libraries and CM system; checks items and groups of items into the CM tools
- Accepts baselined products from third parties and distributes products
- Builds system baselines for promotion and release
- Maintains project status information and status accounting records and reports
- Monitors problems (test incidents) and maintains database for collection and reporting of metrics.

The configuration administrator/librarian

The configuration administrator/librarian is the custodian and guardian of all master copies of software, assets and documentation CIs registered with Asset and Configuration Management. The major tasks of this role are to:

- Control the receipt, identification, storage, and withdrawal of all supported CIs
- Provide information on the status of CIs
- Number, record, store and distribute Asset and Configuration Management issues.

The configuration administrator/librarian has the following specific responsibilities:

- Assists Asset and Configuration Management to prepare the Asset and Configuration Management Plan
- Creates an identification scheme for Configuration Management libraries and the Definitive Media Library (DML)
- Creates an identification scheme for assets and the Definitive Spares (DS)
- Creates libraries or other storage areas to hold CIs
- Assists in the identification of products and CIs
- Maintains current status information on CIs
- Accepts and records the receipt of new or revised configurations into the appropriate library
- Archives superseded CI copies
- Holds the master copies
- Administers configuration control process:
  - Distributes change requests to individual team members for impact assessment
  - Validates completeness of change requests
  - Routes change requests to appropriate authority for approval
  - Progresses and tracks change requests through to completion
  - Reports on change requests

- Records decisions about change requests
- Issues copies of products for review, change, correction or information when authorized to do so
- Maintains a record of all copies issued
- Notifies holders of any changes to their copies
- Collects and retains information that will assist in the assessment of what CIs are impacted by a change to a product
- Produces configuration status accounting reports
- Assists in conducting configuration audits
- Liaises with other configuration libraries where CIs are common to other systems.

The CMS/tools administrator

The CMS/tools administrator has the following responsibilities:

- Evaluates proprietary Asset and Configuration Management tools and recommends those that best meet the organization's budget, resource, timescale and technical requirements; directly or indirectly customizes proprietary tools to produce effective Asset and Configuration Management environments in terms of databases and software libraries, workflows and report generation
- Monitors the performance and capacity of existing Asset and Configuration Management systems and recommends improvement opportunities and undertakes standard housekeeping and fine tuning under change control
- Liaises with the configuration analyst and administrator/librarian on population of the asset and CMS; provides technical administration and support for asset and CMS, central libraries, tools' common codes and data; undertakes regular technical housekeeping of the asset and CMS
- Ensures the integrity and operational performance of the CM systems.

The Configuration Control Board

The Configuration Control Board is required to ensure that the overarching intention and policies of Configuration Management are employed throughout the Service Management lifecycle and with specific consideration for every aspect of the complete service. The Board has the following responsibilities:

- Defines and controls the service configuration baselines in terms of core and support services, applications, information, service, technical, infrastructure – ensuring that they meet the requirements established in the Service Design

- Reviews changes in the service configuration for compliance with standards, contractual and internal requirements
- Originates requirement changes for service configuration to comply with contract change requests.

In some organizations, the Configuration Control Board will be combined with change, thereby providing a holistic view of the current and proposed services and service models, enabling better control, change evaluation, impact assessment and understanding.

The change authority

Formal authorization is obtained for each change from a change authority that may be a role, person or a group of people. The levels of authorization for a particular type of change should be judged by the type, size or risk of the change, e.g. changes in a large enterprise that affect several distributed sites may need to be authorized by a higher-level change authority such as a Global Change Board or the Board of Directors.

The culture of the organization dictates, to a large extent, the manner in which changes are authorized. Hierarchical structures may well impose many levels of change authorization, while flatter structures may allow a more streamlined approach.

A degree of delegated authority may well exist within an authorization level, e.g. delegating authority to a change manager according to pre-set parameters relating to:

- Anticipated business risk
- Financial implications
- Scope of the change (e.g. internal effects only, within the finance service, specific outsourced services).

An example of authorization hierarchy is shown in Figure 4.5, Example of a change authorization model.

The change manager

The main duties of the change manager, some of which may be delegated, are listed below:

- Receives, logs and allocates a priority, in collaboration with the initiator, to all RFCs; rejects any RFCs that are totally impractical
- Tables all RFCs for a CAB meeting, issues an agenda and circulates all RFCs to CAB members in advance of meetings to allow prior consideration
- Decides which people will come to which meetings, who gets specific RFCs depending on the nature of the RFC, what is to be changed, and people's areas of expertise
- Convenes urgent CAB or ECAB meetings for all urgent RFCs
- Chairs all CAB and ECAB meetings
- After consideration of the advice given by the CAB or ECAB, authorizes acceptable changes
- Issues change schedules, via the service desk
- Liaises with all necessary parties to coordinate change building, testing and implementation, in accordance with schedules
- Updates the change log with all progress that occurs, including any actions to correct problems and/or to take opportunities to improve service quality
- Reviews all implemented changes to ensure that they have met their objectives; refers back any that have been backed out or have failed
- Reviews all outstanding RFCs awaiting consideration or awaiting action
- Analyses change records to determine any trends or apparent problems that occur; seeks rectification with relevant parties
- Closes RFCs
- Produces regular and accurate management reports.

Change Advisory Board

A Change Advisory Board (CAB) is an advisory body. It needs to have appropriate terms of reference (e.g. meeting regularity, scope of influence, and links to programme management).

To understand more about the specific role and responsibilities of the CAB, see paragraph 4.2.6.8.

6.3.2.4 Performance and risk evaluation management

The following roles all provide input into the performance and risk evaluation of the Service Transition processes and key decision making, e.g. stopping or holding the deployment.

The performance and risk evaluation manager

The performance and risk evaluation manager has the following responsibilities:

- Uses Service Design and release package to develop the evaluation plan to input to service testing
- Establishes risks and issues associated with all aspects of the Service Transition through risk workshops etc.
- Provides evaluation report to input to Change Management.

6.3.2.5 Service Knowledge Management

Knowledge Management requires effective and authoritative ownership within an organization. The role of the Knowledge Management process owner is crucial, in that it will design, deliver and maintain the Knowledge Management strategy, process and procedures.

The Knowledge Management process owner

The Knowledge Management process owner has the following responsibilities:

- Undertakes the Knowledge Management role, ensuring compliance with the organization's policies and processes
- Is the architect of knowledge identification, capture and maintenance
- Identifies, controls and stores any information deemed to be pertinent to the services provided, which is not available via any other means
- Maintains the controlled knowledge items to ensure currency
- Ensures all knowledge items are made accessible to those who need them in an efficient and effective manner
- Monitors publicity regarding the knowledge information to ensure that information is not duplicated and is recognized as a central source of information etc.
- Acts as an adviser to business and IT personnel on Knowledge Management matters, including policy decisions on storage, value, worth etc.

6.3.2.6 Service test manager

Service test management is primarily responsible for the test support and the test team(s) functions involved with the specific Service Transition. The service test manager will report to the Service Transition manager as will the release and deployment manager; however, these roles should always be undertaken by separate people, and never be combined, to ensure that there is always independent testing and test verification.

The service test manager has the following responsibilities:

- Defines the test strategy
- Designs and plans testing conditions, test scripts and test data sets to ensure appropriate and adequate coverage and control
- Allocates and oversees test resources, ensuring test policies are adhered to
- Provides management reporting on test progress, test outcomes, success rates, issues and risks

- Conducts tests as defined in the test plans and design
- Records, analyses, diagnoses, reports and manages test events, incidents, problems and retest dependent on agreed criteria
- Manages test environment requirements
- Verifies tests conducted by release and deployment teams
- Administers test assets and components.

Test support

The prime responsibility of the test support team is to provide independent testing of all components delivered within the Service Transition programme or project. Responsibilities required to deliver successful service testing include the following, however, not all of these are the direct responsibility of the test support team:

- The change manager is responsible for ensuring that tests are developed appropriate to approved changes and that agreed testing strategy and policy is applied to all changes.
- Test analysts carry out the tests as set out in the testing plans and/or service package.
- The developer/supplier is responsible for establishing the root cause of test failures – the fault in the service component that made the test fail. For complex situations this may require collaboration between testing staff and development/build/supplier personnel. It should always be accepted as a possibility that faults can lie within the testing design as well as within design/development.
- Service Design will design the test, as an element of the overall Service Design. For many services, standard tests will exist, perhaps contained within the transition model chosen as already accepted as appropriate for the type of new or changed service under consideration.
- Customers and users perform customer and user acceptance testing. Such user resource should be able to cover the full range of user profile and requirements, and adequately sign off the conformance of a new or changed service. Users will already have played a major role in helping to design the acceptance testing approaches during the design phase.

6.3.2.7 Release and deployment

Release and deployment is primarily responsible for managing all aspects of the end-to-end release process. The release and deployment manager will report to the Service Transition manager as will the service test manager; however these roles should always be undertaken by separate people, and never be combined, to ensure that there is always independent testing and test verification.

The release and deployment manager

The release and deployment manager is responsible for the planning, design, build, configuration and testing of all software and hardware to create the release package for the delivery of, or changes to, the designated service.

The release and deployment manager has the following responsibilities:

- Manages all aspects of the end-to-end release process
- Updates the SKMS and CMS
- Ensures coordination of build and test environment team and release teams
- Ensures teams follow the organization's established policies and procedures
- Provides management reports on release progress
- Service release and deployment policy and planning
- Deals with release package design, build and configuration
- Deals with release package acceptance including business sign-off
- Deals with service roll-out planning including method of deployment
- Deals with release package testing to predefined Acceptance Criteria
- Signs off the release package for implementation
- Deals with communication, preparation and training
- Audits hardware and software before and after the implementation of release package changes
- Installs new or upgraded hardware
- Deals with storage and traceability/auditability of controlled software in both centralized and distributed systems
- Deals with release, distribution and the installation of packaged software.

However, some of these responsibilities will be delegated to the relevant release team sub-process.

The main components to be controlled are:

- Service documentation including:
  - Service Portfolio
  - Service catalogue
  - Service level agreement, OLAs and UCs
  - Service Design and specification
- Application programs developed in-house
- Externally developed software (including standard off-the-shelf software as well as custom-written software)

- Utility software
- Supplier-provided systems software
- Hardware, and hardware specifications
- Assembly instructions and documentation, including user manuals.

All deliverables need to be managed effectively, from development or purchasing, through customization and configuration, through testing and implementation, to operation in the live environment.

6.3.2.8 Release packaging and build

Release packaging and build management is the flow of work (establish requirements, design, build, test, deploy, operate and optimize) to deliver applications and infrastructure that meet the Service Design requirements.

The release packaging and build manager

The release packaging and build manager has the following responsibilities:

- Establishes the final release configuration (e.g. knowledge, information, hardware, software and infrastructure)
- Builds the final release delivery
- Tests the final delivery prior to independent testing
- Establishes and reports outstanding known errors and workarounds
- Provides input to the final implementation sign-off process.

The release packaging and build manager cannot perform this role in isolation; other functions with which there will be significant interface are:

- Security management
- Test management
- Change and Service Asset Configuration Management
- Capacity management
- Availability management
- Incident management
- Quality management.

6.3.2.9 Deployment

Deployment staff have the following responsibilities:

- Deal with the final physical delivery of the service implementation
- Coordinate release documentation and communications, including training and customer, Service Management and technical release notes
- Plan the deployment in conjunction with change and Knowledge Management and SACM

- Provide technical and application guidance and support throughout the release process, including known errors and workarounds
- Provide feedback on the effectiveness of the release
- Record metrics for deployment to ensure within agreed SLAs.

6.3.2.10 Early life support

It is often believed that early life support starts when the service has actually been transitioned into operational use. This is not the case. Early life support should be considered as an integral role within the release and deployment phase.

Early life support staff have the following key responsibilities:

- Provide IT service and business functional support from prior to final acceptance by Service Operations
- Ensure delivery of appropriate support documentation
- Provide release acceptance for provision of initial support
- Provide initial support in response to incidents and errors detected within a new or changed service
- Adapt and perfect elements that evolve with initial usage, such as:
  - User documentation
  - Support documentation including service desk scripts
  - Data management, including archiving
- Embed activities for a new or changed service
- Deal with formal transition of the service to Service Operations and CSI
- Monitor incidents and problems, and undertake problem management during release and deployment, raising RFCs as required
- Provide initial performance reporting and undertake service risk assessment based on performance.

6.3.2.11 Build and test environment management

The build and test environment function is primarily to ensure that all the relevant people have the appropriate environments, test data, versioned software etc. available at the time that they need it and for the right purpose. As environment resources are normally limited, this role performs a coordinating and sometimes arbitrary role to ensure that resources are used to maximum effect.

Build and test environment staff have the following key responsibilities:

- Ensure service infrastructure and application are built to design specification
- Plan acquisition, build, implementation and maintenance of ICT infrastructure
- Ensure build delivery components are from controlled sources
- Develop an integrated application software and infrastructure build
- Deliver appropriate build, operations and support documentation for the build and test environments prior to handover to Service Operations
- Build, deliver and maintain required testing environments.

6.4 SERVICE TRANSITION RELATIONSHIP WITH OTHER LIFECYCLE STAGES

Service Transition is presented as a discrete lifecycle step, but this should not be taken to imply that it can stand alone. Service Transition exists to deliver the concepts documented within Service Design through to Service Operations for day-to-day management, and so without design and operations it has no purpose.

6.4.1 Upstream relationships for Service Transition

6.4.1.1 Logical staff mobility

Service Transition takes its shape and input from the strategy set by the organization and from the new or changed services it is charged with bringing into live operation, i.e. by the output of the Service Design stage. Its very nature is therefore dependent on its relationship with 'upstream areas'.

In most organizations, many staff will deliver tasks appropriate to more than one lifecycle stage. Indeed, the skills and experience accumulated by Service Transition and Service Operations staff will typically be valuable in the stages upstream of their nominal focus.

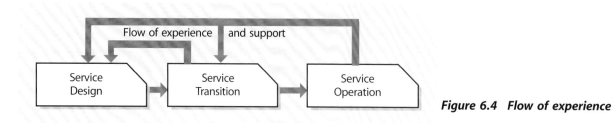

Figure 6.4 Flow of experience

Specifically, Service Transition will depend on appropriate experience from operations skilled staff to deliver much of the knowledge required to make key decisions, based on predicting likely successful practice based on previous behaviour of systems in similar situations, as shown in Figure 6.4.

When Service Design establishes the best transition approach, and when, within Service Transition, the continued viability of that approach is assessed, Service Transition and Service Operation are best placed to play the role of subject matter expert, and provide input to the assessment and evaluation of the design's initial and ongoing viability.

Service Operation people will be involved in (design and) operations tasks directly via population of the Service Knowledge Management System with precedents and experiences detected during Service Operation stages – e.g. through incident-problem-error cycles. This will drive informed and correct decision making processes and facilitate more effective Service Transition.

In order to retain and make effective use of experience, staff may well find themselves allocated (fully or partially) from operations tasks to support a design exercise and then follow that service through Service Transition. They may then, via early life support activities, move into support of the new or changed services they have been involved in designing and implementing into the live environment.

Expert advice on transition (as with design and operations) will also provide expert input to the development and maintenance of Service Strategy.

6.4.1.2 Process communications

Many of the capabilities of a service that require testing and acceptance with transition are established and approach and measures set within design. As described above, this exercise is likely to have involved Service Transition staff, either through direct involvement (perhaps even formal secondment) or through consultation and expert advice.

6.4.2 Downstream process and procedure influence

Many elements initiated or perfected during Service Transition will be established and become key elements within Service Operation.

During transition testing incidents will be detected that reveal errors within the new or changed service. The nature and identified resolution of these errors will provide direct input to the Service Operations procedures for supporting the new or changed service in live use. Service Transition input is likely to affect most areas of the operations stage.

Testing will share processes with operations, possibly with some variations in procedure, e.g. to accommodate the differing requirements and risk environments of analysing and rectifying errors in testing and live environments.

Where testing detects errors in a new or changed service that are not significant enough to prevent the release of the service, these errors are released into the live known error database, and notification is passed to Continual Service Improvement, via the SKMS, which CSI will make extensive use of.

Technology
considerations

7

7 Technology considerations

Technology has a major role to play in Service Transition, and this should be designed in, and mechanisms for maintaining and maximizing benefit from that technology must be in place.

There are two ways in which Service Transition is supported by technology:

- Enterprise-wide tools that support the broader systems and processes within which Service Transition delivers support
- Tools targeted more specifically at supporting Service Transition or parts of Service Transition.

The following systems, supporting the wider scope, will provide automated support for some elements of Service Transition management:

- IT Service Management systems:
  - Enterprise frameworks that provide integration capabilities to integrate and link in the CMDB or tools
  - System, network and application management tools
  - Service dashboards and reporting tools
- Specific ITSM technology and tools that cover:
  - Service Knowledge Management System
  - Collaborative, content management, workflow tools
  - Data mining tools
  - Extract, load and transform data tools
  - Measurement and reporting systems
  - Test management and testing tools
  - Database and test data management tools
  - Copying and publishing tools
  - Release and deployment technology
  - Deployment and logistics systems and tools.

There are many support tools that can assist Change Management, Configuration Management and Release Management. These may come in a variety of combinations and include:

- Configuration Management Systems and tools
- Version control tools
- Document-management systems
- Requirements analysis and design tools, systems architecture and CASE tools, which can facilitate impact analysis from a business perspective

- Database management audit tools to track physical databases
- Distribution and installation tools
- Comparison tools (software files, directories, databases)
- Build and release tools (that provide listings of input and output CIs)
- Installation and de-installation tools (that provide listings of CIs installed)
- Compression tools (to save storage space)
- Listing and configuration baseline tools (e.g. full directory listings with date–time stamps and check sums)
- Discovery and audit tools (also called 'inventory' tools)
- Detection and recovery tools (where the build is returned to a known state)
- Visualization, mapping and graphical representations with drill down
- Reporting tools including those that access objects from several databases, providing integrated reports across systems.

7.1 KNOWLEDGE MANAGEMENT TOOLS

Knowledge Management tools address an organization's need for management for processing information and promulgating knowledge. Knowledge Management tools address the requirements of maintaining records and documents electronically. Records are distinguished from documents by the fact that they function as evidence of activities, rather than evidence of intentions. Examples of documents include policy statements, plans, procedures, service level agreements and contracts.

- **Document management** – defines the set of capabilities to support the storage, protection, archiving, classification and retirement of documents and information
- **Records management** – defines the set of capabilities to support the storage, protection, archiving, classification and retirement of records
- **Content management** – the capability that manages the storage, maintenance and retrieval of documents and information of a system or website. The result is often a knowledge asset represented in written words, figures, graphics and other forms of knowledge presentation. Examples of knowledge services that directly support content management are:

- web publishing tools
- web conferencing, wikis, blogs etc.
- word processing
- data and financial analysis
- presentation tools
- flow-charting
- content management systems (codify, organize, version control, document architectures)
- Publication and distribution.

7.2 COLLABORATION

Collaboration is the process of sharing tacit knowledge and working together to accomplish stated goals and objectives. The following is a list of knowledge services widely available today, which, when properly implemented, can significantly improve the productivity of people by streamlining and improving the way they collaborate:

- Shared calendars and tasks
- Threaded discussions
- Instant messaging
- White-boarding
- Video or teleconferencing
- E-mail.

7.2.1 Communities

Communities are rapidly becoming the method of choice for groups of people spread across time zones and country boundaries to communicate, collaborate and share knowledge. These communities are typically facilitated through an online medium such as an intranet or extranet and the community often acts as the integration point for all knowledge services provided to its members. Well-run communities will typically elect a leader to manage and run the community and a group of subject matter experts to contribute and evaluate knowledge assets within the community. Examples of services and functions provided within the typical online community are:

- Community portals
- E-mail alias management
- Focus groups
- Intellectual property, best practice, work examples and template repository
- Online events and net shows.

Successful communities often implement a reward and recognition programme for their members. Such a programme is a means to acknowledge and reward the contribution of valuable knowledge assets. These assets are submitted by members of the community and are evaluated by the community leader and elected subject matter experts. The author(s) are then recognized within the community and meaningfully rewarded in some fashion for their contribution. This is a highly effective way to encourage members to share their knowledge and move past the old paradigm that knowledge is power and job security and therefore needs to be hoarded. In addition, it is highly recommended that senior management actively participates in these communities to foster a culture and environment that rewards knowledge sharing and collaboration.

7.2.2 Workflow management

Workflow management is another broad area of knowledge services that provides systemic support for managing knowledge assets through a predefined workflow or process. Many knowledge assets today go through a workflow process that creates, modifies, augments, informs, or approves aspects of the asset. For example, within the sphere of application management, a Request for Change (RFC) is a knowledge asset that moves through a workflow that creates it, modifies it, assesses it, estimates it, approves it and ultimately deploys it. Workflow applications provide the infrastructure and support necessary to implement a highly efficient process to accomplish these types of tasks. Typical workflow services provided within this services category include:

- Workflow design
- Routing objects
- Event services
- Gate keeping at authorization checkpoints
- State transition services.

7.3 CONFIGURATION MANAGEMENT SYSTEM

Many organizations have some form of Configuration Management in operation, but it is often paper-based. For large and complex infrastructures, Configuration Management will operate more effectively when supported by a software tool that is capable of maintaining a CMS. The CMS contains details about the attributes and the history of each CI and details of the important relationships between CIs. Ideally, any CMDB should be linked to the DML. Often, several tools need to be integrated to provide the fully automated solution across platforms, e.g. federated CMDB.

The Configuration Management System should prevent changes from being made to the IT infrastructure or service configuration baseline without valid authorization via Change Management. The authorization record should automatically 'drive' the change. As far as possible, all changes should be recorded on the CMS at least by the time that the change is implemented. The status (e.g. 'live', 'archive', etc.) of each CI affected by a change should be updated automatically if possible. Example ways in which this automatic recording of changes could be implemented include automatic updating of the CMS when software is moved between libraries (e.g. from 'acceptance test' to 'live', or from 'live' to an 'archive' library), when the service catalogue is changed, and when a release is distributed.

The Configuration Management System should, in addition, provide:

- Sufficient security controls to limit access on a need-to-know basis
- Support for CIs of varying complexity, e.g. entire systems, releases, single hardware items, software modules
- Hierarchic and networked relationships between CIs; by holding information on the relationships between CIs, Configuration Management tools facilitate the impact assessment of RFCs
- Easy addition of new CIs and deletion of old CIs
- Automatic validation of input data (e.g. are all CI names unique?)
- Automatic determination of all relationships that can be automatically established, when new CIs are added
- Support for CIs with different model numbers, version numbers, and copy numbers
- Automatic identification of other affected CIs when any CI is the subject of an incident report/record, problem record, known error record or RFC
- Integration of problem management data within the CMS, or at least an interface from the Configuration Management System to any separate problem management databases that may exist
- Automatic updating and recording of the version number of a CI if the version number of any component CI is changed
- Maintenance of a history of all CIs (both a historical record of the current version – such as installation date, records of Changes, previous locations, etc. – and of previous versions)
- Support for the management and use of configuration baselines (corresponding to definitive copies, versions

etc.), including support for reversion to trusted versions
- Ease of interrogation of the CMS and good reporting facilities, including trend analysis (e.g. the ability to identify the number of RFCs affecting particular CIs)
- Ease of reporting of the CI inventory so as to facilitate configuration audits
- Flexible reporting tools to facilitate impact analyses
- The ability to show graphically the configuration models and maps of interconnected CIs, and to input information about new CIs via such maps
- The ability to show the hierarchy of relationships between 'parent' CIs and 'child' CIs.

For software, support tools should allow control to be maintained, for applications software, from the outset of systems analysis and design right through to live running. Ideally, organizations should use the same tool to control all stages of the lifecycle, although this may not be possible if all the platforms cannot be supported by one software tool. If this is not possible, then the ITSM infrastructure Configuration Management tool should at least allow Configuration Management information to be transferred from a software development Configuration Management System into the CMS without the need for re-keying.

These individual tools and solutions may be integrated with the main Service Management system or the Configuration Management System where the effort of integration is beneficial. Otherwise, the integration may be undertaken at the procedural or data level.

Automating the initial discovery and configuration audits significantly increases the efficiency and effectiveness of Configuration Management. These tools can determine what hardware and software is installed and how applications are mapped to the infrastructure.

This means a greater coverage of audited CIs with the resources available, and staff can focus on handling the exceptions rather than doing the audits. If the DML is not integrated with the CMDB it may be worth automating the comparison of the DML contents with the CMDB.

Implementing Service
Transition

8 Implementing Service Transition

Implementing Service Transition in a Greenfield situation, i.e. a starting point where no Service Transition exists at all, would only be likely if a new service provider is being established. Therefore the task for most service provider organizations will be one of service improvement, a matter of assessing their current approach to the Service Transition processes and establishing the most effective and efficient improvements to make, prioritized according to the business benefit that can be achieved. Considerable guidance on this topic is contained within the ITIL Continual Service Improvement publication, but the cycle will be as illustrated in Figure 8.1.

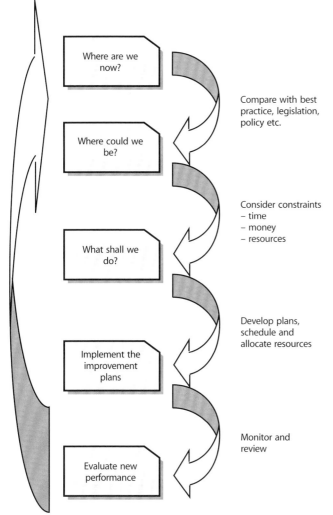

Figure 8.1   Steps to improving Service Transition processes

Introducing new or improved ST processes will be a significant organizational change and an introduction of improved services delivered by the service provider. From that context, much of the guidance in this publication on delivering new or changed services is directly applicable to introducing Service Transition itself. Doing so is, in itself, a Service Transition exercise, since it is changing the services delivered by the service provider.

8.1   STAGES OF INTRODUCING SERVICE TRANSITION

The stages of introducing Service Transition will match that of other services, requiring a justification for their introduction (strategic considerations), designing of the Service Transition components and then their introduction to the organization (transitioning) before they can run in normal mode (operations).

8.1.1   Justifying Service Transition

Service Transition is a key contributor to the service provider's ability to deliver quality services to the business. They are the delivery mechanism between the work of design, and the day-to-day care delivered by operations. However, the Service Transition processes are not always visible to the customers, and this can make financial justification difficult. When setting up Service Transition, attention needs to be paid to ways of quantifying and measuring the benefits, typically as a balance between impact to the business (negative and positive) and cost (in terms of money/staff resources) and in terms of what would be prevented by applying resource to any specific transition, such as diverting staff resources or delaying implementation.

Gathering of evidence on the cost of current inadequate Service Transition is a valid and useful exercise, addressing such issues as:

- Cost of failed changes
- Extra cost of actual transition compared with budgeted costs
- Errors found in live running that could have been detected during test transition.

8.1.2   Designing Service Transition

Design of the Service Transition processes and how they fit within an organization are addressed throughout this publication. Useful factors to consider when designing Service Transition are described below.

8.1.2.1 Applicable standards and policies

Consider how agreed policies, standards and legislation will constrain the design of Service Transition. Considerations might include requirements for independence and visible accountability, such as are commonly found controlling financial sector companies or within legislation such as Sarbanes-Oxley (SOX).

8.1.2.2 Relationships

Other internal support services

In many situations Service Transition must work together with other areas that are transitioning other elements of a business change, such as HR, facilities management, telecoms, production control, education and training. The processes will be designed to facilitate these relationships.

The aim should be to ensure that ownership for each component of the overall service package is defined and subsequently management responsibility is clear.

Programme and project management

Major transitions may be managed as programmes or projects, and Service Transition will deliver their role within the appropriate umbrella. Clear areas of delineation and collaboration between programmes, projects and Service Transition will be required, and these need to be set out and agreed within the organization. To ensure appropriate transition is delivered, Service Transition staff will be involved in agreeing key programme and project milestones and timelines and ST should be set up to adopt this role. For example if a project is due to deliver a major release at the end of the month, ST must provide sufficient and timely resources to baseline and release the service package, at the agreed time and according to agreed quality levels.

To be effective, Service Transition needs to take a broader view across projects, combining transitions and releases to make the best use of available resources.

Service Transition will set up and maintain (working through CSI) an approach to dealing with an ongoing influx of tasks (Service Transitions) that must be delivered, scheduling, combining and sharing resources as appropriate. The strategy should seek to establish this role for ST together with the delegated authority and escalation channels that enable it to deliver.

Internal development teams and external suppliers

Communication channels will need to deal with defects, risks and issues discovered during the transition process, e.g. errors found during testing. Channels to both internal

teams and external suppliers will need to be identified and maintained.

Customers/users

Communication with customers and users is important to ensure that the transitioned service will remain focused on current business requirements. The requirements at actual transition may evolve from the needs identified at design stage and communication channels with the customer will be the source of identifying those changes. Effective communication will benefit from an agreed strategic stakeholder contact map (see paragraph 5.3.2). In many circumstances this communication will be routed through service or account management or SLM, but these channels need to be identified and designed into the Service Transition processes also.

Other stakeholders

Other stakeholders will need to interface with ST, and these should be identified for all foreseeable circumstances, including in disaster recovery scenarios, and so liaison with ITSCM should be catered for. Other possible considerations might include:

- IT, e.g. networks, IT security, data management
- Outside of IT but within the organization, e.g. facilities management, HR, physical security
- Outside of the organization, e.g. landlords, police and regulatory bodies.

8.1.2.3 Budget and resources

The tasks required to deliver Service Transition should deliver an overall net benefit to the organization (or they should be revisited and revised) but nonetheless they do require funding, and the ST strategy should address the source and control of financial provision.

Funding approach

A mechanism for controlling the funding of the transition infrastructure must be established, including:

- **Testing environments** – In many organizations testing groups (including specialist testing aspects such as usability testing) are not under the direct control of transition. The relationship and authority to engage and allocate resources needs to be established, understood, maintained and managed.
- **SCM and Service Knowledge Management Systems** – These will specifically require funding for the technology and skills essential to their effectiveness.

The costing of transition objectives must be an integral part of design. This applies whatever the funding mechanism may be, and will involve serviced transition and customers working with design. Typically the transition options will be costed and a business risk-based decision reached.

Resources

Similarly to the options and issues faced when considering funding, supply and control of other resources will need to be addressed within the ST strategy such as:

■ Staff, for example the allocation of project resource to transition activities
■ Central infrastructure, e.g.:
  ● Central test data, compromise between broadly applicable and re-usable against focused on individual services/features
  ● Network resources for distribution of software, documentation and for testing of networked elements of services to be transitioned.

Test environment management is a major item of expenditure and a significant resource element in many organizations. Under-funding and/or under-resourcing here (either through lack of numbers or lack of requisite skills) can cause very expensive errors and problems in supporting live services, and have severe detrimental effects on an organization's overall business capability.

8.1.3 Introducing Service Transition

Experience shows that it is not advisable to attempt to retrofit a new transition's practices onto projects under way; the benefits from the improved (and still unproven) practices are unlikely to outweigh the disruption caused by changing horses in midstream. If a particular transition is especially problematical, and it may be relevant to force a change of attitude, then an exception could be justified.

One technique that has worked in organizations is capturing 'in flight' initiatives and bringing them into line with the new approach. This involves adjusting projects currently going through design/transition and adjusting their planning to fit in with the new procedures, typically at acceptance test/go live stage. For this to be successful, conversion strategies form 'old transition routes' to the new procedures should be considered, designed (and tested where possible) as part of the design responsibility.

8.1.4 Cultural change aspects

Even formalization of mostly existing procedures will deliver cultural change; if implementing Service Transition into an organization means installing formal processes that were not there before the cultural change is significant. Experience shows that staff working in Change Management, and even those evangelizing change among others, are potentially as resistant to change in their own areas as anyone else.

While it important to focus on gaining the support of Service Transition staff working directly in Service Transition it is equally important that those supporting, and being supported by, Service Transition understand why the changes to procedures are being made, the benefits to themselves and to the organization and their changed roles. The cultural change programme should address all stakeholders and should continue throughout and after transition, to ensure the changed attitudes are firmly embedded and not seen as a fashion accessory that can be dispensed with after the initial high profile has faded.

Considerably more information on cultural change can be found in Chapter 5.

8.1.5 Risk and value

As with all transitions, decisions around transitioning the transition service should not be made without adequate understanding of the expected risks and benefits. In this specific situation the risks might include:

■ Alienation of support staff
■ Excessive costs to the business
■ Unacceptable delays to business benefits.

The risks and beneficial values require a baseline of the current situation, if the changes are to be measurable. Measures of the added value from Service Transition might include:

■ Customer and user satisfaction
■ Reduced incident and failure rates for transitioned services
■ Reduced cost of transitioning.

Challenges, critical
success factors and risks

9 Challenges, critical success factors and risks

9.1 CHALLENGES

The complexity of services across the supply chain is increasing and this leads to challenges for any service provider that implements new services or changes existing services. IT within e-business not only supports the primary business processes, but is part of the primary business processes.

This prime position brings a wide range of challenges to successful Service Transition, such as:

- Enabling almost every business process and service in IT, resulting in a large customer and stakeholder group that is involved and impacted by Service Transition
- Managing many contacts, interfaces and relationships through Service Transition, including a variety of different customers, users, programmes, projects, suppliers and partners
- There being little harmonization and integration of the processes and disciplines that impact Service Transition, e.g. finance, engineering, human resource management
- There being inherent differences among the legacy systems, new technology and human elements that result in unknown dependencies and are risky to change
- Achieving a balance between maintaining a stable production environment and being responsive to the business needs for changing the services
- Achieving a balance between pragmatism and bureaucracy
- Creating an environment that fosters standardization, simplification and knowledge sharing
- Being an enabler of business change and, therefore, an integral component of the business change programmes
- Establishing leaders to champion the changes and improvements
- Establishing 'who is doing what, when and where' and 'who should be doing what, when and where'
- Developing a culture that encourages people to collaborate and work effectively together and an atmosphere that fosters the cultural shifts necessary to get buy-in from people
- Developing standard performance measures and measurement methods across projects and suppliers

- Ensuring that the quality of delivery and support matches the business use of new technology
- Ensuring that the Service Transition time and budget is not impacted by events earlier in the service lifecycle (e.g. budget cuts)
- Understanding the different stakeholder perspectives that underpin effective risk management within an organization
- Understanding, and being able to assess, the balance between managing risk and taking risks as it affects the overall strategy of the organization and potential mismatch between project risks and business risk
- Evaluating the effectiveness of reporting in relation to risk management and corporate governance.

9.2 CRITICAL SUCCESS FACTORS

Service provision, in all organizations, needs to be matched to current and rapidly changing business demands. The objective is to improve continually the quality of service, aligned to the business requirements, cost-effectively. To meet this objective, the following critical success factors need to be considered for Service Transition:

- Understanding and managing the different stakeholder perspectives that underpin effective risk management within an organization and establishing and maintaining stakeholder 'buy-in' and commitment
- Maintaining the contacts and managing all the relationships during Service Transition
- Integrating with the other service lifecycle stages, processes and disciplines that impact Service Transition
- Understanding the inherent dependencies among the legacy systems, new technology and human elements that result in unknown dependencies and are risky to change
- Automating processes to eliminate errors and reduce the cycle time
- Creating and maintaining new and updated knowledge in a form that people can find and use
- Developing good-quality systems, tools, processes and procedures required to manage a Service Transition practice
- Good Service Management and IT infrastructure tools and technology

- Being able to appreciate and exploit the cultural and political environment
- Being able to understand the service and technical configurations and their dependencies
- Developing a thorough grasp of the hard factors (processes and procedures) and soft (skills and competencies) factors required to manage a Service Transition practice
- Developing a workforce with the right knowledge and skills, appropriate training and the right service culture
- Defining clear accountabilities, roles and responsibilities
- Establishing a culture that enables knowledge to be shared freely and willingly
- Demonstrating improved cycle time to deliver change and less variation in time, cost and quality predictions during and after transition
- Demonstrating improved customer and user satisfaction ratings during Service Transition
- Demonstrating that the benefits of establishing and improving the Service Transition practice and processes outweigh the costs (across the organization and services)
- Being able to communicate the organization's attitude to risk and approach to risk management more effectively during Service Transition activities
- Building a thorough understanding of risks that have impacted or may impact successful Service Transition of services in the Service Portfolio.

9.3 RISKS

Implementing the Service Transition practice should not be made without recognizing the potential risk to services currently in transition and those releases that are planned. A baseline assessment of current Service Transitions and planned projects will help Service Transition to identify implementation risks.

These risks might include:

- Change in accountabilities, responsibilities and practices of existing projects that de-motivate the workforce
- Alienation of some key support and operations staff
- Additional unplanned costs to services in transition
- Resistance to change and circumvention of the processes due to perceived bureaucracy.

Other implementation risks include:

- Excessive costs to the business due to overly risk-averse Service Transition practices and plans
- Knowledge sharing (as the wrong people may have access to information)
- Lack of maturity and integration of systems and tools resulting in people 'blaming' technology for other shortcomings
- Poor integration between the processes – causing process isolation and a silo approach to delivering ITSM
- Loss of productive hours, higher costs, loss of revenue or perhaps even business failure as a result of poor Service Transition processes.

9.4 SERVICE TRANSITION UNDER DIFFICULT CONDITIONS

In some circumstances, Service Transitions will be required under atypical or difficult conditions, such as:

- Short timescale
- Restricted finances
- Restricted resource availability – not enough people or lack of test environments, inadequate tools etc.
- Absence of anticipated skills sets
- Internal political difficulty, staff disincentives, such as:
  - Redundancy/outsourcing or similar threats
  - Difficult corporate culture of confrontational management style
  - Internal rivalries and competitiveness
- External difficulties such as weather, political instability, post-disaster, legislation.

Clearly, some of these circumstances overlap with continuity planning, and many of the approaches set out in the Service Design publication will be relevant to successful transition in difficult circumstances.

If the difficulties are anticipated, then alleviating measures will be identified and form part of the service package, planning the route through transition within the transition model, as would any foreseen factors likely to influence transition.

It is quite possible, however, that the difficulties will be unanticipated, perhaps due to changed circumstances, and will require 'on the fly' adaptation. This section sets out some of the constraining circumstances that might require adaptation, modification or compromise, and elements of approach that would aid success. A key element common to most (if not all) of these situations is having a clear understanding of what will constitute success. When circumstances are difficult priorities are often focused on specific aspects of service, customer base etc. – then to deliver accepted priorities in the constrained circumstances will often require compromises in other areas.

9.4.1 When speed is more important than accuracy or smoothness

In time critical situations, implementation of a new or changed service may be more important than a degree of disruption. This is effectively a risk management decision, and general risk management principles apply. Some of the key factors that assist with delivering success in this context are:

■ Empowerment – with staff given the authority to take appropriate levels of risk. In volatile industries Service Transition must act in a way that reflects the corporate risk culture and not suppress or undermine business risk decisions.

■ A need to know the absolute cut off date/time that Service Transition must deliver by – too often either 'safety margins' are built in meaning a product is delivered early that could have been improved, or people assume there is some leeway and there isn't – meaning critical deadlines are missed. It is often better to be totally open and trust key staff.

■ Deciding which components of the transitioned service must be available at the cut-off date, and which could be added later.

■ How separable are the components and what are the dependencies? What elements might be required although not initially on the 'essentials' list?

■ Which users/customers/locations etc. must be in place at the cut-off date?

■ What actually happens if you fail? Again, honesty is often the best policy here. Consider:
  ● Business impact
  ● Money
  ● Lives
  ● Political embarrassment
  ● Reputation.

Understanding crisis management can be very helpful in coping and especially understanding that the rules for crisis management are different from those for everyday management. Just being aware of the first two laws of crisis management (after Larry Niven) can help to reassure people that the situation is survivable:

Rule 1: Don't panic.

Rule 2: A good crisis manager makes decisions instantly and acts on them. If they later turn out to have been correct, so much the better, but speed is often more important than efficiency in a crisis situation.

Success in these circumstances depends on:

■ Empowerment and subsequent support, and a belief in that support. Staff must be aware of their empowerment levels and actually believe that the organization will support their choices – not be in fear of a 'court martial' approach.

■ Authorization channels and those channels being open and rapid. There must be agreed actions if the channels don't function – e.g. increased delegated authority, escalation, alternative support channels.

■ Following the procedures, realizing there is risk, and no blame afterwards – if not the required flexibility and speed of response is constrained.

9.4.2 Restricted resources

When resources are in short supply, a key aspect here is deciding what to measure and sticking to that decision and the framework for delivery, e.g.:

■ What is the important parameter – speed, or low cost or whatever? And knowing that will be the measure of importance afterwards, e.g. no blame for it being expensive when the understanding was 'get it in by 3 p.m. whatever the cost'.

■ Establish an applicable hierarchy of measures – speed – money – full functionality etc. with some subordinate ones having absolute limits, e.g. as quickly as possible, but not more that £12,500; or as cheaply as possible but must be in by 30 September. This requires involving budget holders, business decision makers etc. to ensure the correct parameters are built in.

■ Awareness and documentation. All actually and potentially aware staff need to be aware of requirements, and a mechanism for keeping staff informed quickly about changes to those requirements is essential.

9.4.3 Safety critical services and high risk environments

Ever-increasingly, IT services directly support or actually deliver services on which lives depend, such as hospital services, emergency services call-taking, flood control and aircraft 'fly-by-wire'. Extra security and foolproof approaches are required, with features such as:

- Appropriate documentation, which is essential and often includes counter-signatures and extra checks on stage approval; however, excessive documentation can be counter-productive; high risk can often be found in conjunction with time-restricted situations (e.g. emergency services coordination) meaning careful balancing of safety and speed is required; in such circumstances skill and experience and/or extensive training is a major factor
- Accuracy typically taking priority over speed
- More rigorous testing, longer time periods and more detailed data collected and maintained within the CMS
- Measures of safety accurately assessed by an accepted authority, e.g. what constitutes acceptable levels, such as safe radiation doses within X-ray or radioactive environments
- Setting the sign-off authority, and ensuring those responsible are not overly influenced by inappropriate pressures, such as concern about company profit or staff bonuses as opposed to risking human lives
- In extreme circumstances ensuring more than one individual must be involved for certain actions to be taken (e.g. typically the procedures for launching nuclear weapons require simultaneous confirmation by two trained officers)
- Consider 'veto' rights for sub-groupings whereby those controlling any key component of the service can stop implementation – as a 'no-go' from one of a dozen teams can stop a launch of a the space shuttle.

9.4.4 Working with difficult customers

Of course there is no such thing as a bad customer, really, but often there are customers who are unclear of their role as a customer and so act in a way that prevents rather than supports successful implementation. Examples include customers who:

- Feel the need to get too involved in the detail of how things are done, instead of judging by the service delivered
- Are not able to deliver the decisions and choose options to suit their business needs

- Do not make staff and resources available to facilitate effective Service Transition, for example providing data and staff to assess the transitioned service, or to effect user testing.

These kinds of situation can often be improved by awareness and education of:

- Customers
- Users
- Transition staff (e.g. patience and diplomacy skills)
- Account management working with the customers to reassure customers and ascertain their requirements
- Careful budgetary control, so that customers can see the value returning for their investment of staff time and other resources.

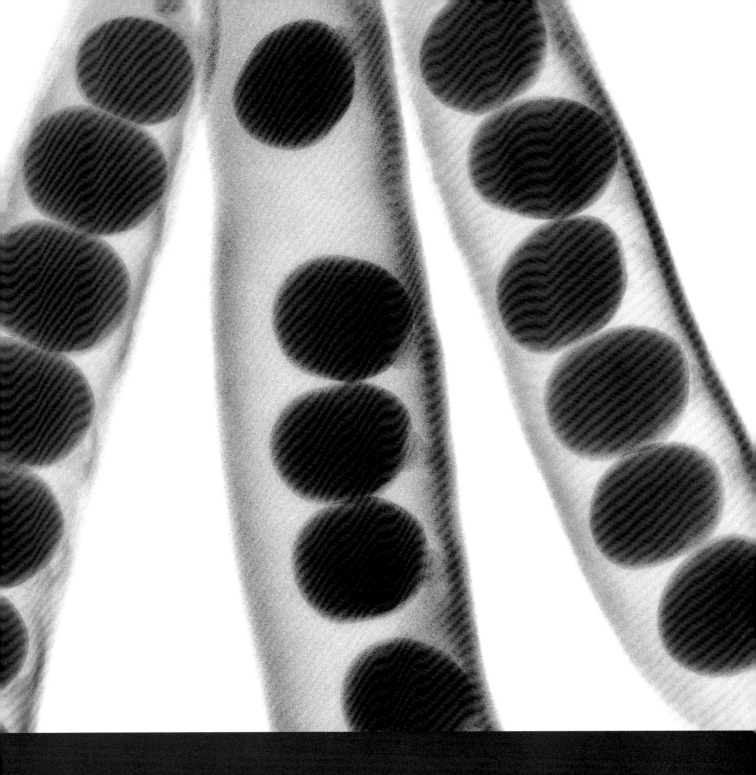

Afterword

Afterword

This publication is part of the ITIL series that sets out good practice and sound advice for organizations that recognize the importance of Service Management to their overall success.

This publication, like the others, offers sound general advice, but this – in itself – is not enough. That advice must be understood within the context that organization finds itself.

IT service managers must manage services within the circumstances they find themselves – for some safety will be the pre-eminent concern, others will consider speed, profitability or usability or some other factor as their prime driver. Delivering effective Service Transition is a challenge for all; delivering effective Service Transition in any specific organization requires understanding of the Service Transition principle, and understanding the business supported and the services being introduced, changed or retired.

This publication has been written to supply a foundation for ITSM professionals to implement solid and effective services to support their customers in their business, and to go on doing that in the longer term.

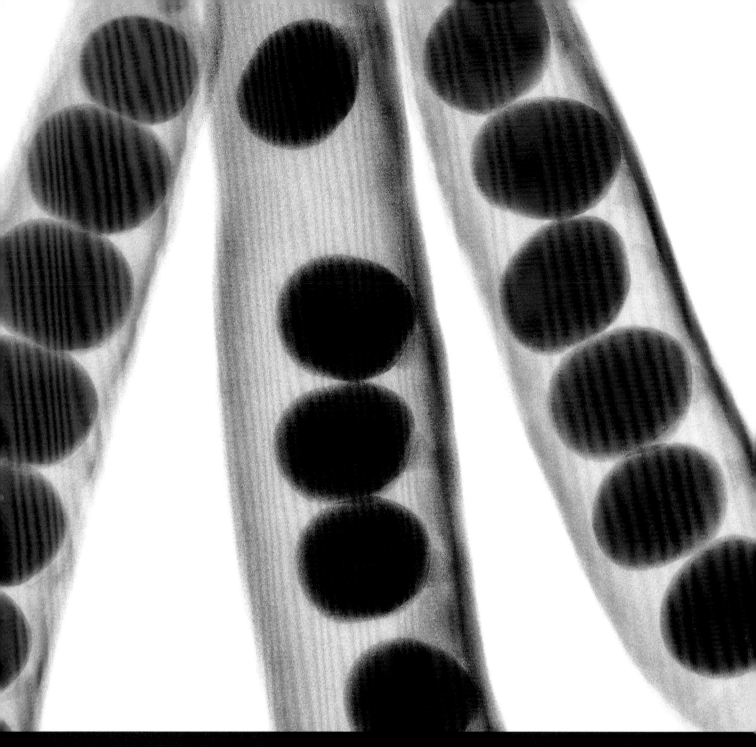

Appendix A:
Description of
asset types

A

Appendix A: Description of asset types

Management

Management is a system that includes leadership, administration, policies, performance measures and incentives. This layer cultivates, coordinates and controls all other asset types. Management includes idiosyncratic elements such as philosophy, core beliefs, values, decision-making style and perceptions of risk. It is also the most distinctive and inimitable type of asset deeply rooted in the organization. [The term organization is used here to refer to the enterprise or firm rather than the organization asset type. The most likely manner in which management assets can be partially extracted from an organization is by the poaching of key individuals who were instrumental in defining and developing a particular management system.] Service Management itself is a type of specialized management asset like others such as project management, research and development, and manufacturing management.

Organization

Organization assets are active configurations of people, processes, applications and infrastructure that carry out all organizational activity through the principles of specialization and coordination. This category of assets includes the functional hierarchies, social networks of groups, teams and individuals, and the systems they use to work in alignment towards shared goals and incentives. Organization assets include the patterns in which people, applications, information and infrastructure deploy either by design or by self-adaptive process to maximize the creation of value for stakeholders. Some service organizations are superior to others simply by virtue of organization. For example, networks of wireless access points, storage systems, point-of-sale terminals, databases, hardware stores, and remote backup facilities. Strategic location of assets by itself is a basis for superior performance and competitive advantage.

Process

Process assets are made of algorithms, methods, procedures, and routines that direct the execution and control of activities and interactions. There is a great diversity in process assets, which are specialized to various degrees from very generic management processes to sophisticated low-level algorithms embedded in software applications and other forms of automation. Process assets are the most dynamic of types. They signify action and transformation. Some of them are also the means by which organization and management assets coordinate and control each other and interact with the business environment. Process people and application assets execute them; knowledge and information assets enrich them; applications and infrastructure assets enable them. Examples of process assets are order fulfilment, accounts receivables, incident management, Change Management and testing.

Knowledge

Knowledge assets are accumulations of awareness, experience, information, insight and intellectual property that are associated with actions and context. Management, organization, process and applications assets use and store knowledge assets. People assets store tacit knowledge in the form of experience, skills and talent. Such knowledge is primarily acquired through experience, observation and training. Movement of teams and individuals is an effective way to transfer tacit knowledge within and across organizations (Argote 2000). Knowledge assets in tacit form are hard for rivals to replicate but easy for owners to lose. Organizations seek to protect themselves from loss by codifying tacit knowledge into explicit forms such as knowledge embedded in process, applications and infrastructure assets. Knowledge assets are difficult to manage but can be highly leveraged with increasing returns and virtually zero opportunity costs (Baruch Lev. 2001). Knowledge assets include policies, plans, designs, configurations, architectures, process definitions, analytical methods, service definitions, analyses, reports and surveys. They may be owned as intellectual property and protected by copyrights, patents and trademarks. Knowledge assets can also be rented for use under licensing arrangements and service contracts.

People

The value of people assets is the capacity for creativity, analysis, perception, learning, judgement, leadership, communication, coordination, empathy and trust. Such capacity is in teams and individuals within the organization, due to knowledge, experience and skills. Skills can be conceptual, technical and social skills. People assets are also the most convenient absorbers and carriers of all forms of knowledge. They are the most versatile and potent of all asset types because of their ability to learn and adapt. People assets represent an organization's capabilities and resources. If capabilities are capacity for action, people assets are the actors. From the capabilities perspective, people assets are the only type that can create, combine and consume all other asset types. Their tolerance of ambiguity and uncertainty also compensates for the limitations of processes, applications and infrastructure. Because of their enormous potential, people assets are often the most expensive in terms of development, maintenance and motivation. They also are assets that can be hired or rented but cannot be owned. Customers highly value services that enhance the productivity or potential of people assets.

People assets are also resources with productive capacity. Units of cost, time and effort measure their capacity as teams and individuals. They are mobile, multi-purpose and highly adaptive with the innate ability to learn. Staffing contracts, software agents and customers using self-service options augment the capacity of people assets.

Information

Information assets are collections, patterns, and meaningful abstractions of data applied in contexts such as customers, contracts, services, events, projects and operations. They are useful for various purposes including communication, coordination and control of business activities. Information assets exist in various forms such as documents, records, messages and graphs. All asset types produce them but management, processes, knowledge, people and applications primarily consume them. The value of information assets can vary with time, location and format, and depreciate very quickly. Some services create value by processing information and making it available as needed by management, processes, people and applications assets. The criteria of effectiveness, efficiency, availability, integrity, confidentiality, reliability and compliance can be used to evaluate the quality of information assets.

Applications

Applications assets are diverse in type and include artefacts, automation and tools used to support the performance of other asset types. Applications are composed of software, hardware, documents, methods, procedures, routines, scripts and instructions. They automate, codify, enable, enhance, maintain or mimic the properties, functions, and activities of management, organization, processes, knowledge, people and information assets. Applications derive their value in relation to these other assets. Process assets in particular commonly exist inside applications. Applications assets consume, produce and maintain knowledge and

information assets. They can be of various types such as general-purpose, multi-purpose and special-purpose. Some applications are analogous to industrial tools, machinery and equipment because they enhance the performance of processes. Others are analogous to office equipment and consumer appliances because they enhance the personal productivity of people assets. Examples of applications are accounting software, voice mail, imaging systems, encryption devices, process control, inventory tracking, electronic design automation, mobile phones and bar code scanners. Applications are themselves supported by infrastructure, people and process assets. One of the most powerful attributes of applications is they can be creatively combined and integrated with other asset types, particularly other applications to create valuable new assets.

Infrastructure

Infrastructure assets have the peculiar property of existing in the form of layers defined in relation to the assets they support, especially people and applications. They include information technology assets such as software applications, computers, storage systems, network devices, telecommunication equipment, cables, wireless links, access control devices and monitoring systems. This category of assets also includes traditional facilities such as buildings, electricity, Heat, Ventilation, Air Conditioning (HVAC) and water supply without which it would be impossible for people, applications, and other infrastructure assets to operate. Infrastructure assets by themselves may be composed of mostly applications and other infrastructure assets. Assets viewed as applications at one level can be used as infrastructure at another. This is an important principle that allows service-orientation of assets.

Financial capital

Financial assets are required to support the ownership or use of all types of assets. They also measure the economic value and performance of all types of assets. Financial assets include cash, cash equivalents and other assets such as marketable securities and receivables that convert into cash with degrees of certainty and ease. Adequacy of financial assets is an important concern for all organizations including government agencies and non-profits. The promise and potential of other assets is not realized in full without financial assets.

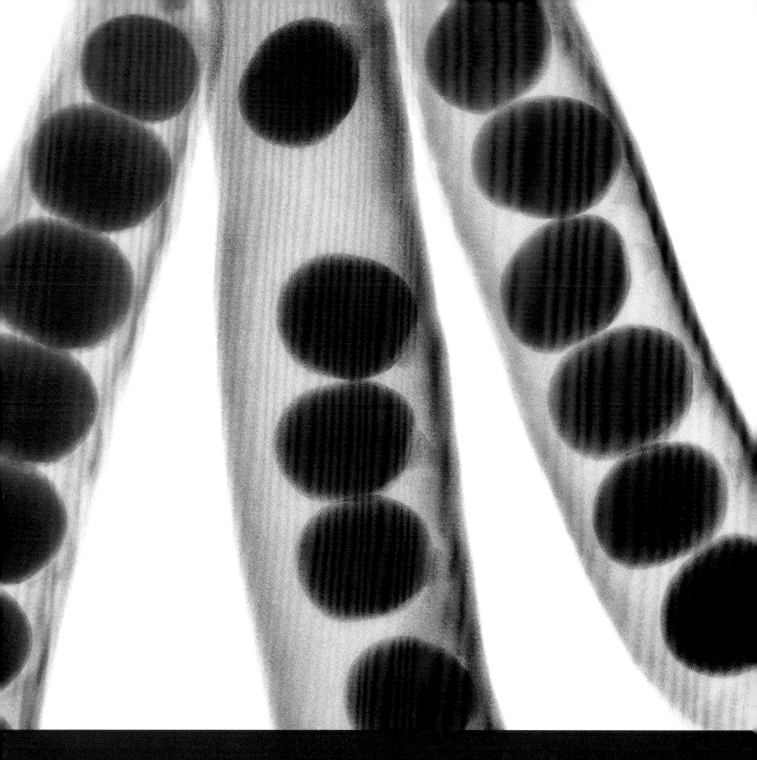

Further information

Further information

REFERENCES

Argote, Linda (2000) Knowledge Transfer: A Basis for Competitive Advantage in Firms. Organizational Behaviour and Human Decision Processes. Vol. 82, No. 1, May, pp. 150–169.

Baruch Lev. (2001) Intangibles: Management, Measurement, and Reporting. The Brookings Institution.

BS 7799-3:2006, Information Security Management Systems – Guidelines for Information Security Risk Management.

BSI (2003) *Managing Culture and Knowledge – A Guide to Good Practice*, Committee KMS/1, Rob Young (Chairman), PD 7501, British Standards Institution, London.

BSI (2003) *Guide to Measurements in Knowledge Management*, Committee KMS/1, Rob Young (Chairman), PD 7502, British Standards Institution, London.

BSI (2001) *Knowledge Management. A Guide to Good Practice*, British Standards Institution, London.

COBIT® (2005) *COBIT Framework, Control Objectives for Information and Related Technology*, Information Systems Audit and Control Association (ISACA) and the IT Governance Institute (ITGI), Rolling Meadows, Illinois, US.

CMMI (2006) *Capability Maturity Model® Integration (CMMI)* version 1.2, August, Software Engineering Institute (SEI), Carnegie Mellon University, Pittsburgh.

Drake, P. (2005a) *Communicative Action in Information Security Systems: An Application of Social Theory in a Technical Domain*, Hull Business School, University of Hull, Hull.

Drake, P. (2005b) Socialising the domain of information security, *OR Insight*, Vol. 18, No. 3, pp. 15–23, Operational Research Society, University of Hull, Hull.

Duck, J. D. (2000) Managing change: the art of balancing, *Harvard Business Review*, November–December.

Dugmore, J. and Lacy, S. (2006), *Achieving ISO/IEC 20000*, British Standards Institution, London.

BIP 0005 A Manager's Guide to Service Management
BIP 0030 Management Decisions and Documentation
BIP 0031 Why People Matter
BIP 0032 Making Metrics Work
BIP 0033 Managing End to End Service
BIP 0034 Finance for Service Managers

BIP 0035 Enabling Change
BIP 0036 Keeping the Service Going
BIP 0037 Capacity Management
BIP 0038 Integrating Service Management

Hambling, B. (ed.) (2007) *Software Testing, An ISEB Foundation*, with P. Morgan, A. Samaroo, G. Thompson and P. Williams, British Computer Society, Swindon.

Hackman, J. R. and Oldham, G. R. (1980) *Work Redesign (Organization Development)*, Addison-Wesley, Reading, Mass., US.

IEEE 829–1998, Standard for Software Documentation.

Institute of Internal Auditors (2005) *Global Technology Audit Guide 2: Change and Patch Management Controls: Critical for Organizational Success*, Institute of Internal Auditors, Altamonte Springs, Florida, US.

ISO 9001:2000, Quality Management Systems – Requirements.

ISO 10007:2003, Quality Management Systems – Guidelines for Configuration Management.

ISO 14001:2004, Environmental Management.

ISO 15489-1:2001, Information and Documentation – Records Management – General.

ISO/IEC 12207:1995, Information Technology – Software Lifecycle Processes.

ISO/IEC 15288:2002, Systems Engineering – System Lifecycle Processes.

ISO/IEC 19770-1:2006, Software Asset Management – Processes.

ISO/IEC 20000-1:2005, Information Technology – Service Management Part 1: Specification.

ISO/IEC 20000-2:2005, Information Technology – Service Management Part 2: Code of Practice.

ISO/IEC 27001:2005, Information Technology – Security Techniques – Information Security Management Systems – Requirements.

ISO/IEC 17799:2005, Information Technology – Security Techniques – Code of practice for information security management.

Kanter, R. M. (2001) *Evolve! Succeeding in the Digital Culture of Tomorrow*, Harvard Business School Press, Boston, MA.

Kotter, J. P. (1996) *Leading Change*, Harvard Business School Press, Boston, MA.

Kotter, J. P. and Schlesinger, L. A. (1979) Choosing strategies for change, *Harvard Business Review*, Vol. 57, No. 2, p. 106.

Kotter, J. P. (1999) Making change happen, in F. Hesselbein and P. Cohen, *Leader to Leader*, Drucker Foundation, New York.

Kotter, J. P. (2000) Leading change: why transformation efforts fail, *Harvard Business Review*, January–February.

McKinsey 7S model: Peters, T., Waterman, R. (1982) *In Search of Excellence*, Harper & Row, New York and London.

Magretta, J. (2002) *What Management Is: How it works and why it's everyone's business*. The Free Press, New York.

OGC (2003) *Managing Successful Programmes*, Office of Government Commerce, TSO (The Stationery Office), Norwich.

OGC (2007) *Management of Risk: Guidance for Practitioners*, Office of Government Commerce, TSO, Norwich.

OGC (2005) *Managing Successful Projects with PRINCE2*, Office of Government Commerce, TSO, Norwich.

PMBOK® (2006) *Project Management Body of Knowledge*, 3rd edn, Project Management Institute, Pennsylvania.

Szulanski, G. (1992) *Sticky Knowledge: Barriers to Knowing in the Firm*, Sage Publications, London.

Szulanski, G. (1996) Exploring internal stickiness: impediments to the transfer of best practice within the firm, *Strategic Management Journal*, 17 (summer special issue), pp. 27–43.

Sirkin, H. L., Keenan, P. and Jackson, A. (2005) The hard side of Change Management, *Harvard Business Review*, October.

Vogel (2005) *Effective Regulatory Compliance Requires IT Configuration Management*, Gartner Inc. Research ID: G00127752, Gartner Inc., Stamford, Connecticut.

Whitmore (1992) *Coaching for Performance*, Nicholas Brealey Publishing, London.

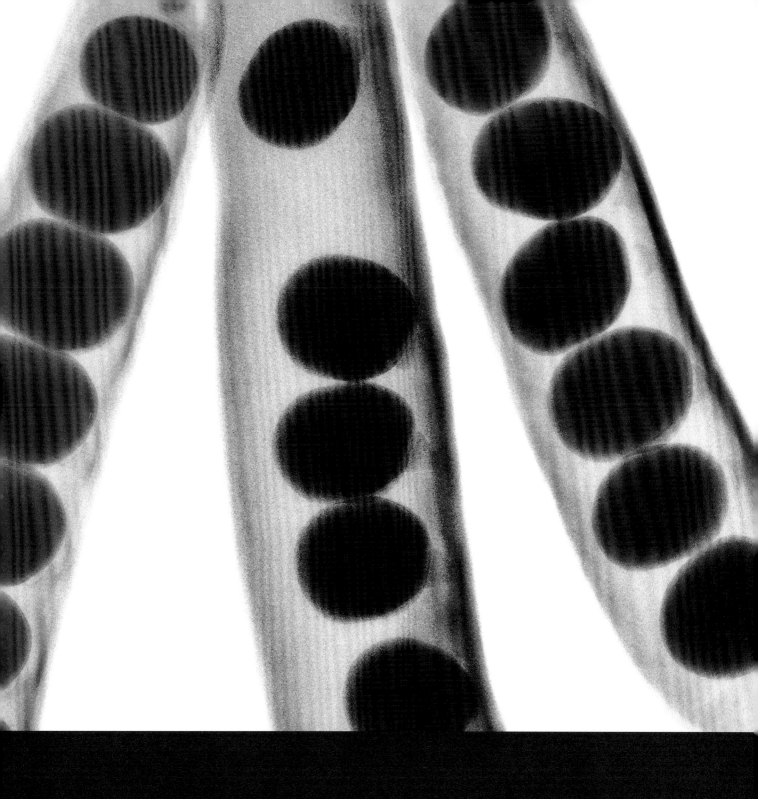

Glossary

Acronyms list

ACD	Automatic Call Distribution
AM	Availability Management
AMIS	Availability Management Information System
ASP	Application Service Provider
BCM	Business Capacity Management
BCM	Business Continuity Management
BCP	Business Continuity Plan
BIA	Business Impact Analysis
BRM	Business Relationship Manager
BSI	British Standards Institution
BSM	Business Service Management
CAB	Change Advisory Board
CAB/EC	Change Advisory Board/Emergency Committee
CAPEX	Capital Expenditure
CCM	Component Capacity Management
CFIA	Component Failure Impact Analysis
CI	Configuration Item
CMDB	Configuration Management Database
CMIS	Capacity Management Information System
CMM	Capability Maturity Model
CMMI	Capability Maturity Model Integration
CMS	Configuration Management System
COTS	Commercial off the Shelf
CSF	Critical Success Factor
CSI	Continual Service Improvement
CSIP	Continual Service Improvement Plan
CSP	Core Service Package
CTI	Computer Telephony Integration

DIKW	Data–to–Information–to–Knowledge–to–Wisdom
eSCM–CL	eSourcing Capability Model for Client Organizations
ELS	Early Life Support
eSCM–SP	eSourcing Capability Model for Service Providers
FMEA	Failure Modes and Effects Analysis
FTA	Fault Tree Analysis
IRR	Internal Rate of Return
ISG	IT Steering Group
ISM	Information Security Management
ISMS	Information Security Management System
ISO	International Organization for Standardization
ISP	Internet Service Provider
IT	Information Technology
ITSCM	IT Service Continuity Management
ITSM	IT Service Management
itSMF	IT Service Management Forum
IVR	Interactive Voice Response
KEDB	Known Error Database
KPI	Key Performance Indicator
LOS	Line of Service
M_o_R	Management of Risk
MTBF	Mean Time Between Failures
MTBSI	Mean Time Between Service Incidents
MTRS	Mean Time to Restore Service
MTTR	Mean Time To Repair
NPV	Net Present Value

OGC	Office of Government Commerce		TCO	Total Cost of Ownership
OLA	Operational Level Agreement		TCU	Total Cost of Utilization
OPEX	Operational Expenditure		TO	Technical Observation
OPSI	Office of Public Sector Information		TOR	Terms of Reference
PBA	Pattern of Business Activity		TQM	Total Quality Management
PFS	Prerequisite for Success		UC	Underpinning Contract
PIR	Post-Implementation Review		UP	User Profile
PSO	Projected Service Outage		VBF	Vital Business Function
QA	Quality Assurance		VOI	Value on Investment
QMS	Quality Management System		WIP	Work in Progress
RCA	Root Cause Analysis			
RFC	Request for Change			
ROI	Return on Investment			
RPO	Recovery Point Objective			
RTO	Recovery Time Objective			
SAC	Service Acceptance Criteria			
SACM	Service Asset and Configuration Management			
SCD	Supplier and Contract Database			
SCM	Service Capacity Management			
SDP	Service Design Package			
SFA	Service Failure Analysis			
SIP	Service Improvement Plan			
SKMS	Service Knowledge Management System			
SLA	Service Level Agreement			
SLM	Service Level Management			
SLP	Service Level Package			
SLR	Service Level Requirement			
SMO	Service Maintenance Objective			
SoC	Separation of Concerns			
SOP	Standard Operating Procedures			
SOR	Statement of requirements			
SPI	Service Provider Interface			
SPM	Service Portfolio Management			
SPO	Service Provisioning Optimization			
SPOF	Single Point of Failure			

Definitions list

The publication names included in parentheses after the name of a term identify where a reader can find more information about that term. This is either because the term is primarily used by that publication or because additional useful information about that term can be found there. Terms without a publication name associated with them may be used generally by several publications, or may not be defined in any greater detail than can be found in the glossary, i.e. we only point readers to somewhere they can expect to expand on their knowledge or to see a greater context. Terms with multiple publication names are expanded on in multiple publications.

Where the definition of a term includes another term, those related terms are highlighted in a second colour. This is designed to help the reader with their understanding by pointing them to additional definitions that are all part of the original term they were interested in. The form "*See also* Term X, Term Y" is used at the end of a definition where an important related term is not used with the text of the definition itself.

Acceptance

Formal agreement that an IT Service, Process, Plan, or other Deliverable is complete, accurate, Reliable and meets its specified Requirements. Acceptance is usually preceded by Evaluation or Testing and is often required before proceeding to the next stage of a Project or Process. *See also* Service Acceptance Criteria.

Access Management

(Service Operation) The Process responsible for allowing Users to make use of IT Services, data, or other Assets. Access Management helps to protect the Confidentiality, Integrity and Availability of Assets by ensuring that only authorized Users are able to access or modify the Assets. Access Management is sometimes referred to as Rights Management or Identity Management.

Account Manager

(Service Strategy) A Role that is very similar to Business Relationship Manager, but includes more commercial aspects. Most commonly used when dealing with External Customers.

Accounting

(Service Strategy) The Process responsible for identifying actual Costs of delivering IT Services, comparing these with budgeted costs, and managing variance from the Budget.

Activity

A set of actions designed to achieve a particular result. Activities are usually defined as part of Processes or Plans, and are documented in Procedures.

Agreement

A Document that describes a formal understanding between two or more parties. An Agreement is not legally binding, unless it forms part of a Contract. *See also* Service Level Agreement, Operational Level Agreement.

Alert

(Service Operation) A warning that a threshold has been reached, something has changed, or a Failure has occurred. Alerts are often created and managed by System Management tools and are managed by the Event Management Process.

Application

Software that provides Functions that are required by an IT Service. Each Application may be part of more than one IT Service. An Application runs on one or more Servers or Clients. *See also* Application Management.

Application Management

(Service Design) (Service Operation) The Function responsible for managing Applications throughout their Lifecycle.

Architecture

(Service Design) The structure of a System or IT Service, including the Relationships of Components to each other and to the environment they are in. Architecture also includes the Standards and Guidelines that guide the design and evolution of the System.

Assembly

(Service Transition) A Configuration Item (CI) that is made up of a number of other CIs. For example a Server CI may contain CIs for CPUs, Disks, Memory, etc.; an IT Service CI may contain many Hardware, Software and other CIs. *See also* Build.

Assessment

Inspection and analysis to check whether a Standard or set of Guidelines is being followed, that Records are accurate, or that Efficiency and Effectiveness targets are being met. *See also* Audit.

Asset

(Service Strategy) Any Resource or Capability. Assets of a Service Provider including anything that could contribute to the delivery of a Service. Assets can be one of the following types: Management, Organization, Process, Knowledge, People, Information, Applications, Infrastructure, and Financial Capital.

Asset Management

(Service Transition) Asset Management is the Process responsible for tracking and reporting the value and ownership of financial Assets throughout their Lifecycle. Asset Management is part of an overall Service Asset and Configuration Management Process. *See also* Asset Register.

Asset Register

(Service Transition) A list of Assets that includes their ownership and value. Asset Management maintains the Asset Register.

Attribute

(Service Transition) A piece of information about a Configuration Item. Examples are: name, location, Version number, and Cost. Attributes of CIs are recorded in the Configuration Management Database (CMDB). *See also* Relationship.

Audit

Formal inspection and verification to check whether a Standard or set of Guidelines is being followed, that Records are accurate, or that Efficiency and Effectiveness targets are being met. An Audit may be carried out by internal or external groups. *See also* Certification, Assessment.

Availability

(Service Design) Ability of a Configuration Item or IT Service to perform its agreed Function when required. Availability is determined by Reliability, Maintainability, Serviceability, Performance, and Security. Availability is usually calculated as a percentage. This calculation is often based on Agreed Service Time and Downtime. It is Best Practice to calculate Availability using measurements of the Business output of the IT Service.

Availability Management

(Service Design) The Process responsible for defining, analysing, Planning, measuring and improving all aspects of the Availability of IT services. Availability Management is responsible for ensuring that all IT Infrastructure, Processes, Tools, Roles, etc. are appropriate for the agreed Service Level Targets for Availability.

Back-out

See Remediation.

Backup

(Service Design) (Service Operation) Copying data to protect against loss of Integrity or Availability of the original.

Baseline

(Continual Service Improvement) A Benchmark used as a reference point. For example:

- An ITSM Baseline can be used as a starting point to measure the effect of a Service Improvement Plan
- A Performance Baseline can be used to measure changes in Performance over the lifetime of an IT Service
- A Configuration Management Baseline can be used to enable the IT Infrastructure to be restored to a known Configuration if a Change or Release fails.

Benchmark

(Continual Service Improvement) The recorded state of something at a specific point in time. A Benchmark can be created for a Configuration, a Process, or any other set of data. For example, a benchmark can be used in:

- Continual Service Improvement, to establish the current state for managing improvements
- Capacity Management, to document performance characteristics during normal operations.

See also Baseline.

Best Practice

Proven Activities or Processes that have been successfully used by multiple Organizations. ITIL is an example of Best Practice.

British Standards Institution (BSI)

The UK National Standards body, responsible for creating and maintaining British Standards. See www.bsi-global.com for more information. *See also* ISO.

Budget

A list of all the money an Organization or Business Unit plans to receive, and plans to pay out, over a specified period of time. *See also* Budgeting, Planning.

Budgeting

The Activity of predicting and controlling the spending of money. Consists of a periodic negotiation cycle to set future Budgets (usually annual) and the day-to-day monitoring and adjusting of current Budgets.

Build

(Service Transition) The Activity of assembling a number of Configuration Items to create part of an IT Service. The term Build is also used to refer to a Release that is authorized for distribution. For example Server Build or laptop Build.

Build Environment

(Service Transition) A controlled Environment where Applications, IT Services and other Builds are assembled prior to being moved into a Test or Live Environment.

Business

(Service Strategy) An overall corporate entity or Organization formed of a number of Business Units. In the context of ITSM, the term Business includes public sector and not-for-profit organizations, as well as companies. An IT Service Provider provides IT Services to a Customer within a Business. The IT Service Provider may be part of the same Business as its Customer (Internal Service Provider), or part of another Business (External Service Provider).

Business Case

(Service Strategy) Justification for a significant item of expenditure. Includes information about Costs, benefits, options, issues, Risks, and possible problems.

Business Continuity Plan (BCP)

(Service Design) A Plan defining the steps required to Restore Business Processes following a disruption. The Plan will also identify the triggers for Invocation, people to be involved, communications, etc. IT Service Continuity Plans form a significant part of Business Continuity Plans.

Business Customer

(Service Strategy) A recipient of a product or a Service from the Business. For example, if the Business is a car manufacturer then the Business Customer is someone who buys a car.

Business Objective

(Service Strategy) The Objective of a Business Process, or of the Business as a whole. Business Objectives support the Business Vision, provide guidance for the IT Strategy, and are often supported by IT Services.

Business Operations

(Service Strategy) The day-to-day execution, monitoring and management of Business Processes.

Business Perspective

(Continual Service Improvement) An understanding of the Service Provider and IT Services from the point of view of the Business, and an understanding of the Business from the point of view of the Service Provider.

Business Process

A Process that is owned and carried out by the Business. A Business Process contributes to the delivery of a product or Service to a Business Customer. For example, a retailer may have a purchasing Process that helps to deliver Services to its Business Customers. Many Business Processes rely on IT Services.

Business Relationship Management

(Service Strategy) The Process or Function responsible for maintaining a Relationship with the Business. Business Relationship Management usually includes:

- Managing personal Relationships with Business managers
- Providing input to Service Portfolio Management
- Ensuring that the IT Service Provider is satisfying the Business needs of the Customers.

This Process has strong links with Service Level Management.

Business Service

An IT Service that directly supports a Business Process, as opposed to an Infrastructure Service, which is used internally by the IT Service Provider and is not usually visible to the Business.

The term Business Service is also used to mean a Service that is delivered to Business Customers by Business Units. For example, delivery of financial services to Customers of a bank, or goods to the Customers of a retail store. Successful delivery of Business Services often depends on one or more IT Services.

Business Service Management (BSM)

(Service Strategy) (Service Design) An approach to the management of IT Services that considers the Business Processes supported and the Business value provided.

This term also means the management of Business Services delivered to Business Customers.

Business Unit

(Service Strategy) A segment of the Business that has its own Plans, Metrics, income and Costs. Each Business Unit owns Assets and uses these to create value for Customers in the form of goods and Services.

Call

(Service Operation) A telephone call to the Service Desk from a User. A Call could result in an Incident or a Service Request being logged.

Capability

(Service Strategy) The ability of an Organization, person, Process, Application, Configuration Item or IT Service to carry out an Activity. Capabilities are intangible Assets of an Organization. *See also* Resource.

Capacity

(Service Design) The maximum Throughput that a Configuration Item or IT Service can deliver whilst meeting agreed Service Level Targets. For some types of CI, Capacity may be the size or volume, for example a disk drive.

Capacity Management

(Service Design) The Process responsible for ensuring that the Capacity of IT Services and the IT Infrastructure is able to deliver agreed Service Level Targets in a Cost Effective and timely manner. Capacity Management considers all Resources required to deliver the IT Service, and plans for short-, medium- and long-term Business Requirements.

Capacity Plan

(Service Design) A Capacity Plan is used to manage the Resources required to deliver IT Services. The Plan contains scenarios for different predictions of Business demand, and costed options to deliver the agreed Service Level Targets.

Category

A named group of things that have something in common. Categories are used to group similar things together. For example, Cost Types are used to group similar types of Cost, Incident Categories are used to group similar types of Incident, CI Types are used to group similar types of Configuration Item.

Certification

Issuing a certificate to confirm Compliance to a Standard. Certification includes a formal Audit by an independent and Accredited body. The term Certification is also used to mean awarding a certificate to verify that a person has achieved a qualification.

Change

(Service Transition) The addition, modification or removal of anything that could have an effect on IT Services. The Scope should include all IT Services, Configuration Items, Processes, Documentation, etc.

Change Advisory Board (CAB)

(Service Transition) A group of people that advises the Change Manager in the Assessment, prioritization and scheduling of Changes. This board is usually made up of representatives from all areas within the IT Service Provider, representatives from the Business and Third Parties such as Suppliers.

Change History

(Service Transition) Information about all changes made to a Configuration Item during its life. Change History consists of all those Change Records that apply to the CI.

Change Management

(Service Transition) The Process responsible for controlling the Lifecycle of all Changes. The primary objective of Change Management is to enable beneficial Changes to be made, with minimum disruption to IT Services.

Change Model

(Service Transition) A repeatable way of dealing with a particular Category of Change. A Change Model defines specific pre-defined steps that will be followed for a change of this Category. Change Models may be very simple, with no requirement for approval (e.g. Password Reset) or may be very complex with many steps that require approval (e.g. major software release). *See also* Standard Change, Change Advisory Board.

Change Record

(Service Transition) A Record containing the details of a Change. Each Change Record documents the Lifecycle of a single Change. A Change Record is created for every Request for Change that is received, even those that are subsequently rejected. Change Records should reference the Configuration Items that are affected by the Change. Change Records are stored in the Configuration Management System.

Change Request

See Request for Change.

Change Schedule

(Service Transition) A Document that lists all approved Changes and their planned implementation dates. A Change Schedule is sometimes called a Forward Schedule of Change, even though it also contains information about Changes that have already been implemented.

Change Window

(Service Transition) A regular, agreed time when Changes or Releases may be implemented with minimal impact on Services. Change Windows are usually documented in SLAs.

Charging

(Service Strategy) Requiring payment for IT Services. Charging for IT Services is optional, and many Organizations choose to treat their IT Service Provider as a Cost Centre.

CI Type

(Service Transition) A Category that is used to Classify CIs. The CI Type identifies the required Attributes and Relationships for a Configuration Record. Common CI Types include: Hardware, Document, User, etc.

Classification

The act of assigning a Category to something. Classification is used to ensure consistent management and reporting. CIs, Incidents, Problems, Changes, etc. are usually classified.

Client

A generic term that means a Customer, the Business or a Business Customer. For example, Client Manager may be used as a synonym for Account Manager.

The term client is also used to mean:

- A computer that is used directly by a User, for example a PC, Handheld Computer, or Workstation
- The part of a Client-Server Application that the User directly interfaces with. For example an e-mail Client.

Closed

(Service Operation) The final Status in the Lifecycle of an Incident, Problem, Change, etc. When the Status is Closed, no further action is taken.

Closure

(Service Operation) The act of changing the Status of an Incident, Problem, Change, etc. to Closed.

COBIT

(Continual Service Improvement) Control Objectives for Information and related Technology (COBIT) provides guidance and Best Practice for the management of IT Processes. COBIT is published by the IT Governance Institute. See www.isaca.org for more information.

Code of Practice

A Guideline published by a public body or a Standards Organization, such as ISO or BSI. Many Standards consist of a Code of Practice and a Specification. The Code of Practice describes recommended Best Practice.

Commercial Off-The-Shelf (COTS)

(Service Design) Application software or Middleware that can be purchased from a Third Party.

Compliance

Ensuring that a Standard or set of Guidelines is followed, or that proper, consistent accounting or other practices are being employed.

Component

A general term that is used to mean one part of something more complex. For example, a computer System may be a component of an IT Service, an Application may be a Component of a Release Unit. Components that need to be managed should be Configuration Items.

Confidentiality

(Service Design) A security principle that requires that data should only be accessed by authorized people.

Configuration

(Service Transition) A generic term, used to describe a group of Configuration Items that work together to deliver an IT Service, or a recognizable part of an IT Service. Configuration is also used to describe the parameter settings for one or more CIs.

Configuration Item (CI)

(Service Transition) Any Component that needs to be managed in order to deliver an IT Service. Information about each CI is recorded in a Configuration Record within the Configuration Management System and is maintained throughout its Lifecycle by Configuration Management. CIs are under the control of Change Management. CIs typically include IT Services, hardware, software, buildings, people, and formal documentation such as Process documentation and SLAs.

Configuration Management

(Service Transition) The Process responsible for maintaining information about Configuration Items required to deliver an IT Service, including their Relationships. This information is managed throughout the Lifecycle of the CI. Configuration Management is part of an overall Service Asset and Configuration Management Process.

Configuration Management Database (CMDB)

(Service Transition) A database used to store Configuration Records throughout their Lifecycle. The Configuration Management System maintains one or more CMDBs, and each CMDB stores Attributes of CIs, and Relationships with other CIs.

Configuration Management System (CMS)

(Service Transition) A set of tools and databases that are used to manage an IT Service Provider's Configuration data. The CMS also includes information about Incidents, Problems, Known Errors, Changes and Releases; and may contain data about employees, Suppliers, locations, Business Units, Customers and Users. The CMS includes tools for collecting, storing, managing, updating, and presenting data about all Configuration Items and their Relationships. The CMS is maintained by Configuration Management and is used by all IT Service Management Processes. *See also* Configuration Management Database, Service Knowledge Management System.

Configuration Record

(Service Transition) A Record containing the details of a Configuration Item. Each Configuration Record documents the Lifecycle of a single CI. Configuration Records are stored in a Configuration Management Database.

Configuration Structure

(Service Transition) The hierarchy and other Relationships between all the Configuration Items that comprise a Configuration.

Continual Service Improvement (CSI)

(Continual Service Improvement) A stage in the Lifecycle of an IT Service and the title of one of the Core ITIL publications. Continual Service Improvement is responsible for managing improvements to IT Service Management Processes and IT Services. The Performance of the IT Service Provider is continually measured and improvements are made to Processes, IT Services and IT Infrastructure in order to increase Efficiency, Effectiveness, and Cost Effectiveness. *See also* Plan–Do–Check–Act.

Contract

A legally binding Agreement between two or more parties.

Contract Portfolio

(Service Strategy) A database or structured Document used to manage Service Contracts or Agreements between an IT Service Provider and their Customers. Each IT Service delivered to a Customer should have a Contract or other Agreement that is listed in the Contract Portfolio. *See also* Service Portfolio, Service Catalogue.

Control

A means of managing a Risk, ensuring that a Business Objective is achieved, or ensuring that a Process is followed. Example Controls include Policies, Procedures, Roles, RAID, door locks, etc. A control is sometimes called a Countermeasure or safeguard. Control also means to manage the utilization or behaviour of a Configuration Item, System or IT Service.

Control Objectives for Information and related Technology (COBIT)

See COBIT.

Control Perspective

(Service Strategy) An approach to the management of IT Services, Processes, Functions, Assets, etc. There can be several different Control Perspectives on the same IT Service, Process, etc., allowing different individuals or teams to focus on what is important and relevant to their specific Role. Example Control Perspectives include Reactive and Proactive management within IT Operations, or a Lifecycle view for an Application Project team.

Core Service

(Service Strategy) An IT Service that delivers basic Outcomes desired by one or more Customers. *See also* Supporting Service, Core Service Package.

Core Service Package (CSP)

(Service Strategy) A detailed description of a Core Service that may be shared by two or more Service Level Packages. *See also* Service Package.

Cost

The amount of money spent on a specific Activity, IT Service, or Business Unit. Costs consist of real cost (money), notional cost such as people's time, and Depreciation.

Cost Effectiveness

A measure of the balance between the Effectiveness and Cost of a Service, Process or activity. A Cost Effective Process is one that achieves its Objectives at minimum Cost. *See also* KPI, Return on Investment, Value for Money.

Countermeasure

Can be used to refer to any type of Control. The term Countermeasure is most often used when referring to measures that increase Resilience, Fault Tolerance or Reliability of an IT Service.

Course Corrections

Changes made to a Plan or Activity that has already started to ensure that it will meet its Objectives. Course corrections are made as a result of Monitoring progress.

Crisis Management

(IT Service Continuity Management) Crisis Management is the Process responsible for managing the wider implications of Business Continuity. A Crisis Management team is responsible for Strategic issues such as managing media relations and shareholder confidence, and decides when to invoke Business Continuity Plans.

Critical Success Factor (CSF)

Something that must happen if a Process, Project, Plan, or IT Service is to succeed. KPIs are used to measure the achievement of each CSF. For example a CSF of 'protect IT Services when making Changes' could be measured by KPIs such as 'percentage reduction of unsuccessful Changes', 'percentage reduction in Changes causing Incidents', etc.

Culture

A set of values that is shared by a group of people, including expectations about how people should behave, their ideas, beliefs, and practices. *See also* Vision.

Customer

Someone who buys goods or Services. The Customer of an IT Service Provider is the person or group that defines and agrees the Service Level Targets. The term Customers is also sometimes informally used to mean Users, for example 'this is a Customer-focused Organization'.

Customer Portfolio

(Service Strategy) A database or structured Document used to record all Customers of the IT Service Provider. The Customer Portfolio is the Business Relationship Manager's view of the Customers who receive Services from the IT Service Provider. *See also* Contract Portfolio, Service Portfolio.

Dashboard

(Service Operation) A graphical representation of overall IT Service Performance and Availability. Dashboard images may be updated in real-time, and can also be included in management reports and web pages. Dashboards can be used to support Service Level Management, Event Management or Incident Diagnosis.

Data–to–Information–to–Knowledge–to–Wisdom (DIKW)

A way of understanding the relationships between data, information, knowledge, and wisdom. DIKW shows how each of these builds on the others.

Definitive Media Library (DML)

(Service Transition) One or more locations in which the definitive and approved versions of all software Configuration Items are securely stored. The DML may also contain associated CIs such as licences and documentation. The DML is a single logical storage area even if there are multiple locations. All software in the DML is under the control of Change and Release Management and is recorded in the Configuration Management System. Only software from the DML is acceptable for use in a Release.

Deliverable

Something that must be provided to meet a commitment in a Service Level Agreement or a Contract. Deliverable is also used in a more informal way to mean a planned output of any Process.

Demand Management

Activities that understand and influence Customer demand for Services and the provision of Capacity to meet these demands. At a Strategic level Demand Management can involve analysis of Patterns of Business Activity and User Profiles. At a tactical level it can involve use of Differential Charging to encourage Customers to use IT Services at less busy times. *See also* Capacity Management.

Dependency

The direct or indirect reliance of one Process or Activity on another.

Deployment

(Service Transition) The Activity responsible for movement of new or changed hardware, software, documentation, Process, etc. to the Live Environment. Deployment is part of the Release and Deployment Management Process. *See also* Rollout.

Depreciation

(Service Strategy) A measure of the reduction in value of an Asset over its life. This is based on wearing out, consumption or other reduction in the useful economic value.

Design

(Service Design) An Activity or Process that identifies Requirements and then defines a solution that is able to meet these Requirements. *See also* Service Design.

Detection

(Service Operation) A stage in the Incident Lifecycle. Detection results in the Incident becoming known to the Service Provider. Detection can be automatic, or can be the result of a user logging an Incident.

Development

(Service Design) The Process responsible for creating or modifying an IT Service or Application. Also used to mean the Role or group that carries out Development work.

Diagnosis

(Service Operation) A stage in the Incident and Problem Lifecycles. The purpose of Diagnosis is to identify a Workaround for an Incident or the Root Cause of a Problem.

Document

Information in readable form. A Document may be paper or electronic. For example, a Policy statement, Service Level Agreement, Incident Record, diagram of computer room layout. *See also* Record.

Downtime

(Service Design) (Service Operation) The time when a Configuration Item or IT Service is not Available during its Agreed Service Time. The Availability of an IT Service is often calculated from Agreed Service Time and Downtime.

Driver

Something that influences Strategy, Objectives or Requirements. For example, new legislation or the actions of competitors.

Early Life Support

(Service Transition) Support provided for a new or Changed IT Service for a period of time after it is Released. During Early Life Support the IT Service Provider may review the KPIs, Service Levels and Monitoring Thresholds, and provide additional Resources for Incident and Problem Management.

Effectiveness

(Continual Service Improvement) A measure of whether the Objectives of a Process, Service or Activity have been achieved. An Effective Process or activity is one that achieves its agreed Objectives. *See also* KPI.

Efficiency

(Continual Service Improvement) A measure of whether the right amount of resources has been used to deliver a Process, Service or Activity. An Efficient Process achieves its Objectives with the minimum amount of time, money, people or other resources. *See also* KPI.

Emergency Change

(Service Transition) A Change that must be introduced as soon as possible. For example, to resolve a Major Incident or implement a Security patch. The Change Management Process will normally have a specific Procedure for handling Emergency Changes. *See also* Emergency Change Advisory Board (ECAB).

Emergency Change Advisory Board (ECAB)

(Service Transition) A sub-set of the Change Advisory Board that makes decisions about high-impact Emergency Changes. Membership of the ECAB may be decided at the time a meeting is called, and depends on the nature of the Emergency Change.

Environment

(Service Transition) A subset of the IT Infrastructure that is used for a particular purpose. For example: Live Environment, Test Environment, Build Environment. It is possible for multiple Environments to share a Configuration Item, for example Test and Live Environments may use different partitions on a single mainframe computer. Also used in the term Physical Environment to mean the accommodation, air conditioning, power system, etc.

Environment is also used as a generic term to mean the external conditions that influence or affect something.

Error

(Service Operation) A design flaw or malfunction that causes a Failure of one or more Configuration Items or IT Services. A mistake made by a person or a faulty Process that affects a CI or IT Service is also an Error.

Escalation

(Service Operation) An Activity that obtains additional Resources when these are needed to meet Service Level Targets or Customer expectations. Escalation may be needed within any IT Service Management Process, but is most commonly associated with Incident Management, Problem Management and the management of Customer complaints. There are two types of Escalation, Functional Escalation and Hierarchic Escalation.

eSourcing Capability Model for Service Providers (eSCM–SP)

(Service Strategy) A framework to help IT Service Providers develop their IT Service Management Capabilities from a Service Sourcing perspective. eSCM–SP was developed by Carnegie Mellon University, US.

Estimation

The use of experience to provide an approximate value for a Metric or Cost. Estimation is also used in Capacity and Availability Management as the cheapest and least accurate Modelling method.

Evaluation

(Service Transition) The Process responsible for assessing a new or Changed IT Service to ensure that Risks have been managed and to help determine whether to proceed with the Change.

Evaluation is also used to mean comparing an actual Outcome with the intended Outcome, or comparing one alternative with another.

Event

(Service Operation) A change of state that has significance for the management of a Configuration Item or IT Service.

The term Event is also used to mean an Alert or notification created by any IT Service, Configuration Item or Monitoring tool. Events typically require IT Operations personnel to take actions, and often lead to Incidents being logged.

Event Management

(Service Operation) The Process responsible for managing Events throughout their Lifecycle. Event Management is one of the main Activities of IT Operations.

External Customer

A Customer who works for a different Business to the IT Service Provider. *See also* External Service Provider.

External Service Provider

(Service Strategy) An IT Service Provider that is part of a different Organization to its Customer. An IT Service Provider may have both Internal Customers and External Customers.

Facilities Management

(Service Operation) The Function responsible for managing the physical Environment where the IT Infrastructure is located. Facilities Management includes all aspects of managing the physical Environment, for example power and cooling, building Access Management, and environmental Monitoring.

Failure

(Service Operation) Loss of ability to Operate to Specification, or to deliver the required output. The term Failure may be used when referring to IT Services, Processes, Activities, Configuration Items, etc. A Failure often causes an Incident.

Fault

See Error.

Fault Tolerance

(Service Design) The ability of an IT Service or Configuration Item to continue to Operate correctly after Failure of a Component part. *See also* Resilience, Countermeasure.

Financial Management

(Service Strategy) The Function and Processes responsible for managing an IT Service Provider's Budgeting, Accounting and Charging Requirements.

Fit for Purpose

An informal term used to describe a Process, Configuration Item, IT Service, etc. that is capable of meeting its objectives or Service Levels. Being Fit for Purpose requires suitable design, implementation, control and maintenance.

Fulfilment

Performing Activities to meet a need or Requirement. For example, by providing a new IT Service, or meeting a Service Request.

Function

A team or group of people and the tools they use to carry out one or more Processes or Activities. For example the Service Desk.

The term Function also has two other meanings:

- An intended purpose of a Configuration Item, Person, Team, Process, or IT Service. For example one Function of an e-mail Service may be to store and forward outgoing mails, one Function of a Business Process may be to dispatch goods to Customers.
- To perform the intended purpose correctly, 'The computer is Functioning'.

Gap Analysis

(Continual Service Improvement) An Activity that compares two sets of data and identifies the differences. Gap Analysis is commonly used to compare a set of Requirements with actual delivery.

Governance

Ensuring that Policies and Strategy are actually implemented, and that required Processes are correctly followed. Governance includes defining Roles and responsibilities, measuring and reporting, and taking actions to resolve any issues identified.

Guideline

A Document describing Best Practice, which recommends what should be done. Compliance with a guideline is not normally enforced. *See also* Standard.

Help Desk

(Service Operation) A point of contact for Users to log Incidents. A Help Desk is usually more technically focused than a Service Desk and does not provide a Single Point of Contact for all interaction. The term Help Desk is often used as a synonym for Service Desk.

High Availability

(Service Design) An approach or design that minimizes or hides the effects of Configuration Item Failure on the users of an IT Service. High Availability solutions are designed to achieve an agreed level of Availability and make use of techniques such as Fault Tolerance, Resilience and fast Recovery to reduce the number of Incidents, and the Impact of Incidents.

Impact

(Service Operation) (Service Transition) A measure of the effect of an Incident, Problem or Change on Business Processes. Impact is often based on how Service Levels will be affected. Impact and Urgency are used to assign Priority.

Incident

(Service Operation) An unplanned interruption to an IT Service or reduction in the Quality of an IT Service. Failure of a Configuration Item that has not yet affected Service is also an Incident. For example Failure of one disk from a mirror set.

Incident Management

(Service Operation) The Process responsible for managing the Lifecycle of all Incidents. The primary Objective of Incident Management is to return the IT Service to Customers as quickly as possible.

Incident Record

(Service Operation) A Record containing the details of an Incident. Each Incident record documents the Lifecycle of a single Incident.

Indirect Cost

(Service Strategy) A Cost of providing an IT Service, which cannot be allocated in full to a specific Customer. For example, the Cost of providing shared Servers or software licences. Also known as Overhead.

Information Security Management (ISM)

(Service Design) The Process that ensures the Confidentiality, Integrity and Availability of an Organization's Assets, information, data and IT Services. Information Security Management usually forms part of an Organizational approach to Security Management that has a wider scope than the IT Service Provider, and includes handling of paper, building access, phone calls, etc., for the entire Organization.

Information Technology (IT)

The use of technology for the storage, communication or processing of information. The technology typically includes computers, telecommunications, Applications and other software. The information may include Business data, voice, images, video, etc. Information Technology is often used to support Business Processes through IT Services.

Infrastructure Service

An IT Service that is not directly used by the Business, but is required by the IT Service Provider so they can provide other IT Services. For example directory services, naming services, or communication services.

Insourcing

See Internal Sourcing.

Integrity

(Service Design) A security principle that ensures data and Configuration Items are modified only by authorized personnel and Activities. Integrity considers all possible causes of modification, including software and hardware Failure, environmental Events, and human intervention.

Internal Metric

A Metric that is used within the IT Service Provider to Monitor the Efficiency, Effectiveness or Cost Effectiveness of the IT Service Provider's internal Processes. Internal Metrics are not normally reported to the Customer of the IT Service.

Internal Sourcing

(Service Strategy) Using an Internal Service Provider to manage IT Services.

International Organization for Standardization (ISO)

The International Organization for Standardization (ISO) is the world's largest developer of Standards. ISO is a non-governmental organization that is a network of the national standards institutes of 156 countries. See www.iso.org for further information about ISO.

ISO 9000

A generic term that refers to a number of international Standards and Guidelines for Quality Management Systems. See www.iso.org for more information. *See also* ISO.

ISO 9001

An international Standard for Quality Management Systems. *See also* ISO 9000, Standard.

ISO/IEC 17799

(Continual Service Improvement) ISO Code of Practice for Information Security Management. *See also* Standard.

ISO/IEC 20000

ISO Specification and Code of Practice for IT Service Management. ISO/IEC 20000 is aligned with ITIL Best Practice.

ISO/IEC 27001

(Service Design) (Continual Service Improvement) ISO Specification for Information Security Management. The corresponding Code of Practice is ISO/IEC 17799. *See also* Standard.

IT Infrastructure

All of the hardware, software, networks, facilities, etc. that are required to develop, Test, deliver, Monitor, Control or support IT Services. The term IT Infrastructure includes all of the Information Technology but not the associated people, Processes and documentation.

IT Operations

(Service Operation) Activities carried out by IT Operations Control, including Console Management, Job Scheduling, Backup and Restore, and Print and Output Management. IT Operations is also used as a synonym for Service Operation.

IT Operations Management

(Service Operation) The Function within an IT Service Provider that performs the daily Activities needed to manage IT Services and the supporting IT Infrastructure. IT Operations Management includes IT Operations Control and Facilities Management.

IT Service

A Service provided to one or more Customers by an IT Service Provider. An IT Service is based on the use of Information Technology and supports the Customer's Business Processes. An IT Service is made up from a combination of people, Processes and technology and should be defined in a Service Level Agreement.

IT Service Continuity Management (ITSCM)

(Service Design) The Process responsible for managing Risks that could seriously affect IT Services. ITSCM ensures that the IT Service Provider can always provide minimum agreed Service Levels, by reducing the Risk to an acceptable level and Planning for the Recovery of IT Services. ITSCM should be designed to support Business Continuity Management.

IT Service Continuity Plan

(Service Design) A Plan defining the steps required to Recover one or more IT Services. The Plan will also identify the triggers for Invocation, people to be involved, communications, etc. The IT Service Continuity Plan should be part of a Business Continuity Plan.

IT Service Management (ITSM)

The implementation and management of Quality IT Services that meet the needs of the Business. IT Service Management is performed by IT Service Providers through an appropriate mix of people, Process and Information Technology. *See also* Service Management.

IT Service Provider

(Service Strategy) A Service Provider that provides IT Services to Internal Customers or External Customers.

ITIL

A set of Best Practice guidance for IT Service Management. ITIL is owned by the OGC and consists of a series of publications giving guidance on the provision of Quality IT Services, and on the Processes and facilities needed to support them. See www.itil.co.uk for more information.

Key Performance Indicator (KPI)

(Service Design) (Continual Service Improvement) A Metric that is used to help manage a Process, IT Service or Activity. Many Metrics may be measured, but only the most important of these are defined as KPIs and used to actively manage and report on the Process, IT Service or Activity. KPIs should be selected to ensure that Efficiency, Effectiveness, and Cost Effectiveness are all managed. *See also* Critical Success Factor.

Knowledge Base

(Service Transition) A logical database containing the data used by the Service Knowledge Management System.

Knowledge Management

(Service Transition) The Process responsible for gathering, analysing, storing and sharing knowledge and information within an Organization. The primary purpose of Knowledge Management is to improve Efficiency by reducing the need to rediscover knowledge. *See also* Data–to–Information–to–Knowledge–to–Wisdom, Service Knowledge Management System.

Known Error

(Service Operation) A Problem that has a documented Root Cause and a Workaround. Known Errors are created and managed throughout their Lifecycle by Problem Management. Known Errors may also be identified by Development or Suppliers.

Known Error Database (KEDB)

(Service Operation) A database containing all Known Error Records. This database is created by Problem Management and used by Incident and Problem Management. The Known Error Database is part of the Service Knowledge Management System.

Known Error Record

(Service Operation) A Record containing the details of a Known Error. Each Known Error Record documents the Lifecycle of a Known Error, including the Status, Root Cause and Workaround. In some implementations a Known Error is documented using additional fields in a Problem Record.

Lifecycle

The various stages in the life of an IT Service, Configuration Item, Incident, Problem, Change, etc. The Lifecycle defines the Categories for Status and the Status transitions that are permitted. For example:

- The Lifecycle of an Application includes Requirements, Design, Build, Deploy, Operate, Optimize
- The Expanded Incident Lifecycle includes Detect, Respond, Diagnose, Repair, Recover, Restore
- The Lifecycle of a Server may include: Ordered, Received, In Test, Live, Disposed, etc.

Live

(Service Transition) Refers to an IT Service or Configuration Item that is being used to deliver Service to a Customer.

Live Environment

(Service Transition) A controlled Environment containing Live Configuration Items used to deliver IT Services to Customers.

Maintainability

(Service Design) A measure of how quickly and Effectively a Configuration Item or IT Service can be restored to normal working after a Failure. Maintainability is often measured and reported as MTRS.

Maintainability is also used in the context of Software or IT Service Development to mean ability to be Changed or Repaired easily.

Major Incident

(Service Operation) The highest Category of Impact for an Incident. A Major Incident results in significant disruption to the Business.

Management Information

Information that is used to support decision making by managers. Management Information is often generated automatically by tools supporting the various IT Service Management Processes. Management Information often includes the values of KPIs such as 'Percentage of Changes leading to Incidents', or 'first-time fix rate'.

Management of Risk (M_o_R)

The OGC methodology for managing Risks. M_o_R includes all the Activities required to identify and Control the exposure to Risk, which may have an impact on the achievement of an Organization's Business Objectives. See www.m-o-r.org for more details.

Management System

The framework of Policy, Processes and Functions that ensures an Organization can achieve its Objectives.

Market Space

(Service Strategy) All opportunities that an IT Service Provider could exploit to meet business needs of Customers. The Market Space identifies the possible IT Services that an IT Service Provider may wish to consider delivering.

Maturity

(Continual Service Improvement) A measure of the Reliability, Efficiency and Effectiveness of a Process, Function, Organization, etc. The most mature Processes and Functions are formally aligned to Business Objectives and Strategy, and are supported by a framework for continual improvement.

Mean Time To Repair (MTTR)

The average time taken to repair a Configuration Item or IT Service after a Failure. MTTR is measured from when the CI or IT Service fails until it is repaired. MTTR does not include the time required to Recover or Restore. MTTR is sometimes incorrectly used to mean Mean Time to Restore Service.

Mean Time to Restore Service (MTRS)

The average time taken to restore a Configuration Item or IT Service after a Failure. MTRS is measured from when the CI or IT Service fails until it is fully restored and delivering its normal functionality. *See also* Maintainability, Mean Time to Repair.

Middleware

(Service Design) Software that connects two or more software Components or Applications. Middleware is usually purchased from a Supplier, rather than developed within the IT Service Provider. *See also* Off-The-Shelf.

Model

A representation of a System, Process, IT Service, Configuration Item, etc. that is used to help understand or predict future behaviour.

Modelling

A technique that is used to predict the future behaviour of a System, Process, IT Service, Configuration Item, etc. Modelling is commonly used in Financial Management, Capacity Management and Availability Management.

Monitoring

(Service Operation) Repeated observation of a Configuration Item, IT Service or Process to detect Events and to ensure that the current status is known.

Near-shore

(Service Strategy) Provision of Services from a country near the country where the Customer is based. This can be the provision of an IT Service, or of supporting Functions such as Service Desk. *See also* Off-shore.

Objective

The defined purpose or aim of a Process, an Activity or an Organization as a whole. Objectives are usually expressed as measurable targets. The term Objective is also informally used to mean a Requirement. *See also* Outcome.

Off-The-Shelf

See Commercial Off-The-Shelf.

Office of Government Commerce (OGC)

OGC owns the ITIL brand (copyright and trademark). OGC is a UK Government department that supports the delivery of the government's procurement agenda through its work in collaborative procurement and in raising levels of procurement skills and capability with departments. It also provides support for complex public sector projects.

Off-shore

(Service Strategy) Provision of Services from a location outside the country where the Customer is based, often in a different continent. This can be the provision of an IT Service, or of supporting Functions such as Service Desk. *See also* Near-shore.

Operate

To perform as expected. A Process or Configuration Item is said to Operate if it is delivering the Required outputs. Operate also means to perform one or more Operations. For example, to Operate a computer is to do the day-to-day Operations needed for it to perform as expected.

Operation

(Service Operation) Day-to-day management of an IT Service, System, or other Configuration Item. Operation is also used to mean any pre-defined Activity or Transaction. For example, loading a magnetic tape, accepting money at a point of sale, or reading data from a disk drive.

Operational

The lowest of three levels of Planning and delivery (Strategic, Tactical, Operational). Operational Activities include the day-to-day or short-term Planning or delivery of a Business Process or IT Service Management Process. The term Operational is also a synonym for Live.

Operational Cost

Cost resulting from running the IT Services. Often repeating payments. For example, staff costs, hardware maintenance and electricity (also known as 'current expenditure' or 'revenue expenditure').

Operational Level Agreement (OLA)

(Service Design) (Continual Service Improvement) An Agreement between an IT Service Provider and another part of the same Organization. An OLA supports the IT Service Provider's delivery of IT Services to Customers. The OLA defines the goods or Services to be provided and the responsibilities of both parties. For example, there could be an OLA:

- Between the IT Service Provider and a procurement department to obtain hardware in agreed times
- Between the Service Desk and a Support Group to provide Incident Resolution in agreed times.

See also Service Level Agreement.

Operations Management

See IT Operations Management.

Opportunity Cost

(Service Strategy) A Cost that is used in deciding between investment choices. Opportunity Cost represents the revenue that would have been generated by using the Resources in a different way. For example, the Opportunity Cost of purchasing a new Server may include not carrying out a Service Improvement activity that the money could have been spent on. Opportunity cost analysis is used as part of a decision making processes, but is not treated as an actual Cost in any financial statement.

Optimize

Review, Plan and request Changes, in order to obtain the maximum Efficiency and Effectiveness from a Process, Configuration Item, Application, etc.

Organization

A company, legal entity or other institution. Examples of Organizations that are not companies include International Standards Organization or itSMF. The term Organization is sometimes used to refer to any entity that has People, Resources and Budgets. For example, a Project or Business Unit.

Outcome

The result of carrying out an Activity; following a Process; delivering an IT Service, etc. The term Outcome is used to refer to intended results, as well as to actual results. *See also* Objective.

Outsourcing

(Service Strategy) Using an External Service Provider to manage IT Services. *See also* Service Sourcing.

Overhead

See Indirect cost.

Pareto Principle

(Service Operation) A technique used to prioritize Activities. The Pareto Principle says that 80% of the value of any activity is created with 20% of the effort. Pareto Analysis is also used in Problem Management to prioritize possible Problem causes for investigation.

Partnership

A relationship between two Organizations that involves working closely together for common goals or mutual benefit. The IT Service Provider should have a Partnership with the Business, and with Third Parties who are critical to the delivery of IT Services.

Pattern of Business Activity (PBA)

(Service Strategy) A Workload profile of one or more Business Activities. Patterns of Business Activity are used to help the IT Service Provider understand and plan for different levels of Business Activity. *See also* User Profile.

Performance

A measure of what is achieved or delivered by a System, person, team, Process, or IT Service.

Performance Management

(Continual Service Improvement) The Process responsible for day-to-day Capacity Management Activities. These include monitoring, threshold detection, Performance analysis and Tuning, and implementing changes related to Performance and Capacity.

Pilot

(Service Transition) A limited Deployment of an IT Service, a Release or a Process to the Live Environment. A pilot is used to reduce Risk and to gain User feedback and Acceptance. *See also* Test, Evaluation.

Plan

A detailed proposal that describes the Activities and Resources needed to achieve an Objective. For example, a Plan to implement a new IT Service or Process. ISO/IEC 20000 requires a Plan for the management of each IT Service Management Process.

Plan–Do–Check–Act

(Continual Service Improvement) A four-stage cycle for Process management, attributed to Edward Deming. Plan–Do–Check–Act is also called the Deming Cycle.

PLAN: Design or revise Processes that support the IT Services.

DO: Implement the Plan and manage the Processes.

CHECK: Measure the Processes and IT Services, compare with Objectives and produce reports.

ACT: Plan and implement Changes to improve the Processes.

Planned Downtime

(Service Design) Agreed time when an IT Service will not be available. Planned Downtime is often used for maintenance, upgrades and testing. *See also* Downtime.

Planning

An Activity responsible for creating one or more Plans. For example, Capacity Planning.

PMBOK

A Project management Standard maintained and published by the Project Management Institute. PMBOK stands for Project Management Body of Knowledge. See www.pmi.org for more information. *See also* PRINCE2.

Policy

Formally documented management expectations and intentions. Policies are used to direct decisions, and to ensure consistent and appropriate development and implementation of Processes, Standards, Roles, Activities, IT Infrastructure, etc.

Post-Implementation Review (PIR)

A Review that takes place after a Change or a Project has been implemented. A PIR determines if the Change or Project was successful, and identifies opportunities for improvement.

Practice

A way of working, or a way in which work must be done. Practices can include Activities, Processes, Functions, Standards and Guidelines. *See also* Best Practice.

PRINCE2

The standard UK government methodology for Project management. See www.ogc.gov.uk/prince2 for more information. *See also* PMBOK.

Priority

(Service Transition) (Service Operation) A Category used to identify the relative importance of an Incident, Problem or Change. Priority is based on Impact and Urgency, and is used to identify required times for actions to be taken. For example, the SLA may state that Priority 2 Incidents must be resolved within 12 hours.

Problem

(Service Operation) A cause of one or more Incidents. The cause is not usually known at the time a Problem Record is created, and the Problem Management Process is responsible for further investigation.

Problem Management

(Service Operation) The Process responsible for managing the Lifecycle of all Problems. The primary objectives of Problem Management are to prevent Incidents from happening, and to minimize the Impact of Incidents that cannot be prevented.

Problem Record

(Service Operation) A Record containing the details of a Problem. Each Problem Record documents the Lifecycle of a single Problem.

Procedure

A Document containing steps that specify how to achieve an Activity. Procedures are defined as part of Processes. *See also* Work Instruction.

Process

A structured set of Activities designed to accomplish a specific Objective. A Process takes one or more defined inputs and turns them into defined outputs. A Process may include any of the Roles, responsibilities, tools and management Controls required to reliably deliver the outputs. A Process may define Policies, Standards, Guidelines, Activities, and Work Instructions if they are needed.

Process Control

The Activity of planning and regulating a Process, with the Objective of performing the Process in an Effective, Efficient, and consistent manner.

Process Manager

A Role responsible for Operational management of a Process. The Process Manager's responsibilities include Planning and coordination of all Activities required to carry out, monitor and report on the Process. There may be several Process Managers for one Process, for example regional Change Managers or IT Service Continuity Managers for each data centre. The Process Manager Role is often assigned to the person who carries out the Process Owner Role, but the two Roles may be separate in larger Organizations.

Process Owner

A Role responsible for ensuring that a Process is Fit for Purpose. The Process Owner's responsibilities include sponsorship, Design, Change Management and continual improvement of the Process and its Metrics. This Role is often assigned to the same person who carries out the Process Manager Role, but the two Roles may be separate in larger Organizations.

Production Environment

See Live Environment.

Programme

A number of Projects and Activities that are planned and managed together to achieve an overall set of related Objectives and other Outcomes.

Project

A temporary Organization, with people and other Assets required to achieve an Objective or other Outcome. Each Project has a Lifecycle that typically includes initiation, Planning, execution, Closure, etc. Projects are usually managed using a formal methodology such as PRINCE2.

Projected Service Outage (PSO)

(Service Transition) A Document that identifies the effect of planned Changes, maintenance Activities and Test Plans on agreed Service Levels.

Qualification

(Service Transition) An Activity that ensures that IT Infrastructure is appropriate, and correctly configured, to support an Application or IT Service. *See also* Validation.

Quality

The ability of a product, Service, or Process to provide the intended value. For example, a hardware Component can be considered to be of high Quality if it performs as expected and delivers the required Reliability. Process Quality also requires an ability to monitor Effectiveness and Efficiency, and to improve them if necessary. *See also* Quality Management System.

Quality Assurance (QA)

(Service Transition) The Process responsible for ensuring that the Quality of a product, Service or Process will provide its intended Value.

Quality Management System (QMS)

(Continual Service Improvement) The set of Processes responsible for ensuring that all work carried out by an Organization is of a suitable Quality to reliably meet Business Objectives or Service Levels. *See also* ISO 9000.

RACI

(Service Design) (Continual Service Improvement) A Model used to help define Roles and Responsibilities. RACI stands for Responsible, Accountable, Consulted and Informed. *See also* Stakeholder.

Record

A Document containing the results or other output from a Process or Activity. Records are evidence of the fact that an activity took place and may be paper or electronic. For example, an Audit report, an Incident Record, or the minutes of a meeting.

Recovery

(Service Design) (Service Operation) Returning a Configuration Item or an IT Service to a working state. Recovery of an IT Service often includes recovering data to a known consistent state. After Recovery, further steps may be needed before the IT Service can be made available to the Users (Restoration).

Redundancy

See Fault Tolerance.

The term Redundant also has a generic meaning of obsolete, or no longer needed.

Relationship

A connection or interaction between two people or things. In Business Relationship Management it is the interaction between the IT Service Provider and the Business. In Configuration Management it is a link between two Configuration Items that identifies a dependency or connection between them. For example Applications may be linked to the Servers they run on, IT Services have many links to all the CIs that contribute to them.

Release

(Service Transition) A collection of hardware, software, documentation, Processes or other Components required to implement one or more approved Changes to IT Services. The contents of each Release are managed, tested, and deployed as a single entity.

Release and Deployment Management

(Service Transition) The Process responsible for both Release Management and Deployment.

Release Identification

(Service Transition) A naming convention used to uniquely identify a Release. The Release Identification typically includes a reference to the Configuration Item and a version number. For example, Microsoft Office 2003 SR2.

Release Management

(Service Transition) The Process responsible for Planning, scheduling and controlling the movement of Releases to Test and Live Environments. The primary Objective of Release Management is to ensure that the integrity of the Live Environment is protected and that the correct Components are released. Release Management is part of the Release and Deployment Management Process.

Release Process

The name used by ISO/IEC 20000 for the Process group that includes Release Management. This group does not include any other Processes.

Release Process is also used as a synonym for Release Management Process.

Release Record

(Service Transition) A Record in the CMDB that defines the content of a Release. A Release Record has Relationships with all Configuration Items that are affected by the Release.

Release Unit

(Service Transition) Components of an IT Service that are normally Released together. A Release Unit typically includes sufficient components to perform a useful Function. For example, one Release Unit could be a Desktop PC, including Hardware, Software, Licences, Documentation, etc. A different Release Unit may be the complete Payroll Application, including IT Operations Procedures and user training.

Release Window

See Change Window.

Reliability

(Service Design) (Continual Service Improvement) A measure of how long a Configuration Item or IT Service can perform its agreed Function without interruption. Usually measured as MTBF or MTBSI. The term Reliability can also be used to state how likely it is that a Process, Function, etc. will deliver its required outputs. *See also* Availability.

Remediation

(Service Transition) Recovery to a known state after a failed Change or Release.

Repair

(Service Operation) The replacement or correction of a failed Configuration Item.

Request for Change (RFC)

(Service Transition) A formal proposal for a Change to be made. An RFC includes details of the proposed Change, and may be recorded on paper or electronically. The term RFC is often misused to mean a Change Record, or the Change itself.

Request Fulfilment

(Service Operation) The Process responsible for managing the Lifecycle of all Service Requests.

Requirement

(Service Design) A formal statement of what is needed. For example, a Service Level Requirement, a Project Requirement or the required Deliverables for a Process.

Resilience

(Service Design) The ability of a Configuration Item or IT Service to resist Failure or to Recover quickly following a Failure. For example, an armoured cable will resist failure when put under stress. *See also* Fault Tolerance.

Resolution

(Service Operation) Action taken to repair the Root Cause of an Incident or Problem, or to implement a Workaround. In ISO/IEC 20000, Resolution Processes is the Process group that includes Incident and Problem Management.

Resource

(Service Strategy) A generic term that includes IT Infrastructure, people, money or anything else that might help to deliver an IT Service. Resources are considered to be Assets of an Organization. *See also* Capability, Service Asset.

Responsiveness

A measurement of the time taken to respond to something. This could be Response Time of a Transaction, or the speed with which an IT Service Provider responds to an Incident or Request for Change, etc.

Restore

(Service Operation) Taking action to return an IT Service to the Users after Repair and Recovery from an Incident. This is the primary Objective of Incident Management.

Retire

(Service Transition) Permanent removal of an IT Service, or other Configuration Item, from the Live Environment. Retired is a stage in the Lifecycle of many Configuration Items.

Return on Investment (ROI)

(Service Strategy) (Continual Service Improvement) A measurement of the expected benefit of an investment. In the simplest sense it is the net profit of an investment divided by the net worth of the assets invested.

Return to Normal

(Service Design) The phase of an IT Service Continuity Plan during which full normal operations are resumed. For example, if an alternate data centre has been in use, then this phase will bring the primary data centre back into operation, and restore the ability to invoke IT Service Continuity Plans again.

Review

An evaluation of a Change, Problem, Process, Project, etc. Reviews are typically carried out at predefined points in the Lifecycle, and especially after Closure. The purpose of a Review is to ensure that all Deliverables have been provided, and to identify opportunities for improvement. *See also* Post-Implementation Review.

Rights

(Service Operation) Entitlements, or permissions, granted to a User or Role. For example, the Right to modify particular data, or to authorize a Change.

Risk

A possible event that could cause harm or loss, or affect the ability to achieve Objectives. A Risk is measured by the probability of a Threat, the Vulnerability of the Asset to that Threat, and the Impact it would have if it occurred.

Risk Assessment

The initial steps of Risk Management. Analysing the value of Assets to the business, identifying Threats to those Assets, and evaluating how Vulnerable each Asset is to those Threats. Risk Assessment can be quantitative (based on numerical data) or qualitative.

Risk Management

The Process responsible for identifying, assessing and controlling Risks. *See also* Risk Assessment.

Role

A set of responsibilities, Activities and authorities granted to a person or team. A Role is defined in a Process. One person or team may have multiple Roles, for example the Roles of Configuration Manager and Change Manager may be carried out by a single person.

Rollout

(Service Transition) See Deployment.

Most often used to refer to complex or phased Deployments or Deployments to multiple locations.

Root Cause

(Service Operation) The underlying or original cause of an Incident or Problem.

Root Cause Analysis (RCA)

(Service Operation) An Activity that identifies the Root Cause of an Incident or Problem. RCA typically concentrates on IT Infrastructure failures. *See also* Service Failure Analysis.

Scope

The boundary, or extent, to which a Process, Procedure, Certification, Contract, etc. applies. For example the Scope of Change Management may include all Live IT Services and related Configuration Items, the Scope of an ISO/IEC 20000 Certificate may include all IT Services delivered out of a named data centre.

Second-line Support

(Service Operation) The second level in a hierarchy of Support Groups involved in the resolution of Incidents and investigation of Problems. Each level contains more specialist skills, or has more time or other resources.

Security

See Information Security Management.

Security Management

See Information Security Management.

Server

(Service Operation) A computer that is connected to a network and provides software Functions that are used by other Computers.

Service

A means of delivering value to Customers by facilitating Outcomes Customers want to achieve without the ownership of specific Costs and Risks.

Service Acceptance Criteria (SAC)

(Service Transition) A set of criteria used to ensure that an IT Service meets its functionality and Quality Requirements and that the IT Service Provider is ready to Operate the new IT Service when it has been Deployed. *See also* Acceptance.

Service Asset

Any Capability or Resource of a Service Provider. *See also* Asset.

Service Asset and Configuration Management (SACM)

(Service Transition) The Process responsible for both Configuration Management and Asset Management.

Service Catalogue

(Service Design) A database or structured Document with information about all Live IT Services, including those available for Deployment. The Service Catalogue is the only part of the Service Portfolio published to Customers, and is used to support the sale and delivery of IT Services. The Service Catalogue includes information about deliverables, prices, contact points, ordering and request Processes. *See also* Contract Portfolio.

Service Continuity Management

See IT Service Continuity Management.

Service Contract

(Service Strategy) A Contract to deliver one or more IT Services. The term Service Contract is also used to mean any Agreement to deliver IT Services, whether this is a legal Contract or an SLA. *See also* Contract Portfolio.

Service Culture

A Customer-oriented Culture. The major Objectives of a Service Culture are Customer satisfaction and helping Customers to achieve their Business Objectives.

Service Design

(Service Design) A stage in the Lifecycle of an IT Service. Service Design includes a number of Processes and Functions and is the title of one of the Core ITIL publications. *See also* Design.

Service Design Package

(Service Design) Document(s) defining all aspects of an IT Service and its Requirements through each stage of its Lifecycle. A Service Design Package is produced for each new IT Service, major Change, or IT Service Retirement.

Service Desk

(Service Operation) The Single Point of Contact between the Service Provider and the Users. A typical Service Desk manages Incidents and Service Requests, and also handles communication with the Users.

Service Improvement Plan (SIP)

(Continual Service Improvement) A formal Plan to implement improvements to a Process or IT Service.

Service Knowledge Management System (SKMS)

(Service Transition) A set of tools and databases that are used to manage knowledge and information. The SKMS includes the Configuration Management System, as well as other tools and databases. The SKMS stores, manages, updates, and presents all information that an IT Service Provider needs to manage the full Lifecycle of IT Services.

Service Level

Measured and reported achievement against one or more Service Level Targets. The term Service Level is sometimes used informally to mean Service Level Target.

Service Level Agreement (SLA)

(Service Design) (Continual Service Improvement) An Agreement between an IT Service Provider and a Customer. The SLA describes the IT Service, documents Service Level Targets, and specifies the responsibilities of the IT Service Provider and the Customer. A single SLA may cover multiple IT Services or multiple customers. *See also* Operational Level Agreement.

Service Level Management (SLM)

(Service Design) (Continual Service Improvement) The Process responsible for negotiating Service Level Agreements, and ensuring that these are met. SLM is responsible for ensuring that all IT Service Management Processes, Operational Level Agreements, and Underpinning Contracts, are appropriate for the agreed Service Level Targets. SLM monitors and reports on Service Levels, and holds regular Customer reviews.

Service Level Package (SLP)

(Service Strategy) A defined level of Utility and Warranty for a particular Service Package. Each SLP is designed to meet the needs of a particular Pattern of Business Activity.

Service Level Requirement (SLR)

(Service Design) (Continual Service Improvement) A Customer Requirement for an aspect of an IT Service. SLRs are based on Business Objectives and are used to negotiate agreed Service Level Targets.

Service Level Target

(Service Design) (Continual Service Improvement) A commitment that is documented in a Service Level Agreement. Service Level Targets are based on Service Level Requirements, and are needed to ensure that the IT Service design is Fit for Purpose. Service Level Targets should be SMART, and are usually based on KPIs.

Service Management

Service Management is a set of specialized organisational capabilities for providing value to Customers in the form of Services.

Service Management Lifecycle

An approach to IT Service Management that emphasizes the importance of coordination and Control across the various Functions, Processes, and Systems necessary to manage the full Lifecycle of IT Services. The Service Management Lifecycle approach considers the Strategy, Design, Transition, Operation and Continuous Improvement of IT Services.

Service Manager

A manager who is responsible for managing the end-to-end Lifecycle of one or more IT Services. The term Service Manager is also used to mean any manager within the IT Service Provider. Most commonly used to refer to a Business Relationship Manager, a Process Manager, an Account Manager or a senior manager with responsibility for IT Services overall.

Service Operation

(Service Operation) A stage in the Lifecycle of an IT Service. Service Operation includes a number of Processes and Functions and is the title of one of the Core ITIL publications. *See also* Operation.

Service Owner

(Continual Service Improvement) A Role that is accountable for the delivery of a specific IT Service.

Service Package

(Service Strategy) A detailed description of an IT Service that is available to be delivered to Customers. A Service Package includes a Service Level Package and one or more Core Services and Supporting Services.

Service Pipeline

(Service Strategy) A database or structured Document listing all IT Services that are under consideration or Development, but are not yet available to Customers. The Service Pipeline provides a Business view of possible future IT Services and is part of the Service Portfolio that is not normally published to Customers.

Service Portfolio

(Service Strategy) The complete set of Services that are managed by a Service Provider. The Service Portfolio is used to manage the entire Lifecycle of all Services, and includes three Categories: Service Pipeline (proposed or in Development); Service Catalogue (Live or available for Deployment); and Retired Services. *See also* Service Portfolio Management, Contract Portfolio.

Service Portfolio Management (SPM)

(Service Strategy) The Process responsible for managing the Service Portfolio. Service Portfolio Management considers Services in terms of the Business value that they provide.

Service Provider

(Service Strategy) An Organization supplying Services to one or more Internal Customers or External Customers. Service Provider is often used as an abbreviation for IT Service Provider.

Service Provider Interface (SPI)

(Service Strategy) An interface between the IT Service Provider and a User, Customer, Business Process, or a Supplier. Analysis of Service Provider Interfaces helps to coordinate end-to-end management of IT Services.

Service Reporting

(Continual Service Improvement) The Process responsible for producing and delivering reports of achievement and trends against Service Levels. Service Reporting should agree the format, content and frequency of reports with Customers.

Service Strategy

(Service Strategy) The title of one of the Core ITIL publications. Service Strategy establishes an overall Strategy for IT Services and for IT Service Management.

Service Transition

(Service Transition) A stage in the Lifecycle of an IT Service. Service Transition includes a number of Processes and Functions and is the title of one of the Core ITIL publications. *See also* Transition.

Service Utility

(Service Strategy) The Functionality of an IT Service from the Customer's perspective. The Business value of an IT Service is created by the combination of Service Utility (what the Service does) and Service Warranty (how well it does it). *See also* Utility.

Service Validation and Testing

(Service Transition) The Process responsible for Validation and Testing of a new or Changed IT Service. Service Validation and Testing ensures that the IT Service matches its Design Specification and will meet the needs of the Business.

Service Warranty

(Service Strategy) Assurance that an IT Service will meet agreed Requirements. This may be a formal Agreement such as a Service Level Agreement or Contract, or may be a marketing message or brand image. The Business value of an IT Service is created by the combination of Service Utility (what the Service does) and Service Warranty (how well it does it). *See also* Warranty.

Shift

(Service Operation) A group or team of people who carry out a specific Role for a fixed period of time. For example there could be four shifts of IT Operations Control personnel to support an IT Service that is used 24 hours a day.

Single Point of Contact

(Service Operation) Providing a single consistent way to communicate with an Organization or Business Unit. For example, a Single Point of Contact for an IT Service Provider is usually called a Service Desk.

Snapshot

(Service Transition) The current state of a Configuration as captured by a discovery tool. Also used as a synonym for Benchmark. *See also* Baseline.

Specification

A formal definition of Requirements. A Specification may be used to define technical or Operational Requirements, and may be internal or external. Many public Standards consist of a Code of Practice and a Specification. The Specification defines the Standard against which an Organization can be Audited.

Stakeholder

All people who have an interest in an Organization, Project, IT Service, etc. Stakeholders may be interested in the Activities, targets, Resources, or Deliverables. Stakeholders may include Customers, Partners, employees, shareholders, owners, etc. *See also* RACI.

Standard

A mandatory Requirement. Examples include ISO/IEC 20000 (an international Standard), an internal security standard for Unix configuration, or a government standard for how financial Records should be maintained. The term Standard is also used to refer to a Code of Practice or Specification published by a Standards Organization such as ISO or BSI. *See also* Guideline.

Standard Change

(Service Transition) A pre-approved Change that is low Risk, relatively common and follows a Procedure or Work Instruction. For example, password reset or provision of standard equipment to a new employee. RFCs are not required to implement a Standard Change, and they are logged and tracked using a different mechanism, such as a Service Request. *See also* Change Model.

Status

The name of a required field in many types of Record. It shows the current stage in the Lifecycle of the associated Configuration Item, Incident, Problem, etc.

Status Accounting

(Service Transition) The Activity responsible for recording and reporting the Lifecycle of each Configuration Item.

Strategic

(Service Strategy) The highest of three levels of Planning and delivery (Strategic, Tactical, Operational). Strategic Activities include Objective setting and long-term Planning to achieve the overall Vision.

Strategy

(Service Strategy) A Strategic Plan designed to achieve defined Objectives.

Supplier

(Service Strategy) (Service Design) A Third Party responsible for supplying goods or Services that are required to deliver IT services. Examples of suppliers include commodity hardware and software vendors, network and telecom providers, and outsourcing Organizations. *See also* Underpinning Contract, Supply Chain.

Supplier Management

(Service Design) The Process responsible for ensuring that all Contracts with Suppliers support the needs of the Business, and that all Suppliers meet their contractual commitments.

Supply Chain

(Service Strategy) The Activities in a Value Chain carried out by Suppliers. A Supply Chain typically involves multiple Suppliers, each adding value to the product or Service. *See also* Value Network.

Support Group

(Service Operation) A group of people with technical skills. Support Groups provide the Technical Support needed by all of the IT Service Management Processes. *See also* Technical Management.

Supporting Service

(Service Strategy) A Service that enables or enhances a Core Service. For example, a Directory Service or a Backup Service. *See also* Service Package.

System

A number of related things that work together to achieve an overall Objective. For example:

- A computer System including hardware, software and Applications
- A management System, including multiple Processes that are planned and managed together. For example, a Quality Management System
- A Database Management System or Operating System that includes many software modules that are designed to perform a set of related Functions.

Tactical

The middle of three levels of Planning and delivery (Strategic, Tactical, Operational). Tactical Activities include the medium-term Plans required to achieve specific Objectives, typically over a period of weeks to months.

Technical Management

(Service Operation) The Function responsible for providing technical skills in support of IT Services and management of the IT Infrastructure. Technical Management defines the Roles of Support Groups, as well as the tools, Processes and Procedures required.

Technical Support

See Technical Management.

Terms of Reference (TOR)

(Service Design) A Document specifying the Requirements, Scope, Deliverables, Resources and schedule for a Project or Activity.

Test

(Service Transition) An Activity that verifies that a Configuration Item, IT Service, Process, etc. meets its Specification or agreed Requirements. *See also* Service Validation and Testing, Acceptance.

Test Environment

(Service Transition) A controlled Environment used to Test Configuration Items, Builds, IT Services, Processes, etc.

Third Party

A person, group, or Business that is not part of the Service Level Agreement for an IT Service, but is required to ensure successful delivery of that IT Service. For example, a software Supplier, a hardware maintenance company, or a facilities department. Requirements for Third Parties are typically specified in Underpinning Contracts or Operational Level Agreements.

Threat

Anything that might exploit a Vulnerability. Any potential cause of an Incident can be considered to be a Threat. For example a fire is a Threat that could exploit the Vulnerability of flammable floor coverings. This term is commonly used in Information Security Management and IT Service Continuity Management, but also applies to other areas such as Problem and Availability Management.

Throughput

(Service Design) A measure of the number of Transactions, or other Operations, performed in a fixed time. For example, 5,000 e-mails sent per hour, or 200 disk I/Os per second.

Total Cost of Ownership (TCO)

(Service Strategy) A methodology used to help make investment decisions. TCO assesses the full Lifecycle Cost of owning a Configuration Item, not just the initial Cost or purchase price. *See also* Total Cost of Utilization.

Total Cost of Utilization (TCU)

(Service Strategy) A methodology used to help make investment and Service Sourcing decisions. TCU assesses the full Lifecycle Cost to the Customer of using an IT Service. *See also* Total Cost of Ownership.

Transaction

A discrete Function performed by an IT Service. For example, transferring money from one bank account to another. A single Transaction may involve numerous additions, deletions and modifications of data. Either all of these complete successfully or none of them is carried out.

Transition

(Service Transition) A change in state, corresponding to a movement of an IT Service or other Configuration Item from one Lifecycle status to the next.

Transition Planning and Support

(Service Transition) The Process responsible for Planning all Service Transition Processes and coordinating the resources that they require. These Service Transition Processes are Change Management, Service Asset and Configuration Management, Release and Deployment Management, Service Validation and Testing, Evaluation, and Knowledge Management.

Trend Analysis

(Continual Service Improvement) Analysis of data to identify time-related patterns. Trend Analysis is used in Problem Management to identify common Failures or fragile Configuration Items, and in Capacity Management as a Modelling tool to predict future behaviour. It is also used as a management tool for identifying deficiencies in IT Service Management Processes.

Tuning

The Activity responsible for Planning changes to make the most efficient use of Resources. Tuning is part of Performance Management, which also includes Performance monitoring and implementation of the required Changes.

Underpinning Contract (UC)

(Service Design) A Contract between an IT Service Provider and a Third Party. The Third Party provides goods or Services that support delivery of an IT Service to a Customer. The Underpinning Contract defines targets and responsibilities that are required to meet agreed Service Level Targets in an SLA.

Unit Cost

(Service Strategy) The Cost to the IT Service Provider of providing a single Component of an IT Service. For example, the Cost of a single desktop PC, or of a single Transaction.

Urgency

(Service Transition) (Service Design) A measure of how long it will be until an Incident, Problem or Change has a significant Impact on the Business. For example, a high Impact Incident may have low Urgency, if the Impact will not affect the Business until the end of the financial year. Impact and Urgency are used to assign Priority.

Usability

(Service Design) The ease with which an Application, product, or IT Service can be used. Usability Requirements are often included in a Statement of Requirements.

Use Case

(Service Design) A technique used to define required functionality and Objectives, and to design Tests. Use Cases define realistic scenarios that describe interactions between Users and an IT Service or other System.

User

A person who uses the IT Service on a day-to-day basis. Users are distinct from Customers, as some Customers do not use the IT Service directly.

User Profile (UP)

(Service Strategy) A pattern of User demand for IT Services. Each User Profile includes one or more Patterns of Business Activity.

Utility

(Service Strategy) Functionality offered by a Product or Service to meet a particular need. Utility is often summarized as 'what it does'. *See also* Service Utility.

Validation

(Service Transition) An Activity that ensures a new or changed IT Service, Process, Plan, or other Deliverable meets the needs of the Business. Validation ensures that Business Requirements are met even though these may have changed since the original design. *See also* Verification, Acceptance, Qualification, Service Validation and Testing.

Value for Money

An informal measure of Cost Effectiveness. Value for Money is often based on a comparison with the Cost of alternatives.

Variance

The difference between a planned value and the actual measured value. Commonly used in Financial Management, Capacity Management and Service Level Management, but could apply in any area where Plans are in place.

Verification

(Service Transition) An Activity that ensures a new or changed IT Service, Process, Plan, or other Deliverable is complete, accurate, Reliable and matches its design specification. *See also* Validation, Acceptance, Service Validation and Testing.

Verification and Audit

(Service Transition) The Activities responsible for ensuring that information in the CMDB is accurate and that all Configuration Items have been identified and recorded in the CMDB. Verification includes routine checks that are part of other processes. For example, verifying the serial number of a desktop PC when a User logs an Incident. Audit is a periodic, formal check.

Version

(Service Transition) A Version is used to identify a specific Baseline of a Configuration Item. Versions typically use a naming convention that enables the sequence or date of each Baseline to be identified. For example, Payroll Application Version 3 contains updated functionality from Version 2.

Vision

A description of what the Organization intends to become in the future. A Vision is created by senior management and is used to help influence Culture and Strategic Planning.

Warranty

(Service Strategy) A promise or guarantee that a product or Service will meet its agreed Requirements. *See also* Service Validation and Testing, Service Warranty.

Work Instruction

A Document containing detailed instructions that specify exactly what steps to follow to carry out an Activity. A Work Instruction contains much more detail than a Procedure and is only created if very detailed instructions are needed.

Workaround

(Service Operation) Reducing or eliminating the Impact of an Incident or Problem for which a full Resolution is not yet available. For example, by restarting a failed Configuration Item. Workarounds for Problems are documented in Known Error Records. Workarounds for Incidents that do not have associated Problem Records are documented in the Incident Record.

Workload

The Resources required to deliver an identifiable part of an IT Service. Workloads may be Categorized by Users, groups of Users, or Functions within the IT Service. This is used to assist in analysing and managing the Capacity, Performance and Utilization of Configuration Items and IT Services. The term Workload is sometimes used as a synonym for Throughput.

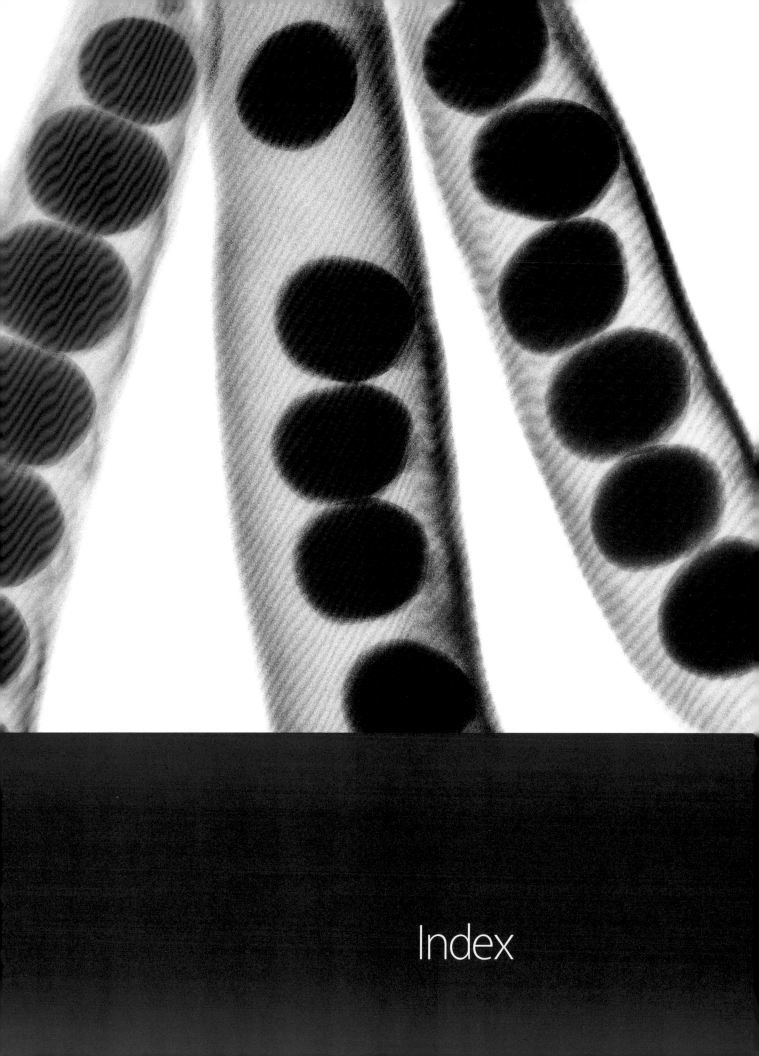

Index

Index